1970

University of St. Francis
GEN 846.6 S778m
Stal el Holstein
D/

W9-ADI-701

3 0301 0000 ...

This b   may be kept

de Staël-du Pont Letters

De Staël-Du Pont Letters

Correspondence

of Madame de Staël and

Pierre Samuel du Pont de Nemours

And

of Other Members of the Necker

and du Pont Families

Edited and Translated by

JAMES F. MARSHALL

The University of Wisconsin Press

Madison, Milwaukee, and London

1968

LIBRARY
College of St. Francis
JOLIET, ILL.

Published by
The University of Wisconsin Press
Box 1379, Madison, Wisconsin 53701

The University of Wisconsin Press, Ltd.
27–29 Whitfield Street, London, W.1

Copyright © 1968 by the Regents of the University of Wisconsin
All rights reserved

Printed in the United States of America by
The Colonial Press Inc., Clinton, Massachusetts

Library of Congress Catalog Card Number 68–9020

846.6
8778m

Contents

THE CORRESPONDENCE

52379

Illustrations

Introduction

Among the many friends of Mme. de Staël, one of the most neglected has been Pierre Samuel du Pont de Nemours. To be sure, the Comte Jean Le Marois published, some twenty years ago, an article entitled "Du Pont de Nemours et Madame de Staël," [1] which is based on some of the du Pont letters preserved in the archives of the château of Coppet. Ambrose Saricks, Gustave Schelle, and B. G. du Pont mention Mme. de Staël in their respective biographies of du Pont, and she is referred to in B. G. du Pont's *Life of E. I. du Pont*.[2] Richmond L. Hawkins also alludes to the relations between these two colorful characters in his *Madame de Staël and the United States* (Cambridge, Mass., 1930). Nevertheless, their friendship has not received its due recognition. For example, in J. Christopher Herold's excellent recent biography of Mme. de Staël, *Mistress to an Age* (Indianapolis, 1958), du Pont de Nemours is not even mentioned. One must recognize, of course, that this extraordinary woman had many prominent friends who influenced her life more than du Pont did. In the present volume, however, we see a rather slighted aspect of her life: her role as a businesswoman concerned with preserving the fortune she had inherited from her father. I believe that the correspondence also sheds some new light on certain other aspects of her life.

[1] *Cahiers de politique étrangère du Journal des nations américaines,* Cahier LV–LVI (Nouvelle Série, 1946–50), 499–512.

[2] Ambrose Saricks, *Pierre Samuel Du Pont de Nemours* (Lawrence, Kans., 1965); Gustave Schelle, *Du Pont de Nemours et l'école physiocratique* (Paris, 1888); B. G. du Pont, *Du Pont de Nemours, 1739–1817,* 2 vols. (Newark, Del., 1933); B. G. du Pont, ed. and tr., *Life of Eleuthère Irénée du Pont from Contemporary Correspondence,* 11 vols. (Newark, Del., 1923–27).

In this work, there appear for the first time thirty-six letters from Mme. de Staël to du Pont de Nemours. All but one of these are to be found in the Eleutherian Mills Historical Library at Greenville, Delaware.[3] That library also contains twelve drafts or copies of du Pont's letters to Mme. de Staël, plus nine copies of his letters to her which are in the archives of the château of Coppet. Gustave Schelle made these copies in 1919 and presented them to the late Colonel Henry A. du Pont. Also included are two letters from du Pont which are in the Archives Nationales in Paris and one at Coppet which the Comte Le Marois copied for Mr. Lammot du Pont Copeland and presented to him. Excerpts from Le Marois' article fill in some gaps in this correspondence. Until the time when all the letters in the Coppet archives which du Pont wrote to Mme. de Staël can be studied, his side of the correspondence must remain incomplete. Nevertheless, I believe that enough of it is available to present adequately the relations between the two.

In order to present a more comprehensible picture of Mme. de Staël's business dealings with du Pont de Nemours, I have included letters written by other members of the du Pont and Necker-de Staël families, as well as some letters written by Mme. de Staël's notary and other persons. Letters between Jacques Necker and du Pont (and in 1801, between Necker and Victor du Pont), in particular, reveal du Pont's early acquaintance with the Necker family and Necker's investment in the du Pont business ventures.

Essentially, this work reveals both the friendship between Mme. de Staël and du Pont de Nemours, and the involvement of Jacques Necker, Mme. de Staël, and other members of the Necker family in the early history of the du Pont enterprises in the United States. Much of this correspondence is therefore concerned with financial matters. Although her passionate nature often caused Mme. de Staël to show poor judgment in various ways, this rarely extended to the realm of finance. Friendship was a sort of religion with her, and perhaps because of her strong attachment to her father, she seems to have had an especial fondness for older men. Her affection for du Pont, twenty-seven years older than she, was obviously sincere, although it became rather strained at times because of his

[3] The one in question is in the Historical Society of Pennsylvania.

difficulties in paying his debts to her, with the result that each distrusted the other somewhat. She worried about the fate of her
father's investment; he was disturbed about his financial problems,
and at one time, even feared imprisonment for debt at her hands.
Business problems, however, did not prevent their discussing the
political, social, and literary events of the times. Thus, their letters
often contain a rather bizarre mixture of eighteenth-century
galanterie and *esprit* with extreme frankness.

It is impossible to say when the two first met. He must have
encountered her at the Court and in Mme. Necker's salon, where
the precocious child conversed with the most distinguished leaders
of French life before the Revolution. The present correspondence
shows that du Pont knew Necker as early as 1778. The tone of the
letter from Mme. Necker included in this collection, which was
written about 1790, indicates that friendly relations had existed
between the Necker family and du Pont for some years.

Du Pont's first known comment about Mme. de Staël is far from
flattering. On March 15, 1796, he wrote to Carl Friedrich, the
Margrave of Baden:

> Mr Necker, dont vous me parlez, est enfermé dans son
> château de Coppet, à peu près invisible et vivant dans la mo-
> rosité et la solitude. Sa fille revenue de Paris avec deux estafiers,
> partage son temps entre la demeure de son père et les bals de
> Lausanne. Elle est plus impudique, plus effrontée, plus folle
> que jamais. Son nom est d'un tel scandale et ses extravagances
> sont si dangereuses que les constitutionnels l'ont totalement
> abandonnée et la laissent s'ébattre sur son républicanisme. Elle
> n'a au reste pas plus d'influence à Paris que la Reine Berthe.[4]

But in 1797, a year after he made his observations about Mme. de
Staël's disreputable behavior, du Pont, a member of the Council

---

[4] "M. Necker, of whom you speak to me, is shut up in his château at Coppet,
seeing almost no one and living in moroseness and solitude. His daughter, who has
returned from Paris with two armed valets, divides her time between the home of
her father and the balls of Lausanne. She is more lewd, brazen, and mad than ever.
Her name is so scandalous and her extravagant actions so dangerous that the con-
stitutionals have completely abandoned her and left her to frolic with her repub-
licanism. Moreover, she has no more influence in Paris than Queen Bertha." (Carl
Friedrich, *Carl Friedrichs von Baden Brieflicher Verkehr mit Mirabeau und du Pont*
[Heidelberg, 1892], I, 226.)

of Ancients, was evidently in some danger of being deported to
French Guiana as a result of the *coup d'état* of the 18 Fructidor,
which had been essentially an effort to eliminate conservative or
royalist members from the government.[5] Mme. de Staël claimed to
have helped save him from this fate. In her *Considérations sur la
Révolution,* she wrote:

> La proscription s'étendit de toutes parts après le 18 fruc-
> tidor; et cette nation, qui avoit déjà perdu sous le règne de la
> terreur les hommes les plus respectables, se vit encore privée
> de ceux qui lui restoit. On fut au moment de proscrire Dupont
> de Nemours, le plus chevaleresque champion de la liberté qu'il
> y eût en France, mais qui ne pouvoit la reconnoître dans la
> dispersion des représentans du peuple par la force armée. J'ap-
> pris le danger qu'il couroit, et j'envoyai chercher Chénier le
> poête, qui deux ans auparavant, avoit à ma prière prononcé le
> discours auquel M. de Talleyrand dut son rappel. Chénier,
> malgré tout ce qu'on peut reprocher à sa vie, étoit susceptible
> d'être attendri, puisqu'il avoit du talent, et du talent dra-
> matique. Il s'émut à la peinture de la situation de Dupont de
> Nemours et de sa famille, et courut à la tribune, où il parvint
> à le sauver, en le faisant passer pour un homme de quatre-
> vingts ans, quoiqu'il en eût à peine soixante. Ce moyen déplut
> à l'aimable Dupont de Nemours, qui a toujours eu de grands
> droits à la jeunesse par son âme.[6]

---

[5] Du Pont de Nemours was in danger several times during the Revolution. In 1790
he had almost been killed by a mob because of his opposition to the *assignats;* in
1792 he was forced to go into hiding as a result of his loyalty to Louis XVI; in 1793
during the Terror he was imprisoned for several months.

[6] "Banishment extended everywhere after the 18 Fructidor; and this nation, which
had already lost the most respectable men under the Reign of Terror, saw itself
deprived again of those who were left. Du Pont de Nemours was about to be exiled
—du Pont, who was the most chivalrous champion of liberty there was in France,
but who could not recognize liberty in the dispersion of the people's representatives
by armed force. I learned about the danger in which he found himself, and I sent
for Chénier the poet, who, two years before, had at my request given the speech to
which M. de Talleyrand owed his recall. Chénier, in spite of all that one may
criticize about his life, was capable of being touched, since he had some talent, and
some dramatic talent. He was moved by the picture of the situation of du Pont de
Nemours and his family, and ran to the tribune, where he succeeded in saving him
by claiming that he was a man eighty years old, although he was scarcely sixty. This
means displeased the lovable du Pont de Nemours, who has always had great rights
to be considered young because of his soul." (Paris, 1818, II, 188–89.)

Du Pont was sufficiently well known so that the ruse about his advanced years probably deceived no one. Ironically enough, Mme. de Staël played some part in effecting the *coup d'état* of the 18 Fructidor, though she claimed in later years that her role had been limited to the appointment of Talleyrand as minister of foreign affairs.

After this episode, du Pont de Nemours decided to emigrate to the United States, although he made no real preparations to do so until 1799. His subsequent relations with Mme. de Staël and the Necker family from that time until 1817, when both du Pont and Mme. de Staël died, are described in this correspondence.

In 1820, Auguste de Staël, Mme. de Staël's son, published his *Notice sur M. Necker*. The following passage in that work is a fitting epilogue to the correspondence between his family and the du Pont family:

> Lorsque l'on parle des économistes, le mot de secte est presque toujours celui qu'on emploie, et ce n'est pas sans raison; car tous les caractères des sectes religieuses se retrouvent dans les disciples de Quesnay: même zèle, même croyance aveugle à de certains dogmes, même intolérance pour les opinions différentes des leurs, même indulgence pour toutes les erreurs de leurs partisans, pourvu qu'elles ne comprommettent pas la doctrine; enfin même persévérance inébranlable dans leur foi. Aujourd'hui que l'économie politique a changé de face, on trouveroit encore tel homme, fort instruit d'ailleurs des progrès de la science, qui ne laisseroit échapper aucune occasion de protester en faveur de l'impôt territorial unique. Il seroit toutefois fort injuste de ne pas convenir que les physiocrates sont les premiers qui aient commencé à donner à l'économie publique le caractère d'une science, et de ne pas reconnoître que cette école compte parmi ses membres quelques hommes de génie, et plusieurs citoyens vertueux, animés pour le bien public de la passion la plus désintéressé. Qui pourroit prononcer sans respect les noms de Turgot et de Dupont de Nemours? [7]

[7] "When one speaks of economists, the word 'sect' is almost always the one that is used, and it is not without reason, for all the characteristics of religious sects are found in the disciples of Quesnay: the same zeal, the same blind belief in certain

When working from manuscript material to establish the text of these letters, I have reproduced them with each writer's peculiarities of spelling and incorrect accents, or complete lack of accents. This, of course, was not possible when it was necessary to work from modernized and corrected copies made by the Comte Le Marois or Gustave Schelle. It should be noted that the copies made by the latter are not always reliable, and I have therefore corrected certain obvious errors. Since the punctuation of the correspondents, especially that of Mme. de Staël, was often either capricious or nonexistent, I have inserted periods at the ends of sentences where they are missing, capitalized first letters of words at the beginning of sentences when necessary, and inserted apostrophes when omitted by the writers. This was done in order to facilitate reading of the text. Some of the drafts made by du Pont de Nemours are illegible in a few places. Ellipsis points within square brackets indicate these portions. I have kept accepted contractions such as Ier for *premier* and M^r for *Monsieur,* but certain contractions peculiar to the writers, such as p and p^r for *pour,* v^s for *vous,* and $n/^e$ for *notre* have been expanded. These occur most frequently in the letters of Victor du Pont, du Pont de Nemours' elder son. Square brackets indicate emendations by the editor.

Where the text for a letter has been taken from a source other than the original letter, I have so indicated in the heading to the letter. Otherwise, the text has been derived from the original.

I believe that careful and repeated collation of the French text with the manuscripts has kept inaccurate readings to a minimum. I repeat that the letters abound in the errors and peculiarities of spelling and grammar of the correspondents, but I have avoided the tiresome and constant repetition of *sic* to indicate them and

---

dogmas, the same intolerance for opinions different from theirs, the same indulgence for all the errors of their believers, provided that they do not compromise doctrine; finally, the same unshakeable perseverance in their faith. Now that political economy has changed, one could still find some men, well informed moreover of the progress of the science, who would not let any opportunity escape to protest in favor of taxes based solely on land. It would, however, be very unjust not to agree that the physiocrats are the first ones who began to give to public economy the character of a science, and not to recognize that that school counts among its members some men of genius, and several virtuous citizens, animated by the most disinterested passion for the public good. Who could pronounce the names of Turgot and du Pont de Nemours without respect?" (Pp. xlix–l.)

hope that the reader will recognize them as the work of the writers
and not as mistakes of the editor. Only in the case of errors which
might seem completely egregious have I inserted *sic*.

Simone Balayé, Georges Solovieff, and Beatrice Jasinski have all
indicated the characteristics of Mme. de Staël's spelling in their
excellent editions of her various letters.[8] Du Pont de Nemours had
fewer idiosyncracies. Perhaps the most interesting of those revealed
in these letters was his obsession with the circumflex accent. The
past participle of *être* becomes *été,* and the imperfect forms are
written with that accent, except when he neglects to use any accent
at all. In a letter to his son Eleuthère-Irénée du Pont dated December 19, 1794, he explained that since the circumflex represents an *s*
which has disappeared, it should be used in all forms where that
letter was originally used.[9]

Since this correspondence may interest students of economics,
government, and American history who may object to deciphering
the often antiquated or incorrect French spellings, I have included
an English translation of each letter. I have attempted, in these
translations, to keep the style and flavor of the original French as
much as possible and yet avoid a too literal translation.

I wish to thank all those persons and organizations that gave assistance in this project. First, thanks are due the University of
Wisconsin Graduate School and the Eleutherian Mills-Hagley
Foundation for the financial assistance which made the basic
research possible. I greatly appreciate the invaluable aid and sug-
gestions of the staff of the Eleutherian Mills Historical Library. I
must also thank the University of Wisconsin-Milwaukee Graduate School for providing certain clerical help.

On behalf of the Société d'Etudes Staëliennes and the de Staël
heirs, the Countess Jean de Pange has kindly granted permission
to reproduce the letters of Mme. de Staël. The du Pont family
letters taken from the collections of the Eleutherian Mills Historical Library are reproduced by that library's permission. Finally,

---

[8] Madame de Staël, *Lettres à Ribbing,* ed. Simone Balayé (Paris, 1960); Madame de
Staël, *Lettres à Narbonne,* ed. Georges Solovieff (Paris, 1960); Madame de Staël,
Correspondance générale, ed. Béatrice W. Jasinski (Paris, 1960).

[9] B. G. du Pont, *E. I. du Pont,* III, 129–30.

although most of the material used in this work is located at the
Eleutherian Mills Historical Library, I must recognize the Archives Nationales in Paris, the Historical Society of Pennsylvania,
and the Comte Le Marois for their permission to use certain letters
indicated in the text.

Milwaukee, Wisconsin   JAMES F. MARSHALL
June, 1968

Short Titles and Abbreviations

E. I. du Pont
> B. G. du Pont, ed. and tr., *Life of Eleuthère Irénée du Pont from Contemporary Correspondence,* 11 vols. (Newark, Del., 1923–27).

1801 Journey
> Victor Marie du Pont, *Journey to France and Spain, 1801,* ed. Charles W. David (Ithaca, 1961).

Journaux intimes
> Benjamin Constant, *Journaux intimes,* ed. Alfred Roulin and Charles Roth (Paris, 1952).

Le Marois, *Cahiers*
> Jean Le Marois, "Du Pont de Nemours et Madame de Staël," *Cahiers de politique étrangère du Journal des nations américaines,* Cahier LV–LVI (Nouvelle Série, 1946–50), 499–512.

LMSS
> The Longwood Manuscripts, Eleutherian Mills Historical Library, Greenville, Delaware.

WMSS
> The Henry Francis du Pont Collection of Winterthur Manuscripts, Eleutherian Mills Historical Library, Greenville, Delaware.

de Staël-du Pont Letters

❁

1

du Pont de Nemours to Necker

25 December 1778

From a draft, WMSS 2/1

From a draft, WMSS 2/1

Paris, 25 X^{bre} 1778[1]

Monsieur,

Mr Blondel [2] m'a fait l'honneur de m'ecrire de votre part que vous aviez examiné le tableau de la balance du commerce formé selon l'usage d'après les états de la ferme générale[3] et les estimations des chambres du commerce, que vous y aviez remarqué plusieurs imperfections, et que vous aviez jugé qu'il ne suffisait pas d'operer avec exactitude sur des materiaux quelconques, mais que le Rédacteur, en s'appliquant à rejetter les materiaux imparfaits devait indiquer les moyens de s'en procurer de meilleurs, qu'enfin vous aviez bien voulu jetter les yeux sur moi pour remplir cette fonction sous les ordres de MM. les Intendans du Commerce.[4]

Je ne puis qu'être reconnaissant, Monsieur, de la justice que vous avez rendue à mon zêle. Je me suis hâté de quitter la campagne pour prendre d'une maniere plus détaillée vos ordres et ceux de MM. les Intendans du Commerce.

Il me semble que pour entrer dans vos vues je dois commencer par faire des observations sur le travail actuel et chercher autant qu'il dépendra de moi à l'eclaircir et à le perfectionner. C'est à quoi je ne puis réussir qu'après en avoir eu communication et avoir profité de vos instructions sur les reformes que vous y jugez necessaires.

Peut-être faudra-t-il ensuite former un plan de travail plus etendu et selon lequel une partie des materiaux qu'on se procurerait pût servir à rectifier ce qui manque à l'exactitude des autres.

Vous n'exigez pas, Monsieur, qu'on arrive dans ce travail à une perfection complete. Il est infiniment difficile de controller toutes les estimations et même par rapport aux quantités la contrebande presente un obstacle qui ne peut jamais être entierement surmonté.[5]

Mais peut-être y a-t-il moyen de diminuer beaucoup l'obscurité dont s'enveloppe la contrebande, et d'acquerir des renseignemens sur une grande partie des objets qu'elle soustrait aujourd'hui aux Etats qu'on vous a présentés.

Plusieurs marchandises sorties de france en fraud sont obligées de payer à leur entrée chez l'etranger. Plusieurs autres qui entrent dans le Royaume pareillement en contrebande n'ont pu eviter les droits de sortie du pays qui les a produites ou envoyées.

Si nous avions donc les états des exportations et des importations de l'Etranger, nous y retrouverions une partie des objets échappés aux nôtres, et nous approcherions certainement davantage de la verité. Il ne resterait plus que les articles qui pourraient être exempts chez l'etranger de formalités et de droits, et ceux par rapport auxquels la contrebande a lieu des deux cotés dont on ne pourrait avoir de notion precise. Il est vraisemblable qu'à leur égard on sera toujours réduits aux conjectures.

Peut-être serait-il pratiquable de se procurer par les Ministres du Roi dans les pays etrangers et surtout par les consuls de France les états du commerce des pays où ils sont employés. J'en ai vu que M[r] le M[arqu]is de Noailles[6] avaient envoyés de hambourg et qui êtaient très curieux.

Il n'est pas douteux qu'en rassemblant une quantite suffisante de ces etats, on acquerrerait la connaissance d'un grand nombre de faits propres non seulement à diminuer l'imperfection du tableau de la balance du commerce nationnal mais même à donner une idée generale de celui de l'Europe entière. Il est vrai que cette recherche augmenterait beaucoup le travail, mais s'il a quelque utilité, cette utilité augmenterait dans la même proportion.

Je suis prêt, Monsieur, à me livrer, soit à ce travail, si vous le jugez convenable, soit à tout autre qui vous paraitrait approcher davantage du but que vous vous proposez. Je n'ai point oublié cependant l'esperance que vous m'avez donnée d'une retraite absolue, que je n'avais point désirée, que j'ai du accepter avec soumission, dont j'ai eu lieu de croire les arrangemens prêts à être consommés, à laquelle j'ai du me préparer de toutes manieres, et que j'attends encore avec une juste reconnaissance pour les bontés que vous y avez jointes. Mais si vous me faisiez en effet la grace de terminer ces arrangemens selon le plan que vous avez bien voulu me faire esperer, je ne m'en croirais que plus oblige de continuer avec le meme zêle le travail dont vous m'auriez chargé.

Je vous prie, Monsieur, de m'accorder un rendez vous pour mieux m'instruire de vos intentions. J'en attendrai l'ordre avant de rien entreprendre.

Je suis avec respect &

[Sans signature]

TRANSLATION

Paris, December 25, 1778[1]

Sir,

M. Blondel[2] has done me the honor of writing to me on your behalf that you had examined the table of the trade balance prepared according to custom from the conditions of the general farming of taxes[3] and the estimates of the Chambers of Commerce; that you had noticed in it several imperfections; and that you had decided that one could not operate accurately on just any data, but that the editor, taking care to reject incomplete material, should indicate the means of procuring better data; that finally you had been so kind as to consider my serving in this capacity under the orders of the Intendants of Commerce.[4]

I can only be grateful, Sir, for the justice that you have rendered to my zeal. I have hastened to leave the countryside in order to receive in a more detailed way your orders and those of the Intendants of Commerce.

It seems to me that, in order to understand your views, I must begin by making some observations on the present work and seeking, insomuch as it depends on me, to clarify it and perfect it. I cannot succeed in that until I have been informed about it and have profited from your instructions about the reforms which you consider necessary.

Perhaps it will be necessary afterwards to form a more extensive working plan, according to which part of the materials obtained could serve to rectify what is lacking in the exactness of the others.

You do not demand, Sir, that one attain complete perfection in this work. It is extremely difficult to check all the estimates, and even in relation to amounts, contraband presents an obstacle which can never be entirely overcome.[5]

But perhaps there is a way to diminish greatly the confusion in which contraband is enveloped and to acquire information about a large number of the objects which it now removes from the accounts which have been presented to you.

Various products which have left France fraudulently are obliged to pay duty on their entry abroad. Several others which enter France likewise as contraband have not been able to avoid the export duties of the country which produced or exported them.

If we had, therefore, the accounts of the exports and imports from abroad, we would find in them some of the objects which have evaded ours, and we would certainly approach the truth more nearly. There would remain only those articles which might be exempt from formalities and taxes abroad and those which are smuggled from both sides, about which one could not have any precise notion. It is likely that, in regard to them, we will always be reduced to conjecture.

Perhaps it would be feasible to obtain from the King's ministers in foreign countries, and especially from the French consuls, statements of commerce of the countries in which they are employed. I have seen some which the Marquis de Noailles[6] had sent from Hamburg which were very interesting.

There is no doubt that by collecting a sufficient number of these statements, one would learn a great many facts capable not only of lessening the imbalance of national commerce but even of giving a general idea of that of Europe as a whole. It is true that this research would mean a great increase in work, but if it has some usefulness, this usefulness would increase in the same proportion.

I am ready, Sir, to devote myself either to this work, if you consider it suitable, or to any other which would seem to approach more nearly the goal which you propose for yourself. I have not forgotten, however, the expectation that you gave me of a complete retirement, which I had not wanted, which I had to accept with submission, whose arrangements I had occasion to believe were about to be completed, to which I had to prepare myself in every way, and which I still await with a just gratitude for the kindness that you have shown. But if, in fact, you have done me the favor of ending these arrangements according to the plan which you kindly allowed me to hope for, I should believe myself only more obliged to continue with the same zeal the work which you had given me.

I beg you, Sir, to grant me an appointment in order to inform me better of your intentions. I shall await orders before undertaking anything.

I am with respect, etc.

[No signature]

NOTES

1 At the top of the page: *Cart[on]* (*Aff. g^{ales} du Commerce 1er dossier*). In pencil and in another hand: *Duplicate. N° 233*. At the bottom of the first page: *M^r le directeur général.*

2 Probably Jean Blondel (1733–1810), French jurisconsult and one of the editors of the *code criminel*. He wrote, among other things, an introduction to Necker's work, *De l'administration des finances*, published in 1785.

3 One of the tax agencies of the old regime in France.

4 Du Pont de Nemours had been recalled from Poland, where he had a lucrative position in the service of Prince Czartoryski, to serve as Inspector General of Commerce under Turgot. On the latter's dismissal as Controller General of Finances in 1776, which was due in large part to the enmity of Marie Antoinette, du Pont de Nemours lost his position also.

In 1778, Jacques Necker, who had found the statistics on foreign commerce completely inadequate, decided to recall du Pont to put them in order. Although du Pont distrusted Necker, Turgot advised him to accept the appointment. See Gustave Schelle, *Du Pont de Nemours et l'école physiocratique* (Paris, 1888), p. 203, and Ambrose Saricks, *Pierre Samuel Du Pont de Nemours* (Lawrence, Kans., 1965), pp. 70–73.

5 Much smuggling, especially from England, went on at this time. The treaty of commerce with England of 1786, in whose preparation du Pont played an important role, represented an effort to end this illicit trade. See Saricks, *Du Pont de Nemours*, pp. 91–98.

6 Emmanuel-Marie-Louis, Marquis de Noailles (1743–1822), French minister to North Germany in 1786, and in 1770, ambassador to the Netherlands.

2

du Pont de Nemours to Necker

18 May 1789

Archives Nationales, Paris

A Monsieur Necker
Ministre d'Etat, directeur
général des finances[1]

Monsieur,

J'ai l'honneur de vous envoyer une petite brochure dont l'objet est de faire adopter à nos chambres une forme de deliberation qui puisse apporter à la fois plus de perfection et de célérité dans leur travail.[2]

J'ai êté aujourd'hui pour vous la présenter; mais vous veniez de rentrer.

Je suis avec le plus profond respect
Monsieur,

Votre tres humble
et tres obeissant serviteur
du Pont

Versailles, 18 may 1789

TRANSLATION

To Monsieur Necker
Minister of State,
Director General of Finances[1]

Sir,

I have the honor of sending you a small brochure whose object is to have our chambers adopt a form of deliberation which may bring both more perfection and speed in their work.[2]

I went today to present it to you, but you had just gone home.

I am with the most profound respect
Sir,

Your very humble
and very obedient servant
du Pont

Versailles, May 18, 1789

NOTES
   This letter is reproduced by permission of the Archives Nationales.
   1 At the head of the letter in another handwriting is the notation R[*épon*]d[*u*], *18 may 1789, M. Dupont.*
   2 The work in question must be du Pont de Nemours' *De la meilleure manière de délibérer et de voter dans une grand assemblée,* 15 pages, 8°, published without the author's name in 1789.

3

Suzanne Necker to du Pont de Nemours

26 December [1790?]

WMSS 2/22

a Geneve le 26 d[écem]bre [1790?]
Je viens Monsieur de relire pour la troisieme fois la lettre surprenante que vous m'avez fait l'honneur de m'écrire, heureusement ce n'est pas le chant du cygne, ce sont les paroles de la Sybille sur son trépied, ou plustot celles d'anchise quand il presageoit les destins de Rome et la suite de ses descendants; je vais essayer de vous répondre, car malgré l'affaissement où mes maux m'ont reduite vous m'avez fait sentir que ma mort n'etoit pas *complette.* et tant qu'on évoquera mon ombre de cette maniere elle ne pourra s'empecher de reparoitre, mais elle est sourde a la voix des furies, et elle s'est cachée a Copet pour ne plus entendre leurs hurlements; vous êtes trop sage Monsieur pour vouloir des sacrifices inutiles, Mr Necker n'etoit plus qu'une colonne ébranlée qui soutenoit un édifice qu'on vouloit renverser; la colonne seroit tombée sous les decombres du bâtiment, si le Ciel ne m'avoit permis et suggéré de la transporter toute entiere, ainsi que ces beaux monuments qui decoreront à jamais les temples de Rome, quoi qu'ils fussent destinés par leur figure colossale a s'elever au milieu des vastes contrées de l'Egipte.[1] Je reconnois votre amitié dans l'attention que vous avez donnée a cet informe mémoire des *inhumations,*[2] je l'ai dicté rapidement pour acquitter un triste devoir, je voulois au moment où j'allois quitter la france suivre l'humanité jusques vers les confins qui la séparent des barrieres du jour; si j'avois eu a parler a des ames sensibles comme la vôtre j'aurois pu montrer la

mienne toute entiere, mais je donnois a des gens simples des conseils qui devoient être simples comme eux pour qu'ils pussent les suivre. Avec quelle inquietude, avec quelle profonde indignation nous avons appris les nouvelles de l'insurection que vous avez éprouvée.[3] Que les francois me paroissent à plaindre d'être ainsi sans cesse armés contre leurs plus zelés défenseurs, un jour ils auront les remords d'Atis[4] aprez avoir été fascinés comme lui; mais vous avez un grand courage et de grandes vertus et malgré les presages dechirants dont votre lettre est remplie, ce sera vous qui verres un jour le triomphe de la raison que vous esperés encor, et vous raconterés a vos neveux tout ce qu'elle vous doit et tout ce que vous lui devez.

J'ai reçu avec reconnoissance vos nouveaux et excellents écrits; votre esprit a autant de force que de souplesse, vous embrassés tous les objets tantot en leur servant d'appui et tantot en les faisant plier sous le joug de la reflexion et des circonstances. Vos ouvrages ont de plus ce caractère d'honnêteté, et de simplicité morale, toujours nécéssaire même aux esprits superieurs pour inspirer la confiance, c'est ici Monsieur ou nous sentons mieux tout ce que vous mérités, c'est à travers un air pur que les objets se montrent tels qu'ils sont, recevés donc de notre part un nouvel hommage avec l'assurance de tous les sentiments dont vous nous avez pénétrés et avec lesquels j'ai l'honneur d'être Monsieur votre tres humble et tres obeissante servante.

C[urchod] de Na[a]s Necker

TRANSLATION

at Geneva, December 26 [1790?]

I have just reread, Sir, for the third time the surprising letter that you have done me the honor of writing to me. Fortunately it is not the swan song: it is the words of the sibyl on her tripod, or rather those of Anchises when he predicted the destiny of Rome and the continuation of his descendants. I am going to try to answer you, for in spite of the prostration to which my ailments have reduced me, you have made me feel that my death was not *complete*. And as long as someone evokes my spirit in this way, it will not be able to prevent itself from reappearing. But it is deaf to the voice of the Furies, and it has concealed itself at Coppet in order not to hear their howling any more. You are too wise, Sir, to want useless sacrifices. M. Necker was nothing more than a shaken column which held up a building that men wanted to knock down. The column would have fallen under the ruins of the building if Heaven had not permitted and suggested to me to transport it in its entirety, like those beautiful monuments which will decorate forever the temples of Rome, although they were destined by their colossal size to rise in the midst of the vast countryside of Egypt.[1] I recognize your friendship in the attention that you have given to that unpolished memoir on *burials*.[2] I dictated it rapidly to carry out a sad duty. I wanted, at the moment when I was going to leave France, to follow humanity to the confines which separate it from the gates of life. If I had had to speak to sensitive souls like yours, I could have shown mine in its entirety, but I was giving to simple people some advice which had to be simple like them so that they could follow it. With what uneasiness, with what profound indignation, we learned the news of the insurrection that you experienced.[3] How much the French seem to me to be pitied for being thus unceasingly in arms against their most zealous defenders. One day they will have the remorse of Atys[4] after having been fascinated like him; but you have great courage and great virtues, and despite the heart-rending prophecies with which your letter is filled, it will be you who will see one day the triumph of reason for which you still hope, and you will tell your nephews all that it owes to you and all that you owe to it.

I have received with gratitude your new and excellent writings. Your mind has as much strength as adaptability. You embrace all subjects, sometimes serving as a support for them and sometimes making them bend under the yoke of thought and circumstances. Your works have, moreover, that character of honesty and moral simplicity always necessary, even to superior minds, in order to inspire confidence. It is here, Sir, that we appreciate more all that you deserve. It is through a pure air that things show themselves as they are. Receive, therefore, on our behalf a new homage with the assurance of all the sentiments with which you have filled us and with which I have the honor of being, Sir, your very humble and very obedient servant.

Curchod de Naas Necker

NOTES

1 Necker had resigned, under pressure, as minister in 1790 and retired to Switzerland.

2 Mme. Necker was haunted by a fear of being buried alive. In Paris hospitals,
she had seen persons not entirely dead removed from their beds and buried. Ill
at this time and feeling death approaching, Mme. Necker published in 1790 a
work entitled *Les Inhumations précipitées*. Her death occurred in 1794. Her
body was then placed in a basin filled with alcohol at the château of Coppet,
where her husband's body was also eventually deposited at the time of his death.

3 On September 2, 1790, du Pont, who had been president of the National Assembly during August, had been seized on leaving the Assembly by a mob which
wished to throw him into the Seine. Only the arrival of the National Guard
saved him. The Left provoked this incident because of du Pont's opposition to
the issuing of more assignats. As a disciple of Turgot, he had always opposed
paper money.

4 Atys, or Attis, a young Phrygian shepherd, was loved by the goddess Cybele. He,
however, was unfaithful to her. On learning of this, Cybele struck him with
madness. The shepherd mutilated himself and was changed into a pine tree.

4

Necker to du Pont de Nemours

3 August 1799

WMSS 2/12

Vous quittez donc notre Europe;[1] vous quittez notre france que
vous avez tant aimé, qui [*sic*] vous aimerez toujours, et à qui de si
bonne heure vous avez dévoué vos talents et vos services. Emportez
avec vous, Monsieur, le souvenir et la reconnoissance des amis de
la morale et des sentiments généreux. Je fais des vœux pour le
succes de votre entreprise; je fais des vœux pour votre bonheur; et
souvent, pendant ma courte carrière, je demanderai de vos nouvelles à ceux qui pourront m'en donner. J'ai à New York des correspondants d'une excellente réputation et qui m'en ont paru
dignes sous tous les rapports, autant du moins que j'ai pu en juger;
si vous avez besoin de leurs services, il seroit possible que mon
interest a vous anima leur caractère obligeant. Ainsy gardez cette
lettre comme une recommandation de plus auprès de ces estimables negotiants M[rs] Le Roy Bayard & Everts.[2]

Necker

Coppet le 3 aoust 1799

Postscript written by Madame de Staël:

Je veux joindre à cette lettre encor un adieu d'amitié; mon père n'a pas en ce moment d'affaires en amérique, mais qui sait moi si je n'en aurai pas? Vous serez mon avenir dans ce nouveau monde, où sans vous je n'aurois cherché que l'oubli de l'ancien. Adieu mon cher du pont. Je vous embrasse avec la plus tendre affection.

N[ecker] St[aël]

On the reverse:

Au Citoyen
Dupont de Nemours, rue
de l'oratoire à l'oratoire
a Paris

Postmark:

99 Genève

TRANSLATION

So you are leaving our Europe;[1] you are leaving our France that you have loved so much, that you will always love, and to which so early you devoted your talents and services. Take with you, Sir, the remembrance and the gratitude of the friends of morality and generous sentiments. I express wishes for the success of your undertaking; I express wishes for your happiness; and often, during the short course of my life, I shall ask for news of you from those who can give me some. I have in New York correspondents of excellent reputation, who have seemed worthy of it to me in every respect, at least as far as I have been able to judge; if you need their services, it is possible that my interest in you might encourage their obliging character. Thus keep this letter as an additional recommendation to those estimable businessmen, Messrs. Le Roy, Bayard and Everts.[2]

Necker

Coppet, August 3, 1799

Postscript written by Madame de Staël:

I wish to add to this letter another friendly farewell; my father has not, at this time, any business in America, but who knows whether I shall not have some? You will be my future in that new world, where, without you, I should have sought only to forget of the old. Goodbye, my dear du Pont. I embrace you with the most tender affection.

Necker Staël

On the reverse:

To Citizen
Dupont de Nemours, rue
de l'Oratoire at the Oratoire
in Paris

Postmark:

99 Geneva

NOTES
1 Du Pont de Nemours sailed for America in September 1799.
2 The correct name of this company was Le Roy, Bayard and McEvers. According to the *DAB* William Bayard (1761–1826) was the son of Colonel William and Catherine (McEvers) Bayard. Colonel Bayard was a colonial merchant, land-owner, and ardent Tory who raised a Loyalist regiment during the American Revolution. This resulted in the loss of his property by confiscation, and he sailed for England in 1783 with his family. His son William, however, remained in the United States and formed a trading company with Herman Le Roy in 1786. This became the most important commercial house of New York until its failure in 1827. James McEvers, Bayard's cousin, became a partner in the company some time after its founding. At the end of the War of 1812, this company was prospering greatly and was engaged in trading with countries all over the world. Its credit was excellent. The company later engaged in land speculation and was active in developing the Genesee country in New York. The town of Le Roy in that area was named for Herman Le Roy.

5

du Pont de Nemours to Madame de Staël

8 February 1800

From Le Marois, *Cahiers*, pp. 503–4

le 19 pluviose an 8

Madame,

Je vous écris en toute confiance et même en toute sûreté à Paris ou à Saint-Ouen. Vous avez une si vive passion pour les grands hommes, les grandes choses, et même les choses nouvelles qui, comme dit Cacambo,[1] sont toujours très curieuses à voir, que certainement vous n'êtes pas restée à Coppet quand on donne à la France sa dernière espérance et même une espérance raisonnable d'arriver enfin à un Gouvernement sous lequel on puisse vivre, qui connaisse les intérêts de la nation, et le prix de la liberté civile.[2]

Je n'ai pas besoin de vous avouer que si les événements qui ont eu lieu avaient précédé mon entreprise américaine, je ne me serais pas exilé à l'autre bout du monde; et je serais vraisemblablement avec vous à causer sur ce qu'on a fait, ce qu'on peut faire, ce qu'on doit faire et ce qu'on fera.

Mais c'est un bonheur qui ne m'est plus réservé.

Il n'y a aucune apparence aujourd'hui que je vous voie en Amérique.

Et lorsque j'y suis, chargé de la confiance et des capitaux d'une Société commerçante, qui ne me les aurait pas donnés si elle ne m'eût pas cru un homme de tête et un homme de bien, je ne puis abandonner ces affaires qui souffriraient beaucoup de ma retraite.

Les vertus publiques se composent de vertus privées. Celui-là ferait un mauvais administrateur politique ou d'État, qui n'aurait pas pu, ou pas su, ou pas voulu être un bon administrateur particulier pour ses associés, ses amis et ses parents.

Pourquoi m'accordez-vous une bienveillance qui m'est très précieuse? C'est que vous m'avez toujours vu très fidèle à mes patrons, à mes compagnons, à mes alliés et confédérés. Je ne saurais donc revenir en Europe qu'après avoir fait la fortune de ma Compagnie et la mienne: car c'est là ce que j'ai promis: c'est à cette condition que de fort honnêtes gens ont réuni leurs forces pour m'envoyer ici: c'est ce qu'ils attendent de moi.

J'ai lu, dans les Mille et une Nuits, autorité respectable et qui nous vient de l'Orient comme beaucoup d'autres, qu'après les princes, les conquérants et les vizirs, c'étaient les riches marchands que l'on considérait le plus, et qui passaient dans le monde pour les plus grands personnages.

J'ai très beau jeu dans ce pays-ci pour que la confiance et les affaires des négociants de l'Europe viennent m'y chercher: il ne s'en faut que d'un bien petit nombre de têtes que j'y aie le privilège exclusif de la prudence et de la sûreté.

Le caractère américain est l'*entreprenance*, presque tout le

monde excède ses forces, on *hasarde*. Surtout moi, qui n'ai la prétention de ressembler à personne, j'entreprendrai peu, et l'on aura
beaucoup de peine à me faire *hasarder* un écu. J'en ai déjà vu assez
ici pour juger que le métier de l'araignée y vaut mieux que celui
de l'hirondelle. J'y fais et ferai ma toile avec soin, précaution et
tout ce que Dieu m'a donné d'intelligence. Il n'y a pas, comme en
Europe, de servantes appelées Corps législatifs ou Puissances bel-
ligérantes qui donnent des coups de balai.

Du reste, le ciel, la terre, les eaux et les hommes champêtres y
sont d'une beauté et d'une bonté rares.

J'ai à me louer de la réception bienveillante de tout le monde
et des procédés libéraux même des employés de la douane, qui sont
en Europe une si mauvaise Compagnie.

J'espère que j'y conserverai votre amitié; et je la supplie de faire
toujours cas de mon respectueux attachement.

Du Pont (de Nemours)

Rappelez-moi au souvenir de nos amis, je les salue bien tendrement.

TRANSLATION

19 Pluviôse, year VIII

Madame,

I am writing to you in all confidence and even in all safety at
Paris or at Saint-Ouen. You have so strong a passion for great men,
great things, and even new things which, as Cacambo[1] says, are
always very curious to see, that certainly you did not remain at
Coppet when France is being given its last hope, and even a reasonable hope, of finally attaining a government under which one
can live, which knows the interests of the nation and the value of
civil liberty.[2]

I do not need to confess to you that if the events which have
taken place had preceded my American undertaking, I should not
have exiled myself to the other end of the world; and I should
probably be with you to talk about what we have done, what we
can do, what we must do and what we shall do.

But that is a happiness which is no longer reserved for me.

There is no likelihood now that I shall see you in America.

And when I am there, charged with the confidence and the capital of a company which would not have entrusted them to me if it had not believed me to be a capable and upright man, I cannot abandon this business, which would suffer a great deal from my withdrawal.

Public virtues are composed of private virtues. That man would make a bad political or state administrator who would not have been able, or not have known how, or not have wished to be a good private administrator for his associates, his friends, and his relatives.

Why do you accord me a benevolence which is very precious to me? It is because you have always seen me very faithful to my employers, to my companions, to my allies and associates. I could not return to Europe until I have made the fortune of my company and that of my own, for that is what I have promised: it is on that condition that some very respectable people have joined forces to send me here. That is what they expect from me.

I have read in the *Arabian Nights,* a respectable authority which comes to us from the Orient like many others, that after princes, conquerors, and viziers, it was rich merchants whom people respected most and who passed in the world for the greatest persons.

I am in very favorable circumstances in this country, so that the confidence and business of European merchants will probably come to seek me out; except for a very small number of heads, I almost have the exclusive privilege of prudence and safety.

The American characteristic is *venture:* almost everyone exceeds his strength; people *take risks.* Above all, I—who do not claim to resemble anyone—I shall venture little, and people will have a great deal of difficulty in making me risk an *écu.* I have already seen enough here to decide that the spider's job is better than the swallow's. I am making and shall continue to make my web with care, precaution, and all the intelligence that God has given me. There are not, as in Europe, any servant girls called legislative bodies or belligerent Powers who sweep about with brooms.

Moreover, the sky, the earth, the water, and the men of the fields are of a rare beauty and kindness here.

I must congratulate myself on the benevolent reception of everyone and on the liberal behavior even of the employees of the customs, who are in Europe such a bad group.

I hope that I shall keep your friendship there; and I beg you to value always my respectful attachment.

Du Pont (de Nemours)

Remember me to our friends; I send them kind regards.

NOTES
1 The valet in Voltaire's *Candide*.
2 Mme. de Staël had indeed returned to Paris from Switzerland in November, 1799. The allusion in this paragraph is to the events of 18 Brumaire (November 9, 1799), when Bonaparte, having returned from Egypt, overthrew the government of the Directory and established the Consulate the following day, with himself as one of the three Consuls.

6

Madame de Staël to du Pont de Nemours

2 May 1800

WMSS 2/13

ce 12 floréal an 8[1]

J'ai èté bien heureuse mon cher du pont de recevoir une lettre de vous. Ce que j'ai le plus souvent rèpèté depuis le 18 brumaire c'est que vous ne seriez pas parti et s'il vous avoit ramennè ce 18 il auroit bien mérité quelques èloges de plus. Nèanmoins je trouve que vous avez raison d'attendre jusqu'à la paix mais seulement jusqu'alors. Vous rapporterez fidèlement à vos associes ce qu'ils vous ont confié mais à la paix vous trouverez en france plus de moyens de faire valoir leur argent qu'en amèrique. Ce n'est pas mon cher du pont que si vous conservez votre ancien et fidele amour pour la liberté vous ne deviez trouver quelque chose à dire à notre constitution de l'an 8. Mais les hommes sont si bas qu'ils vous feroient oublier les choses. Je n'en dis pas autant de moi. Je suis un peu plus que vous encor enthousiaste de quelques idèes. Au reste quand tout vous paroit dècidè là bas tout nous semble encor incertain ici, et les èvènements de la guerre ont acquis une importance ènorme par l'influence qu'ils auront ici sur l'intérieur. Il paroit un ouvrage de moi sur la littérature que je vous prie de lire s'il vous parvient là bas.[2] Dans un gros livre on s'entend bien autant que dans une petite lettre et beaucoup de sentiments s'apperçoivent à travers les idèes gènèrales. Je pars pour la suisse où je vais passer mes six mois accoutumés. Vous saurez des nouvelles de la paix ou de la guerre cette anneè et vous reviendrez le printems de l'anneè suivante ayant bien ètabli vos correspondances avec l'amèrique et pouvant ètablir à paris une maison de commerce vraiment utile. Mais pouvez vous vous rèsigner là bas à ne jamais revoir vos amis qui sont tous rèunis ici maintenant et pour qui votre nom est si cher et si respectè. La fayette vit à la campagne nullement en faveur mais nullement persécuté. Il en est de mème des amis les plus vifs de la liberté. Les modèrès sont employès ainsi que les aristocrates et les terroristes. Toutes les nuances excepté celle qu'on peut considérer comme purement philosophique sont employèes par le gouvernement. Les partis ne s'en aiment pas mieux mais ils se voyent, et nous savons ce qu'il faut prèfèrer du divorce ou du marriage forcé. C'est une nation bien difficile à gouverner que la nòtre et je crois qu'il existe bien peu de moyens de conserver long-tems son enthousiasme. Les deux hommes que bonaparte paroit traiter le mieux c'est rœderer[3] et talleyrand.[4] Je suis mal avec tous les deux parce que benjamin[5] s'est placè dans l'espèce de petite opposition que comporte l'ordre de choses actuel et que les courtisans de bonaparte sont plus irritables que lui mème comme il convient dans un pays bien gouverné et ce n'est pas de gouvernement que nous manquons. Bonaparte qui est certainement malgré les èloges qu'on lui donne un trés grand homme, B[onaparte] fera je n'en doute pas quelque chose d'extraordinaire soit dans la guerre soit à la paix. Attendez donc les èvènements de cette anneè et prèparez vous pour nous revoir l'annèe prochaine. Avec quel plaisir je vous retrouverai vous que j'ai craint d'avoir perdu pour toujours—vous qui ètes le meilleur et le plus spirituel, le plus animè et le plus ferme et qui rèunissez tant de qualités presqu'opposèes que rèunit un bon coeur et une intelligence supèrieure. Parlez de moi à tout ce que vous aimez. Il n'est pas encor si dècidè que personne de nous n'ira vous rejoindre en amèrique.

[Sans signature]

TRANSLATION

12 Floréal, year VIII [1]

I was very happy, my dear du Pont, to receive a letter from you. What I have repeated most often since the 18 Brumaire is that you would not have left and if it had brought you back, this 18 would have deserved some additional praise. Nevertheless, I find that you are right to wait until peace, but only until then. You will bring back faithfully to your associates what they have entrusted to you, but after the peace you will find in France more ways to make the most of their funds than in America. This does not mean, my dear du Pont, that if you keep your ancient and faithful love of liberty, you should not find something to criticize in our constitution of the year VIII. But men are so base that they would make you forget things. I do not say the same about myself. I am, a little more than you, still enthusiastic about a few ideas. Moreover, while everything seems decided to you over there, everything still seems uncertain to us here, and the events of the war have acquired an enormous importance by the influence that they will have here on the interior. A work of mine about literature is being published which I beg you to read if it reaches you over there.[2] In a big book people understand each other as well as in a little letter, and many sentiments are glimpsed through general ideas. I am leaving for Switzerland, where I am going to spend my usual six months. You will have news of peace or war this year, and you will return in the spring of the following year, having well established your connections with America and being able to establish a truly useful business house in Paris. But can you resign yourself over there to never again seeing your friends who now are all reunited here and to whom your name is so dear and so respected? Lafayette lives in the country, not in favor but not persecuted. It is the same with the most ardent friends of liberty. The moderates are employed, as are the aristocrats and the terrorists. All shades of political belief, except the one that may be considered purely philosophical, are employed by the government. The parties do not like each other better, but they see each other, and we know which one must prefer, divorce or forced marriage. Ours is a very difficult nation to govern, and I believe that there exist very few ways of keeping its enthusiasm for a long time. The two men whom Bonaparte seems to treat best are Rœderer[3] and Talleyrand.[4] I am on bad terms with both, because Benjamin[5] placed himself in the sort of small opposition which the present state of things allows and because the courtiers of Bonaparte are more irritable than he himself, as is fitting in a well governed country, and it is not government that we lack. Bonaparte, who is certainly, in spite of the praise that one gives him, a very great man, B[onaparte] will do, I do not doubt, something extraordinary either in war or at the time of peace. Wait then for the events of this year and prepare yourself to see us again next year. With what pleasure I shall find you again, you whom I feared to have lost forever—you who are the best and the wittiest, the most animated and the most firm, who combine so many almost opposite qualities which a good heart and a superior intelligence join together. Speak of me to all you love. It is not yet so definite that one of us will not go to join you in America.

[No signature]

NOTES
1 The date 3 May 1800 appears on the manuscript and is in another hand, probably that of Mrs. S. F. du Pont. The correct date is 2 May.
2 Her *De la littérature, considérée dans ses rapports avec les institutions sociales.*
3 Pierre-Louis, Count Rœderer (1754–1835), one of the most active agents in the *coup d'état* of the 18 Brumaire, which he described as "une généreuse et patriotique conspiration." Napoleon appointed him Councilor of State on December 25, 1799.
4 Charles-Maurice de Talleyrand-Périgord, Prince de Bénévent (1754–1838), who had also been an active supporter of the *coup d'état* of the 18 Brumaire. He was reappointed to the Ministry of Foreign Affairs on November 22, 1799.
5 Benjamin Constant. He had been appointed to the Tribunate, one of the assemblies created under the Constitution of the Year VIII for the purpose of discussing proposed legislation. Constant, obviously prompted by Mme. de Staël, angered Napoleon by his attacks on tyranny in speeches given in the Tribunate. Fouché, the Minister of Police, thereupon advised Mme. de Staël to retire to the Necker country house at Saint-Ouen. She still hoped, however, to ingratiate herself with Napoleon. It should be noted that most moderates originally looked with favor upon the 18 Brumaire, as Mme. de Staël did.

7

Necker to du Pont de Nemours

7 May 1800

WMSS 2/13

J'ai eu beaucoup de plaisir Monsieur en apprenant par vous même votre heureuse arrivée a New York. Je souhaite de tout mon cœur que vous y soyez heureux; et s'il en etoit autrement après une année d'experience ne vous laissez pas enchainer par une premiere resolution et revenez dans notre Europe où vous serez tout aussy bien receu que si vous ne l'aviez jamais quittée.

Certainement vous obtiendrez Monsieur toutes les marques de confiance dues a la juste reputation de votre parfaite moralité. Je crois que si vous vous determinez a l'establissement d'une maison de commerce dans toutes les regles il vous conviendra de prendre un associé et de joindre son nom au vôtre. J'ai vu constamment qu'un homme seul en sa qualité de mortel inspiroit un peu de retenue et cette circonspection vous seroit applicable comme a un autre puisque dans la commerce on n'admet pas la longue durée des noms par la reconnoissance publique.

Je désire une fois de scavoir votre opinion sur la solidité de la dette americaine et de la banque de New York en particulier.[1] On voudroit aussy connoitre avec quel degré de sureté et quel interest on place en Amerique sur hypotheques. On n'est point pressé d'avoir ces informations et vous les donnerez a votre loisir si vous jugez a propos. Dites moi aussy par occasion ce qu'on pense a New York de la solidité de Mʳˢ Le Roy Bayard et Everts. Vous voyez Monsieur que dans les deux hemispheres on met a contribution vos lumieres. Mais ce qui m'interesse le plus c'est d'etre sur que vous êtes content du parti que vous avez pris et j'espere que non seulement vous vous garantirez de la fievre jaune[2] mais que vous mettrez encor les americains sur la voye de quelque sauvegarde ou de quelque precaution contre ce terrible fleau. Je vous prie Monsieur d'agreer mes vœux et les assurances de mon inviolable attachement.

Necker

Coppet le 7 may 1800

Je scais que ma fille a receu aussy une lettre de vous Monsieur.
Je l'attends icy dans huit jours.

TRANSLATION

I was very pleased, Sir, to learn from you of your safe arrival in
New York. I wish with all my heart that you may be happy there;
and if it is otherwise after a year of experience, do not let yourself
be chained by a first resolve, and return to our Europe, where you
will be as well received as if you had never left it.

Certainly you will obtain, Sir, all the marks of confidence due
your just reputation of perfect morality. I believe that if you
decide to establish a business house according to all the rules, it
will be fitting for you to take an associate and add his name to
yours. I have constantly seen that one man, alone in his quality as
a mortal man, inspired a little reserve, and this caution would be
applicable to you as to any other, since in commerce one does not
take for granted a long recognition of names by the public.

I wish sometime to know your opinion about the solidity of the
American debt and of the Bank of New York in particular.[1] We
should like also to know with what degree of safety and what interest one invests in mortgages in America. We are not in a hurry
to have this information, so send it at your leisure if you consider
it apropos. Tell me occasionally also what people in New York
think of the solidity of Messrs. Le Roy, Bayard and Everts. You
see, Sir, that in both hemispheres we press your knowledge into
service. But what interests me most is to be sure that you are
pleased with the decision that you have made, and I hope that not
only will you protect yourself against yellow fever[2] but that you
will also set the Americans on the way to some safeguard or some
precaution against this terrible scourge. I beg you, Sir, to accept
my best wishes and the assurances of my eternal attachment.

Necker

Coppet, May 7, 1800

I know that my daughter also received a letter from you, Sir.
I expect her here in a week.

NOTES

1 The Bank of New York began operations in 1784. Both William Bayard and
Herman Le Roy of the company Le Roy, Bayard and McEvers were directors of

the Bank—Bayard, from 1792 to 1794, and Le Roy, from 1795 to 1820 (Allan Nevins, *History of the Bank of New York and Trust Company* [New York, 1934], p. iii).

Necker's concern about the stability of the Bank probably resulted from the founding of the rival Manhattan Company in 1799. According to Allan Nevins

> With the closing of the century, New York, with a population of 60,000, had grown to be easily the largest of American cities. . . . The Bank of New York, still the only organization of its kind in the city incorporated under the State Law, and with only the Branch Bank of the Bank of the United States as a competitor, enjoyed unusual opportunities. Others had been eager to share them. Two attempts had been made in 1792 to secure bank charters for New York City groups. . . . But these organizations remained mere paper hopes, to die in the legislature. However, in 1799, under the leadership of Aaron Burr and Brockholst Livingston, a banking charter for a rival company was secured.
>
> It was Burr who was the active leader of this successful attack, and he won his victory by a ruse. New York City . . . was desperately in need of an adequate water supply. . . . Burr and his associates petitioned the legislature to grant a charter for a water company. A capitalization of $2,000,000 was requested. . . .
>
> But the wily Burr had tucked a clause into the bill which specified that surplus capital could be used "in the purchase of public or other stocks, or in any other moneyed transactions or operations not inconsistent with the laws and constitution of the State of New York." . . . The legislature . . . passed the bill and Governor Jay signed it, without suspecting that permission to establish a bank was being granted. . . .
>
> The Manhattan Company forthwith gave notice that it would begin banking operations in September with a capital of $500,000. The new company was a formidable rival . . . it had distinct advantages over its well-established rival, for its legal capitalization was $2,000,000 as against $900,000, and its charter was a perpetual one, while that of the Bank of New York ran until 1811 only. (Nevins, *Bank of New York*, pp. 30–31.)

2 Yellow fever had caused 2,086 deaths in New York in the summer of 1798. There was an even more fatal epidemic in the summer of 1799.

8

du Pont de Nemours to Madame de Staël

8 May 1800

From excerpts in Le Marois, *Cahiers*, pp. 504–5

18 floréal, an 8
Good Stay[1]

.   .   .   .

Mais je me trouve au bout du monde, lié aux intérêts d'une compagnie qui dans un temps de calamité m'a confié ses capitaux. . . .

On dit ici que les Français ressemblent un peu aux lièvres qui, après avoir bien couru, reviennent au gîte mais au moins ne ressemblent-ils pas aux lièvres dans la guerre.[2]

.   .   .   .

Si ma Compagnie peut servir, et elle le peut, je concilierai avec un extrême plaisir mes différents devoirs.

.   .   .   .

Ils n'auront point tort ceux qui voudront une portion de leur fortune en sécurité au delà des mers! [3]

.   .   .   .

Tous les négociants[4] me témoignent la plus entière confiance. Je recueille un peu le fruit de ma bonne renommée! . . . Vous sourirez en apprenant que ma maison de commerce à New-York est Liberty Street, N° 91 . . . on ne peut pas trouver un meilleur emplacement pour un ex-président de la Constituante comme lui.[5]

.   .   .   .

J'ai idée que M. de Staël redeviendra ambassadeur de France.[6] Je ne puis m'accoutumer à ne vous voir que baronne. Je n'ai commencé à être amoureux de vous que depuis que vous avez été ambassadrice: auparavant vous étiez trop jeunette, je n'aurais pas osé. Agréez au moins mon respect très tendre.

Du Pont de Nemours

Mme Du Pont de Nemours demande si je vous ai écrit mille choses pour elle; j'assure que oui.

52379

LIBRARY
College of St. Francis
JOLIET, ILL.

TRANSLATION

18 Floréal, year VIII
Good Stay[1]

. . . .

But I find myself at the end of the world, tied to the interests of a company which, in a time of calamity, confided its capital to me. . . .

People here say that the French are a little like hares, which, after having run a great deal, return to the form; but at least they do not resemble hares in war.[2]

. . . .

If my company can serve, and it can, I shall reconcile with an extreme pleasure my different duties.

. . . .

They will not be wrong, those who will want a portion of their fortune in safety beyond the seas! [3]

. . . .

All business men[4] show me the most complete confidence. I am picking a bit of the fruit of my good reputation! . . . You will smile to learn that my business in New York is at 91 Liberty Street . . . a better address than that cannot be found for an ex-president of the Constituent Assembly.[5]

. . . .

I have an idea that M. de Staël will become ambassador to France again.[6] I cannot accustom myself to seeing you only as a baroness. I have begun to fall in love with you only since you have been the wife of the ambassador: before that you were too young; I should not have dared. Accept at least my very tender respect.

Du Pont de Nemours

Mme. du Pont de Nemours asks whether I have remembered her to you; I assure her that I have.

NOTES
The entire text of this letter does not appear in Le Marois' article.
1 Property of the du Pont family at Bergen Point, New Jersey.
2 Le Marois indicates that du Pont de Nemours goes on to offer foodstuffs and war materiels to France in the omitted passage which follows.
3 A reference to du Pont de Nemours' friends in France.
4 In the United States.
5 Du Pont de Nemours was president of the Constituent Assembly in 1790.

According to Le Marois' summary of the omitted passage which follows, du Pont proposes a way of establishing an order of succession in a republic. This is the same method which he indicates was considered in Poland in his letter of November 27, 1800, to Mme. de Staël (see Letter 10).

6 The Baron de Staël had been dismissed as Swedish minister in October 1798 and had never regained the position.

9

Madame de Staël to du Pont de Nemours

6 August 1800

WMSS 2/13

Coppet, ce 18 thermidor, an 8[1]

J'ai reçu votre lettre ici mon cher du pont, et je ne retournerai a paris que dans trois mois. Cependant j'ècris à nos amis ce qui peut vous intéresser. Mon opinion est que vous avez besoin d'un voyage à paris pour ètablir les correspondances nècessaires à votre maison. J'ai vu à mon dèpart que l'intention des tribuns nos amis ètoit de vous porter comme candidat au sènat conservateur,[2] et j'espère que vous aurez les voix des deux nuances qui sèparent le tribunat, les gouvernementistes parce qu'ils sont composés en grande partie des anciens constitutionels, les rèpublicains parce que ceux d'entre eux qui ne sont pas fous vous ont toujours cru rèpublicain. Ce projet est formé pour l'hyver prochain. Je ne sais s'il s'accomplira mais ce que vous savez bien au moins c'est que j'y ferai tout qu'il dèpendra de moi. Ce qui vous ramenneroit en france me rendroit vraiment heureuse et jamais je ne pourrai remplacer le vuide que vous avez laissé dans ma sociètè. J'ai dèja quitté la france depuis plus de trois mois. Ainsi je ne vous dirai rien de bien piquant en politique. Ce que je sais de nous c'est la victoire[3] et la paix. Pour l'intérieur vous devez en juger comme nous. C'est une dictature glorieuse par les armes à côté de laquelle rien n'existe et rien ne paroit. Mais comment n'ètre pas enthousiaste de tant d'exploits mèmorables! A la paix nous saurons comment on organisera l'intérieur, car il me paroit peu probable que l'on ne modifie pas l'organisation actuelle. Cette paix est presque faite du moins sur le continent mais nous autres pauvres suisses nous n'y gagnons gueres car on établit chez nous 60 mille hommes à nos frais commandès par brune[4] et dumas[5] votre ancien collègue. Si cela duroit les habitants quitteroient le pays faute de nourriture. Nos amis sont tous rentrés. C'est de tous les biens du 18 brumaire celui auquel j'ai ètè le plus sensible. J'espère que mon père viendra réclamer au printems prochain ce qu'on lui doit. Si comme je le crois la paix est dècidèe revenez à cette èpoque pour un simple voyage ne fut ce que pour cela. Ce que vous direz de l'amèrique fera beaucoup plus d'effet que ce que vous en ècrirez. Vous rèchaufferez vos amis puissants. Les autres n'en ont pas besoin et vous arrangerez en deux mois ce qui ne se fera pas en deux ans si vous vous bornez à ècrire. Voila barbè marbois[6] conseiller d'ètat au dep[artement] de la marine. C'est avec lui que vous pourriez le mieux concerter ce qui concerne votre maison. Ce ne sont donc pas les intérets de vos associès que vous sacrifierez mais ce sont ces intérets mèmes que vous servirez en rendant heureux vos amis. Je suis reconnoissante et flattée du souvenir de Mad. du pont. Je vois souvent à genève sa sœur Mad. boulay.[7] Je la soigne par religion pour tout ce qui tient à vous plus que par gout s'il faut vous l'avouer. La liste d'éligibles[8] ne se fera que dans le cours de l'annèe prochaine—et j'ai de la peine à concevoir comment cette liste s'exècutera. L'institut[9] n'est past fort aimé par quelques dominateurs du jour mais votre nom concilie tout. Je ne crois donc pas que l'institut soit mis en masse sur la liste mais bien vous—si le titre de sènateur n'arrangeoit pas tout. Je suis convaincue que bonaparte aime les lumières mais quelques personnes se persuadent que c'est lui faire sa cour que de ne louer dans le monde que le pouvoir, et d'ècarter ceux qui ont l'habitude de l'analyser. La paix arrangera tout, mais la guerre nous a accablè de tant de malheurs que la nation entière est comme les hommes malheureux fatiguèe de tout ce qui demande du tems, de tous les remèdes dont l'effet est èloignè. Adieu mon cher du pont. Venez nous voir ne fut ce que pour causer, cela vaut un voyage.

[Sans signature]

Mon père me charge de le rappeler à votre souvenir. Votre lettre porte le n° 3. Je n'ai reçu que deux lettres de vous.[10]

TRANSLATION

Coppet, 18 Thermidor, year VIII [1]

I received your letter here, my dear du Pont, and I shall not
return to Paris for three months. However, I write to our friends
things that may interest you. In my opinion, you need a trip to
Paris in order to establish the relations necessary to your business.
I saw, on my departure, that the intention of the tribunes, our
friends, was to support you as a candidate for the *Sénat conservateur*,[2] and I hope that you will have the votes of the two nuances
which divide the Tribunate: the supporters of the government,
because they are composed in large part of the former members of
the constitutional party, [and] the republicans, because those
among them who are not mad have always believed you to be a
republican. This plan has been formed for next winter. I do not
know whether it will be accomplished, but you know well at least
that I shall do all that will depend on me. Whatever would bring
you back to France would make me really happy; never will I be
able to replace the void that you have left in my society. It has
already been more than three months since I left France. Thus I
shall not tell you anything very piquant about politics. All I know
about us is victory[3] and peace. As for internal affairs, you must
judge as we do. It is a glorious dictatorship of arms beside which
nothing exists and nothing appears, but how not to be enthusiastic
about so many memorable achievements! When peace comes, we
shall find out how the interior will be organized, for it seems unlikely to me that the present organization will not be modified.
This peace is almost made, at least on the continent, but we poor
Swiss scarcely gain by it, for 60,000 men are being stationed here
at our expense commanded by Brune[4] and Dumas,[5] your former
colleague. If this were to continue, the inhabitants would leave the
country for lack of food. Our friends have all returned. Of all the
good results of the 18 Brumaire, this is the one which I have appreciated most. I hope that my father will come next spring to claim
what is owed him. If, as I believe, peace is decided on, come back
at that time for a simple trip, even if it should be only for that.
What you will say about America will produce much more effect
than what you write about it. You will arouse again the enthusiasm of your powerful friends. The others do not need this, and

you will arrange in two months what would not be done in two
years if you limit yourself to writing. Barbé-Marbois[6] is now Councillor of State in the Navy Department. You could best arrange
what concerns your company with him. It is not, therefore, the
interests of your associates that you will sacrifice, but it is these
very interests that you will serve by making your friends happy.
I am grateful for and flattered by the kind remembrance of Mme.
du Pont. I see her sister, Mme. Boulay,[7] often in Geneva. I show
her attention as a sort of religious duty out of respect for you
rather than by inclination, if I must confess it. The List of Eligibles[8] will not be formed until some time during the next year,
and I have difficulty in conceiving how that List will be realized.
The Institute[9] is not very well liked by a few rulers of the times,
but your name conciliates everything. I do not believe, consequently, that the Institute will be placed in a body on the List, but
you certainly will be—if the title of senator did not settle everything. I am convinced that Bonaparte loves enlightenment, but
some persons are convinced that one courts him by praising only
power in the world and by driving away those who are accustomed
to analyzing it. Peace will arrange everything, but war has overwhelmed us with so many misfortunes that the entire nation is,
like unhappy men, tired of everything that demands time, of all
remedies whose effect is distant. Goodbye, my dear du Pont. Come
see us, even if it should be only to converse. That is worth a trip.

[No signature]

My father asks me to remember him kindly to you. Your letter
bears the number 3. I have received only two letters from you.[10]

NOTES

 1 In another hand, probably that of Mrs. S. F. du Pont, is *5 Aout 1800*. The correct
   date is August 6.
 2 One of the legislative bodies created by the Constitution of the year VIII. On the
   4 Nivôse of the year VIII (December 25, 1799), Sieyès, Roger Ducros, Cambacérès
   and Lebrun appointed the majority of the members of the Sénat, who, in turn,
   chose the remaining members. The Sénat never played an important role in the
   government and was always subject to Napoleon's will. Du Pont de Nemours
   was never appointed to it.
 3 The successful battle of Marengo had taken place on June 14, 1800.
 4 Guillaume-Marie-Anne Brune (1763–1815), marshal of France. He commanded
   the army sent to Switzerland in 1798 to overthrow the autocratic, aristocratic

government of Bern. The Canton of Vaud, in which Coppet is located, had been controlled by Bern until that time.

5 Comte Mathieu Dumas (1753–1837). Banished at the time of the *coup d'état* of 18 Fructidor, he took refuge in Germany. He returned to France after the fall of the Directory, and although under a cloud of suspicion at first, soon won the favor of Napoleon. Dumas regained his rank as a general and organized the Army of the Grisons, which invaded Switzerland in 1800 under the leadership of General Macdonald.

Both du Pont and Dumas had been members of the National Assembly during the Revolution, and later, of the Council of Ancients.

6 François, Marquis de Barbé-Marbois (1745–1837), a member of the Council of Ancients during the Directory and one of the group led by Mathieu Dumas, which included du Pont de Nemours, Royer-Collard, Portalis, and Lebrun. An opponent of the Directory, he was arrested as a royalist during the *coup d'état* of the 18 Fructidor and deported to French Guiana. After the 18 Brumaire, Napoleon released him, appointing him Councillor of State and Director of the Treasury in 1801. He was one of the early subscribers of the firm of Du Pont de Nemours, Père et Fils & Cie., though he later withdrew his support from the company. He is remembered mainly for his role in the Louisiana Purchase, in which he was the principal negotiator for Napoleon.

7 Susanne Boullée, the wife of Philibert Boullée (1760–1836). The address of a letter in the Eleutherian Mills Historical Library (A. Pictet to Boullée, 24 Messidor, year XIII [July 13, 1805]) identifies Boullée as director of the registry in Bourg. Another letter in the Library, written from Bourg (Boullée to du Pont, 28 Vendémiaire, year XIV [October 20, 1805]), indicates that he had served in a government position in Geneva.

8 Under the Constitution of the year VIII, the voters of each commune selected one tenth of their number as persons most suitable to direct public affairs. From these lists, one tenth were chosen for each department. Those designated from the department composed the list of citizens eligible for national public office.

9 Du Pont de Nemours had been a member of the Institut de France since 1795.

10 This postscript appears on the duplicate of the letter, in Mme. de Staël's handwriting.

10

du Pont de Nemours to Madame de Staël

27 November 1800

Archives Nationales, Paris

Good-Stay près New York
6 Frimaire, an 9

à Mme de Stael

Vous êtes bien bonne. Vous êtes dans les femmes que j'aime et qu'il faut aimer. Avec vous les Absens n'ont point tort. Vous n'oubliez pas vos amis. Faites des filles, afin qu'il en reste de la graine.

J'ai en France des philosophes qui me sont très chers, des amis très intimes, qui ne m'ont pas écrit autant que vous, ni aussi instructivement.

Cependant, je n'irai pas encore vous voir cette année.

J'envoie à ma place mon fils *le superbe*.[1]

La raison n'est point que je ne pusse être réellement aussi utile aux affaires de mes Associés en Europe qu'ici, supposé qu'il me fût possible de persuader au Gouvernement Français et au Commerce, que je ne viens en effet que pour l'interêt de mes Amis et de nos commettans, et nullement pour planter là leurs affaires et *quêter* des places: quoiqu'on dût savoir que je ne suis pas *quêteur*.

Mais ma réputation d'Administrateur, de Législateur, de Philosophe, êtant déja vieille, et plus que je ne voudrais, tandis que ma réputation de Négociant est toute jeunette, j'ai besoin de laisser prendre à celle-ci sa puberté, et de lui procurer quelques Bonnes-fortunes bien évidentes, afin que l'on sache, ce qui est vrai, que je veux et dois vouloir mourir dans la *République commerçante* où je suis entré, et qu'on y peut compter sur l'emploi de toutes mes forces.

Je ne renonce pas pour cela aux idées que votre amitié daigne avoir de faire contracter quelques rapports entre *ma République* qui peut très utilement en servir *d'autres,* et ces *Autres* qui peuvent très utilement la protéger. Je me vois ici le moyen de faire gâgner ou épargner bien des millions à la France comme marchande et cultivatrice, à la France comme Nation, à la France comme Gouvernement.

Et puisque je le peux, je le veux. Car ce sera en même tems le bien de ma Patrie et celui de ma Société.

Quand je pense avec combien d'économie et de succès nous pouvons hâter le rétablissement de la Marine et la résurrection des colonies, je ne puis m'empêcher de croire qu'il entrait dans les bonheurs si multipliés de *Buonaparte* que, un peu avant que l'Autorité fut réunie dans ses mains *réparatrices* quatre hommes aussi unis, aussi intelligens, aussi probes, aussi bons citoyens que Pusy,[2] moi, et mes deux enfans, se soient trouvés jettés par les circonstances sur le principal magasin des *Réparations*.[3]

En France, nous n'aurions pas mieux valu que d'autres. Et l'on aurait envoyé ici, *trop tard,* des hommes *tels quels,* qui auraient eu leur éducation à y faire, et qui par impéritie, *ou autrement,* auraient avec moitié moins de frait[4] gaspillé trente millions à la République.

Si je parle du *bonheur* de Buonaparte, ne croyez pas que ce soit pour ne pas rendre au *bonheur* tous les égards qui lui sont dus: moi, qui suis dans les hommes les plus heureux qu'il y ait au monde: moi qui regarde quelques uns des bonheurs comme l'effet de la protection des *Bons-Génies,* qu'on n'obtient pas sans la mériter; et la pluspart des bonheurs comme des données assez généralement répandues, dont il n'y a que les Gens d'esprit et de tête qui sachent profiter.

Tous les hommes ont des *bonheurs* qui amenent le volant sur leur Raquette. Mais les maladroits la laissent tomber, et ne la relevent pas. Les vigoureux et les habiles l'envoient percer les nues.

C'est *un bonheur* pour Buonaparte que d'être revenu d'Egypte sans accident. Ce bonheur n'est comparable qu'à celui qu'eut son Patron, *César,* de traverser l'Adriatique durant la tempête dans son Bateau-pêcheur. Et il est plus grand, en raison de ce que la traversée est plus étendue.

Mais il n'y a que *le Génie* qui ait dit: "Je passerai les Alpes dans un tems invraisemblable, par une Route à peu près impraticable; donc je n'aurai que la Nature à vaincre, et je ne rencontrerai pas l'Ennemi. J'arriverai au milieu de ses quartiers. J'enleverai ses magasins de vivres, d'habillemens, d'artillerie, de munitions, de fourrages, pendant qu'il s'amuse à prendre Massena et à poursuivre Suchet.[5] Je le séparerai de tous ses secours. Il n'aura de ressource qu'une Bataille. Et, comme dit le Comte Almaviva, BATAILLE! *c'est mon fort."* [6]

Ce sont le Génie et le Talent qui, d'une Armée de recrues, ont fait une Armée de Héros.—Il est vrai que ces Recrues êtaient des Français.—Respect à ma Nation! et revenons en Amérique.

C'est, comme je vous le disais, un lieu dont je ne puis sortir avant qu'on soit très certain que je n'abandonnerai jamais les devoirs que m'impôse le Contrat qui m'y a conduit; et avant que j'aie préparé toutes les mesures qui pourront faire réussir les affaires dont j'y suis et dois naturellement y être chargé, de façon qu'elles y marchent sans moi avec la même perfection, et que ce soit à celles de leurs branches qui doivent être déployées en Europe que mon travail devienne le plus utile.

J'aurais pu négocier aussi bien que mon Fils les opèrations que nous avons à suivre à Paris. Et le très doux plaisir de vous voir, l'avantage de m'y trouver au Printems avec M^r votre Pere, de savoir de lui même s'il approuve mes plans, ce qu'il y ajouterait, ce qu'il y changerait, êtaient de puissantes tentations.

Mais mon maudit visage aurait détruit l'effet de mes bons discours. Plusieurs de nos meilleurs amis, à commencer par *Talleyrand,* auraient empêché d'ajouter foi, de donner confiance à mes propositions, en croyant, en disant, que c'aurait êté *le Théatre du Vaudeville* ou *le Conseil d'Etat*[7] que je serais venu chercher, pour me sauver de l'ennui qu'ils ont trouvé en Amérique,[8] où je ne l'ai pas même entrevu dans mon jardin, dans mon Bureau, dans ma Maison patriarchale.

Et les Commerçans distingués dont je veux l'estime raisonnée, auraient trouvé *léger* que ce fût moi qui dans notre Société me chargeasse des voyages. Ils auraient cru avec le ministere et plus encore que lui, qu'il ne fallait pas compter sur ma vocation pour l'Etat de Négociant.

Cependant, il n'y aurait qu'un Fou qui pût abandonner mon *très libre* métier, dans lequel je suis à portée de traiter avec les Cours en Allié et en Coopérateur Secourable, pour attendre ou recevoir *de leur* GRANDEUR, *des Places* laborieuses et subordonnées.

Il faut être *justus et tenax propositi Vir.*[9]

De toutes vos dignités *françaises,* partagées entre mes compagnons et mes Amis, la seule qui ne me fût pas disconvenable aujourd'hui (et j'aimerais mieux la recevoir en absence qu'en présence) est celle sur laquelle vous me dites qu'on a eu une pensée dont je suis reconnaissant: l'entrée au *Sénat conservatoire.*[10] J'aurais tort d'annoncer pour elle *une Prétention* déplacée; j'aurais plus grand tort de faire des sollicitations ridicules. Mais j'aurais tort aussi de ne point accepter cet honneur, si l'estime de mes concitoyens me le faisait accorder. D'un côté, je suis *conservateur* par Principes, par expérience, par haine contre les secousses et les bouleversemens. De l'autre je ne pourrais trouver d'objection dans l'interêt de ma Compagnie, attendu que le Senat demande rarement un emploi de tems considérable, et qu'il y a exemple, au moins celui de *Le Couteulx,*[11] de Sénateurs qui etaient négocians et n'ont point quitté leurs affaires.

Je n'ôserais donc et ne voudrais pas refuser a l'Etat *ma* FERMETÉ *stationaire.* Mon travail journalier est à ma Société. Ce n'est que celui de ma Société que je puis offrir. Mais il peut en valoir un autre; et je désire qu'on en profite plus que d'un autre.

Quant à *la conservation,* elle tient uniquement à ce que le Premier Consul fera, ou fera faire, ou laissera faire, pour la succession, après sa mort, de sa place qui necessairement et sans difficulté doit être à vie, si l'on ne veut pas de grands et dangereux troubles périodiques et une corruption générale.

Il faut éviter l'Election par les Armées, que les *Sénats* sont toujours obligés de confirmer.

Il faut également éviter la succession héréditaire qui donne quelquefois des *Nérons* et presque toujours des imbéciles.

Je vous ai marqué à ce sujet ce que nous avons êté au moment d'établir en Pologne.[12] Une Election annuelle au scrutin secret dans toutes les *diétines,*[13] le même jour, à la même heure; les scrutins portés au Sénat et conservés sans être ouverts jusqu'à l'année suivante; jettés au feu, sans les ouvrir, et remplacés par un nouveau scrutin également général et secret, si au bout de l'année le Premier Magistrat vit encore; ouverts et dépouillés le jour de sa mort; et donnant *nécessairement* pour successeur un des hommes les plus marquans dans l'opinion publique.

C'est cette lettre de moi que vous n'avez point reçue: ce qui me donne à penser.

J'en ai écrit à *Maret*[14] avec plus de détail. Et j'ignore s'il a lu ma lettre.

Je suis buté d'en faire *un Ouvrage* régulier et en forme. Le Premier Magistrat, le Peuple, tous les corps sont sur un volcan, tant qu'il n'y a point d'héritier désigné, et quand la force militaire peut en donner un du soir au matin, comme à Rome. Et il est insupportable pour les Nations d'obéir à *Charles Six* ou même à *Louis Treize,* parcequ'ils sont, ou paraissent, de tel sang et lignée.

Le magistrat actuel est jeune: on a le tems d'y songer. Mais la chose importe. Et je ne serai point tranquille si elle ne se décide pas de manière à nous assurer la perpétuité d'un Gouvernement d'hommes éclairés.

Ce serait pour moi une forte raison de me claquemurer encore plus dans le magasin de mon indépendante République commerciale.

J'ai écrit fort au long à M[r] votre Pere sur des questions qu'il m'a faites relativement au Pays que j'habite; ce qui m'a conduit à lui exposer comment je compte y piloter ma Barque. Pourrez vous me dire, sans le lui demander formellement, s'il m'a trouvé raisonnable?

Je baise vos belles mains; et j'ai pour vous un attachement respectueux, fidele et tendre.

D. P. d. N.

Mes enfans vous verront et parleront pour eux mêmes.[15]

Ma Femme est sensible à vos bontés pour elle, et même pour sa sœur;[16] et surtout à celles dont vous m'avez donné des preuves si actives, quand j'avais l'honneur d'être au cachot avec trois voleurs et un assassin, quoique je n'aie jamais ni volé, ni assassiné personne.[17]

P.S. Il faut que je vous ajoute un mot sur les *Listes des Eligibles*. Il est impossible de les former par *Elections positives* autrement qu'entre les *présens* aux Assemblées Electorales: sans quoi les grandes réputations occasionneraient des doubles emplois, et il y aurait des voix perdues. Et l'on élirait aussi des morts, ce qui perdrait d'autres voix.

Mais il en résultera que suivant la rigueur de la Loi générale, tous les militaires employés au dehors, le Général Moreau, le Général Le Courbe;[18] tous les marins à bord des vaisseaux; tous les Ambassadeurs, leurs Secretaires, les consuls, les Savans voyageurs par ordre du Gouvernement, comme Broussonet,[19] moi,[20] ceux de l'Institut d'Egypte,[21] le Capitaine Baudin[22] et ses estimables compagnons, seront *exclus*. Et que, même après leur retour, ils demeureront obligés à deux ans au moins de *Stage* avant que le Gouvernement puisse employer leurs talens, ou récompenser leur mérite.

Ainsi le Gouvernement sera privé de très bons et très utiles coopérateurs. Et ils seront *punis* pour avoir très bien servi. Cela n'a pas de sens.

Il faut remarquer que désormais il n'y aura rien de plus désagréable en France que l'état d'un homme *connu* qui ne sera sur aucune liste. Je conseillerais à tous ceux qui seront dans le cas de rester ou de passer chez l'Etranger.

Comment y pourvoir? Et qu'est-ce que disent à cet égard la

raison et la justice? Qu'il faut pour la premiere fois admettre, chacun dans leur grade, ceux dont *l'absence* est l'accomplissement d'un devoir. Voici la Loi que je proposerais.

"Tous les citoyens *absens* par ordre du gouvernement et pour le service de la République seront compris dans les *Listes natio-nales* ainsi qu'il suit. Les Soldats et Matelots en service ou prison-niers de guerre seront *de droit* sur la *premiere liste,* ou celle des six cent mille. Les sous officiers et officiers jusques et compris le grade de capitaine, et les officiers des navires marchands dans la *Seconde Liste* ou celle des *soixante mille.* Les militaires au dessus du grade de capitaine, les marins commandans des vaisseaux de l'Etat, les Ambassadeurs, ministres, consuls, secretaires de légation, les chanceliers des consulats, et les Savans qui sont en voyage par ordre du Gouvernement pour l'avancement des sciences, dans la *Troisieme Liste,* ou celle des *Six mille.*"

TRANSLATION

Good Stay near New York
6 Frimaire, year IX

To Madame de Staël:

You are very good. You are one of the women whom I love and whom it is necessary to love. With you, absent ones are not in the wrong. You do not forget your friends. Have some daughters so that some seed will be left.

I have in France some philosophers who are very dear to me, very close friends, who have not written to me as much as you, nor as instructively.

However, I shall not be going to see you this year.

I am sending in my place my son, *the superb.*[1]

The reason is not that I could not be really as useful in the business of my associates in Europe as here, supposing that I could persuade the French government and the world of commerce that I come in fact only in the interest of my friends and our principals and not at all to abandon their business and *seek* positions, al-though people ought to know that I am not a *seeker.*

But my reputation as an administrator, legislator, and philos-opher being already old, and more so than I should like, while my reputation as a businessman is quite young, I need to let the latter reach its puberty and obtain for it some very evident successes, so that people will know that which is true, that I want and must resolve to die in the *commercial republic* which I have entered and that they can count on the employment of all my strength in it.

I do not renounce for that reason the ideas that you deign to have, because of your friendship, of contracting some relationships between *my republic,* which can very usefully serve *others,* and these *others,* who can very usefully protect it. I see myself here as the means of earning or saving many millions for France in its role as a merchant and agriculturist, for France as a nation, for France as a government.

And since I can do so, I will do so. For it will be at the same time the good of my country and that of my company.

When I think with how much economy and success we can hasten the reestablishment of the Navy and the revival of the colonies, I cannot help but believe that it was part of the many good fortunes of *Bonaparte* that, a little before authority was gathered in his *restoring* hands, four men as united, as intelligent, as honest, as good citizens as Pusy,[2] I, and my two children should find ourselves cast by circumstances on the principal storehouse of *reparations.*[3]

In France, we would not have been any better than others. And they would have sent here, *too late,* some *ordinary* men, who would have had their education to get, and who, by incompetence due to lack of experience, *or otherwise,* would have, with half the cargo, wasted thirty millions for the Republic.

If I speak of the *good fortune* of Bonaparte, do not think that it is in order not to render to *good fortune* all the respect that is due it—I, who am among the happiest men in the world; I, who regard some good fortune as the effect of the protection of *Good Spirits,* which one does not obtain without deserving it, and most good fortune as a rather generally widespread fact, from which only people of wit and intelligence know how to profit.

All men have *good fortunes* which bring the shuttlecock onto their battledore. But the awkward ones let it fall and do not pick it up again. The vigorous and skillful ones send it to pierce the clouds.

It is a *good fortune* for Bonaparte to have returned from Egypt without accident. This good fortune is comparable only to that which his patron, *Caesar,* had in crossing the Adriatic during the storm in his fishing boat. And he is greater because the crossing is longer.

But it is only *Genius* who said: "I shall cross the Alps in unbelievable weather, by an almost impassable route; thus I shall have only nature to vanquish, and I shall not encounter the enemy. I shall arrive in the midst of his quarters. I shall carry off his stores of food, clothing, artillery, munitions, fodder, while he amuses himself by taking Masséna and pursuing Suchet.[5] I shall separate him from all help. His only resource will be a battle. And, as Count Almaviva says, Battle! *that is my strong point.*"[6]

It is Genius and Talent which, of an army of recruits, have made an army of heroes.—It is true that these recruits were French.— Respect for my country! and let us come back to America.

It is, as I was saying, a place that I cannot leave before people are very certain that I shall never abandon the duties that the contract which brought me here imposes on me, and before I have prepared all the measures which can make a success of the business of which I am, and must naturally be, in charge, so that it will proceed with the same perfection without me, and so that my work will become most useful to those of its branches which must be spread to Europe.

I could have negotiated as well as my son the operations that we have to effect in Paris. And the very sweet pleasure of seeing you, the advantage of being there in the spring with your father, of learning from him whether he approves of my plans, what he would add to them, what he would change in them, were powerful temptations.

But my accursed face would have destroyed the effect of my good words. Several of our best friends, beginning with *Talleyrand,* would have prevented people from crediting, from relying on my proposals, by believing, by saying, that it was the *Théâtre du Vaudeville* or the *Council of State*[7] that I had come to seek, in order to save myself from the boredom that they found in America,[8] but which I have not even glimpsed in my garden, in my office, [or] in my patriarchal house.

And the distinguished merchants whose reasoned esteem I want would have found it *frivolous* that I should be the one in our company who should concern myself with traveling. They would have believed with the ministry, and even more than it, that my vocation as a businessman could not be counted on.

However, only a madman could abandon my *very free* business, in which I am within reach of dealing with the courts as an ally and helpful cooperator, in order to await or receive *from their* LORDSHIPS arduous and subordinate *positions*.

One must be *justus et tenax propositi Vir*.[9]

Of all your *French* honors, shared among my companions and friends, the only one which would not be unsuitable for me today (and I would prefer to receive it in absentia rather than in presence) is the one about which you say there has been a thought, for which I am grateful: entry into the *Sénat conservatoire*.[10] I should be wrong to reveal an improper *ambition* for it; I should be more wrong to make ridiculous solicitations. But I should be wrong also not to accept this honor if the esteem of my fellow citizens caused it to be granted to me. On the one hand, I am *conservative* in principle, from experience, from hatred of jolts and upsets. On the other, I could not find any objection in the interest of my company, considering that the Sénat rarely requires a considerable amount of time and that there is an example, at least that of *Le Couteulx*,[11] of senators who were businessmen and did not leave their business.

I should not dare and should not wish to refuse the state *my steady* FIRMNESS. My daily work belongs to my company. It is only the efforts of my company that I can offer. But they can be as good as any other, and I want people to profit from them more than from another.

As for *conservation*, it depends only on what the First Consul will do, or will have done, or will allow to be done after his death for the succession to his position, which necessarily and without difficulty must be for life, if we do not want periodic great and dangerous troubles and general corruption.

We must avoid election by the armies, which *Senates* are always obliged to confirm.

We must also avoid hereditary succession, which sometimes produces *Neros* and almost always imbeciles.

On this subject, I have indicated to you what we were about to establish in Poland:[12] An annual election, with a secret ballot, in all the *diétines*,[13] the same day, at the same time; the ballots brought to the Senate and kept without being opened until the next year; thrown into the fire, without opening them, and re-placed by a new ballot equally general and secret, if at the end of the year the First Magistrate is still living; opened and counted the day of his death; and giving *necessarily* as successor one of the most prominent men in public opinion.

It is that letter from me that you did not receive which makes me pause to think.

I wrote to *Maret*[14] about it in more detail. And I do not know whether he has read my letter.

I am dead set on making of it *a work,* regular and in form. The First Magistrate, the common people, all groups are on a volcano as long as there is no designated heir and when the military force may produce one overnight, as in Rome. And it is un-bearable for countries to obey *Charles VI* or even *Louis XIII* because they are, or appear to be, of a certain blood and lineage.

The present magistrate is young; we have time to think about it. But the matter is important. And I shall not be at ease if it is not decided in such a way as to assure us of the perpetuity of a govern-ment of enlightened men.

That would be, for me, a strong reason to shut myself up still more in the store of my independent commercial republic.

I have written your father at great length on some questions which he asked me about the country in which I am living, which led me to expose to him how I expect to pilot my ship. Can you tell me, without asking him expressly, if he found me reasonable?

I kiss your beautiful hands, and I have for you a respectful, faithful, and tender attachment.

D. P. d. N.

My children will see you and speak for themselves.[15]

My wife is grateful for your kindness to her, and even to her sister,[16] and especially for that of which you gave me such active proof when I had the honor of being in prison with three thieves and a murderer, although I have never robbed or murdered anyone.[17]

P.S. I must add a word about the *Lists of Eligibles.* It is im-possible to form them by *positive elections* except among the *persons present* in Electoral Assemblies: without this, great reputations would result in double positions, and votes would be lost. And dead men would also be elected, which would lose other votes.

But the result will be that, following the strictness of the general law, all soldiers employed outside the country, General Moreau, General Le Courbe;[18] all sailors on board ships; all ambassadors, their secretaries, consuls, scientists traveling by order of the government, like Broussonet,[19] myself,[20] those of the Institute of Egypt,[21] Captain Baudin[22] and his respectable companions, will be *excluded.* And even after their return, they will remain obliged to spend two years at least on *probation* before the government can use their talents or reward their merit.

Thus the government will be deprived of very good and very useful cooperators. And they will be *punished* for having served very well. That makes no sense.

I must remark that, henceforth, there will be nothing more disagreeable in France than the condition of a *well known* man who is not on any list. I should advise all in that position to stay abroad or go abroad.

How to provide for that? And what do reason and justice say in that regard? That it is necessary for the first time to admit, each one in his rank, those whose *absence* is the accomplishment of a duty. Here is the law that I should propose:

"All citizens *absent* by order of the government and for the service of the Republic will be included in the *national lists* as follows. Soldiers and sailors in service or prisoners of war will be *by right* on the *first list,* or that of the 600,000. Non-commissioned officers and officers up to and including the rank of captain, and officers of merchant ships on the *second list,* or that of the *60,000.* Soldiers above the rank of captain, captains of ships of the State, ambassadors, ministers, consuls, secretaries of legations, chancellors of consulates, and scientists who are traveling by order of the government for the advancement of science, in the *third list,* or that of the *6,000.*"

NOTES

This letter is reproduced by permission of the Archives Nationales. The Eleutherian Mills Historical Library has a draft of the first eight paragraphs (WMSS 2/3).

1 Victor du Pont. He had received this nickname from Mme. de Staël. Mme. Victor du Pont states that "Mad^e de Stael, qui goutait si bien l'esprit vif et penetrant de

Du Pont de Nemours, qui l'aimait beaucoup, . . . avait baptisé son fils Victor *le superbe.*" ("Mme. de Staël, who enjoyed so much the lively and penetrating mind of Du Pont de Nemours, who liked her very much, . . . had given the name of *the superb one* to his son Victor.") (Mme. Victor du Pont, "Notre Transplantation en Amérique" [unpubl. MS, Eleutherian Mills Historical Library], p. 12.)

2 Jean Xavier Bureaux de Pusy (1750–1806), the son-in-law of the second Mme. du Pont de Nemours. A distinguished army engineer, he had served on the staff of Lafayette. The Austrians captured both Bureaux de Pusy and Lafayette in 1792 and imprisoned them at Olmütz. Released in 1797 on the condition that he not return to France, he sailed from Holland in 1799 for the United States with his daughter Sara and Mme. du Pont de Nemours, several months before the departure of the other members of the family. He returned to France after the 18 Brumaire and was appointed prefect of the Department of Allier in 1801.

3 The United States, which could send supplies to troops in the West Indies more easily than could France.

4 Probably a misspelling of *fret* ("cargo").

5 André Masséna, Duc de Rivoli, Prince d'Essling (1756–1817), marshal of France who distinguished himself in 1800 at the siege of Genoa; and Louis Suchet, Duc d'Albufera (1772–1826), marshal of France.

6 Count Almaviva, a character in Beaumarchais' *Barber of Seville* and *Marriage of Figaro.* In Act II, Scene xiv of the *Barber of Seville,* he exclaims: "Bataille? Ah, volontiers, bataille! c'est mon métier à moi." ("Battle? Ah, gladly, battle! that is my trade.")

7 The Théâtre du Vaudeville, founded during the Revolution, presented *vaudevilles,* brief, light comedies of manners. Du Pont de Nemours had been a member of the Council of State before the Revolution and had served as Commissioner General of Commerce.

8 It is well known that Talleyrand had found life in the United States extremely tiresome during his stay there.

9 "A just and tenacious man of purpose."

10 Du Pont de Nemours means the Sénat conservateur.

11 Jean Barthélemy Le Couteulx de Canteleu (1749–1818), a banker and politician who had been a member of the States-General and of the National Constituent Assembly. An ardent admirer of Napoleon, he was appointed to the Sénat at the time of its creation. He had been president of the Caisse d'Escompte, a bank founded in 1776, and was one of the founders of the Banque de France. He and J. F. Perrégaux were presidents of the latter from 1800 to 1806. Always interested in questions of economics and taxation, he published, among other works, a *Réfutation de la lettre de Dupont de Nemours adressée à la Chambre de Commerce de Normandie* in 1788. The Franco-British commercial treaty of 1786, in which du Pont de Nemours had played a major part, aroused much criticism because of its easing of restrictions on trade, and one of the most famous protests came from the Chamber of Commerce of Rouen in Normandy. Du Pont's reply attracted attention also because of his attack on the doctrine of protectionism.

12 Du Pont de Nemours had gone to Poland in 1774, with a generous salary, as preceptor of the son of Prince Czartoryski; he had also been promised the position as secretary of the King of Poland, Stanislaus II, in the Council of Public Instruction. Polish education was practically nonexistent, however, and du Pont was able only to plan some secondary schools.

At this time, Stanislaus was attempting to strengthen his decaying country by constitutional and educational reforms. It appears, from this passage, that he consulted du Pont about constitutional reforms also.

13 Polish legislative assemblies.

14 Hugues-Bernard Maret, Duc de Bassano (1763–1839). He founded the *Bulletin de l'Assemblée Nationale,* which later became the *Moniteur universel.* After the 18 Brumaire, he became Napoleon's secretary, and soon after, Secretary of State. Victor du Pont mentions Maret as an old friend of his father (*1801 Journey,* p. 34).

15 Both of du Pont de Nemours' sons were to return to France in 1801. Victor du Pont was to seek more capital for the recently formed company of Du Pont de Nemours, Père et Fils & Cie., as well as to promote its interests in various other ways. Eleuthère-Irénée du Pont was to return to Essonnes, the location of the government's powder mills, in order to learn the newest techniques and to obtain the machinery for the proposed powder mills to be built on the banks of the Brandywine in Delaware.

16 Mme. Boullée.

17 Du Pont de Nemours is alluding to his second sojourn at the prison of La Force, which occurred in 1797 after the *coup d'état* of the 18 Fructidor, when he was charged with conspiring to overthrow the republic and restore the monarchy. Mme. de Staël was indignant at these charges, and she claims that she and Marie-Joseph Chénier obtained du Pont's release by maintaining that he was an inoffensive octogenarian. He was, in reality, 58 years old at this time and was somewhat offended by this ruse of Mme. de Staël, which probably deceived no one.

18 Jean-Victor Moreau (1763–1813), French general whose army had crossed the Rhine, April 25, 1800, and was then in Germany and Austria; and Claude Lecourbe (1759–1815), French general whose assistance assured the victory of Masséna at the battle of Zurich in 1799.

19 Pierre-Auguste Broussonet (1761–1807). This distinguished French naturalist had fled from France during the Revolution but returned secretly in 1795. After his name was removed from the list of *émigrés* in 1797, he obtained the post of vice-consul at Mogador in Morocco, as well as a mission as traveler for the *Institut de France.* He reached Tangier in 1798 but left for the Canary Islands in 1799 after an outbreak of the plague. In 1800 he was appointed vice-consul in Teneriffe.

20 Du Pont de Nemours had come to America as an official voyager for the Institut. He was to prepare reports on subjects connected with natural history.

21 A scientific society founded in Cairo by Napoleon on August 22, 1798, whose main purpose was the study of Egyptian life, history, and natural history. Various prominent persons were members of this Institute, including Geoffroy Saint-Hilaire, Denon, Kléber, Monge, Fourier, Andréossy, and Say.

22 Nicolas Baudin (1750–1803), naval officer and botanist who made trips to India and the West Indies for research in natural history. In 1800 the Directory appointed him a post captain and placed him in charge of two ships sent to explore the South Seas. His departure took place October 19, 1800. The voyage ended in near-disaster and scandal.

11

Necker to du Pont de Nemours

3 January 1801

WMSS 2/15

3 janvier 1801

Ayant appris Monsieur par une lettre de vous a ma fille que vous n'ayez rien receu de moi je vous envoye la copie de ma lettre du mois de may de l'année derniere & je ne scais trop si ce n'est pas un triplicat.

J'ai receu la lettre que vous m'avez fait l'honneur de m'ecrire le 12 floreal. Cette grande baisse des terres dont vous me parlez doit embarrasser les speculateurs qui pour en acheter ont emprunté a de gros interests. Il sembloit que l'accroissement de la population et du commerce de l'Amerique devoit prevenir cette baisse; mais on a ecarté les etrangers en leur interdisant les achapts de terre et meme les prets sur l'hypotheque de ces terres qui se font a la verite par forme d'achapt.

On voudroit scavoir quelle est la constitution de votre maison si c'est par actions et combien il y en a de prises ou de negotiables et je vois qu'on observe comme je vous l'ai dit dans la lettre dont je vous envoye copie qu'on voudroit pour la plenitude de la confiance que votre maison fut composée de deux ou trois persones en vous y comprenant.

Avez vous deja le tems de domicile necessaire en Amerique pour acheter des terres ou pour placer a hypotheque en votre nom?[1] Quel est l'interest de ces hypotheques? Quel interest bonifiez vous en compte courant?

Il y a en Hollande une compagnie considerable qui a achete il y a plusieurs annees des terres dans le Comte de Geneseè en New York et qui en a divisé la propriete par actions.[2] Si ces terres avoient considerablement baissé vous pourriez peut être former quelque entreprise dans ce genre. Je vous dis comme vous voyez Monsieur en vous ecrivant tout ce qui me passe par la tete.

Je laisse aux gens de france le soin de vous parler de guerres et de victoires et de la paix de terre qui ne tardera pas a etre faite. Agreez Monsieur les assurances de mon inviolable attachement.

Necker

On the reverse in du Pont de Nemours' handwriting:

3 J^{er} 1801
Mr. Necker et la reponse

TRANSLATION

January 3, 1801

Having learned, Sir, by a letter from you to my daughter that you have received nothing from me, I send you the copy of my letter of May of the past year, and I am not too sure that it is not a triplicate.

I have received the letter that you did me the honor of writing the 12 Floréal [May 2]. This great decline in the price of land of which you speak must disturb the speculators who, in order to purchase land, have borrowed at high rates of interest. It seemed that the increase in the population and commerce of America should prevent that decline; but foreigners were brushed aside, having been forbidden to purchase land and even to make mortgage loans on these lands, which are made, in truth, as a kind of purchase.

We should like to know how your company is constituted, whether it is by shares and how many have been taken or are negotiable; and I see that people note, as I told you in the letter of which I am sending you a copy, that they would like your company to be formed of two or three persons, including you, in order to have complete confidence in it.

Have you already spent the necessary time in America to buy land or to invest in mortgages in your name?[1] What is the interest rate on these mortgages? What interest do you allow currently?

There is a large company in Holland which bought, several years ago, some land in Genesee County in New York and which divided the property by shares.[2] If this land had gone down appreciably in value, you might perhaps form some enterprise of that kind. As you see, Sir, I am telling you everything that passes through my head while writing to you.

I leave to the French the matter of telling you about wars and victories and peace on land, which will soon be concluded.

Accept, Sir, the assurance of my inviolable attachment.

Necker

On the reverse in du Pont de Nemours' handwriting:

January 3, 1801
M. Necker and the reply

NOTES

1 Aliens could not own land in the United States. Accordingly, in 1800, Victor du Pont went to Virginia, where the naturalization laws were least stringent, and obtained his citizenship.

2 The Holland Land Company, founded in 1796 by Dutch bankers who had foreclosed on Robert Morris, the great land speculator, had thus acquired extensive lands in western New York which the company developed.

12

Necker de Germany to Victor du Pont

5 March 1801

WMSS 3/9

J'ai reçu Monsieur une lettre de Messieurs Dupont (de Nemours) pere fils & comp. du 8 Nivose dont vous avez été vraisemblablement le porteur par laquelle ils m'invitent attendu que leur établissement est formé & que la paix entre la France et l'Amerique est signée[1] à prendre une détermination sur les deux actions que j'avois eu l'intention de prendre dans leurs entreprises et de m'entendre avec Messieurs Bidermann[2] ou Roman[3] ou avec vous sur les fonds de ces actions.

Je ne retrouve pas sous ma main les documens que j'ai eu autrefois de Mons. votre pere sur la nature de la maison de commerce que vous avez formé ensemble. Le plan n'en est surement pas le même qu'il étoit dans l'origine et j'aurois besoin de recevoir de votre complaisance des notions un peu exactes sur la nature et les conditions de votre etablissement. Je prends donc la liberte de vous demander

1° De quelle somme est son fond capital?

2° En combien d'actions est-il partagé?

3° Les societés en commandite sont elles permises en Amerique de façon que chaque associe commanditaire ne soit responsable que de sa mise en fond?

4° quelle est la part des associés commanditaires dans les pertes et les bénéfices?

5° quels avantages prélevent les gèrans?

6° les actionnaires recoivent ils l'intéret annuel de leur mise en fond?

7° pour combien d'années est la société?

8 a quelle epoque se repartissent les benefices?

9 quelle est la valeur des actions? Est-ce 10 ou 20 mille livres?

10 chez qui se payeront les dividendes? Sera-ce en Europe ou en Amerique?

11 quels sont les associés gerans ayant la signature de la raison de commerce?

12 devez vous monsieur etre longtems absent?

J'ai dessein d'aller passer 3 mois à Paris. J'espere d'y arriver vers le 10 Germinal. Puis je esperer d'avoir le plaisir de vous y trouver?

Y a-t-il encore beaucoup d'actions qui ne soient pas encore distribuées & pourrois je en parler a quelques amis qui ont des fonds à placer? Quel terme et quelles facilités accordez vous le payement? Doit-il se faire à Mess. Gros Davillier & Cie ou à vous?

Excusez je vous prie la peine que je vous donne et agreez monsieur mes cordiales salutations.

Necker de Germany

Geneve le 14 ventose

On the reverse:

A Monsieur Victor
Dupont chez
Mess Gros & Davillier
à Paris

This has been crossed out and the following address added:

M. Dupont de Nemours
hotel de Paris rue de la loy[4]
vis avis la biblioteque

In Victor du Pont's handwriting:

Mr Necker Germany
Geneve 14 ventose
demande de renseignemens. Repondu 10 Germinal.

TRANSLATION

I have received, Sir, a letter from Messieurs Dupont (de Nemours) Père et Fils & Cie., dated 8 Nivôse [December 29] which you probably conveyed and in which they invite me, since their establishment has been formed and peace between France and America has been signed,[1] to decide about the two shares of stock which I had intended to buy in their enterprise, and to come to an agreement with Messrs. Bidermann[2] or Roman,[3] or with you, about the funds for these shares of stock.

I do not find the documents which I received earlier from your father about the nature of the business which you have formed. The plan is surely not the same as it was originally, and I should need to receive from you rather exact notions about the nature and conditions of your company. I take, therefore, the liberty of asking you:

1. What is the amount of its capital fund?

2. Into how many shares is it divided?

3. Are limited-liability companies permitted in America in such a way that each silent partner is responsible only for his share in the capital?

4. What is the share of the silent partners in the losses and profits?

5. What profits do the managers deduct?

6. Do the shareholders receive annual interest on their investment?

7. For how many years is the company to last?

8. When are the dividends distributed?

9. What is the value of the shares? Is it ten or twenty thousand livres?

10. Where will the dividends be paid? Will it be in Europe or in America?

11. Who are the managing partners having the right to sign for the company?

12. Are you to be absent for a long time, Sir?

I plan to spend three months in Paris. I hope to arrive there about the 10 Germinal [March 31]. May I hope to have the pleasure of finding you there?

Are there still many shares which are not yet allotted and could I speak about this to some friends who have funds to invest? What terms and what facilities for payment do you grant? Is payment to be made to Messrs. Gros, Davillier and Company or to you?

Please excuse the trouble that I cause you, and accept, Sir, my cordial greetings.

Necker de Germany

Geneva, 14 Ventôse

On the reverse:

To Monsieur Victor
Dupont in care of
Messieurs Gros and Davillier
in Paris

This has been crossed out and the following address added:

M. Dupont de Nemours
Hôtel de Paris, rue de la Loy,[4]
opposite the Library

In Victor du Pont's handwriting:

M. Necker Germany
Geneva, 14 Ventôse,
request for information.
Answered 10 Germinal

NOTES

Louis Necker (1730–1804), called Necker de Germany from an estate he owned in Switzerland, was the elder brother of Jacques Necker. He too had made a fortune in banking and speculation.

1 The Convention of Mortefontaine, signed September 30, 1800, ended the difficulties with France which had arisen from the Genêt affair, from French resentment at Jay's treaty of 1795 with England, and from the XYZ affair.

2 Jacques Bidermann (1751–1817), a Swiss banker living in Paris, friend of du Pont de Nemours, and one of the original investors in the latter's business ventures in the United States.

3 Jacques Roman, one of the partners in the Paris banking company of Gros, d'Avilliers & Cie., and Bidermann's brother-in-law.

4 The old name of the present Rue de Richelieu.

13

Necker to Victor du Pont

21 March 1801

WMSS 3/9

21 mars 1801

Ma fille m'a fait parvenir Monsieur la lettre que M[r] votre pere vous avoit remis pour moi et en vous remerciant de votre attention j'ai l'honneur de vous envoyer ma reponse. J'espere beaucoup que votre etablissement reussira et si je pouvois dans ma retraite y concourir je le ferois avec beaucoup d'interest et de plaisir. M[r] de Germani mon frere vous a ecrit pour avoir quelques renseignements sur la constitution de votre maison[1] qui est je crois en entier par actions mais dont nous ignorons le nombre et le fonds exigible pour chacune, de meme la part attribuee a chacune dans les profits & la duree de la societe, et quelle quantite de ces actions est actuellement payée.

Oserois-je vous demander Monsieur quand vous comptez retourner en Amerique et si vous permettriez que je vous fasse remettre une ou deux lettres pour ce pays la. Je vous prie monsieur de recevoir mes vœux pour vos succès et les assurances de mon attachement a vous Monsieur et a votre famille.

Necker

On the reverse in Victor du Pont's handwriting:

21 mars 1801
Mr Necker
Repondu le 5 avril

TRANSLATION

March 21, 1801

My daughter, Sir, has forwarded the letter that your father had given you for me, and thanking you for your attention, I have the honor of sending you my answer. I hope very much that your establishment will succeed, and if I could help out in my retreat, I should do so with much interest and pleasure. M. de Germany, my brother, has written to you to get some information about the formation of your company,[1] which is, I believe, entirely in shares of stock; but we do not know the number of these and the price of each share, nor the portion allotted to each share in the profits and the duration of the company, and what number of these shares are presently paid for.

Dare I ask you, Sir, when you expect to return to America and whether you would permit me to give you one or two letters for that country? I beg you, Sir, to receive my wishes for your success and the assurances of my attachment to you, Sir, and to your family.

Necker

On the reverse in Victor du Pont's handwriting:

March 21, 1801
M. Necker
Answered April 5

NOTE
1 See Letter 12.

14

Victor du Pont to Necker de Germany

21 March 1801

From Victor du Pont's Letter Book, WMSS 3/3

30 Ventose [an 9]

Mr Necker Germany
de Geneve

M^r une absence de quelques jours ne m'a pas permis de repondre sur le champ a votre lettre du 14 courrant et de vous donner les details que vous desirez sur un etablissement qui commencé sous d'heureux auspices doit avoir des succès d'autant plus grands que des hommes tels que vous voudront bien y cooperer de leur nom & de leurs moyens.

Vous avez raison de penser que le plan d'operations actuel de

N[otr]e Maison n'est pas le même que celui qui avait été concu lors de la formation de la societe. Notre capital devait etre formé par 400 actions a 10,000 francs. Quatre millions qui auraient suffi à la grande operation de terres dans le genre de celle executée dans le Genessee Etat de New York par le Cap[itain]e Williamson p[ou]r le c[ompt]e de la C[ie] Pultney de Londres.[1] Il y a 14 ans Monsieur que j'ai campé dans ce pays ou il n'y avait alors ni un sentier de tracé ni un arbre d'abattu. Les terres y valaient de 3 a 5 sols l'acre. A present a force de travaux publics qui y ont attiré la population ce pays est devenu un des plus riches des plus peuplés des mieux cultivès de l'amerique. Les terres y valent jusqu'a 100 et 120 francs l'acre. Cette progression de richesse & de prosperité est si rapide que depuis que Mr de Liancour[2] y a passé ce pays a encore une fois changé de face et qu'il y existe a present une superbe route en *turnpike* jusqu'à la chute de Niagara. Mais pour forcer et accelerer ainsi cet etat de prosperité il a fallu des capitaux très considerables et nous voyons que les Compagnies hollandaises et francaises etablies sous les mêmes principes, mais qui n'ont pas les mêmes moyens ou ne veulent pas les mettre dehors prosperent peu.

Au lieu d'avoir placé 400 actions, nous n'en avons pas eu plus de 80 souscrites et 60 de payées jusqu'a ce jour. Il a donc fallu necessairement renoncer aux grandes idées d'amelioration et de culture, se contenter de placer une partie du capital en terres, qui au lieu de centupler de valeur pendant la durée de la société se trouveront seulement triplèes ou quatruplées par l'augmentation naturelle de la population et de la valeur des proprietés. Dans le premier plan la maison de commerce n'etait considerée que comme objet secondaire. A present c'est d'elle que nous attendons les grandes benefices.

Notre plan d'acquisition de terres a eté extrêmement favorisé par les circonstances, lors de n[otr]e arrivèe en Amerique nous avons trouvé plusieurs des grands proprietaires de terres en etat de faillite et toutes leurs proprietes mises a la fois à l'encan, autant les terres avaient eté portées par les Speculateurs en Amerique et en Europe au dela de leur veritable valeur autant elles sont a present tombèes au dessous par suite de ces evenremens et de l'activite des joueurs à la baisse. On nous a proposé a 10 sols l'acre, 100,000 acres dans la Caroline du nord dans un pays beau & deja traversé par des chemins. Ces terres ont eté estimées 30 sols il y a trois ans, il est vraisemblable qu'elles nous appartiennent a present pour huit sols que nous en avons offert comptant. En achetant ainsi sur les lieux, choisissant bien le moment et connaissant d'avance la situation et la qualitè des terres—il est impossible que l'argent placé ainsi ne produise pas un très fort interet à l'expiration de notre societé.

Nos autres capitaux seront employès dans un commerce sagement dirigé. Nous tacherons en ne faisant que des operations sures de contraster avec l'audace americaine qui ne connaissant point de bornes ne saurait inspirer de confiance aux Etrangers, notre reputation de sagesse et de probité nous fera donner necessairement la plus grande partie des commissions de france et une portion de celles de suisse et de hollande.

Si dans quelques années nous trouvions a vendre une moitié de nos terres avec un benefice très considerable nous pourrions employer cet argent a mettre l'autre moitié en valeur, mais les fonds qui resteront dans le commerce et les benefices qu'ils auront produits ne seront pas detournés pour l'operation des terres sans la volontè des actionnaires ayant voix deliberative dans la societé, et qui a son expiration seront maîtres de les retirer ou de laisser le tout ou partie dans une nouvelle societé purement territoriale. Voila a peu près Monsieur, nos idées que des causes majeures et imprevues pourront seulement changer.

La Reponse a vos deux premieres questions se trouve ci dessus. Quant à la 3me il est bien vrai que quelques anciennes loix anglaises qui ne sont pas abrogées sont contraires aux commandites et rendent les commanditaires responsables. Mais l'attorney general de l'Etat de New York[3] homme très habile a etè consultè a ce sujet et Mr de lessert [4] a ici sa consultation. Il assure qu'il n'y a jamais eu d'exemple de l'application de ces loix dans les Etats Unis ou cependant une grande partie des maisons de commerce ne sont que des commandites d'Angleterre. Mais quand à la notre le cas est encore different. La societè est francaise l'acte de societè a ete signè a Paris et y est deposé. C'est à Paris que l'on paye les dividendes, toute contestation relative a la societé doit etre determinée en france & d'après les loix francaises. Les actionnaires ne sont designés sur les livres de la maison de New York que comme creanciers pour la valeur de leurs actions. Il ne doit exister aucune inquietude à ce sujet.

Les actionnaires recoivent l'interet annuel de leur mise de fonds d'abord a 4 p[ou]r cent ensuite a 6 ensuite a 8 pourvu que ce dernier taux n'excede pas la moitié des benefices. La societé doit expirer le 20 juin 1812. Les actions sont de deux mille dollars americains ou piastre fortes d'espagne. Les associés gerans ont un traitement fixe de 1200 dollars par an et le droit d'opter d'ici a la sixieme année entre ce traitement et le partage entreux du tiers des benefices.

La circulaire cy jointe vous donne Monsieur les signatures des administrateurs, le quatrieme irenée du Pont se retire; les capitaux actuels de la societé et ses nouveaux plans n'exigeant pas un aussi grand nombre d'administrateurs, il va se mettre à la tete d'une manufacture de poudre a canon et de chasse, que nous etablissons sous la protection du Gouvernement des Etats Unis et avec l'assurance de sa fourniture. Mon frere a eté pendant six ans eleve des poudres sous Mr Lavoisier. Il possede a fond cette partie, c'est de toute les manufactures celle qui exigeant le moins de bras doit reussir le mieux en amerique. Deux ou trois de ces fabriques qui prosperent sont a cinquante ans des procedès actuels et de tout ce qui a été inventé depuis pour simplifier la fabrication. L'avance du salpètre faite par le gouvernement qui l'envoye chercher dans l'inde par ses fregates facilite beaucoup. Les debouchès du commerce interieur sont aussi très considerables, & tout assure un benefice de 50 p^r o/o sur les fonds placès dans cette entreprise, les deux tiers des fonds seront faits par notre maison et pour l'autre tiers nous avons donné des actions particulieres a quelques uns de nos principaux interessés. Il nous en reste encore deux a placer et nous pourrions vous en reserver une Monsieur dans le cas ou vous auriez [l']intention de prendre plusieurs actions dans n[otr]e Compagnie.

Les fonds peuvent se faire indifferement ou aux Etats Unis, ou en ouvrant un credit a hambourg, ou en payant ici chez Mess^r Gros Davilliers & Cie. Mr Roman est chargé de delivrer les actions.

J'espere Monsieur, avoir l'honneur de vous voir encore ici avant mon depart pour l'Espagne ou au moins a mon retour dans 2 ou 3 mois. J'aurai l'honneur alors de vous communiquer l'acte de societé et de vous donner de vive voix tous les renseignemens ulterieurs qui pourront vous interesser.

Agreez l'assurance de mon respectueux devouemen[t].

TRANSLATION

30 Ventôse [year IX]

M. Necker Germany
of Geneva

Sir, an absence of a few days did not permit me to answer immediately your letter of the 14th inst. giving you the details that you wish about an establishment which, started auspiciously, must have all the greater success, since men like you are willing to cooperate in it with their name and their means.

You are right in thinking that the present plan of operations of our company is not the same as the one which had been conceived at the time of its formation. Our capital was to be formed by 400 shares at 10,000 francs: four million, which would have been sufficient for a great land development similar to that carried out in the Genesee region of New York State by Captain Williamson for the account of the Pulteney Company of London.[1] It has been fourteen years, Sir, since I camped in that country, where there was then neither one path traced nor one tree cut down. The land was worth three to five sols an acre. At present, as a result of public works which have brought population there, this country has become one of the richest, most populated, best cultivated areas of America. Land there is worth up to 100 and 120 francs an acre. This increase in wealth and prosperity is so rapid that, since M. de Liancourt[2] passed through there, this country has once more changed in appearance, and there exists at present a superb turnpike as far as Niagara Falls. But to impel and thus to accelerate this state of prosperity took very considerable capital, and we see that the Dutch and French companies, established on the same principles, but not having the same means or not wanting to use them, prosper little.

Instead of having disposed of 400 shares, we have not had more than eighty subscribed and sixty paid for up to this time. It has therefore been necessary to abandon great ideas of improvement and cultivation, [and] to be content with investing a part of the capital in land, which, instead of increasing a hundredfold during the life of the company, will be only tripled or quadrupled by the natural increase of population and the value of the property. In the first plan, the business house was considered only as a secondary object. At present, it is from it that we expect large profits.

Our plan of land acquisition has been extremely favored by circumstances. At the time of our arrival in America, we found several of the large landowners bankrupt and all their land put up at the same time for auction; the land had been brought by speculators in America and in Europe to a price as much beyond its real value as it has now fallen below because of these events and the activity of short sellers. We were offered, at ten sols an acre, 100,000 acres in North Carolina in a beautiful region already crossed by roads. This land was valued at thirty sols three years ago. It is likely that it belongs to us now for eight sols, which we offered in cash for it. By buying thus on the spot, choosing the time well, and knowing in advance the situation and the quality of the land, it is impossible for money invested in this way not to produce a very high interest at the expiration of our company.

Our other capital will be used in a wisely directed business house. We shall try, by conducting only safe transactions, to be a contrast to American boldness, which, not recognizing any limits, could not inspire confidence in foreigners. Our reputation for wisdom and probity will necessarily give us the greatest amount of brokerage business from France and a portion of that from Switzerland and Holland.

If, in a few years, we found it possible to sell half of our land at a very considerable profit, we could use this money to develop the other half, but the funds which will remain in the commercial world and the profits that they produce will not be turned aside for work on the land without the approval of the shareholders who have a vote in the company, and who, at its expiration, will be free to withdraw the money or leave all or part in a new company concerned entirely with land. There, approximately, Sir, are our ideas, which only major and unexpected causes can change.

The reply to your first two questions is found above. As for the third, it is quite true that some old English laws which have not been repealed are opposed to limited-liability companies and make silent partners responsible. But the Attorney General of the State of New York,[3] a very able man, has been consulted on this subject and M. Delessert[4] has his opinion here. He assures us that there has never been any example of the application of these laws in the United States, where, however, a large number of commercial firms are only silent partners from England. But as for ours, the case is still different. The company is French, the deed of partnership was signed in Paris and is registered there. The dividends are paid in Paris. Any question concerning the company must be settled in France according to French laws. The stockholders are designated on the books of the New York office only as creditors for the value of their shares. There need be no uneasiness on this subject.

The stockholders receive annual interest on their investment, at first at four per cent, then at six, afterwards at eight, provided that this latter rate does not exceed half of the profits. The company is to go out of existence on June 20, 1812. The shares cost 2,000 American dollars or Spanish hard piasters. The managing directors have a fixed salary of $1,200 per year and the right to choose, up to the sixth year, between this salary and a share among them of a third of the profits.

The enclosed circular gives you, Sir, the signatures of the administrators. The fourth one, Irénée du Pont, is withdrawing. Since the present capital of the company and its new plans do not require so large a number of administrators, he is going to head a gunpowder factory that we are establishing under the protection of the United States government and with the assurance of supplying it. My brother was for six years a student of gunpowder under M. Lavoisier. He understands that business thoroughly. Of all factories, it is the one which must succeed best in America, requiring the fewest employees. Two or three of these factories, which are prospering, are fifty years behind the present procedures and all that has been invented since then to simplify manufacture. An advance of saltpeter by the government, which sends its frigates to purchase it in India, helps very much. The domestic market is also very considerable, and everything assures a profit of fifty per cent on funds invested in this enterprise. Two thirds of the funds will be contributed by our company, and for the other third, we have given private shares to some of our interested partners. We still have two for sale and could reserve one for you, Sir, in case you might intend to buy several shares in our company.

The funds can be paid in the United States, or by opening a credit account in Hamburg, or by paying here at Messrs. Gros, Davilliers and Company. M. Roman is in charge of delivering the shares.

I hope, Sir, to have the honor of seeing you again here before my departure for Spain, or at least, on my return in two or three months. I shall then have the honor of giving you the contract of the company and of telling you all the subsequent information that may interest you.

Accept the assurance of my respectful devotion.

NOTES

This is the reply to Letter 12.

The Letter Book from which the text is taken was Victor du Pont's record of his correspondence during his trip to France and Spain in 1801.

1 Captain Charles Williamson (1757–1808), a British officer and land promoter.

In 1791, an English group headed by Sir William Pulteney placed Williamson in charge of the development of a tract of 1,200,000 acres in western New York which the group had acquired from Robert Morris. Filled with ambitious plans, Williamson designed the town of Bath, N. Y., and constructed there a theater, race track, and elegant hotel. He founded a newspaper, *The Bath Gazette,* and built another sumptuous hotel at Geneva, N. Y. Fairs, horse races, dances, and theatrical performances were presented in an effort to attract settlers. From 1792 to 1799, Williamson spent $1,374,470, while the income from land sold amounted to only $147,974. Eventually, the English owners of the land disapproved of his activities and dismissed him in 1802. See *DAB* and A. M. Sakolski, *The Great American Land Bubble* (New York, 1932), pp. 74–78.

2 François Alexandre Frédéric, Duc de La Rochefoucauld-Liancourt (1747–1827), the French philanthropist, whose *Voyage dans les Etats-Unis d'Amérique, fait en 1795, 1796 et 1797* had been published by the Du Pont presses in 1799.

Victor du Pont may be alluding to the discouraging reports Mme. de Staël had received from La Rochefoucauld-Liancourt about land investments in the United States. Jared Sparks mentions that, about 1796, Mme. de Staël had persuaded her father to allocate $20,000 for her use in the purchase and improvement of American land. Sparks states: "A negotiation to this effect had been arranged with M. Leray de Chaumont, and was to be closed immediately, when Madame de Staël received a letter from the Duke de Liancourt, then traveling in the United States, which contained representations that seemed to her discouraging" (Jared Sparks, *The Life of Gouverneur Morris* [Boston, 1832], I, 489–90). On November 6, 1796, she wrote to Le Ray de Chaumont: "J'ai vu une lettre du duc de Liancourt datée d'Amérique, et une autre d'un négociant bien informé; ils s'accordent pour ne conseiller à personne, soit d'aller en Amérique, soit d'y faire des acquisitions. Ces lettres sont de nature à guérir les Suisses de ces spéculations." ("I have seen a letter written in America from the Duke de Liancourt, and another from a well-informed businessman; they agree in advising no one either to go to America, or to make any purchases there. These letters are of such a kind as to cure the Swiss of these speculations.") (Quoted in Richmond Laurin Hawkins, *Madame de Staël and the United States* [Cambridge, Mass., 1930], p. 12.)

3 Josiah Ogden Hoffman (1766–1837), Attorney General of the State of New York from 1798 until 1801 and a land speculator in New York City and Saint Lawrence County. In 1798, Aaron Burr, who was then a member of the New York Assembly, effected passage of a bill giving aliens the conditional right to own land

in New York. Apparently the Holland Land Company backed this legislation and gave bribes to Burr and Hoffman. See Sakolski, *Great American Land Bubble*, pp. 79–80.

4 Etienne Delessert (1735–1816), a Paris banker and businessman who owned 1800 acres of land near Kingston, N. Y. In 1801, he assisted E. I. du Pont in introducing Merino sheep to the United States, importing them from Spain.

Victor du Pont's Letter Book contains a copy of his letter to Bidermann (see Letter 12, note 2) dated July 28, 1801, in which he states that Necker de Germany "a été beaucoup ebranlé par tout ce que Mr de Lessert lui aura dit sur la responsabilité solidaire des actionnaires" ("was much disturbed by all that M. Delessert has probably told him about the joint responsibility of shareholders").

❁

15

Necker to du Pont de Nemours

21 March 1801

WMSS 2/15

21 mars 1801

M. votre fils en arrivant a Paris m'a fait parvenir une lettre de vous Monsieur où je vois avec un grand plaisir que la mienne du mois de may ne s'est point egarée. Cette lettre que vous avez eu la bonté de m'ecrire est un chef d'œuvre d'instruction, ordre idées justes sage prevoyance tout y est et je reste honteux seulement que vous ayez pris tant de peine pour moi. J'ai très bonne idée de votre affaire particuliere et je m'en expliquerai dans ce sens toutes les fois que l'occasion s'en presentera. Il me semble que c'est assez de quatre person[n]es pour reponder a toute espece d'inquietude de la part de vos correspondans & un associé de plus seroit inutile a ce but.

M. votre fils me donnera je l'espere les notions qui me manquent sur le nombre et le capital des actions qui forment votre societe; et si je puis vous etre bon a quelque chose j'y serai engagé par divers motifs.

Je ne scais pas pourquoi dans un pays etranger vous dattez vos lettres selon l'almanach de france. Peu de gens vous en scauront gré et vous deplairez hors de france a tous vos correspondants.

Je vous prie Monsieur d'agreer mes vœux pour votre bonheur et les assurances du plus sincere et du plus parfait attachement.

Necker

March 21, 1801

Your son, on arriving in Paris, delivered a letter to me from you, Sir, in which I see with great pleasure that mine of the month of May did not get lost. This letter which you had the kindness to write to me is a masterpiece of information, order, correct ideas, [and] wise foresight; everything is in it, and I am ashamed only that you took so much trouble for me. I have a very good idea of your particular business, and I shall understand it in that sense every time the occasion presents itself. It seems to me that four persons are enough to reply to any kind of uneasiness on the part of your correspondents, and another partner would be useless for that purpose.

Your son will give me, I hope, the information which I lack about the number and the capital of the shares which form your company; and if I can help you in some way, I shall do so for various reasons.

I do not know why, in a foreign country, you date your letters according to the French calendar. Few people will be grateful to you for doing so, and you will displease all your correspondents outside of France.

I beg you, Sir, to accept my wishes for your happiness and assurances of a most sincere and perfect attachment.

Necker

16

du Pont de Nemours to Madame de Staël

6 April 1801

From an excerpt in Le Marois, *Cahiers*, p. 505

New York, 16 Germinal, an 9

J'ai trois ou quatre bagatelles a faire avant de mourir.

L'Éducation Nationale dans les Républiques américaines;[1] un million à gagner pour la part de ma Compagnie; l'ordre de succession à la première magistrature, que je suppose rendue à vie, ordre qui sera le plus efficace moyen de prévenir les attentats contre le premier Magistrat.

Et en fin l'enchaînement complet des plans nécessaires à l'instruction publique chez les Français.

Après quoi, je pourrai m'endormir avec mes pères, pour me réveiller avec mes amis.

TRANSLATION

New York, 16 Germinal, year IX

I have two or three trifles to complete before dying.

National education in the American republics;[1] a million to make on behalf of my company; the order of succession to the first consulate, which I suppose to be for life, an order which will be the most efficacious way of preventing attacks against the First Consul.

And finally, the complete chain of plans necessary for public education in France.

After which, I shall be able to go to sleep with my ancestors, in order to awaken with my friends.

NOTES

The entire text of this letter was not reproduced in the Le Marois article.

1 Du Pont de Nemours' *Sur l'éducation nationale dans les Etats-Unis d'Amérique* had been published in Philadelphia in 1800. Jefferson had requested that he write a letter containing his views on this subject; Du Pont de Nemours, filled with enthusiasm, wrote instead an entire book on the topic.

17

Victor du Pont to Necker

8 April 1801

From Victor du Pont's Letter Book, WMSS 3/3

Paris ce 18 G^{al} 8 avril 1801

Monsieur Necker
a Coppet près Geneve

Monsieur,

Madame votre fille me dit vous avoir annoncé l'époque *fixée* pour le départ du Parlementaire[1] sur lequel nous sommes arrivés d'Amérique, ce depart tenant néanmoins à des circonstances et à des affaires indeterminées. J'ai désiré être à même de vous donner au sujet quelque chose de certain, et je crois pouvoir vous assurer que vous avez encore le tems d'écrire jusqu'à la fin du mois,[2] le batiment ne pouvant mettre à la voile avant le 25 ou 30 d'avril. Mon frere[3] qui repart se chargera avec grand plaisir de toutes les commissions que vous voudrez bien nous donner. Quant à moi Monsieur, je pars pour l'Espagne, et dans les differentes courses que je me propose de faire cet été afin d'établir des liaisons avantageuses à notre maison j'espere avoir l'honneur de vous voir quelques instans, une des premières instructions de mon pere qui croyait que j'aurais le bonheur de vous rencontrer a Paris était de vous voir aussi souvent que vous me le permettriez de solliciter vos conseils sur notre entreprise et de mériter votre bienveillance. Il disait souvent, *Nôtre Etablissement aura les plus grands succès si Monsieur Necker en augure bien.*

J'ai l'honneur d'addresser sous votre couvert une reponse que j'avais faite à Monsieur de Germany sur différentes questions relatives à notre Société. Sa lettre ne mettant parvenue qu'au retour d'un petit voyage j'ai hésité a faire partir ma reponse espérant— d'après ce qu'il m'avait marqué le voir arriver de jour en jour, mais puisque vous desirez Mr connoitre aussi ces détails je ne crois pouvoir mieux faire que de vous les addresser.

Agréez Mr l'assurance de mon respect et du plus entier dévouement.

TRANSLATION

Paris, 18 Germinal, April 8, 1801

Monsieur Necker
at Coppet, near Geneva

Sir,

Your daughter tells me that she has informed you of the time arranged for the sailing of the cartel ship[1] on which we arrived from America, this departure depending, nevertheless, on undetermined circumstances and affairs. I wanted to be able to give you something definite about the matter, and I believe I can assure you that you still have time to write until the end of the month,[2] the ship not being able to sail before April 25 or 30. My brother,[3] who is leaving, will attend to all the messages that you care to give us with great pleasure. As for me, Sir, I am leaving for Spain, and during the various trips that I propose to take this summer in order to establish connections advantageous to our company, I hope to have the honor of seeing you for a few moments. One of the first instructions of my father, who believed that I should have the happiness of meeting you in Paris, was to see you as often as you would permit it, in order to request your advice about our enterprise and to deserve your good wishes. He has often said, "Our establishment will have the greatest success if M. Necker augurs well of it."

I have the honor of enclosing a reply that I had made to M. de Germany about various questions concerning our company. His letter having reached me only on my return from a short trip, I hesitated to send a reply, hoping, according to what he had indicated to me, to see him arrive from one day to the next; but since you desire, Sir, to know those details also, I do not believe that I can do better than to address them to you.

Accept, Sir, the assurance of my respect and most complete devotion.

NOTES

1 The ship in question was the *Benjamin Franklin,* owned by Francis Breuil of Philadelphia, which Victor du Pont also describes as a cartel ship (*parlementaire*) in his *Journey to France and Spain* (p. 3, n. 6). Such a ship had a guarantee of safe passage from the enemy, the English in this case.
2 See Letter 13.
3 Eleuthère Irenée du Pont. He sailed for America about May 1 (*E. I. du Pont,* V, 224).

18

du Pont de Nemours to Necker

8 April 1801

From a draft, WMSS 2/4

8 avril
New York 18 Germinal An 9

A Mr Necker

Je reçois avec une nouvelle reconnaissance votre lettre du 3 janvier. J'ai déja repondu avec étendue et peut-être avec trop d'etendue a celle du 7 may 1800. Et ma lettre ayant ete portée par mes enfans je suppose qu'il y a près de deux mois qu'elle est entre vos mains.[1]

Je suis entré dans de grands détails sur les Finances des Etats Unis. Elles ont été conduites depuis quatre ans d'une maniere dont la prolongation les eut mises en danger. Mais l'administration éclairée, économique et ferme de Mr Jefferson les réparera certainement. Mr Jefferson est un Homme très rare, il doit compter parmi les grands gouverneurs des nations. On présume qu'il destine le ministère des Finances à Mr Galatin votre digne compatriote dont je vous ai envoyé une brochure fort bien faite.[2]

Je vous ai parlé dans le Post Scriptum que mon fils vous aura remis du vol qui avait été fait à la banque de New York.[3] Vous verrez par le prix courant que je vous envoie des stocks américains que l'effet de cet accident est presque entierement dissipé, et que les actions sont revenues a peu près au pair de celles de la banque des Etats Unis. Elles rehausseront encore mais je ne crois pas qu'elles reprennent la superiorité qu'elles avaient l'année dernière, parce que l'on sait que sous Mr Jefferson la Banque des Etats Unis n'aura aucun service à rendre au Gouvernement.

Vous aurez vu par notre circulaire que le nom de nos enfans se trouve dans la raison de notre maison de commerce et celui de Pusy[4] dans les personnes qui en ont la signature. Je vous ai déja prié de me dire si vous pensiez que quelque chose de plus fut necessaire.

Notre maison a êtè formée en actions de deux mille dollars ou piastres fortes. Chacune en a fait quatre cents et l'on ne peut pas en faire davantage sans une nouvelle et formelle deliberation de la société. Ces actions portent pour les quatre premieres années qui échoiront dans deux ans quatre pour cent de dividende fixe pour les quatre annees suivantes six pour cent pour les quatre dernieres huit. Le surplus des benefices est remis a la comp[agn]ie pour etendre les operations. La societé sera dissoute et liquidée le premier prairial de l'an 19, et je crois qu'alors son capital sera decuplé. Cinq actions y donnent voix de ce benefice. Les actionnaires plus faibles nomment des syndics pour les représenter. C'est actuellement le Citoyen Johannot[5] bien connu de vous et de Madame votre fille et interessé lui meme pour huit actions qui [. . . .][6] C'est lui et le citoyen Roman beau-frere et associe de

Bidermann [. . .] [7] à Paris qui sont depositaires des actions dont nous pouvons encore disposer, et qui les delivreront aux nouveaux souscripteurs qui se presenteraient. La caisse d'Europe et le centre de la correspondance sont chez le citoyen Roman. Lors de la formation de la societé j'ai eu des propositions pour placer jusques a deux cent et soixante dix-huit actions et sur ces demandes. J'en regardais *deux cent vingt sept* comme tres assurees. Mais un des soumissionnaires qui avait retenu *soixante et quinze* est mort sans avoir conclu son engagement[8] et je ne sais pas à quel point ses enfans pourront et voudront tenir sa promesse. Un autre qui devait faire remettre les fonds de *trente* actions chez mes correspondants de Hollande vers le tems de mon départ[9] a été retenu par la descente que les Anglais et les Russes ont fait alors.[10] J'ignore ce qui depuis l'a fait suspendre. Je n'ai point recu de ses nouvelles. Je crains qu'il ne soit mort. Aussi c'etait un homme agé. D'autres parmi lesquels est *Monsieur votre frere* qui m'avait annoncé l'envoi tres prochain des fonds de deux actions et en avait fait esperer trois à mon voyageur m'ont ecrit qu'ils suspendraient jusqu'à la paix entre les deux Republiques francaise et americaine.

C'est en partie pour recueillir leurs fonds que j'ai envoyé mon fils ainé[11] en Europe. Avant son retour je ne puis pas savoir au juste ma veritable force.

Son voyage a encore un autre objet. Je l'ai chargé de proposer au gouvernement de France relativement au service de banque de la legation en ce pays ainsi qu'aux approvisionnemens de sa marine et de ses colonies des vues sur lesquelles il doit vous consulter. Et ce n'est pas le seul point pour lequel il invoquera vos lumieres. Madame votre fille nous a fait esperer que vous seriez à Paris au printems.

Si mes propositions sont acceptees, il y aura peu de maisons plus puissantes que la nôtre, et aucune qui soit exposée à moins de danger; parce que j'ai disposé mes plans de maniere à n'être jamais sans gage entre les mains.[12]

Pendant que mes enfans traitent les affaires en Europe, un evenement tres heureux qui a ete uniquement l'effet de la confiance personnelle m'a mis a portée d'en commencer l'execution sans les attendre en me procurant un gage d'un million en lettres de change de la République Batave.

Je n'ai point accepté ce dépot comme une avance de fonds qui se serait consumée d'elle même et n'aurait donné lieu qu'à une seule operation; mais comme un cautionnement qui sera successivement applicable à toutes les expeditions qui pourront avoir lieu, et dont les retours de chacune liberant le gage le rendra susceptible de servir aussi efficacement pour la suivante.

Je conserverai ainsi à la République son moyen de puissance. Il pourra etre pour elle la base d'un service beaucoup plus considerable que celui qu'elle désirait, et pour notre maison l'occasion le vehicule d'une suite d'affaires qui pourront s'elever très haut et dont il n'y en aura pas une seule qui n'ait sa complette garantie.

Je crois que vous trouverez cela dans les meilleurs principes et d'economie politique, d'administration, de patriotisme et de commerce.

Vous voyez que si vous avez la bonté de me dire tout ce qui vous passe par la tête, je ne vous cache rien non plus de ce que j'ai dans l'esprit et dans le cœur.

Vous me faites encore quelques questions.

1° Si j'ai le tems de domicile nécessaire pour achetter des terres.

Les loix à cet ègard sont très variées dans les différens Etats. J'ai sous mon nom pour ma compagnie cinquante six mille acres de terre dans le Kentucky qui ont êté mis par un de nos actionnaires[13] dans la Société pour le nombre d'actions que leur vent[e] et a leur valeur a lui et à nous encore inconnue pourra solder.

J'ai c'est a dire la societé a dans la ville d'Alexandrie près Washington City une maison et un magasin sous le nom de mon fils ainé, qui a êté obligé pour les acquerir de preter *allegeance* à l'Etat de Virginie qui n'a sur ce point aucun egard à la loi générale concernant la naturalisation. C'est une propriété dont la valeur augmente parce qu' Alexandrie sera pour longtems encore le port de commerce de la capitale.

J'ai dans le Jersey à trois lieues de New York une maison de campagne et un terrain que j'ai acquis parce que j'ai sçu d'avance que la nouvelle route de New York a Philadelphie devait y passer.

Ce terrain touche le port que l'on va faire sur le goulet de la baie de Newark. Je pourrai y bâtir deux jolies maisons et huit mediocres chacune avec leur clos et leur cour et leur jardin, lesquelles jointes à la mienne qui est assez belle et à une douzaine d'autres telles qu'elles qui existent deja et avec une église que les proprietaires et les fideles des differens cultes feront par souscription par devouement pour ameliorer leurs heritages formeront le commencement d'une petite ville tres agreable que j'ai nommée *Biderman's Town* en l'honneur de mon ami et de mon principal actionnaire *Bidermann*. Je lui devais les prémices.

Si jamais je bâtis une autre ville *pour vous* et de votre nom je la placerai de maniere qu'elle doive devenir plus grande.

Si je fais un *Nemours* je le mettrai dans une isle de riviere à portée des bois et un *Genêve,* ce sera sur la debouche d'un lac. Il faut en tout de l'analogie. C'est la base du gout.

En parlant de gout on me mande que vous venez de faire un livre *religieux* en trois volumes,[14] et vous ne m'en dites pas un mot. L'auteur de la *Philosophie de l'univers*[15] n'est cependant point excommunié dans votre église, et vous etes au moins aussi tolérant que le Pape que Buonaparte a plus d'à moitie converti.

Mais revenons à vos questions. Vous me demandez iterativement comment on place sur hypotheque que l'on appelle ici *mortgage*. Je vous ai déja répondu là dessus qu'on y place six pour cent avec parfaite sureté quand on prend bien ses renseignemens. Et j'ajouterai que si un tel emploi de fonds vous faisait plaisir je vous *mortgagerais* nos proprietés pour augmenter nos fonds disponibles. C'est l'esprit du pays et c'est, en commerce, un très bon esprit.

Vous me demandez combien je bonifierais en compte courant— Six pour cent.

Vous me parlez des compagnies hollandaises. Il y en a plusieurs dont les deux plus puissants sont:

Celle de MM. Willinks et Van Staphorst[16] laquelle soutient aujourd'hui contre l'Etat de Pensylvanie un procès qui est au moins une des causes les plus celebres en Amerique, et qui partage les plus grands jurisconsultes, les plus eloquens orateurs du pays.

L'Etat de Pensylvanie reclame les terres que MM. Willinks et Van Staphorst lui ont achettées [et] attendu qu'ils n'ont pas bati le nombre de maisons, defriché la quantité de terres, ou etabli le nombre de familles à quoi ils s'etaient obligés dans l'acte de concession.

Leurs defenseurs répondent que ces conditions doivent être regardées comme comminatoires; qu'on les a toujours faites; qu'on n'en a jamais exigé l'execution rigoureuse; qu'il n'y a pas de raison de commencer par leurs cliens que si la severite de ces conditions difficiles a remplir rompait le contract l'acquisition des terres en serait generalement decouragée.

Les defenseurs de l'Etat de Pensylvanie repliquent qu'un contrat est un contract, que celui là est conforme à l'interet public, qu'aucun administrateur n'a le droit d'en dispenser au detriment de la Pensylvanie; que si d'autres Administrateurs ont a cet égard négligé leur devoir, c'est une raison de plus pour ceux d'aujourd'hui de faire le leur.

On plaide dans la cour federale. L'influence de la République est grande, celle de tous les acquereurs de terres dont il n'y en a peut-être pas un qui ne soit dans le cas de MM. Willinks et Van Staphorst ne l'est pas moins. Il est impossible de prévoir le jugement. L'existence même de la cause parait tenir au jeu à la baisse.

L'autre compagnie est celle des MM. Casenove.[17] Elle a beaucoup gagné non pas sur ses terres mais par un jeu habile sur les fonds publics. Il y a environ deux [. . .][18] qu'elle commence à s'occuper serieusement de son territoire. Elle parait le faire avec intelligence. Mais il est difficile qu'elle ne souffre pas du cours general de baisse que rien ne peut plus arreter que son excès.

Oui certainement la déconvenue de ces *pauvres riches* compagnies peut nous fournir plus d'une matiere à speculation. Je serais fâché d'y contribuer. Ma politique commerciale est *mon bien resultant du bien de tous;* et vous l'aurez reconnu dans ce que je vous ai dit tout a l'heure sur l'approvisionnement des colonies. Mais je serais un imbecile, et je manquerais a la confiance de mes commettans, si je n'attendais pas pour achetter au moment où le marché sera au plus bas et dans la necessité d'un rehaussement ulterieur.

Salut et bien respectueux attachement.

TRANSLATION

April 8 [1801]
New York, 18 Germinal, year IX

To Monsieur Necker,

I receive your letter of January 3 with a new gratitude. I have already replied at length, and perhaps at too much length, to that of May 7, 1800. And my letter having been brought by my children, I suppose that it has been in your hands nearly two months now.[1]

I entered into great detail about the finances of the United States. They have been directed for four years in a manner the continuation of which would have endangered them. But the enlightened, economic, and firm administration of Mr. Jefferson will certainly reestablish them. Mr. Jefferson is a very rare man. He must be considered among the great governors of nations. We assume that he plans to entrust the Department of the Treasury to Mr. Gallatin, your worthy compatriot, whose very well-done pamphlet I have sent you.[2]

I mentioned to you, in the postscript that my son has given to you, the theft that had taken place at the Bank of New York.[3] You will see from the current price which I am sending you of American stocks that the effect of this accident has almost entirely dissipated, and that the shares have almost returned to a par with those of the Bank of the United States. They are still rising, but I do not believe that they will have again the superiority which they had last year because people know that under Mr. Jefferson the Bank of the United States will have no service to render to the government.

You will have seen from our circular that the name of our children is in the name of our business house and that of Pusy[4] among the persons who can sign for it. I have already requested you to tell me if you thought that something more was necessary.

Our company was formed by shares of two thousand dollars or hard piasters. They added up to four hundred, and no more can be offered without a new and formal deliberation by the company. For the first four years these shares, which fall due in two years, bear four per cent fixed dividend; for the four following years, six per cent; for the last four, eight. The remainder of the profits is returned to the company to extend its operations. The company will be dissolved and liquidated on 1 Prairial of the year XIX [May 21, 1811], and I believe that at that time its capital will have increased tenfold. Five shares give a vote on this profit. The smaller shareholders name agents to represent them. This is presently Citizen Johannot,[5] well known to you and your daughter, who has himself eight shares which [. . . .][6] It is he and Citizen Roman, brother-in-law and associate of Bidermann [. . .][7] in

Paris who are the agents for the shares which we can still sell, and who will deliver them to the new subscribers who may appear. The cashier's office for Europe and the center for correspondence are at Citizen Roman's office. When the company was formed, I had propositions for selling up to 278 shares, and of these requests, I considered 227 as assured. But one of the tenderers, who had reserved *seventy-five,* died without having concluded his arrangement,[8] and I do not know to what extent his children will be able and willing to keep his promise. Another, who was to pay the money for *thirty* shares to my correspondents in Holland about the time of my departure,[9] was prevented from doing so by the raid that the English and Russians made then.[10] I do not know what has made him delay since then. I have not received any news from him. I fear that he has died. Moreover, he was an old man. Others, among whom is *your brother,* who had announced to me their intention to send very soon funds for two shares and had caused my envoy to hope for three, have written me that they would wait until there is peace between the French and American republics.

It is, in part, to collect their funds that I have sent my elder son to Europe.[11] Before his return, I cannot know exactly my real strength.

His trip has also another purpose. I instructed him to propose to the government of France, in regard to the banking service of the legation in this country, as well as to the supplying of its navy and colonies, some plans about which he is to consult you. And that is not the only point about which he will call upon your knowledge. Your daughter caused us to hope that you would be in Paris in the spring.

If my propositions are accepted, there will be few companies more powerful than ours, and none which is exposed to less danger, because I have arranged my plans so as never to be without security.[12]

While my children are dealing with business in Europe, a very fortunate event which was uniquely the effect of personal confidence has put me within reach of starting business without delay by procuring for me a pledge of a million in bills from the Batavian Republic.

I did not accept this deposit as an advance of funds which would be used up by itself and would have applied to only one single operation, but as a guarantee which will be successively applicable to all the shipments which may take place, and whose returns for each one, freeing the guarantee, will make it possible for it to serve as efficaciously for the following shipment.

I shall thus preserve for the Republic its means of power. It can be for the Republic the base of a service much more considerable than the one it desired, and for our company, the opportunity and the vehicle for a series of business affairs which can rise very high and of which there will not be a one that does not have its complete guarantee.

I believe that you will find this in the best principles of political economy, administration, patriotism, and commerce.

You see that if you have the kindness to tell me all that passes through your head, neither do I conceal anything of what I have in my mind and heart.

You ask me some other questions.

1. If I have lived in America long enough to purchase land.

The laws, in this regard, are very different in the various states. I have in my name, for my company, 56,000 acres of land in Kentucky, which were placed by one of our shareholders[13] in the company for the number of shares which their sale, at a value still unknown both to him and to us, may bring.

I have—that is, the company has—in the city of Alexandria near Washington a house and a store in the name of my elder son, who was obliged, in order to acquire them, to pledge *allegiance* to the State of Virginia, which has no relation to the general law concerning naturalization in this matter. It is a property whose value is increasing, because Alexandria will be the port of the capital for a long time yet.

In New Jersey, three leagues from New York, I have a country house and a plot of land which I acquired because I knew in advance that the new road from New York to Philadelphia was to pass by there.

This plot of land borders the port which is going to be made on the narrows of Newark Bay. I can build two pretty houses and eight ordinary ones there, each with its own enclosure, court, and garden, which, added to mine (which is rather beautiful) and to a dozen others such as exist already, along with a church that the landowners and members of the various sects will build by subscription and by devotion in order to improve their heritage, will form the beginning of a very pleasant small town which I have named *Bidermann's Town* in honor of my friend and principal shareholder *Bidermann.* I owed the first honors to him.

If I ever build another town *for you* and with your name, I shall locate it in such a way that it will have to become larger.

If I found a *Nemours,* I shall put it on an island in a river near the woods, and if I establish a *Geneva,* it will be on the outlet of a lake. There must be analogy in everything. That is the basic element of taste.

Speaking of taste, I have been informed that you have just written a *religious* book in three volumes,[14] and you do not tell me a word about it. The author of the *Philosophy of the Universe*[15] is not, however, excommunicated from your church, and you are at least as tolerant as the Pope, whom Bonaparte has more than half converted.

But let us return to your questions. You ask me again how one invests in what is called a *mortgage* here. I have already replied about that matter, that one can invest at six per cent with perfect safety when one investigates carefully. And I shall add that if such a use of funds pleased you, I should give you a *mortgage* on our property in order to increase our available funds. That is the spirit of the country, and it is, in commerce, a very good spirit.

You ask me how much I should make good on current accounts. Six per cent.

You speak to me of the Dutch companies. There are several of them, of which the two most powerful are:

That of Messrs. Willinks and Van Staphorst,[16] which is engaging the State of Pennsylvania in a suit that is among the most famous cases in America and divides the greatest legal experts, the most eloquent speakers of the country.

The State of Pennsylvania claims the land which Messrs. Willinks and Van Staphorst bought from it, inasmuch as they have not built the number of houses, cleared the quantity of land, or established the number of families to which they had obligated themselves in the concession.

Their defenders reply that these conditions must be considered as comminatory; that they have always been made, that their rigorous execution has never been demanded, and that there is no reason to begin with their clients; that if the severity of these conditions, difficult to fulfill, broke the contract, the purchase of land would be generally discouraged.

The defenders of the State of Pennsylvania reply that a contract is a contract, that this one conforms to the public interest, that no administrator has the right to give a dispensation to the detriment of Pennsylvania; that if other administrators have neglected their duty in this regard, that is an additional reason for the present ones to do theirs.

The case is being heard in the Federal court. The influence of the Republic is great; that of all the purchasers of land, of which there is perhaps not one who is not in the same position as Messrs. Willinks and Van Staphorst, is not less so. It is impossible to predict the decision. The very existence of the suit may cause prices to decline.

The other company is that of Messrs. Cazenove.[17] It has made a great deal of money, not on its land, but on skillful speculation with government stocks. About two [. . .] [18] ago, it began to concern itself seriously with its land. It seems to do so with intelligence. But it is hard for it not to suffer from the general decline in prices, which nothing can stop any longer except its excess.

Yes, certainly, the discomfiture of these *poor rich* companies can offer us more than one object for speculation. I should be sorry to contribute to it. My politics in business is *my good resulting from the good of all,* and you will have recognized it in what I said to you earlier about the supplying of the colonies. But I should be an imbecile, and I should betray the confidence of my principals, if I did not wait to buy at the moment when the market will be at its lowest and will have to have a later rise in price.

Greetings and very respectful attachment.

NOTES

1 This letter seems to have been lost.

2 Probably Gallatin's *Views of the Public Debt, Receipts and Expenditures of the United States* (New York, 1800). Albert Gallatin (1761–1849), a native of Geneva, served as Secretary of the Treasury from 1801 to 1814.

3 Probably an allusion to the founding of the Manhattan Company in New York, which was due to the trickery of Aaron Burr. See Letter 7, note 1.

4 Bureaux de Pusy.

5 Jean Johannot (1748–1829), a Swiss businessman established in Paris. After serv-

ing as a member of the National Convention and of the Council of Ancients, he withdrew from political life in 1797.

6 The rest of this sentence is illegible. The following reading has been suggested: "qui occup[ent] et ont d' . . . aux petits actionnaires."

7 An illegible portion.

8 Pierre-Augustin Caron de Beaumarchais (1732–99), the famous playwright. Always interested in America, he had lent a considerable sum of money to the Americans to help finance the revolution against England.

9 Probably a certain Praire, of whom little is known except that he had promised to invest 300,000 francs in the new company. See *E. I. du Pont,* V, 97, 101, 104, 164, 165, 178, 179.

10 An allusion both to Nelson's naval triumph over Napoleon at Aboukir in 1798 and to the defeat of the French by the Russians in Italy in 1799, when Russian forces invaded Italy under the command of General Suvarov.

11 Victor du Pont.

12 The following paragraph has been crossed out:

> J'ai aussi quelques idées relativement à l'Espagne pour lesquelles j'ai lieu de compter sur l'appui de M^r d'Iranda aussi zélé que puissant de M^r d'Iranda.

> (I also have some ideas concerning Spain for which I have reason to count on the zealous and powerful support of M. d'Iranda.)

Simon de Arragorry, marqués d'Iranda, a Spanish banker, had secretly advanced funds to aid the Americans during the American Revolution.

Before this paragraph, the following is inserted between the lines and crossed out: "de plus dans le cas où la guerre se prolongerait" ("moreover, in case the war should be prolonged").

13 Jacques Bidermann. See Letter 12, note 2.

14 Necker's *Cours de morale religieuse* (Genève et Paris, an IX [1800]).

15 Du Pont de Nemours himself.

16 Two of the six partners in the Holland Land Company, founded in 1796 for speculation in land in Western New York and Western Pennsylvania.

17 Théophile Cazenove (1740–1811), an agent of the Holland Land Company, was sent to the United States in 1789 to develop that company's holdings in the Genesee region. He was later active in a company formed for settlement at Cazenovia, New York, and the development of the surrounding territory, south of the Mohawk. See A. M. Sakolski, *The Great American Land Bubble* (New York, 1932), pp. 60–62, 66, 78–81; and Paul D. Evans, *The Holland Land Company* (Buffalo, 1924).

18 A word missing, probably *ans* ("years").

19

Necker to Victor du Pont

19 April 1801

WMSS 3/9

19 avril 1801

J'ai lu avec beaucoup d'interet Monsieur la lettre que vous avez ecrite a mon frere. Il etoit parti et quoiqu'il vous verra je la lui envoye, ne doutant point quelle ne fasse sur lui la même impression que sur moi. On y voit de l'ordre dans les idées de la sagesse dans les vues et elle m'a donné un degré de confiance de plus dans les succés graduels de votre etablissement. Je vous assure que je les souhaite beaucoup.

Je vois avec plaisir que dans vos projets de voyage vous faites entrer ce Pays. Il faut Monsieur que vous abordiez chez moi et que de là vous fassiez les courses qu'exigeront vos affaires. Nous vous y seconderons dans ce qui dependra de nous.

On desireroit savoir quels interets votre maison alloueroit sur un pret de quelques milles Piastres a deux ou trois ans.

M[r] votre pere m'a repondu brievement sur la Maison Le Roy Bayard & Everts, je vous prie de me dire plus particulierement ce que vous pensez sur sa solidité.

Ce que vous dites du haut prix des terres en Genesey de l'achapt Williamson est bien remarquable. Qu'estimez vous celles en Genesey aussi mais appartenant a la societé par actions fournie a Amsterdam.[1]

Vous m'obligerez Monsieur si en me repondant vous voulez bien me dire s'il est encore tems de vous envoyer ou a Monsieur votre frere une lettre pour Newyork

Agréez les assurances du plus sincere et du plus parfait attachement.

Necker[2]

On the reverse:

Au Citoyen Victor Dupont
Chez les Citoyens Gros d'Avilier et C[i]e
a Paris
M[r] Necker
19 avril 1801
ans[we]r[e]d from Spain[3]

TRANSLATION

April 19, 1801

I have read with much interest, Sir, the letter that you wrote to my brother. He had left, and although he will see you, I am sending it to him, not doubting that it will make the same impression on him as on me. One sees in it order in ideas, wisdom in views, and it gave me another degree of confidence in the gradual success of your establishment. I assure you that I wish it very much.

I see with pleasure that in your travel plans, you include this country. You must come, Sir, to my house and make from there the trips that your business requires. We shall support you in anything that depends on us.

We should like to know what interest your company would pay on a loan of several thousand piasters for two or three years.

Your father answered me briefly about the Le Roy, Bayard and McEvers Company. I beg you to tell me in more detail what you think about its soundness.

What you say about the high price of the land of the Williamson purchase in Genesee is very remarkable. What do you estimate the price of that land, in Genesee also, but belonging to the joint-stock company formed in Amsterdam? [1]

You will oblige me, Sir, if, in answering, you will please tell me whether there is still time to send to you or to your brother a letter for New York.

Accept the assurances of my most sincere and most perfect attachment.

Necker[2]

On the reverse:

To Citizen Victor Dupont
in care of Citizens Gros, Davilliers and Co.
in Paris
M. Necker
April 19, 1801
answered from Spain[3]

NOTES
1 The Holland Land Company.
2 Only the signature of this letter is in Necker's handwriting.
3 The last three lines are in the handwriting of Victor du Pont.

20

Madame de Staël to du Pont de Nemours

20 April 1801

WMSS 2/15

ce 30 germinal
an 9[1]

Votre fils vous dira mon cher dupont bien mieux que moi la
situation de ce pays. Comme vous me soupçonnez un peu de l'enthousiasme rèpublicain vous trouveriez que mon opinion est
suspecte. Cependant je crois fermement que nous allons à la
monarchie en 1801—comme on marchoit à la république en 1791
—et qu'entre la contre rèvolution et nous il n'y a plus que bonaparte comme entre la rèpublique et nous il n'y avoit plus que louis
16. La bulle du pape est arrivée,[2] nous allons avoir des èvèques et
des curès une religion dominante. Comment voulez vous que la
religion catholique telle qu'elle est puisse jamais s'accorder avec
la liberté? Si on avoit laissé des èvèques ce n'ètoit rien mais en
faire revenir! C'est a vous à mèditer sur ces questions. Je vous les
indique. Quand à ce qui vous concerne j'avois conçu l'espoir que
vous seriez nommé senateur, mais ils ont tous dit que si vous aviez
été présent vous l'auriez été avant tout le monde mais qu'il falloit
attendre votre retour. Il faut au moins vous faire mettre sur cette

bizarre liste de notabilité.[3] Maret a son père[4] prèfet dans votre dep[artement]. Il me paroit impossible que vous ne soyez pas mis sur la liste des absents mais ils sont tous devenus si occupès d'eux mêmes et si froids pour les autres que je n'en voudrois pas rèpondre. Je vais cependant y travailler encor jusqu'à mon départ pour la suisse et peut ètre que ma persévérance vaudra les grands crèdits. La mort de paul 1er nous a tous frappé. On ne croit pas que son successeur soit aussi favorable à la france.[5] Cependant il est pacifique de caractere et ne fera pas la guerre je crois ni aux anglais ni à la france. Quoiqu'il en soit la coalition du nord est dètruite. Nous sommes encor dans les anxiétés sur l'ègypte. L'es-pèrance domine cependant. Bernadotte part après demain pour essayer si l'on peut tenter une descente. Si l'égypte étoit perdue je ne serois pas etonnée que buonaparte lui mème monta sur les vaisseaux. Ce qui le distingue c'est la haine des obstacles. Vous aimerez cela vous qui allez à 60 ans en amérique. Vous devriez bien en revenir. Le caractere est prouvé. Maintenant il faudroit contenter l'amitié. Votre ami talleyrand qui n'est plus le mien[6] passe pour le plus riche particulier de l'europe. Rœderer ne s'en-richit point et son crédit n'augmente pas non plus mais bonaparte est très stable dans ses choix. Il a senti avec raison qu'un gouverne-ment qui n'étoit pas fondé sur les institutions devoit l'ètre au moins sur les hommes et il n'en change point. Personne cependant ne regarde ceci comme stable parce que la france est en rente viagère sur la tète de bonaparte et que cette idèe ne lui déplait pas. Il en craint les dangers assez visiblement mais il ne voudroit pas se rendre moins nècessaire. Après lui non le dèluge comme disent les enfants mais le cahos. Que dites vous de la louisiane? On croyoit ici que l'amérique verroit avec peine que les françois s'y établis-sent. Croyez vous toujours que le gouv[ernement] des ètats unis est très ferme?[7] J'ai imaginé que jefferson ne suivroit pas le systeme des amis qui l'ont placè si ses amis veulent un changement à la constitution. Ah! quelle peur cela fait un changement à un pays libre. Ils nous diront bientot qu'elle est impossible la liberté. Au moins il en restera quelques petits exemples pour servir d'exemple au raisonnement. Votre ami barbè marbois s'est fait le cerbère du directoire. Je le crois naturellement austère mais je suis convaincue qu'il a exagérè son propre caractére par les èloges qu'il lui a valu. Quand à portalis[8] la loi qu'il a proposé relativement aux tribunaux spèciaux a beaucoup diminué sa considération. Il y avoit un article qu'on a retirè sur la faculté illimitée de déporter accordèe au gouvern[ement]. Cette faculté a paru un peu trop despotique mème aux plus hardis en ce genre et la complaisance de portalis lui a nui. Voila tout ce que je sais sur vos anciens amis; comme il n'y a plus de parti les hommes ont moins d'importance et tous sont plus ou moins effacès ou confondus. Malgrè toutes ces observations c'est un beau pays que la france. Les habitudes sont douces et je vous dèfie de trouver ailleurs rien qui remplace le charme de tous les jours à paris ou dans la société des françois. Y renonceriez vous a jamais et vos amis ne vous reverroient ils plus? La fayette est ici conservant son caractere noble et pur n'acceptant rien désirant encor moins et regrettant toujours cette liberté parfaite l'idole de sa vie. Parlez de moi je vous prie à Mr Bureau de pusi. Se souvient il de moi? Je me rappelle d'avoir eu l'honneur de le voir deux fois chez Mad. de tessè[9] il y a dix ans. Présentez mon hommage à Madame dupont. Les hommages lui sont bien dus pour son caractére ses sentiments et son esprit. Adieu mon cher dupont. Quand vous me manderez que vous revenez votre lettre me causera la plus sensible joye. Voulez vous remettre cette lettre à M^r camille roussillon[10] qui doit ètre près de vous et qui m'a paru mériter votre intéret.

[Sans signature]

TRANSLATION

30 Germinal
year IX [1]

Your son will tell you, my dear du Pont, much better than I, the situation of this country. As you suspect me of republican enthusiasm a little, you would find my opinion questionable. However, I firmly believe that we are going to become a monarchy in 1801, as we proceeded to become a republic in 1791, and that between counterrevolution and us there is nothing but Bonaparte, as between the republic and us there was nothing but Louis XVI. The papal bull has arrived.[2] We are going to have bishops and priests, a dominant religion. How do you expect the Catholic religion, being as it is, ever to agree with liberty? If they had left the bishops alone, that was nothing—but to have some return! I leave it to you to meditate about these questions. I indicate them to you. As for what concerns you, I had conceived the hope that you would be named senator, but everyone said that if you had been present, you would have been named before anyone else, but that it was necessary to await your return. We must, at least, have you put on that strange list of notability.[3] Maret has his father[4] appointed as prefect in your department. It seems impossible to me that you will not be put on the list of absent persons, but everyone has become so concerned with himself and so cold to others that I should not want to swear to it. I am going to work on it, however, until my departure for Switzerland, and perhaps my perseverance will prevail against great influences. The death of Paul I has affected us all. People do not believe that his successor will be as favorable to France.[5] However, he is peaceful in character and will not, I think, declare war either on the English or on France. Be that as it may, the coalition of the North is destroyed. We are still anxious about Egypt. Hope dominates, however. Bernadotte leaves the day after tomorrow to try to make a landing. If Egypt were lost, I should not be surprised if Bonaparte himself should embark. What distinguishes him is his hatred of obstacles. You will like that, you who go at the age of sixty to America. You really should return. Character is proven. Now you should satisfy friendship. Your friend Talleyrand, who is no longer mine,[6] is considered the richest man in Europe. Rœderer does not get rich, and his influence does not increase either, but Bonaparte is very sound in his choices. He felt with reason that a government which was not founded on institutions should be founded at least on men, and he does not change. No one, however, regards this as stable because France depends for her support on the life of Bonaparte and that idea does not displease him. He quite obviously fears the dangers, but he does not want to make himself less necessary. After him, not the deluge, as children say, but chaos. What do you say about Louisiana? People here thought that America would look with disfavor on the French establishing themselves there. Do you still believe that the government of the United States is very solid? [7] I imagined that Jefferson would not follow the system of the friends who put him in power if these friends want a change in the constitution. Ah! what fear that arouses, a change in a free country! People will soon tell us that liberty is impossible. At least, there will remain a few little examples to serve as example for reasoning. Your friend Barbé-Marbois has made himself the Cerberus of the Directory. I believe him to be naturally austere, but I am convinced that he has exaggerated his own character as a result of the praise it has brought him. As for Portalis,[8] the law that he proposed concerning the special tribunals has greatly decreased respect for him. There was an article, which was withdrawn, about the unlimited right of deportation granted to the government. That right seemed a bit too despotic even to the boldest of that group, and Portalis' complaisance on that subject has harmed him. That is all I know about your old friends; [but] as there are no longer any parties, men have less importance, and all are more or less effaced and disconcerted. In spite of all these observations, France is a beautiful country. Manners are gentle, and I defy you to find elsewhere anything that replaces the charm of everyday life in Paris or in French society. Would you give it up forever, and would your friends never see you again? Lafayette is here, maintaining his noble and pure character, accepting nothing, desiring even less, and still regretting perfect liberty, the idol of his life. Please mention me to M. Bureaux de Pusy. Does he remember me? I remember having had the honor of seeing him twice at Mme. de Tessé's[9] ten years ago. Give my regards to Mme. du Pont. Respect is due her for her character, her sentiments, and her mind. Goodbye, my dear du Pont. When you inform me that you are returning, your letter will give me the greatest pleasure. Will you deliver this letter to M. Camille Roussillon,[10] who must be in your vicinity and who seemed to me to deserve your interest.

[No signature]

NOTES

1 The date *20 Avril* has been inserted here by another hand.

2 An allusion to the Concordat of 1801 between Napoleon and the Pope.

3 The List of Eligibles.

4 Jean Philibert, Comte Maret, the father of Hugues-Bernard Maret (see Letter 10, note 14). He had been appointed prefect of Le Loiret.

5 Paul I, Czar of Russia, was assassinated on March 11, 1801 and succeeded by his son, Alexander I.

6 In his *Journey to France and Spain,* under the date of February 21, 1801, Victor du Pont notes: "The Consul does not like Mde de Stael and she has broken with Talleyrand who treats her very ill and did not even ask her to his fête" (p. 34).

7 Jefferson's election as President of the United States has been called "the Revolution of 1800." Aaron Burr had tied Jefferson for the office of President, and the House of Representatives had to choose between the two. After a long deadlock, Hamilton advised the Federalists to support Jefferson as the less dangerous of the two. Fear of anarchy had prevailed for a while.

On May 27, 1800, an unknown correspondent sent from Philadelphia the following report, which was published in *Le Publiciste* in Paris on 21 messidor, year VIII (July 10, 1800):

> Tout est ici dans un état de crise. Le congrès vient de terminer sa session. On est occupé dans tous les états aux élections des nouveaux membres, & l'on procédera en même temps à la nomination d'un nouveau président. Vous savez que les époques d'élections sont des époques d'agitations, de troubles & d'intrigues. Tous les partis sont en mouvement, & plusieurs incidens ont concouru avec le renouvellement du congrès, à donner à l'esprit de faction un nouveau degré d'exaltation. . . .
>
> Si vous voulez avoir la nomenclature des partis qui divisent l'opinion publique, je vous dirai qu'il n'y en a de véritablement influens que deux; les *fédéralistes* et les *républicains*. Les premiers sont fortement attachés au maintien de la constitution fédérale, telle qu'elle existe; les autres voudroient y renforcer l'influence populaire, sans être bien d'accord sur les réformes qu'il faudroit y faire pour cela. Parmi ceux-ci, il y a encore des démocrates qui voudroient réformer la constitution sur les principes de Robespierre & de Babeuf; mais le nombre en est extrêmement diminué, & ils ne sont plus dangereux.

> (Everything here is in a state of crisis. Congress has just ended its session. People are occupied in all the states with the elections of new members, and they will proceed at the same time with the nomination of a new President. You know that the times of elections are times of agitation, trouble, and intrigue. All parties are in a state of excitement, and several incidents have combined with the renewal of Congress in giving to factiousness a new degree of excitement. . . .
>
> If you want to know the nomenclature of the parties which are dividing public opinion, I shall tell you that there are really only two influential ones: the *Federalists* and the *Republicans*. The former are strongly attached to the support of the Federal Constitution, as it now exists; the latter would like to strengthen the influence of the people, without being quite in agreement about the reforms that should be made. Among the latter, there are still some democrats who would like to reform the Constitution according to the principles of Robespierre and Babeuf; but their number has greatly diminished, and they are no longer dangerous.)

8 Jean Etienne Marie Portalis (1746–1807), a prominent jurist who, as a member of the Council of Ancients, had been exiled because of his opposition to the Directory. After the fall of that government, he returned to France and became a member of the Council of State and minister of public worship. He played a major role in the preparation of the Civil Code and in the negotiations for the Concordat of 1801 with the Pope.

The law in question, enacted February 7, 1801, established special criminal tribunals which dispensed with juries, allowed no appeal from their verdict, and could impose any penalty. This repressive measure resulted from the attempt to assassinate Napoleon on December 24, 1800.

9 Adrienne-Catherine, Comtesse de Tessé (1741–1814). The daughter of Louis, duc de Noailles, she had been a prominent figure at the court of Louis XVI. Her niece was Madame de Lafayette.

10 Camille de Roussillon (1769–1805?) is mentioned frequently in Philippe Godet's

Madame de Charrière et ses amis d'après de nombreux documents inédits (Geneva, 1906). There we learn that he entered the French Navy at an early age and was wounded at the siege of Gibraltar. Mme. de Charrière, in letters to A. d'Oleyres and Benjamin Constant written in 1793 and 1794, while he was an *émigré* in Switzerland, mentions his "sensibilité" and praises his intelligence and his charm (II, 34–35). He met Mme. de Staël during his stay in Switzerland (II, 207). Returning to Paris in 1795, he entered naval service again and was a prisoner of the English for two and a half years (II, 209). After his release, he went to sea again (II, 209). We find him in New York in December 1800 (II, 359). About 1804 or 1805, he sailed for Constantinople and presumably died in a shipwreck or at the Battle of Trafalgar (II, 359).

The Eleutherian Mills Historical Library possesses two letters from Roussillon to the du Pont Company in New York. One, dated March 8, 1801, written from Baltimore, deals with commercial and shipping matters and contains an account of Jefferson's inauguration. The second, dated March 17, 1801, also written from Baltimore, contains news of the peace treaty signed between France and Austria and an offer to help the newly formed company in any way possible.

21

Victor du Pont to Necker

14 May 1801

From Victor du Pont's Letter Book, wmss 3/3

14 may
Aranjuez[1]

Mr Necker a Coppet
près Geneve

Mr. Quelques instans avant mon depart j'eus l'honneur de voir Mr de Germany & de recevoir une lettre de vous, je la laissai a mon frere pour y repondre mais comme il etait extrèmement pressé de se rendre au havre pour s'y embarquer peut etre ne l'aura t-il pas fait[2] et dans tous les cas je repeterai ce qu'il vous aura dit ne fut ce que pour trouver une occasion de vous exprimer ma reconnaissance des choses obligeantes qu'elle contient.—Autant que je puis me rappeller vous me demandiez trois choses, d'abord quelques details plus circonstancies sur la maison Le Roy Bayard & McEvers de notre ville.—Mr Le Roy est extrèmement riche. Mr Bayard l'est aussi. Mr McEvers est un jeune homme actif et intelligent, ils font beaucoup d'affaires en Co[mmis]sion pour la hollande telles que

placement de fonds recouvremens d'interets et ventes de cargaisons
en consignations.—Les deux premiers d'origine hollandaise en ont
conservé un peu les mœurs et par consequent cet esprit de sagesse
et de moderation qui existe peu chez le negociant Americain.—En
un mot c'est une des maisons d'Amerique à la quelle j'aimerais
le mieux confier ma fortune et je dois en rendant cet hommage a
la verité vous tranquiliser autant qu'il est en moi sur les interets
que vous avez mis entre leurs mains.—Vous me demandiez aussi si
nous prendrions quelques milliers de piastres a 2 ou 3 ans et combien d'interet nous en donnerions. Nous prefererions beaucoup
qu'elles fussent placées en actions nos principales speculations
portant sur des etablissemens et biens fonds qui ne peuvent se
realiser a jour fixe, cependant comme nous ne serons jamais
embarassés pour en tirer un interet plus considerable que celui
que l'on a droit d'attendre de nous. Nous les prendrons avec plaisir
et serons reconnoissans de la peine que vous voudrez bien prendre
pour nous les faire obtenir. Nous desirerions les avoir a 5 ou 5½
et ne pourrions en donner plus de 6 p[ou]r cent nos banques es-
comptant a ce taux avec beaucoup de facilité.—Vous me demandiez egalement M^r ce que peuvent valoir les terres de la Cie hollandaise situées dans le Genessee, je ne puis vous donner a ce sujet
aucune reponse satisfaisante, je l'ignore.—Elles vaudront certainement beaucoup dans quelques années, et sont peut être deja fort
cheres pour ceux qui voudraient en acheter, sans que pour cela
on put s'en defaire avantageusement surtout par grandes portions.
C'est le cas de toutes les terres incultes d'amerique dont le prix ne
peut se quoter comme celui des effets publics et encore moins a
present qu'elles ont cessé d'etre un objet d'agiotage, tous ceux qui
speculent de cette maniere doivent bien se convaincre qu'autant
le benefice est sur, autant il est quelquefois lent, et qu'il ne faut
placer ainsi que son superflu et des fonds sur l'interet regulier des
quels on ne doit pas compter, et qu'il faut arroser au contraire
pendant nombre d'années tant pour le payement des taxes que
pour d'autres frais imprevus.—Mais je vais vous citer un fait à ma
connaissance qui entre mille autres peut servir de reponse a ceux
qui declament contre ces speculations de terres parcequ'ils y ont
eté lesès soit pour avoir acheté en Europe fort cher des terres qui
n'existaient pas ou dont les titres etaient douteux ou situèe dans
un pays aride soit parce qu'ils ont voulu s'en defaire trop tôt et sans

attendre l'occasion favorable.—En 1757 l'Etat de Massachusset a concedé a neuf de ses citoyens un *tract* de 30 milles quarrèes sur la riviere de Kennebeck à charge par eux de faire quelques legers travaux pour faciliter la navigation de la riviere. En 1760 Mr Apthorp[3] l'un des proprietaires mourut. Sa part fut estimée 800 *dollars* et aucun de ses enfans ne s'en souciait à ce prix, l'ainé ayant deux parts par les loix du pays consentit a prendre ces terres dans l'une de ses parts uniquement pour obliger ses freres et sœurs. Cet ainé Mr Charles Apthorp que j'ai beaucoup connu et qui m'a raconté lui même ce fait[4] est mort a New York en 1797 et le même terrein a ete estimè dans sa succession Cent mille dollars et se realise tous les jours par ses enfans à un taux plus elevè.—Il faut acheter des terres en Amerique comme on plante ici des arbres plus pour ses enfans que pour soi mais comme les saisons favorables avancent quelquefois la pousse de ceux ci de mème les evennemens politiques peuvent accelerer de quelques années le benefice certain que promettent les terres aux Etats Unis.—La guerre arrête en ce moment l'emigration des Allemands qui etait annuellement fort considerable et qui sont les meilleurs et les plus industrieux colons, celle des irlandais est fort restreinte, beaucoup de francais sont retenus par le danger d'etre pris dans la traversèe. —La Revolution de France et celles qui la suivront en Europe avanceront d'un demi siecle la puissance et la prosperitè des Etats Unis.—Je suis convaincu qu'a la paix des milliers de familles se transplanteront en Amerique. L'ouvrier le cultivateur accoureront en foule dans un pays qui offre tant de ressources au travail et a l'industrie, le particulier aisé trouvera l'avantage d'y placer ses fonds avec plus de sureté qu'ailleurs, le Sage le Philosophe l'homme d'Etat viendront y finir leurs jours en paix y jouir de la solution de ce probléme vainement cherchee en Europe *la libertè la plus illimitèe sans aucuns des abus de la liberté.* Ils y trouveront une constitution assez bonne vierge et que personne n'a interet a violer, un peuple pensant, froid, generalement instruit, très peu de taxes, point de pauvres, point de voleurs, point de populace, du savoir vivre chez le matelot et le dernier des ouvriers. Voila des avantages que ne peuvent nier même ces francais qui disent tant de mal de l'amerique parcequ'ils y ont trouvé les femmes severes et l'opera comique mauvais.—Pardon Monsieur de ce long bavardage mais je ne sais jamais m'arrêter quand je parle d'un pays que j'aime beaucoup parceque je le connais bien et qui [*sic*] j'aime toujours davantage quand je puis le comparer avec un autre.— Vous m'eussiez ecouté avec indulgence si dans votre cabinet j'eusse repondu longuement aux questions que vous m'auriez faites sur l'amerique. Daignez me lire de même.—Je crains bien de ne pouvoir repondre a votre obligeante invitation et d'etre forcé de remettre a mon prochain voyage en Europe, l'honneur de vous voir et de faire votre connaissance que j'ambitionne depuis longtems, mais les affaires que j'espere lier ici exigeront un promt retour en Amerique et des lettres que je viens de recevoir de mon pere m'annoncent qu'il nous est arrivé des commissions importantes d'hollande et des isles et tout cela me rappelle au comptoir. —Vous nous avez appris Monsieur, à compter sur votre bienveillance. Elle peut plus que ma presence en Suisse nous y procurer des affaires et des amis.—J'espere etre de retour a Paris dans 5 ou 6 semaines et je m'estimerai heureux d'y trouver vos ordres p[ou]r l'amerique. Je suis avec respect &

TRANSLATION

May 14
Aranjuez[1]

M. Necker at Coppet
near Geneva

Sir,

   A few moments before my departure, I had the honor of seeing M. de Germany and of receiving a letter from you. I left it for my brother to answer; but as he was in a great hurry to go to Le Havre to board ship, perhaps he has not done so,[2] and in any case, I shall repeat what he may have told you, even if it should be only to find an opportunity to express my gratitude to you for the obliging things it contains.—As I remember, you asked me three things, first, some more detailed information about the firm of Le Roy, Bayard and McEvers of our city.—Mr. Le Roy is extremely rich. So is Mr. Bayard. Mr. McEvers is an active and intelligent young man. They do much business on a commission basis for Holland, such as investments of funds, collection of interest, and sales of cargoes on consignment.—The first two, of Dutch origin, have kept somewhat the manners of the Dutch, and consequently, that spirit of wisdom and moderation which is not too common in

American businessmen. In a word, it is one of the American firms to which I should like best to entrust my fortune, and I must, by rendering this homage to truth, set your mind at ease, as much as I can, about the interests that you have placed in their hands.— You asked me also if we would take a few thousand piasters for two or three years and how much interest we would give. We would much prefer to have them invested in shares of stock, since our main speculations are concerned with settlements and real estate which cannot be realized at a fixed date. Nevertheless, we shall never be at a loss to draw from them a more considerable interest than could rightly be expected from us. We shall accept them with pleasure and shall be grateful for the trouble that you take to obtain them for us. We should like to have them at 5 or 5½ per cent and could not give more than 6 per cent, our banks discounting at that rate with great ease.—You asked me also, Sir, what the value of the Dutch company's land in Genesee is. I cannot give you any satisfactory answer on that subject. I do not know.—It will certainly be worth a great deal in a few years and is perhaps already very expensive for those who would like to buy some, although it is not easily disposed of for that reason, especially in large plots. That is the situation with all the uncultivated land in America, whose price cannot be quoted like that of public bonds and even less so now that it has ceased to be a subject for gambling. All those who speculate in this way must be convinced that the more certain the profit is, the slower it sometimes is, and that therefore one must invest only one's superfluous funds and funds on whose regular interest one must not count, and that it is necessary, on the contrary, to expect a loss for a number of years because of the payment of taxes and other unexpected expenses.— But I am going to cite one instance I know about which, among a thousand others, may serve as a reply to those who attack this land speculation because they have been injured either by having bought in Europe, at a very high price, land which did not exist or whose title was doubtful or which was located in an arid region, or because they wanted to get rid of it too soon without waiting for the favorable moment.—In 1757, the State of Massachusetts granted to nine of its citizens a *tract* of thirty square miles on the Kennebec River on the condition that they do some slight things to facilitate navigation on the river. In 1760, Mr. Apthorp,[3] one of the owners, died. His share was estimated at $800, and not one of his children cared for it at that price. The eldest, having two portions in the inheritance by the laws of the country, consented to take this land as one of his portions only to oblige his brothers and sisters. This elder son, Mr. Charles Apthorp, whom I knew well and who told me of this matter himself,[4] died in New York in 1797, and the same land was valued in his estate at $100,000 and every day reaches a higher price for his children.—One must buy land in America as one plants trees here: more for one's children than for oneself. But, as favorable seasons sometimes advance the growth of trees, political events may also accelerate by a few years the certain profit that land in the United States promises.—At the moment, the war stops the very considerable annual emigration of the Germans, who are the best and most industrious colonizers; that of the Irish is very limited; many French people are restrained by the danger of being captured during the crossing.— The Revolution in France, and those which will follow it in Europe, will advance by half a century the power and the prosperity of the United States.—I am convinced that with the coming of peace, thousands of families will move to America. The worker and the farmer will come in swarms to a country which offers so many resources to work and industry; the wealthy man will find the advantage of investing his money there with more security than elsewhere; the Sage, the Philosopher, the Statesman will come to complete their lives there in peace and to enjoy the solution sought in vain in Europe to that problem, *the most unlimited liberty without any of the abuses of liberty*. They will find there a rather good virgin constitution whose violation would profit no one, a thinking people, cold, generally educated, very few taxes, no poor people, no thieves, no rabble, good manners among sailors as well as among the lowest of workers. These are advantages which cannot be denied even by those Frenchmen who say such harsh things about America because they found the women there to be strict and the comic opera bad.—Pardon me, Sir, for all this garrulity, but I never know when to stop when I speak of a country that I love very much because I know it well and love still more when I can compare it with any other.—You would have listened to me with indulgence if, in your study, I had answered at length the questions that you would have asked me about America. Deign to read me in the same way.—I fear very much that I cannot accept your kind invitation and that I am forced to postpone until my next trip to Europe the honor of seeing you and of making your acquaintance, which I have aspired to for a long time; but the business which I hope to accomplish here will require a prompt return to America, and some letters which I have just received from my father announce that some important commissions have arrived for us from Holland and the islands, and all that calls me back to the office.—You have taught us, Sir, to count on your good wishes. They can, more than my presence in Switzerland, obtain business and friends for us there.—I hope to be back in Paris in five or six weeks, and I shall consider myself happy to find there your orders for America. I am with respect, etc.

NOTES

1 Victor du Pont had left France for Spain on April 26, 1801 (*1801 Journey*, p. 66).

2 E. I. du Pont left Paris to return to the United States on April 29, 1801 (*E. I. du Pont*, V, 224).

3 During the mid-eighteenth century, Charles Apthorp of Boston and later his son Charles Ward Apthorp of New York were American correspondents of certain London mercantile firms in international exchange (Philip L. White, *The Beekmans of New York in Politics and Commerce, 1647–1877* [New York, 1956], p. 381).

Charles Ward Apthorp was a member of the Council of New York from 1763 to 1783. He married Mary McEvers, presumably a relative of James McEvers of Le Roy, Bayard and McEvers, in 1775 (*New York Genealogical and Biographical Record* [New York, 1938], LXIX, 277). In 1777 and 1778, his Massachusetts property was confiscated by that state because of his Loyalist sympathies during the Revolution, but his property in New York seems to have avoided this fate, and it seems likely that the property in Maine was returned by Massachusetts (E. B. O'Callaghan, ed., *Documents Relative to the Colonial History of the State of New York* [Albany, 1857], VIII, 765; *Proceedings of the Massachusetts Historical Society*, 2nd series [Boston, 1895–96], X, 163; James Phinney Baxter, ed., *The Baxter Manuscripts*, in *Documentary History of the State of Maine*, XII [Portland, 1908], 51–53).

4 Victor du Pont must have known Apthorp during the former's service with the French diplomatic mission in the United States from 1787 to 1798.

22

Madame de Staël to du Pont de Nemours

29 June 1801

WMSS 2/15

Copet ce 10 messidor [an 9]

J'ai remis une lettre pour vous mon cher du pont à l'un des *superbes*.[1] Mon père a èté en correspondance avec victor et je l'ai trouvé très enchanté de sa manière d'ècrire. Je n'ai point vu votre ministre des beaux arts,[2] et me voici dans mes six mois de retraite dans cette partie de ma vie pendant laquelle je pense bien à mes amis, mais je ne puis leur être utile à rien. Ce que je sais cependant, c'est que quand il seroit possible que vous ne fussiez pas sur la liste[3] vous ne devriez pas y attacher la moindre importance. D'abord personne ne croit à la durée de cette liste. Elle déplait à la nation et le gouv[ernement] se popularisera un de ces jours en la cassant. Il ne la suivra pas pour ses nominations et cette aristo-cratie bourgeoise de cinq mille èlus pèsera autant que le hasard de cent mille nobles. De plus elle se renouvellera tous les trois ans et il y auroit un tel cri d'indignation si vous n'étiez pas de cette liste çi que vous y seriez mis à votre arrivée. Certes vous n'avez pas à craindre d'être protégé républicainement par les nouveaux citoyens, nous aurions de la peine à vous contenir, et vous paroi-triez fougueux à présent à beaucoup de jacobins. Mais ce dont il s'agit c'est de vous revoir, je ne puis supporter l'idée que vous me présentez. Ne pas se revoir. Ah! mes opinions religieuses ne sont pas assez fortes pour que cette pensée ne me paroisse pas la plus terrible de toutes. Je veux vous dire un joli vers de daru:[4]

Il vient marquer sa tombe auprès de son berceau.

Croyez moi mon cher du pont il faut revenir, dans votre pays près de vos souvenirs. Est ce que ces lieux ou vous n'avez rien aimé rien espèré dans votre jeunesse ne vous laissent pas plus seul que la solitude de France. Vous avez encor bien des illusions sur ce pays. Cela vous paroit quelque chose d'être ou de n'être pas sur la liste nationale, mais vous oubliez donc qu'il n'y a qu'un homme en

france par premier par second par troisieme. On apperçoit un
brouillard qu'on appelle la nation, mais on n'y distingue rien. Lui
seul est sur le devant du tableau, qu'importe donc les places du
fond pourvu qu'on soit à côté de ses amis. Je ne puis guères vous
dire des nouvelles depuis mes montagnes, cependant je crois à ce
résultat ci paix cette année avec l'angleterre ou renouvellement de
guerre continentale l'année prochaine. Mais c'est la paix avec
l'angleterre qui me paroit de beaucoup la plus vraisemblable.
Nous possèdons en france un cardinal de gonsalve[5] messager du
pape dinant chez M[r] de talleyrand.[6] Mais il s'agit de nous faire une
religion catholico-consulaire qui ne laisse pas d'être assez difficile
à arranger. Le pape a des scrupules. Le g[énér]al murat se prèpare
à les lever mais nous autres américains nous n'entendons pas trop
la nècessité de ce bizarre mélange de superstition et d'incrédulité
qui saute[7] la vraie religion entre deux, et nous aurions mieux aimé
les principes de jefferson. Qu'il est beau son discours à l'ouverture
du congrès! Est ce que votre vieux cœur rèpublicain n'en a pas
tressailli? Mon père se porte bien. Vous lui annonciez une lettre
dans la mienne qui ne lui est point parvenue. La votre à moi ètoit
du 18 germinal. Je donne l'ordre qu'on vous envoye les ouvrages
de la famille.[8] Le mien a èté l'objet de vingt brochures et de 50
journaux à cause d'un mot sur la perfectibilité de l'espèce humaine. On a criè à la barbarie dans un certain parti, mais j'ai
obtenu d'ailleurs *tout* ce qui pouvoit me flatter le plus. *Tout* c'est
trop car vous ne m'avez pas encor écrit que vous en ètes content.
Cet hyver benjamin [Constant] a mis plusieurs fois en avant l'idèe
de vous nommer pour sénateur, mais on a su que bonaparte ne
vouloit pas que ces places fussent donnèes à des absents. Il est trop
pressé de tout pour attendre un appui mème, s'il vient de loin mais
si vous arriviez je suis sure que l'opinion que Bonaparte ècoute
vous porteroit à l'instant à cette place. Que ne faites vous un
voyage d'une annèe seulement en france? Vous qui ètes si jeune[9]
vous pouvez aller d'un bout du monde à l'autre comme je vais de
suisse à paris. Votre tète vous donne des forces, et vous avez une
puissance de volonté qui vous fera vivre j'espère tant que vous le
jugerez à propos. Vos lettres m'attachent à vous s'il se peut encor
plus. J'y trouve tant d'esprit et de bonhomie de candeur et de
prudence, que vous me paroissez avoir réalisé ce proverbe *si jeunesse savoit et si vieillesse pouvoit.* Les deux ages sont à vous et

vous tirez de chacun des deux ce qu'il y a de meilleur. Mes tendres
hommages à Mad. du pont, et des lettres de vous je vous en prie.
Personne ne vous est plus attachée que moi. Je vous ai ècrit par
votre fils. Soyez sur que mes lettres se noyent quand vous n'en
recevez pas.

[Sans signature]

TRANSLATION

Coppet, 10 Messidor [year IX]

I have given a letter for you, my dear du Pont, to one of the
superbs.[1] My father has been in correspondence with Victor, and
I found him delighted with his way of writing. I have not seen our
Minister of Fine Arts,[2] and here I am in my six months of retreat,
in that part of my life during which I think very much of my
friends, but I cannot be useful to them in any way. What I know,
however, is that if it is possible that you were not on the list,[3] you
should not attach the slightest importance to it. First of all, no one
believes in the duration of that list. It displeases the nation, and
the government will make itself popular some day by doing away
with it. It will not follow it for its nominations, and that bourgeois
aristocracy of 5,000 elect will carry as much weight as chance with
100,000 nobles. In addition, it will be renewed every three years,
and there would be such a cry of indignation if you were not on
this list that you would be put on it upon your arrival. Certainly
you do not have to fear being supported as a republican by the
new citizens. We should have difficulty in restraining you, and you
would appear impetuous, at present, to many Jacobins. But to see
you again, that is the question. I cannot bear the idea that you
present to me. Not to see each other again! Ah! my religious opinions are not strong enough that that thought does not seem to me
the most terrible of all. I want to quote to you a pretty line of
verse from Daru:[4]

"He comes to indicate his tomb near his cradle."

Believe me, my dear du Pont, you must return to your country
and your memories. Do not these places where you have loved
nothing, hoped for nothing in your youth leave you more alone
than the solitude of France? You still have many illusions about
this country. It seems to you to be something, to be or not to be

on the national list, but you forget that there is only one man in France in the first rank, in the second rank, and in the third rank. One notices a fog called the nation, but one can distinguish nothing in it. He alone is in the front of the picture. What do the places in the background matter provided that one is near one's friends? I can scarcely tell you any news from here in my mountains. However, I believe in this result: peace this year with England or renewal of war on the Continent next year. But it is peace with England which seems to me by far the most likely. We have in France a Cardinal Consalvi,[5] a messenger of the Pope, dining at Talleyrand's house.[6] But it is a question of establishing a Catholic-Consular religion for us, which is rather difficult to arrange. The Pope has scruples. General Murat is preparing to remove them, but we Americans do not understand too well the necessity of this bizarre mixture of superstition and incredulity which leaps over true religion between the two, and we would have preferred the principles of Jefferson. How beautiful is his speech at the opening of Congress! Did your old republican heart not thrill to it? My father is well. You announced to him a letter in mine which has not reached him. Your letter to me was written on the 18 Germinal. I am ordering that the works of the family be sent to you.[8] Mine has been the subject of twenty brochures and fifty newspaper articles because of a word about the perfectibility of the human species. People in a certain party shouted barbarism, but in other respects, I obtained *all* that might flatter me the most. *All* is too much, for you have not yet written me that you are pleased with it. Several times this winter Benjamin [Constant] advanced the idea of nominating you for senator, but we learned that Bonaparte did not want these positions to be given to absent persons. He is in too great a hurry in every way to wait for support even, if it comes from a distance; but if you arrived, I am sure that public opinion, which Bonaparte heeds, would carry you at once to that position. Why do you not take a trip of only a year to France? You, who are so young,[9] you can go from one end of the world to the other, as I go from Switzerland to Paris. Your mind gives you strength, and you have a willpower which will cause you to live, I hope, as long as you consider it fitting to do so. Your letters attach me to you, if possible, still more. I find in them so much wit, joviality, ingenuousness, and prudence that you seem to me to have realized that proverb, *If youth knew and old age were able.* Both ages belong to you, and you draw the best from each. My tender respect to Mme. du Pont, and some letters from you, please. No one is more attached to you than I am. I have given your son some letters for you. Be assured that my letters go down with the ship when you do not receive any.

[No signature]

NOTES

1 Probably E. I. du Pont, who had sailed for the United States about May 1, 1801. Madame de Staël is no doubt referring to her letter of April 20 addressed to du Pont de Nemours (Letter 20).

2 Jean-Antoine-Claude Chaptal (1756–1832), the distinguished chemist and public official. A disciple of Lavoisier, he was a professor of chemistry at Montpellier, and later, at the Ecole Polytechnique in Paris. He served also as director of the Grenelle powder works in Paris. Appointed Minister of the Interior in January 1801, he was responsible for fine arts, among other things. Chaptal constructed the rue de Rivoli, three bridges across the Seine, and the quais along that river. He also cleared the space in front of the cathedral of Notre Dame.

3 The List of Eligibles.

4 Comte Pierre-Antoine Daru (1767–1829), a man of letters and prominent political figure during the Napoleonic era. A cousin of Stendhal, he helped advance the novelist's governmental career before Napoleon's downfall. Daru's best known literary work is his *Histoire de la République de Venise.* The line which Madame de Staël is quoting appears in Daru's *Epître à Jacques Delille* (Paris, 1801). Daru considered Delille, who is all but forgotten now, the outstanding French poet of the time. The latter had gone into exile during the Revolution, and in this poem, Daru appeals to him to return home.

5 Cardinal Consalvi (1757–1824), as the minister of Pope Pius VII, negotiated the Concordat of 1801 with Napoleon.

6 Madame de Staël is obviously struck by the irony of this situation, since Talleyrand, before the Revolution, had been the Bishop of Autun, despite his well known immorality. During the Revolution, he had abandoned his ecclesiastical career and was excommunicated in 1791.

7 On the duplicate of this letter, *saute* has been crossed out and *laisse* inserted between the lines.

8 In 1800 Jacques Necker published his *Cours de morale religieuse* and Madame de Staël her *De la littérature.* In 1801 the *Nouveaux Mélanges extraits des manuscrits de Mme Necker* appeared.

9 Du Pont de Nemours was then 62 years old. Madame de Staël is probably thinking again of his irritation, at the time of the *coup d'état* of 18 Fructidor, 1797, when, with the help of Chénier, she claimed to have saved him from possible deportation by describing him as a harmless octogenarian.

23

Victor du Pont to Necker

14 July 1801

From Victor du Pont's Letter Book, wmss 3/3

Paris le 14 juillet 1801

Mons.

Je retrouve a mon retour ici vôtre lettre du 4 et vôtre billet du 5 de ce mois.[1]—Celle que vous m'annonciez avoir été envoyée après mon depart a certainement été ouverte par mon frere, qui se sera chargé de l'incluse selons vos intentions. Le Batiment sur le quel il a passé[2] a été pris & conduit en Angleterre, mais relaché au bout de quinze jours, il doit être arrivé a sa destination.—Je tacherai Monsieur de terminer ici mes affaires avant le 15 du mois prochain. De la j'irai à Amsterdam, et si je n'y trouve pas un bon navire pour Newyork j'irai prendre le paket en Angleterre. Je vous prie de m'adresser vos ordres pour l'Amerique chez vos amis de Paris, d'ici a trois semaines: Je desirerais infiniment que vous puissiez avoir une determination fixe relativement a l'emprunt de quelques mille piastres (avant mon depart). Je pourrais les employer avantageusement en M[es]s[i]dor ou si le crédit nous etait seulement fait a hambourg ou a londres donner des a présent ma reconnaissance dans la forme preferée.—Une seule deliberation des principaux actionnaires de N[o]tre Comp[agn]ie peut autoriser la délivrance d'un certain nombre d'actions au porteur, et si vous croyez Monsieur, qu'il nous devienne facile par ce moyen d'en placer plusieurs.—Je vais solliciter cette déliberation.—J'ai la certitude M. qu'il y a eu plusieurs lettres de mon père d'egarés en mer. Il me manque 2 N.[os] dont l'un certainement de la même datte que la lettre à Mad de Stael qui en annonce une pour vous, qui je pense aura subi le sort des miennes.—J'aurai le plus grand soin, M. de me faire accuser reception de la lettre que vous m'adresserez pour un habitant des environs de Newyork.[3]—Vous me demandez ce qu'on pense en Amerique de sa fortune & de sa solidité.—La premiere doit être enorme si l'on en juge par ses depenses, qui diminueraient la bonne opinion que l'on pourrait avoir de la seconde, si cette bonne opinion n'etait pas deja fort ébranlée par divers abus de confiance qui crient vengeance et qui dans un pays moins tolerant que le nôtre eussent deja fait explosion.—

Comptez toujours, M. sur le devouement le plus entier d'une famille qui vous revere et agreez l'assurance de mon respect.

TRANSLATION

Paris, July 14, 1801

Sir,

I found, on my return here, your letter of the fourth and your note of the fifth of this month.[1]—The one that you indicated had been sent after my departure has certainly been opened by my brother, who will have attended to the enclosure according to your intentions. The ship on which he sailed [2] was seized and taken to England, but released after two weeks. He must have reached his destination.—I shall try, Sir, to finish my business here before the fifteenth of next month. From here, I shall go to Amsterdam, and if I do not find a good ship for New York there, I shall go take the packet in England. I request that you address your orders for America to me at your friends' in Paris within three weeks. I should like it very much if you could make a definite decision concerning the loan of a few thousand piasters (before my departure). I could use them to advantage during Messidor, or if the credit were only made to us in Hamburg or London, I could give my receipt right now in the preferred form.—A single deliberation of the principal stockholders of our company can authorize the delivery of a certain number of shares "to the bearer," and if you believe, Sir, that it will be easy for us to sell several of them in this way, I am going to request this deliberation.—I am certain, Sir, that several of my father's letters have been lost at sea. I am missing two, one certainly of the same date as the letter to Mme. de Staël which mentions one for you, which, I think, must have shared the fate of mine.—I shall take the greatest care, Sir, to have acknowledgment made of the letter that you will send me for a resident living near New York.[3]—You ask me what people in America think of his fortune and of his solidity.—The first must be enormous if one judges by his expenditures, which would diminish the good opinion that people might have of the latter if that good opinion were not already much shaken by various abuses of confidence which call aloud for vengeance and which, in a nation less tolerant than ours, would already have created an explosion.

Count always, Sir, on the most complete devotion of a family which reveres you, and accept the assurance of my respect.

NOTES

1 Necker's two letters seem to have been lost.

2 The *Benjamin Franklin.*

3 Although it is impossible to identify with certainty the person to whom Necker was sending this letter, it seems likely that it was Gouverneur Morris. Morris had encouraged Necker and Mme. de Staël to purchase land in the United States (Richmond Laurin Hawkins, *Madame de Staël and the United States* [Cambridge, Mass., 1930], p. 16, n. 2; Howard Swiggett, *The Extraordinary Mr. Morris* [Garden City, N. Y., 1952], p. 228). Letters in the present volume reveal that this land speculation did not bring the wealth that the investors had expected, which may explain the reference to "abus de confiance." During discussions in the U. S. Senate in 1792 about Morris's qualifications to be U. S. minister to France, James Monroe expressed the opinion that Morris was indiscreet and had gone to Europe to sell land (Swiggett, *Morris,* p. 225). After a nine-year stay in Europe, Morris returned to the United States in 1798 and spent large sums of money on his estate, Morrisania, near New York (*ibid.,* pp. 337–39).

24

Necker to Victor du Pont

20 July 1801

From Victor du Pont's Letter Book, WMSS 3/3

Coppet 20 juillet 1801

J'ai entre les mains de MM. Ger[ar]d & Jos[ep]h Van Neck & Co a Londres 9833.40/100 dollars de six p[ou]r cent differés achettés il y a plus d'un an. Ces differés sont devenus des six p[ou]r cent simples puisque si je ne me trompe pas l'interêt court depuis le premier janvier de cette année. J'offre de vous donner une assignation sur MM. Van Neck pour en disposer & votre maison m'en creditera sous la date du 1er de ce mois au prix au quel sera ce fonds à New York à la dite datte et elle me bonifiera l'interêt a 6 p[our] cent du produit que je lui laisserai pendant trois ans si mieux je n'aime avoir son billet au même terme et dans les deux cas elle s'engagera a me rembourser en especes au titre et poids à nous connus ce jour. L'interet me sera du a compter du premier de ce mois, et l'intérêt du Capital des 6 p[our] cent cedés par moi, appartiendra pareillement a votre maison a compter de la même date. Je dois être dechargé de ces 9833 dollars du moment qu'ils seront remis par Mr Van Neck à votre correspondant car ils ne sont pas en mon nom et comme il serait possible que vous preferassiez de realiser ces fonds en Angleterre ou de voir procurer un credit dessus et d'en faire servir le produit à quelques speculations je vous envoye un ordre pour MM. Van Neck que vous me renverrez si vous n'acceptez pas ma proposition. &

TRANSLATION

Coppet, July 20, 1801

I have, in the hands of Messrs. Gerard and Joseph Van Neck and Company in London, $9,833.40 of 6 per cent deferred stocks bought more than a year ago. These shares have become simple 6 per cent stocks, since, if I am not mistaken, the interest starts from January 1 of this year. I am offering to give you an assignment on Messrs. Van Neck to use them. Your company will credit me with them from the first of this month at the price at which this fund will be in New York at said date, and it will make good the interest at six per cent of the capital which I shall leave with it for three years, if I prefer not to have its note at the same term. In both cases, your company will agree to reimburse me in specie at the standard and weight known to us that day. The interest will be due me starting from the first of this month, and the interest on the capital of the six per cent stocks which I am turning over will belong also to your company starting from the same date. I am to receive a receipt for this $9,833 from the moment it is delivered by Mr. Van Neck to your correspondent, for these stocks are not in my name, and as it might be possible that you preferred to realize these funds in England or obtain a credit on them and use the proceeds in some speculations, I am sending you an order for Messrs. Van Neck which you will return to me if you do not accept my proposition. Etc.

NOTE

In the left-hand corner of the page appears the following notation: *Copy d'une lettre de Mr Necker.*

25

Victor du Pont to Necker

29 July 1801

From Victor du Pont's Letter Book, WMSS 3/3

Mʳ Necker
a Coppet

29 juillet 1801

Mʳ. J'accepte au nom de la maison du Pont de Nemours pere fils & Cⁱᵉ de New York le pret que vous voulez bien lui faire pour trois ans de $9833.40ᶜ de Stocks americains qui sont entre les mains de MM. G[erar]d & Jos[eph] Van Neck & Cⁱᵉ de Londres aux termes et conditions contenues dans votre lettre en date du 20 Courrant, en consequence je garde l'ordre sur MM. Van Neck que je vais addresser a mon correspondant avec injonction de retirer ces *stocks* de leurs mains. J'envoye en même tems copie de votre lettre a ma maison qui attendra vos ordres ulterieurs sur cet objet. J'ai fait partir pour Nantes Mʳ sous le couvert de ma maison et avec ordre de s'en faire accuser reception les deux lettres que vous m'aviez addressées pour la même personne les 5 et 16 de ce mois. Je pense Monsieur que nous allons mettre un très petit nombre de nos actions transferables au porteur par arrêté de la majorité des actionnaires ayant voix deliberatives. Ce moyen pourra nous procurer quelques souscripteurs parmi les personnes qui ne sont retenues que par la crainte d'une responsabilite de commandite. Si vous en connaissez quelques unes dans ce cas qui ayent des placemens a faire, je prends la liberté de solliciter votre recommandation auprès deux. J'ai l'honneur &.

TRANSLATION
M. Necker
at Coppet

July 29, 1801

Sir,

I accept, in the name of du Pont de Nemours, Père et Fils & Cie. of New York, the loan that you are willing to make for three years of $9,833.40 in American stocks which are in the hands of Messrs. Gerard and Joseph Van Neck & Co. of London on the terms and conditions contained in your letter dated the twentieth of this month. Consequently, I am keeping the order on Messrs. Van Neck, which I am going to send to my correspondent with the order to obtain these *stocks* from them. I am sending, at the same time, a copy of your letter to my company, which will await your later orders about this matter. Under the address of my company and with the order to have acknowledgment made, I have dispatched to Nantes, Sir, the two letters that you had sent me for the same person the fifth and sixteenth of this month. I think, Sir, that we are going to designate a very small number of our shares transferable to the bearer by decision of the majority of the shareholders having voting rights. This contrivance can obtain for us a few investors among the people who are held back only by fear of the responsibility for capital invested by silent partners. If you know some persons in this situation who have investments to make, I take the liberty of requesting your recommendation to them. I have the honor, etc.

26

Victor du Pont to Necker de Germany

18 August 1801

From Victor du Pont's Letter Book, WMSS 3/3

18 aoust

M. Necker de Germany
à Genève

M^r

J'ai l'honneur de v[ou]s adresser une action dans la fabrique de Poudre. L'autre que v[ou]s avez prise dans la Compagnie restera à vos ordres chez M. Roman. Elle est endossée au Porteur d'après les changements faits dans l'acte de société. Ceux à qui elles sont délivrées doivent s'engager seulement à ne point les mettre en vente sans en prévenir la société qui se réserve ainsi le droit de les racheter de préfèrence, si ses moyens le lui permettent. Veuillez m'indiquer, Mʳ où vous faites vos fonds. Je me dispose à partir dans le Courant du mois prochain, et je voudrois combiner d'ici là l'envoi des recouvrements que je suis venu faire, et des nouveaux fonds qui sont mis à la disposition de la société. J'espere, Mʳ que l'intérêt que vous voulez bien y prendre, et la mesure des actions au porteur pourront déterminer quelques Capitalistes du pays que vous habitez, à s'intéresser dans notre Entreprise. Plus nos moyens seront considérables et plus les espérances de succès que nous avons, seront faciles à réaliser. Nous sollicitons votre bienveillance &ca.

TRANSLATION

August 18

> M. Necker de Germany
> in Geneva

Sir,

I have the honor of sending you one share in the powder factory. The other which you have bought in the company will remain at your disposition at M. Roman's office. It is endorsed to "to the bearer" according to the changes made in the deed of partnership. Those to whom these are delivered must agree only not to put them up for sale without informing the company, which thus reserves for itself the right to repurchase them first, if its means allow it. Please indicate to me, Sir, where you have your funds. I am preparing to leave during the next month, and I should like to combine before then all the collection of funds that I have come here to make and the new funds which have been placed at the disposition of the company. I hope, Sir, that the interest that you kindly take in it and the action of making the shares out "to the bearer" may convince some capitalists of the country in which you live to take an interest in our enterprise. The more considerable our means are, the more the hopes which we have for success will be easy to realize. We request your good wishes, etc.

27

du Pont de Nemours to Madame de Staël

18 August 1801

From an excerpt in Le Marois, *Cahiers*, p. 506

New York, 30 Thermidor, an 9
Ayant inutilement désiré contribuer au bon gouvernement du monde, auquel j'ai pourtant rendu quelques services quand j'étais au Conseil des Rois, et pour qui je n'ai réussi à rien dans la République; n'étant pas devenu assez grand pour commander—mais étant devenu assez distingué pour n'obéir à rien d'arbitraire—, j'ai besoin de l'indépendance. Je la cherche dans ma vaste République qui embrasse la terre entière et qui se mêle à tous les Gouvernements, et qui n'a ni lois, ni magistrats, qui n'obéit qu'à des mœurs et à des usages. Cette République a, comme toutes les autres, quelque aristocratie: la noblesse y est dans la richesse jointe à la bonne renommée; mais elle y est accessible pour tout le monde. Je suis ambitieux et ne me soucie pas de rester plébéien. Je suis désireux d'être riche, cela est laborieux et ennuyeux (quel credo américain), mais cela est nécessaire. Il faut m'y dévouer, je m'y dévoue; et d'autant plus volontiers qu'auprès de mes associés, c'est un devoir. M. votre Père qui est un grand Maître, dit que je ne m'y prends pas sans intelligence: son suffrage m'est un puissant encouragement.

TRANSLATION

New York, 30 Thermidor, year IX
Having vainly wished to contribute to the good government of the world, to which I nevertheless rendered some services when I was a member of the Council of Kings, and for which I succeeded in no way in the Republic; not having become great enough to command—but having become distinguished enough to obey nothing arbitrary—I need independence. I seek it in my vast Republic, which embraces the whole world and is concerned with all governments, and has neither laws nor magistrates, and obeys only customs and usages. This Republic has, like all the others, some

aristocracy: nobility is there in wealth joined to a good reputation; but it is accessible to everyone. I am ambitious and am not anxious to remain a plebeian. I want to be rich; this is difficult and tiresome (what an American credo!), but necessary. I must devote myself to it; I do devote myself to it, and all the more willingly since, on behalf of my associates, it is a duty. Your father, who is a great Teacher, says that I am not going about it without intelligence; his approval is a powerful encouragement for me.

28

Victor du Pont to Necker de Germany

4 September 1801

From Victor du Pont's Letter Book, WMSS 3/3

4 7ᵇʳᵉ 1801

Mʳ Necker Germany
Genève

Mʳ

J'ai reçu la lettre que v[ou]s m'avez fait l'honneur de m'écrire le 13 dernier.[1] La pluspart des observations qu'elle contient sur l'acte de Societé des moulins à poudre nous avoient déja frapé, et nous avions rédigé un nouveau projet d'acte d'association dont je joins ici copie.[2] Je me fais bon que notre maison de Newyork et mon frere adopteront avec plaisir ces changements: Les deux actionnaires de Paris les ont provoqués et je ne doute pas que M. Bidermann qui arrivera sous peu de sa Campagne ne consente à détruire le premier qu'il avoit signé, et à y substituer celui-ci qui restera déposé chez lui, et où vous pouvez charger quelqu'un de le signer de votre part, si vous en approuvez la teneur. L'art. 10 répond à votre seconde objection. Nous avions d'abord pensé qu'un Directeur de manufacture ne pouvant emprunter que par hipothéque sur son établissement, n'étoit pas dans le cas d'engager les actionnaires au delà de leur mise. Mais cependant si une explosion de Moulins, ou toute autre grande réparation exigeoit de nouveaux fonds, les 5 ou 6 actionn[ai]res de france, en vertu de la rédaction de cet art. 10. seroient les maîtres d'abandonner, ou de consentir aux emprunts que la M[ais]on Du Pont de Nemours Co —administratrice auroit jugé nécessaire, et qui, en cas de non-approbation des autres intéressés resteroient entierem[en]t à sa Charge. Quant à votre 3ᵉ observation, cette part des bénéfices est réservée à un des promoteurs de l'etablissem[en]t qui doit concourir à faire accorder la fourniture du Gouvernement.³ Peut-être ne l'acceptera-t-il point et dans tous les cas on saura à quoi s'en tenir, avant l'époque du 1ᵉʳ dividende; il étoit délicat de donner à ce sujet de plus grands détails. L'art. 9 est rédigé dans le sens proposé par votre 4ᵉ observation. L'art. *11* devenu art. *12* n'a rapport qu'a des formes d'administration intérieure peu importantes dans les résultats et dont on est à même de s'instruire ici, et qu'il eut été trop long de détailler. Si vous gardez la copie que je vous adresse aujourd'hui et me renvoyez l'autre, je remettrai à la personne qui comptera vos fonds un reçu conçu en ces termes. "Nous soussignés Du Pont de Nemours, pere, fils et Cⁱᵉ reconnoissons avoir reçu de M. Necker Germany Mille dollars pour son intérêt dans la manufacture de poudre établie dans les Etats unis, sous la direction de E. I. Du Pont aux Clauses et conditions de l'acte de société déposé à Paris chez le C[itoy]en Roman, Boulevard Montmartre." Ce titre équivaudra, je pense, à la premiere forme de copie certifiée que nous avions adoptée: Veuillez me marquer ce que vous en pensez. Quant à l'action dans la Comp[agn]ie je vous en envoye une copie conforme. On remplit *au Porteur* la place destinée à placer le nom de l'Actionn[ai]re et on raye ce qui avoit rapport au transfer sur les registres. Ceci peut servir jusqu'à ce que l'on ait déterminé si l'on emettra de nouveaux talons d'actions. M. Roman est dépositaire de toutes les actions non placées, et vous remettra certainement la vôtre ou une reconnoissance d'action dans la forme que vous desirerez en touchant le montant de cette dite action. Quant à la signature de l'acte de société les changements qui viennent d'y être faits exigent qu'il soit envoyé en Amérique pour la signature des actionn[ai]res qui y sont résidents, ou que ceux-ci envoyent leur procuration à l'effet de le signer ici. Jusque là, ce qui importoit à la parfaite sureté des actionnaires, est fait par la délivrance du titre au Porteur. La signature des Porteurs est donc moins essentielle et urgente. Je ne pense pas même qu'elle soit de rigueur. Car dans une société où le sociétaire ne veut pas s'engager audelà de ce qu'il a donné de premier abord, les Directeurs qui tiennent sa mise de fonds n'ont plus besoin de sa signature, et l'actionnaire n'a réellement besoin que d'un reçu ou titre quelconque qui l'établisse aux droits et prérogatives que lui ont cédé les administrat[eu]rs par un acte déposé en lieu sûr à leur connoissance. Nous avons pensé à faire signer par quelques uns des princip[au]x actionn[ai]res et par tous, s'il étoit possible, une espéce d'engagem[en]t de donner la préférence à la société p[ou]r le rachat des actions, a fin d'éviter l'inconvénient d'un discrédit public par la trop grande quantité qui pourroit être mise à la fois sur la place; mais si vous y trouver quelque inconvénient, nous n'insisterons pas, quoi que cela puisse en quelque maniere compromettre les actionn[ai]res actuels qui, par la nature de l'action au Porteur représentée telle en Amérique, si on y découvre qu'il y a des actionnaires, seroient toujours à l'abri des poursuites des créanciers amèricains et de l'effet des loix américaines. En général, M. lorsque des entreprises se forment si loin des intéressés, il est bien difficile de prevoir d'avance une infinité de Circonstances. Il faut avoir une grande latitude de confiance dans les administrateurs, et l'argent qu'on leur confie, est, pour-ainsi dire, un prêt sur leur responsabilité. Si nous ne justifions pas cette confiance, ce ne sera pas manque de Zêle, de bonnes intentions, de probité, de travail. Veuillez nous continuer votre bienveillance et vos Conseils, nous tâcherons de justifier l'une et suivront toujours les autres.

TRANSLATION

September 4, 1801

M. Necker Germany
Geneva

Sir,

I have received the letter that you did me the honor of writing the thirteenth of last month.[1] The majority of the observations that it contains about the deed of partnership for the powder mills had already struck us, and we had drawn up a new plan for a deed of partnership, a copy of which I enclose.[2] I am confident that our company in New York and my brother will adopt these changes with pleasure. The two shareholders in Paris prompted them, and I do not doubt that M. Bidermann, who will soon arrive from his country estate, will consent to destroy the first one which he had signed and substitute for it this one which will be left at his house, where you can have someone sign it on your behalf, if you approve its terms. Article 10 answers your second objection. We had thought at first that the director of a factory, being unable to borrow except by a mortgage on his establishment, was not in a position to engage the stockholders beyond their investment. But, nevertheless, if an explosion in the mills or any other great repair required new funds, the five or six shareholders in France, by virtue of the wording of that article 10, would be at liberty to decline or to consent to the loans which the Du Pont de Nemours Company as administrator would have judged necessary, and which, in case of the disapproval of the other interested parties, would remain entirely at its expense. As for your third observation, that portion of the profits is reserved for one of the promoters of the establishment, who is to arrange to have the supplies for the government granted to the company.[3] Perhaps he will not accept, and in any event, we shall know what to do before the time of the first dividend. It was difficult to give greater details about this matter. Article 9 is worded in the sense proposed by your fourth observation. Article *11*, which has become article *12*, relates only to forms of internal administration, of little importance in the results; you can find out about this here, and it would have taken too long to explain it in detail. If you keep the copy which I am sending you today and return the other to me, I shall give the person who will turn over your funds a receipt couched in these terms: "We, the undersigned Du Pont de Nemours, Père et Fils & Cie., acknowledge having received from M. Necker Germany $1,000 for his interest in the powder factory established in the United States under the direction of E. I. du Pont according to the clauses and conditions of the deed of partnership on deposit in Paris at the office of Citizen Roman, Boulevard Montmartre." This certificate will be the equivalent, I think, of the first form of the certified copy which we had adopted. Please tell me what you think of it. As for the share of stock in the Company, I am sending you a certified true copy of it. In the place designated for the name of the shareholder, *to the bearer* is to be filled in, and that which related to the transfer on the registers is to be crossed out. This can serve until we decide whether new stubs for shares will be issued. M. Roman has all the shares not yet sold, and he will certainly turn over to you your shares or a stock receipt in whatever form you wish when he receives payment for said share. As for the signature on the deed of partnership, the changes which have just been made in it require that it be sent to America for the signatures of the shareholders who reside there or that the latter send their proxy to sign it here. Until then, the complete safety of the shareholders is ensured by the delivery of the share made out "to the bearer." The signatures of the bearers are therefore less essential and less urgent. I do not even think that they are required, for in a company where the partner does not want to become responsible beyond what he has given at first, the directors who hold his investment no longer need his signature, and the shareholder really needs only a receipt or warrant of some sort which guarantees him the rights and prerogatives which the administrators have given him by a deed deposited in a place known to be safe. We thought of having some of the principal shareholders, and all of them, if possible, sign a kind of agreement to give the company preference for the repurchase of the shares, in order to avoid the inconvenience of public discredit if too many should be put up for sale at the same time; but if you find some objection to it, we shall not insist, although that may in some way compromise the present shareholders, who, by the very nature of the stock marked "to the bearer" in America, in case it is discovered that there are stockholders, would be safe from the suits of American creditors and from the effect of American laws. In general, Sir, when enterprises are formed so far away from the interested persons, it is very difficult to foresee in advance a great number of circumstances. One must have a great latitude of confidence in the administrators, and the money that one entrusts to them is, so to speak, a loan on their responsibility. If we do not justify that confidence, it will not be for lack of zeal, good intentions, probity, and work. Please continue to show your good will and give us your advice. We shall try to justify the former and will always follow the latter.

NOTES

1 This letter has apparently been lost.

2 In a letter written from Paris on August 8, 1801, to Du Pont de Nemours Père et Fils & Cie. in New York, Victor du Pont states that in order to find more

shareholders for the new company, Bidermann, Johannot, and he had decided to adopt a new plan of organization, without waiting to consult the New York branch. Delessert's reports on the obligations of shareholders under American law had caused the original subscribers to refuse completion of their payments, and those who had merely promised to subscribe, such as Necker de Germany, now refused to do so. Under this new plan, shares would be endorsed "to the bearer," thus avoiding identification of shareholders and possible penalties. The three men thus hoped to increase confidence among possible investors. See *E. I. du Pont*, V, 258-59.

3 Probably Colonel Anne Louis de Tousard (1749-1817). He had served gallantly in the American Revolution and had been commissioned a lieutenant-colonel in the American Army; he had also been given a pension for life by Congress. While serving with the French Army during the uprisings in Santo Domingo in 1792, he was arrested on charges of resistance to orders and counter-revolutionary principles and spent a year in the prisons of L'Abbaye in France. The American Minister obtained his release, and Tousard returned to the United States, where the Army reinstated him and he advanced rapidly. In 1800 he was appointed Inspector of Artillery, and in 1801 he remodeled the garrison at West Point into a military school.

In a letter to Bidermann dated December 1, 1800, Du Pont de Nemours states that the new company was forced to give an interest to Tousard without any payment from him. Du Pont considered this a desirable arrangement, since Tousard had promised that the United States would provide the powder company with government saltpeter and would order its powder from the new company (*E. I. du Pont*, V, 192). Tousard, however, returned to Santo Domingo in 1802, and shortly thereafter, to France.

29

Victor du Pont to Necker de Germany

24 September 1801

From Victor du Pont's Letter Book, WMSS 3/3

2 Vendemiaire an 10

M. Necker de Germany
Genêve

J'ai reçu la lettre dont vous m'avez honoré en date du 27 fructidor. Je suis bien convaincu que c'est moins l'espoir d'un placement avantageux que le desir de nous être agréable, de nous aider dans nos entreprises, et de favoriser nos projets et nos travaux qui vous a déterminé à prendre deux actions. Agréez l'expression de ma reconnoissance, et soyez convaincu que mon Pere ne sera pas moins sensible que moi à ce procedé de v[o]tre part.

J'ai réfléchi, M[r] à la proposition que v[ou]s me faites de changer en un prêt à six ans de pareille somme votre mise de fonds. Je pense que cela pourroit bien convenir au moins pour la moitié, et je vous donnerai conjointement avec M[r] Biderman un reçu provisoire de cette moitié, jusqu'à ce que la réponse des administrateurs de la Comp[agn]ie à New York ait déterminé cette mesure. Mais a présent je n'ai point les pouvoirs nécessaires pour vous donner en leur nom le titre que vous pourriez desirer, et leur ayant annoncé, il y a près de 3 mois, le placement de 2 actions, comme vous m'y aviez autorisé, en me disant avant votre départ que je pouvois regarder cela comme une affaire conclue, je dois les prévenir du Changement proposé et solliciter leur agrement.

Mr Martin[1] que j'ai vu ne m'a pas paru encore suffisament autorisé par vous pour conclure, il m'a proposé de le faire seulement pour une action et à condition de renoncer à l'autre, ou de la laisser en suspens. En fin il s'est résumé à vous demander de nouveaux ordres. Ce délai m'a un peu contrarié, parceque dans les arrangements d'un départ très prochain, j'avois, comptant sur cette rentrée, étendu mes achats en fabriques et au moment même de la réception de votre lettre, pris quelques traites sur les Etats unis à un taux avantageux. J'espere cependant que nous aurons votre réponse avant mon départ de Paris. Le Navire sur lequel j'ai pris passage met à la voile de Nantes du 10 au 15 8[bre] [2] et dans tous les cas mes amis de Paris m'aideront, s'il est nécessaire.

Ne pouvant profiter de l'heure du Courrier p[ou]r prévenir M. votre frere de mon depart, oserois-je vous prier, M[r] si vous en avez l'occasion, de lui dire que j'attendrai ses ordres pour Newyork ainsi que ceux de M[de] de Staël et les vôtres.

TRANSLATION

2 Vendémiaire, year X

M. Necker de Germany
Geneva

I have received the letter dated the 27 Fructidor with which you have honored me. I am quite convinced that it is less the hope for an advantageous investment than the desire to be obliging to us, to aid us in our undertakings, and to favor our plans and work which caused you to decide to buy two shares. Accept my gratitude and be assured that my father will be no less grateful than I am for this action on your part.

I have thought, Sir, about the proposition that you make to me about changing your investment to a six-year loan for the same amount. I think that that might be suitable, at least for half, and I shall give you, jointly with M. Bidermann, a temporary receipt for that half until the reply of the administrators of the company in New York has settled this matter. But, at present, I have not the necessary powers to give you, in their name, the certificate that you might wish; and having announced to them nearly three months ago the sale of two shares, as you had authorized me to do, telling me before your departure that I could consider that as a settled matter, I must warn them of the proposed change and request their approval.

M. Martin,[1] whom I saw, still did not seem to me to have sufficient authorization from you to settle the matter. He proposed doing so for only one share, on condition that the other not be bought, or of leaving the matter undecided. Finally, he resolved to ask you for new orders. This delay annoyed me somewhat, because in my arrangements for my fast approaching departure, counting on that payment, I had extended my purchases of manufactures, and at the very moment I received your letter, had bought a few drafts on the United States at an advantageous rate. I hope, however, that we shall have your reply before my departure from Paris. The ship on which I have booked passage sails from Nantes between the tenth and fifteenth of October,[2] and in any case, my friends in Paris will help me, if it is necessary.

Since I cannot write in time before the mail collection to inform your brother of my departure, may I dare ask you, Sir, if you have the opportunity, to tell him that I shall await his orders for New York, as well as those of Madame de Staël and your own?

NOTES

1 I have been unable to identify this person.
2 Victor du Pont did not leave France until the middle of December, when he sailed on the *Benjamin Franklin* from Bordeaux. See *1801 Journey,* pp. 116–18.

30

Necker to du Pont de Nemours

29 October 1801

WMSS 2/15

J'ai receu Monsieur la lettre que vous m'avez fait l'amitié de m'ecrire le 21 aoust. Toutes vos paroles sont douces et vont a mon cœur. Je souhaite plus que je ne puis vous l'exprimer que vous conserviez longtems tous les biens dont vous jouissez par une heureuse association par des fils estimables et par la serenité de votre ame.

Je ne suis point allé a Paris; la paix est une epoque qui devroit me decider[1] mais je suis encore dechiré entre le desir bien vif d'un rapprochement durable avec ma fille[2] et tant de motifs qui semblent devoir me vouer a la retraite du monde.

Je vois par votre lettre Monsieur que Mr Bureau de Pusy est en france. Il y est precedé par une reputation bien honorable.

M. votre fils vous aura informé ainsy que votre maison du pret que j'ai fait a votre societe. Je le mets sous la garde de votre loyaute et il sera bien là. J'ai ete surpris que M[r] votre fils ne m'ait pas informé avant son depart si l'assignation que je luy avois envoyé sur M[rs]. Van Neck en fonds Americains differes avoit ete acquittée ponctuellement. Ces Messrs de leur coté ne m'ont rien ecrit. Je prie votre maison de m'envoyer le decompte de cette affaire conformement a notre convention. Je souhaite qu'elle ait pu faire un employ avantageux de cette avance.

C'est avec le plus tendre interest Monsieur que je vous adresse les assurances et l'homage de mon inviolable attachement.

[Sans signature]

Le 29 Octobre 1801

On the duplicate of this letter, in Jacques Necker's handwriting:

Le 8 Decembre 1801

Ce qui precede est la copie de ma derniere.

J'ai appris que Mr Bureau de Pusy avoit accepté une place de Prefet.[3] [C']est une acquisition pour la chose publique. Comment conciliera-t-il son nouvel etat avec les services que vous attendiez de son association. Il ne peut la quitter pour les affaires passées et tant que sa retraite du commerce ne sera pas connue par une circulaire il sera toujours lié de sa fortune a votre maison.[4] Je m'en rapporte sur tout cela a votre sagesse.

Je vous renouvelle Monsieur avec le plus tendre interest les assurances de mon inviolable attachement.

Necker

TRANSLATION

I have received, Sir, the letter that you had the kindness to write to me on August 21. All your words are kind and touch my heart. I hope, more than I can express to you, that you may long keep all the good things you enjoy from a fortunate association, from admirable sons, and from the serenity of your soul.

I have not gone to Paris; peace is a time which should make up my mind,[1] but I am still torn between the very strong desire for a lasting reunion with my daughter[2] and so many reasons which seem to force me to retirement from the world.

I see by your letter, Sir, that M. Bureaux de Pusy is in France. He is preceded there by a very honorable reputation.

Your son will have informed you as well as your establishment of the loan that I have made to your company. I put it under the protection of your loyalty, and it will be well off there. I was surprised that your son did not inform me before his departure whether the assignment which I had sent him on Messrs. Van Neck in deferred American funds had been paid promptly. These gentlemen, for their part, have written nothing to me. I beg your company to send me a detailed account of this matter in conformity with our agreement. I hope that it has been able to make advantageous use of that advance.

It is with the most tender interest, Sir, that I send you the assurances and the homage of my inviolable attachment.

[No signature]
October 29, 1801

On the duplicate of this letter, in Jacques Necker's handwriting:

December 8, 1801

What precedes is a copy of my latest letter.

I have learned that M. Bureaux de Pusy had accepted a position as prefect.[3] That is an acquisition for the state. How will he reconcile his new position with the services that you expected from his association? He cannot leave it for past business, and as long as his retirement from business is not announced by a circular, he will still be tied by his fortune to your company.[4] I leave all that to your wisdom.

I repeat, Sir, with the most tender interest the assurances of my inviolable attachment.

Necker

NOTES

1 The Treaty of Lunéville between France and Austria had been signed February 9, 1801. The Preliminaries of London were signed October 1, with the Peace of Amiens being concluded in March of the following year.

2 Madame de Staël returned to Paris in November, 1801.

3 Bureaux de Pusy was appointed prefect of Allier, November 9, 1801.

4 According to B. G. du Pont, Bureaux de Pusy's resignation from the Du Pont Company "was very unsatisfactory to those of the original shareholders who had invested because of their belief in his ability" (*Du Pont de Nemours, 1739–1817* [Newark, Del., 1933], II, 59).

31

du Pont de Nemours to Necker

30 November 1801

From a draft, WMSS 2/4

New York 30 9bre 1801

Monsieur,

Nous avons reçu aujourd'hui en huit certificats de *deferred stocks* devenus 6 p[ou]r cent des Etats unis montant ensemble à \$9833$^{66}/_{100}$ que vous avez passés à notre maison sur le pied du cours que les memes papiers avaient le 1er juillet de la presente année en amerique, suivant votre lettre du 20 du même mois, dont notre victor du Pont a le 29 accepté la proposition.

Nous avons l'honneur de joindre ici les deux prix courans du 27 juin et 4 juillet derniers qui constatent que le cours etait le 27 juin a 90 et le 4 juillet a 91 pour cent d'où suit que le 1er il devait être a 90½.

A ce taux les 9833 dollars 66 cents valaient ce
jour 1er juillet $8889.$^{65}\!/_{100}$
a quoi doivent etre ajoutés les interets echus au
meme jour   295.$^{1}\!/_{100}$
    Total   9184.66
dont nous vous créditons et que nous tiendrons à votre disposition
le 1er juillet 1804 selon vos intentions en vous servant d'ici là les
interets à 6 pour cent.

    Agreez nos remerciemens de votre confiance et notre respect.

P.S. Mr Walpole[1] ayant obmis dans la procuration le pouvoir de
toucher les interets on nous les a refusés au Loan Office. Voudrez
vous bien donner vos ordres pour qu'il nous soit envoyé à ce sujet
une procuration supplementaire car nous vous avons crédité de
ceux des six premiers mois, et c'est votre intention que nous jouis-
sions de ceux des six derniers.

TRANSLATION

                        New York, November 30, 1801
Sir,

    We received today eight certificates of *deferred stocks,* which
have become 6 per cent stocks of the United States, amounting
altogether to $9,833.66, which you have transferred to our com-
pany at the rate of exchange that these same bills had on July 1
of the present year in America, according to your letter of the
twentieth of the same month, the offer of which our Victor du
Pont accepted on the twenty-ninth.

    We have the honor to enclose here the two current prices of last
June 27 and July 4, which state that the rate was at 90 on June 27
and at 91 per cent on July 4, from which it follows that on July 1,
it should have been at 90½.

    At this rate the $9,833.66 was worth that day,
July 1 $8,889.65
to which must be added the interest due on the
same day   295.01
    Total $9,184.66
with which we credit you and which we shall hold at your disposition on July 1, 1804, according to your intentions, while
paying you the interest at 6 per cent until then.

    Accept our thanks for your confidence and our respect.

P.S. Because Mr. Walpole[1] omitted in the proxy the authority to collect the interest, we were refused it at the Loan Office. Would you kindly order that a supplementary proxy be sent to us about this matter, as we have credited you with the first six months' interest and as your intention was that we profit by that of the last six.

NOTE
1 I have been unable to identify this person.

32

du Pont de Nemours to James Casenove and Company

30 November 1801

From a draft, WMSS 2/4

New York 30 9bre 1801

Messrs James Casenove et Co.[1]

Messieurs

Nous recevons les huit certificats de deffered stocks des Etats unis que vous avez bien voulu vous charger de nous faire passer de la part de notre Victor du Pont

Savoir N° 1705 de $1000
1706 — 1000
1707 — 1333.66
1749 — 3000
1750 — 1000
1751 — 1000
1752 — 1000
1753 — 500

} 9833^d.66^c

avec la procuration de Mr Robert Walpole pour en disposer.

Nous vous remercions de cette continuation de bons offices de votre part et nous avons l'honneur de vous saluer.

5 X^bre P.S. nous rouvrons notre lettre pour vous dire que M^r

Walpole ayant négligé d'inserer dans sa procuration le pouvoir de toucher les interets on nous les a refusés au Loan Office. Voudrez vous bien faire ce qui sera necessaire a ce sujet pour nous procurer une procuration supplementaire?

Nous en ecrivons aussi à Mr Necker de qui nous tenions les stocks et a qui nous vous prions de faire passer l'incluse.

TRANSLATION

New York, November 30, 1801

Messrs. James Casenove and Company.[1]

Gentlemen,

We have received the eight certificates of deferred stocks of the United States that you have kindly arranged to send to us on behalf of our Victor du Pont.

To wit: No. 1705 of $1,000
1706 "   1,000
1707 "   1,333.66
1749 "   3,000
1750 "   1,000
1751 "   1,000
1752 "   1,000
1753 "   500

$9,833.66

with the proxy of Mr. Robert Walpole to dispose of them.

We thank you for this continuation of kindness on your part, and we have the honor of sending you greetings.

December 5. P.S. We reopen our letter to tell you that, Mr. Walpole having neglected to enclose in his proxy the power to receive the interest, it was refused us at the Loan Office. Would you be so kind as to do what is necessary about this matter to obtain a supplementary proxy for us?

We are also writing about this to M. Necker, from whom we got the stocks and to whom we beg you to forward the enclosed letter.

NOTE

1 A Swiss banking firm established in London. James Casenove was a cousin of Anthony Charles Casenove, who had left Switzerland and settled in Alexandria, Virginia, in 1794 and whom Victor du Pont met in 1800 on his trip to that city to acquire the citizenship necessary to own land in the United States. See E. I. du Pont, V, 141, 158, et passim.

✺

33

du Pont de Nemours to Madame de Staël

3 December 1801

From a draft, WMSS 2/4

New York 3 X^{bre} 1801

Mme de Stael.

Madame,

Vous apprendrez avec interêt, si vous ne le savez pas déja, que *M^r votre Pere* a donné un assez grand encouragement, une marque de confiance notable à *Du Pont votre ami*. Et cela en quatre mots comme les hommes de tête font les affaires privées.

La Paix me cause un très grand plaisir, quoiqu'elle me dérange absolument une belle affaire que Mr de Pusy allait conclure et où il pouvait y avoir à gagner un petit million.[1]

Mais en compensation, elle me donnera d'autres avantages durables, particulierement celui de n'avoir pas besoin pour mille choses d'acheter assez cher et non sans quelque risque un nom américain.

Elle me donnera vraisemblablement aussi la consolation de vous expedier toutes les six semaines un navire qui vous portera des lettres et me rapportera les vôtres sans qu'elles se noient.

Vous serez instruite de tout ce que notre grave nation du nouveau monde fait de raisonnable et j'apprendrai tous les divertissemens, toutes les gentillesses qui vous amuseront a Paris.

"quelle est la volupté
"qu'inspire un *Te deum* quand il est bien chanté." [2]

Je suis émerveillé de revoir les Français si bons catholiques, et les Jesuites survivre aux Parlemens.

Vous avez sçu dans le tems que quoiqu'huguenot de naissance, Philosophe de profession, et toujours très laïque lors de l'établissement du clergé constitutionnel, j'ai eu quatre voix pour être Archevêque de Rouen.

Puisqu'on paye si bien les oremus, les mitres, les croix et les crosses, j'ai presque regret de n'avoir pas réuni un plus grand nombre de suffrages.

Vous me croyez desolé. Point du tout. Je vois la chose sous un autre aspect.[3]

Pythagore et plusieurs autres philosophes ou législateurs ont eu la doctrine publique et la doctrine secrete. Ma confiance dans le genie de Buonaparte est telle qu'il ne l'a nullement vendue par cette apparente reculade vers le fumier de la theologie qu'il a au reste declare n'avoir faire que *par egard pour la majorite et non dans sa propre opinion.*[4]

Il me semble qu'il se conduit comme q[uelqu']un qui voulant netoyer un tonneau barbouillé d'une lie epaisse et gluante le remplit d'eau et la laisse detremper: en suite de quoi toute l'ordure s'expulse aisement.

Je crois le voir tenant sa parole au Pape et au Légat, et impôsant très bien la nation pour le payement des curés catholiques et Protestans ou de toute autre foi. Puis au bout de quelques années, s'appercevant ou laissant le Tribunat s'appercevoir que ce doit être [une] charge locale et personnelle. Puis ordonnant que le salaire des pretres sera conservé *en son entier,* mais reparti suivant les sectes celui des catholiques sur les catholiques, celui des Protestans sur les Protestans avec liberté même pour les Fideles d'en augmenter le tarif.

D'ou suivra que qui sera catholique devra contribuer pour le Pretre catholique; d'où suivra que si quelques catholiques qui trouveront l'impot lourd changent de croyance, l'impôt deviendra plus lourd encore sur les perseverans; d'ou suivra qu'à la fin l'opinion de la majorité deviendra differente de ce qu'elle est aujourd'hui. D'où suivra que cette opinion generale trouvera juste que l'entretien des Pretres soit l'objet d'une contribution volontaire et particuliere, *d'une souscription.* Or le premier consul respectera dans tous les tems l'opinion générale. Il gouverne, veut gouverner, gouvernera les Français selon leur gré. D'où suivra que son Eminence Mg[r] le cardinal Caprara[5] n'aura *capé*[6] qu'*un rat.*

Et alors la maladie sera guerie sans retour par la vigueur de temperament du malade.

Si c'est ainsi qu'il a vu la chose, ma foi ce guerrier de trente ans a la cervelle bien mure et bien prévoyante et je suis de l'avis de

Sir Roland Meredith[7] qui pensait que *rien* n'est *superieur a la tête d'un vieillard sur les epaules d'un jeune homme.*

Si vous voyez *Chenier* dites lui que sa satire des nouveaux saints[8] m'a paru [. . . .] [9] Comme elle est charmante.

Mais pourquoi m'arrive t'il ceci cela, et jamais votre livre réimprimé trois fois ni celui de votre Papa.[10]

Il y avait un pauvre jardinier qui cultivait des Peches, il recolta des Prunes: la greffe avait manqué.

Ce qui ne manquera jamais, c'est mon respectueux et tendre attachement pour vous.

D. P. d. N.

Madame du Pont me charge de vous dire combien elle vous aime. Autant en font *les superbes.*

TRANSLATION

New York, December 3, 1801

Madame de Staël.

Madame,

You will learn with interest, if you do not know it already, that *your father* has given a rather great encouragement, a notable mark of confidence to *Du Pont your friend.* And that in few words, as capable men do private business.

Peace gives me very great pleasure, although it upsets absolutely a fine business deal which M. de Pusy was going to conclude in which a small million could have been gained.[1]

But in compensation, it will give me other durable advantages, particularly that of not needing to purchase rather dearly, and not without some risk, an American name in order to accomplish so many things.

It will probably also give me the consolation of sending to you every six weeks a ship which will bring you some letters and will bring yours back to me without their being lost at sea.

You will be informed of everything reasonable that our serious nation of the New World does, and I shall learn all the diversions, all the pleasant things which will amuse you in Paris.

"How great the voluptuousness
which a *Te deum* inspires when it is well sung." [2]

I am amazed to see the French such good Catholics again and the Jesuits survive the Parlements.

You have already learned that, although Huguenot by birth, philosopher by profession, and always very secular, when the constitutional clergy was established, I got four votes for Archbishop of Rouen.

Since people pay so well for prayers, miters, crosses, and crosiers, I almost regret not having garnered a larger number of votes.

You think that I am heartbroken. Not at all. I see the thing in another light.[3]

Pythagoras and several other philosophers or legislators had a public doctrine and a secret doctrine. My confidence in the genius of Bonaparte is still such that he did not betray it at all by this apparent retreat to the dung of theology which he has, moreover, declared he had to do only *because of respect for the majority and not because of his own opinion.*[4]

It seems to me that he behaves like someone who, wanting to clean out a barrel filled with thick and sticky dregs, fills it with water and lets it soak, as a result of which all the filth is easily cleaned out.

I believe that I see him keeping his word to the Pope and the Legate, and taxing the nation very heavily to pay the Catholic and Protestant clergy, or that of any other faith. Then, after a few years, noticing, or letting the Tribunate notice, that this must be a local and personal charge. Then ordering that the salary of the priests will be kept *in its entirety,* but divided according to the sects, that of the Catholics to the Catholics, that of the Protestants to the Protestants with liberty, moreover, for the faithful to increase the rate.

From this it will follow that the Catholic will have to contribute for the Catholic priest; from this it will follow that, if some Catholics who find the tax heavy change their belief, the tax will become still heavier for the faithful; from this it will follow that finally the opinion of the majority will become different from what it is today. From this it will follow that this general opinion will find it just that the support of the priests should be the object of a voluntary and private contribution, *of a subscription.* Now the First Consul will respect general opinion at all times. He governs, wants to govern, and will govern the French according to their wishes. From this it will follow that His Eminence the Cardinal Caprara[5] will have *caught* only *a rat.*

And then the disease will be cured forever by the invalid's vigor of temperament.

If it is thus that he has seen the matter, my word, this thirty-year-old warrior has a very mature and far-sighted mind, and I am of the opinion of *Sir Roland Meredith,*[7] who thought that *nothing is superior to the head of an old man on the shoulders of a young man.*

If you see *Chénier,* tell him that his satire on the new saints[8] seemed [. . .] [9] to me. How charming it is!

But why does this and that reach me, and never your book now in its third edition, nor that of your papa? [10]

There was a poor gardener who grew peaches; he harvested plums. The graft had failed.

What will never fail is my respectful and tender attachment for you.

D. P. d. N.

Mme. du Pont requests me to tell you how much she loves you. *The superbs* do the same.

NOTES

1 Probably the mysterious scheme which had prompted Victor du Pont's trip to Spain in 1801. The du Pont Company had proposed to help the Spaniards obtain their resources from their American colonies despite the British naval blockade. See *1801 Journey,* pp. xiii–xv.

2 I have been unable to identify the source of this quotation.

3 This paragraph has been inserted between the lines, with the following crossed out: "Il faut que Buonaparte ait bien de l'esprit car malgré le scandale de cette reculade vers la." ("Bonaparte must have a great deal of intelligence, for in spite of the scandal of this backward movement toward the.")

4 The following has been crossed out: "il a encore toute ma confiance à moi vieux Républicain pour qui le consulat de Valerius avait bien d'auguste." ("He still has all my confidence, I, an old republican for whom the consulate of Valerius was something august.") Valerius Publicola was one of the founders of the Roman Republic, along with Lucius Junius Brutus. They served as the two Roman consuls in 509 B.C.

5 Cardinal Caprara (1733–1810) negotiated the Concordat of 1801.

6 A pun on the cardinal's name. Du Pont de Nemours obviously means *capté.*

7 Du Pont de Nemours probably means Sir William Meredith, who seems to have been an assistant to William Eden (later Lord Auckland) in effecting the commercial treaty of 1786 with France. Du Pont had been the French delegate in these negotiations. See *D.N.B.*

8 Marie-Joseph Chénier (1764–1811), the playwright and brother of the more
famous poet, André Chénier, guillotined during the Terror. Marie-Joseph Chénier
played an active political role during the Revolution.

His *Les Nouveaux Saints* appeared in 1801 and was greatly successful, running
through sixteen editions by 1802. The work was a reply to the neo-Catholic spirit
of Chateaubriand's *Atala*. The "nouveaux saints" ridiculed in this book were
Geoffroy, Esménard, Fontanes, Chateaubriand, Mme. de Genlis, and La Harpe.
See Louis Madelin, *Le Consulat* (Paris, 1939), pp. 137, 322.

9 A word missing here.

10 Mme. de Staël's *De la littérature* and Necker's *Cours de morale religieuse.*

34

Necker to du Pont de Nemours

10 January 1802

WMSS 2/16

M. Dupont de Nemours a New York

Depuis ma derniere lettre a votre Maison monsieur du 8 decembre[1] dont je vous envoye la copie j'ai receu les lettres que vous
m'avez fait l'honneur de m'écrire le 9 & 24 8ᵇʳᵉ et le 9 Novembre.[2]
Je vous remercie Monsieur du soin que vous avez bien voulu
prendre de ma lettre a Mʳ le Gouverneur Morris.[3]

Il ma semble qu'on avoit assez fait pour la tranquilite de vos
actionaires en laissant leurs noms inconnus sous la forme au
porteur et lui auroit pu y joindre quelque declaration formelle
dans le meme sens dans un registre public mais le parti que vous
prenez pourroit fort bien diminuer le credit de la maison de
Newyork car elle ne parvi[en]dra qu'un commissionaire agent de
la maison de Paris et le fonds des actionaires ne constitue plus
directement sa solidité. Ainsy pour ma creance lorsqu'une telle
circulaire me parviendra et dès a present s'il est necessaire je
retiendrai la garantie et le cautionement du fonds des actionaires
d'une maniere speciale ce qui est indisputable pour une affaire
anterieure a votre nouvel arrangement. J'ai fait parvenir indirecte-
ment a M. de Lessert ma façon de penser sur ce projet que peut etre
au reste je n'entends pas suffisamment.

On dit que le prix des terres monte en Amerique & que vous
regretterez peut etre de n'y avoir pas encore place les capitaux de

vos actionaires; mais vos affaires de commerce les auront probable-
men dedomagé. Je le souhaite beaucoup surtout par rapport a
vous Monsieur et les votres. Agreez les assurances de mon inviolable
attachement.

Necker

10 Janvier 1802

> *A duplicate of this letter appears on the triplicate of the letter from Jacques
> Necker dated December 8, 1801. Necker added at the end of the duplicate:*

Le 18 avril 1802

J'ai receu Monsieur la lettre que votre maison m'a ecrite le 30
Novembre et j'ai notté comme vous me l'indiquez l'evaluation de
mes differés. Je fais une grosse perte par l'evenement mais elle est
adoucie pour moi en pensant que vous en profitez. Je n'ai plus
d'objet de correspondance avec M^{rs} van Neck et je prie M. votre
fils qui a dirige cette affaire de demander directement ou par son
correspondant la procuration dont il a besoin. Je suis surpris de ne
pas scavoir encore son arrivée ni par vous Messieurs ni par aucune
reponse au pacquet qui luy a ete envoyé par Mrs de Lessert a
Bordeaux & qui contenoit plusieurs lettres. Agreez tous mes
complimens.

Necker

> *The Eleutherian Mills Historical Library possesses a copy of the letter of
> April 18, 1802, at the end of which, Necker added the following note:*

J'ai receu Monsieur la lettre que vous m'avez fait l'honneur de
m'ecrire le 21 mars[4] et je suis touché de l'interest que vous prenez
a la sureté de ma creance et dèsque vous acceptez la tutele que je
vous ai confié je ne connois rien de plus sur et je n'y pense plus.

J'avois ecrit en recevant votre lettre a Mrs Van Neck et ils
m'envoyent un receu de Mrs Ja^{es} Casenove & C$^{[i]e}$ de £89.13 sterling
pour 9 mois d'interest echus au p[remie]r octobre 1801—sur les
differès que je vous ai cedés. Je comprends que ces Mrs Casenove
sont vos correspondants. Ainsy cette affaire est parfaitement en
regle.

Je partage vos regrets sur Mr Bureau de Pusé. C'est la chose
publique qui vous l'a enlevé et qui abuse ainsy de votre amour
pour elle.

Je vous remercie de ce que vous me dites sur nos livres de famille
tant en votre nom qu'au nom de Madame **Dupont**. Vous êtes bien

l'un & l'autre du petit nombre de persones dont le suffrage m'est précieux.

Ma fille est icy avec moi fort occupée d'un roman en quatre ou cinq volumes dont l'impression se commencera bientost.[5] Vous y trouverez de l'esprit en quantite & des sentimens, de l'interest, des tableaux, enfin c'est un tres bel ouvrage. L'auteur vous croit toujours des siens en politique et cela ne seroit pas que bien d'autres motifs l'attacheroient a vous comme ils unissent a vous son pere et tendrement ainsy que pour la vie. Adieu Monsieur.

[Sans signature]

TRANSLATION

M. Dupont de Nemours in New York

Since my last letter to your company of December 8,[1] Sir, a copy of which I am sending you, I have received the letters that you honored me by writing on October 9 and 24, and on November 9.[2] I thank you, Sir, for the care that you kindly took of my letter for Mr. Gouverneur Morris.[3]

It seems to me that you had done enough for your stockholders' peace of mind by leaving their names unknown under the form "to the bearer," possibly adding some formal declaration in the same sense in a public register; but the decision that you make could very well diminish the credit of the New York office, for it will reach only a commission agent of the Paris office, and the funds of the stockholders no longer directly constitute its solidity. So, for my credit, when such a circular reaches me, and from this moment, if it is necessary, I shall retain the guarantee and the security of the stockholders' funds in a special way which is indisputable for a matter previous to your new arrangement. I have indirectly sent to M. Delessert my thoughts about this project, which perhaps, moreover, I do not understand sufficiently.

People say that the price of American land is rising and that you will perhaps regret not having invested in it the capital of your stockholders; but your commercial affairs will probably have compensated for it. I very much hope so, especially in relation to you, Sir, and your family. Accept the assurances of my inviolable attachment.

Necker

January 10, 1802

A duplicate of this letter appears on the triplicate of the letter from Jacques Necker dated December 8, 1801. Necker added at the end of the duplicate:

April 18, 1802

I have received, Sir, the letter that your company wrote to me on November 30, and I have noted, as you indicated to me, the evaluation of my deferred stocks. I am taking a great loss from this transaction, but it is softened for me when I think that you are profiting from it. I have no more reason for correspondence with Messrs. Van Neck, and I request your son, who managed this affair, to ask directly, or by his correspondent, for the proxy he needs. I am surprised at not yet learning of his arrival either from you gentlemen, or by any answer to the parcel containing several letters which was sent to him at Bordeaux by Messrs. Delessert. Accept all my compliments.

Necker

The Eleutherian Mills Historical Library possesses a copy of the letter of April 18, 1802, at the end of which, Necker added the following note:

I have received, Sir, the letter that you honored me by writing on March 21,[4] and I am touched by the interest that you take in the safety of my credit, and since you accept the guardianship that I entrusted to you, I know of nothing more certain and I think no more about it.

I had written, on receiving your letter, to Messrs. Van Neck, and they are sending me a receipt from Messrs. James Casenove and Company for £89.13 sterling for nine months' interest due October 1, 1801, on the deferred stocks which I turned over to you. I understand that these Messrs. Casenove are your correspondents. Thus this affair is perfectly in order.

I share your regrets about M. Bureaux de Pusy. It is the public good which took him from you and which thus takes advantage of your love for it.

I thank you for what you say to me about our family books, both in your name, and in the name of Mme. Dupont. You are both indeed among the few persons whose approval is precious to me.

My daughter is here with me, very busy with a novel of four or five volumes whose printing will begin soon.[5] You will find in it much wit and sensibility, interest and tableaux; in short, it is a

very fine work. The author still believes you share her views in
politics, and even if that were not true, many other reasons would
attach her to you as they attach her father to you and tenderly, as
well as for life. Adieu, Sir.

[No signature]

NOTES
1 See the postscript to Letter 30.
2 These two letters seem to have been lost.
3 See Letter 23, note 3.
4 This letter is in the Archives at Coppet and was not available for publication.
5 Mme. de Staël's *Delphine*.

35

Madame de Staël to du Pont de Nemours

25 April 1802

WMSS 2/16

Paris ce 5 florèal an 10
Non mon cher du pont toutes vos belles idèes ne seront point
accomplies. Nous avons un but plus direct. Nous voulons recom-
mencer une 4eme dynastie imiter charlemagne etc et pour le mieux
imiter ne faut il pas ramener les esprits au tems où il a vècu? Je
vous aurois souhaité à la grande féte de notre dame,[1] vous auriez
vu les plus étranges contrastes qui ayent jamais frappè les regards
fouchè[2] talleyrand[3] cambaceres[4] faisant le signe de la croix avec
une vraie componction et l'arch[evêque] d'aix prèchant en
mèmoire du sacre etc.[5] Si vous étiez ici mon cher du pont nous
aurions bien des choses à vous dire. Mais de là bas vous vous faites
une france à votre grè. Si du moins cet optimisme vous y ramenoit
ce seroit une erreur dont nous jouirions comme de la vèrité. Mais
vous nous voyez bien plus beaux que nous ne sommes et vous ne
venez pas nous voir. Je pars pour mes six mois de copet. J'emmenne
avec moi Mr de Stael. Il a une paralysie sur le cerveau qui le rend
presque imbècile.[6] J'ai cru devoir me charger de lui quand sa téte
n'y étoit plus et j'espere venir à bout de payer ses dettes sans trop
ruiner mes enfants. Je ne vois que des crèanciers et je ne fais que

des comptes depuis dix jours. C'est un mauvais exercice pour achever un roman [*Delphine*], qui doit ètre publiè dans quelques mois. Aussi ne veux-je le finir que sur le sommet des alpes. Ce n'est que là qu'on retrouve son ame. Pour vous mon cher du pont vous ètes le mème aux pieds des apalaches ou dans les rues de paris. Rien de ce qui vous environne n'agit sur vous. Votre imagination vous entoure quelque soit le lieu que vous habitez. Je vous enverrai cet ouvrage de moi que vous voulez bien désirer par M^r le ray de chaumont.[7] Il vous parlera de l'europe. C'est la france qui en dispose. Notre pauvre suisse se divise.[8] On l'y excite, et l'un de ces jours on lui dira qu'elle n'est pas en ètat de se gouverner elle mème. Enfin mon cher du pont il n'y a plus qu'un homme sur le continent. Mais cet homme choisit pour instrument des personnes que vous aimez, et vous seriez un des premiers et des plus honorablement dèsignès pour ce qu'on appelle les premiers emplois de la rep[ublique]. Je vous le rèpète donc. Revenez. Votre obstination s'est fait assez de gloire. Un retour de foiblesse pour l'amitié ira très bien dans le roman historique de votre vie. Vous aurez vu qu'un de mes amis ètoit èlimine du tribunat,[9] et vous n'entendrez plus parler du tribunat car depuis cette opèration il se tait à faire plaisir. Vous en conclurez que nous sommes ce qu'on nomme ici le parti de l'opposition mais cette opposition ètoit si bènigne lors mème qu'elle avoit toute sa force que les plaintes du consul à cet ègard rappellent un peu ce que me disoit dubuc[10] dans mon enfance, *l'amour se plaignit un jour à sa mère qu'une feuille de rose replièe dans son lit l'avoit empèchè de dormir toute la nuit.* Enfin nous allons, et comme l'anarchie a fait croire qu'il n'y avoit rien à désirer que l'ordre dans l'ètat social, on est content dès qu'il n'y a plus de bruit dans la rue. Il n'y a pas de pays sur la terre je crois ou ce qu'on appelle l'action et la rèaction se fasse mieux sentir. Votre ami crillon[11] va faire un beau marriage pour son fils. Il èpouse la fille d'archambault de pèrigord [12] que tout le monde demandoit voir mème lucien bonaparte. Je cherche s'il y a d'ailleurs quelques mouvements dans la sociètè. Je ne vois rien. Tout est stationaire dans les affaires privèes comme dans les affaires publiques. On n'entend plus vivre personne. Adieu mon cher du pont. Si vous m'ècrivez que vous revenez j'aurai un bien vif mouvement de joye. Vous savez sans doute que ce pauvre baumets[13] est mort aux indes. Quel cruel sort de finir sa vie loin de ses amis. Vous avez de longues annèes à vivre mais il faut nous les donner. Votre cœur ne se serre t'il pas en songeant que vous ètes sur terre ètrangere. Il est vrai que nous n'avons plus de patrie mais il y a encor le site et l'air qui rappelle le tems où l'on espèroit d'en avoir une. Mes compliments aux *superbes*. Mes respects à votre parfaite compagne et pour vous tendre amitiè et vif dèsir de revoir.

[Sans signature]

TRANSLATION

Paris, 5 Floréal, year X

No, my dear du Pont, all your fine ideas will not be accomplished. We have a more direct goal. We want to start a fourth dynasty, to imitate Charlemagne, etc.; and in order to imitate him better, must we not bring our minds back to the time when he lived? I should have liked to see you at the Grande Fête of Notre Dame.[1] You would have seen the strangest contrasts that have ever met the eye: Fouché,[2] Talleyrand,[3] and Cambacérès[4] making the sign of the cross with a real compunction and the Archbishop of Aix preaching in memory of the coronation, etc.[5] If you were here, my dear du Pont, we should have many things to tell you; but from over there, you imagine a France as you wish it. If, at least, that optimism brought you back, it would be an error which we should enjoy as if it were the truth. But you imagine us much more beautiful than we are, and you do not come to see us. I am leaving for my six months at Coppet. I am taking M. de Staël with me. He has a paralysis of the brain which makes him almost an imbecile.[6] I felt obliged to take charge of him when his mind was gone, and I hope to succeed in paying his debts without ruining my children too much. I see only creditors, and I have done nothing but figure accounts for ten days. It is bad exercise for finishing a novel [*Delphine*] which is to be published in a few months. So I want to finish it only on top of the Alps. Only there can one find one's soul again. As for you, my dear du Pont, you are the same at the foot of the Appalachians or in the streets of Paris. Nothing that surrounds you influences you. Your imagination envelops you wherever you may be. I shall send to you, by M. Le Ray de Chaumont,[7] that work of mine that you wish to have. He will speak to you of Europe. France does as she wishes with it. Our poor Switzerland is becoming divided.[8] It is encouraged to do so, and one of these days it will be told that it is not in a condition to govern itself. Indeed, my dear du Pont, there is now only one man on the Continent. But that man chooses as his instruments people whom you love, and you would be one of the first and most honorably designated for what people call the highest positions of the Republic. Therefore, I repeat it to you. Come back. Your obstinacy has acquired enough glory for itself. A return of weakness for friendship will fit very well in the historical novel of your life. You will have seen that one of my friends was eliminated from the Tribunate,[9] and you will not hear any more about the Tribunate, for since that operation, it has kept pleasingly silent. You will conclude that we are what is called here the party of the opposition, but that opposition was so benign, even when it had all its strength, that the complaints of the Consul in that regard rather recall to me what du Buc[10] said to me in my childhood: *"Eros complained one day to his mother that a folded rose petal in his bed had prevented him from sleeping all night."* In the end, we go on our way; and as anarchy has made people believe that there was nothing more to be desired than order in society, they are content as soon as there is no more uproar in the streets. There is no country on earth, I believe, where so-called action and reaction make themselves felt more. Your friend Crillon[11] is going to make a fine marriage for his son. He is marrying the daughter of Archambault de Périgord,[12] whom everyone sought, even Lucien Bonaparte. I try to see whether there is some movement in society. I see nothing. Everything is stationary in private as in public affairs. You no longer hear anyone living. Adieu, my dear du Pont. If you write me that you are coming back, I shall be very joyful! You doubtless know that that poor Beaumez[13] died in India. What a cruel fate to end one's life far away from one's friends. You have many years to live, but you must give them to us. Does not your heart ache on thinking that you are on foreign soil? It is true that we no longer have a country, but there is still the site of it and the air, which recall the time when we hoped to have one. My compliments to the *superbs,* my respects to your perfect wife, and for you, tender friendship and a strong desire to see you again.

[No signature]

NOTES

1 Mass at the Cathedral of Notre Dame on Easter Sunday, 1802, to celebrate the signing of the Concordat.

2 Joseph Fouché (1759–1820), the notorious Minister of Police during the Directory, Consulate, Empire, and part of the Restoration. It has been said of him that "il ne lui manqua rien en habileté, peu en bon sens, tout en vertu." ("He lacked nothing in skill, little in good sense, everything in virtue.")

3 Once more, as in Letter 22, Madame de Staël is struck by Talleyrand's cynicism and hypocrisy.

4 Jean-Jacques Régis de Cambacérès (1753–1824), Second Consul during the Consulate and Archchancellor of the Empire. He had a major part in preparing the Civil Code of Napoleon.

5 Georges Pariset, *Le Consulat et l'Empire*, in *Histoire de France contemporaine*, ed. Ernest Lavisse, III (Paris, 1921), 108, describes this event as follows:

> Le dimanche de Pâques, 18 avril 1802, le gouvernement célébra la première fête religieuse du Consulat. Un long cortège se rendit à Notre-Dame: les vieux carosses royaux et les fiacres aux numéros barbouillés se suivaient à la file. La foule curieuse et amusée regarda passer les uniformes, les domestiques, que pour la première fois on voyait en livrée, les généraux, les diplomates, les membres du gouvernement dans leur costume officiel, les consuls, et Bonaparte, qu'on acclamait, comme toujours. . . . Caprara dit la messe. . . . Boisgelin, ci-devant archevêque d'Aix, maintenant archevêque de Tours, avait été désigné pour le discours, sans doute parce qu'il avait parlé au sacre de Louis XVI.

> (Easter Sunday, April 18, 1802, the government celebrated the first religious ceremony of the Consulate. A long procession went to Notre Dame: the old royal carriages and the cabs with smeared numbers followed one after another. The curious and amused crowd watched the uniforms, the servants, whom they saw in livery for the first time, the generals, the diplomats, the members of the government in their official costumes, and Bonaparte, who was acclaimed as usual, pass by. . . . Caprara said mass. . . . Boisgelin, formerly Archbishop of Aix, now Archbishop of Tours, had been chosen for the speech, doubtless because he had spoken at the coronation of Louis XVI.)

6 The Baron de Staël died en route to Coppet, May 9, 1802.

7 James Donatien Le Ray de Chaumont (1760–1840), who, along with Gouverneur Morris, acted as an agent for Necker and Madame de Staël in the purchase of American lands. His father, the wealthy owner of the château of Chaumont, had been an early supporter of the American Revolution. He put at Benjamin Franklin's disposal, rent free, a house in Passy, in which Franklin lived during his stay in France (1776–85), and also sent munitions and other supplies to the colonists. In 1790 Morris advised the son to speculate in New York land, and the latter acquired extensive holdings in that state. He sold part of his land to various French *émigrés* and exiles, as well as to Necker and Madame de Staël. See Richmond Laurin Hawkins, *Madame de Staël and the United States* (Cambridge, Mass., 1930).

8 In 1797 certain exiled Swiss leaders in France prevailed upon the Directory to interfere in Switzerland and overthrow the cantonal governments, which were ruled by an aristocratic oligarchy. The French invaded Switzerland in 1798, set up a new government, the Helvetic Republic, and annexed Geneva to France.

The Helvetic Republic lasted until 1803, when Napoleon imposed the Act of Mediation, which established a confederation of nineteen cantons. Switzerland was dominated by the French, however, until Napoleon's downfall.

9 Benjamin Constant, who had angered Napoleon by his attacks on tyranny. Madame de Staël had encouraged him to commit these indiscretions.

10 Jean Baptiste du Buc (1717–95), the French economist. Born in Martinique, du Buc was sent to France in 1761 as the delegate of the chambers of agriculture of that colony to the French government. The Duc de Choiseul, Minister of Foreign Affairs, was so favorably impressed with du Buc that he appointed him head of the colonial office. Du Buc was also active in the Compagnie des Indes and accomplished much in effecting a more liberal trade policy between France and her colonies. He was noted for his probity, intelligence, independence, and graciousness. In the *Nouveaux mélanges de Mme Necker* (Paris, 1801), his clever remarks and observations are quoted frequently; the statement mentioned here appears in Vol. I, p. 97, of that work.

11 Probably François Félix Dorothée Balbe de Crillon (1748–1820). He had been a member of the States-General and supported the Revolution until the overthrow of the monarchy. He appeared again in public life in 1815 and was made a peer. Several of Crillon's business connections with du Pont de Nemours are mentioned in *1801 Journey*, pp. 43–44, n. 6: in 1799 he was listed as a stockholder in Du Pont de Nemours, Père et Fils & Cie., to which he offered "paper on a bankrupt"; in 1800 he gave a power of attorney to du Pont for use in negotiations with a certain Homassel, a merchant in Philadelphia; and in 1808 he appears as the holder of one and a half shares in the company.

Crillon had two sons, neither of whom married the woman mentioned.

12 Archambault-Joseph, Duc de Talleyrand-Périgord (1762–?), brother of the more famous Talleyrand. His daughter, Françoise, married the Comte de Noailles, later Duc de Poix, in 1803; see *Mémoires du Prince de Talleyrand* (Paris, 1891), II, 4, n. 2.

13 Bon-Albert Briois de Beaumez (1759–1801?). Elected to the States-General as the deputy of the nobility of Artois in 1789, he joined the liberal group of the Left Center, but he attempted to seek popularity rather than to defend any principles. In 1792, accused of trying to restore the monarchy, he was forced to leave France for Germany. From there he went to England, where he encountered his friend Talleyrand, and the two sailed for America in 1794. In 1796 Beaumez married Mrs. Sarah Lyons Flucker, the daughter of General Knox, who had extensive land holdings in Maine. That same year Beaumez and his wife sailed for India, where he planned to dispose of these American holdings to the Indian potentates. On his arrival in Calcutta, he found a representative of Robert Morris (see Letter 11, note 2) already there, and unable to sell any of the land in question, Beaumez became a sugar and spice merchant. His death must have occurred in 1801. See *Dictionnaire de biographie française;* Paul D. Evans, *The Holland Land Company* (Buffalo, 1924), pp. 92–3; and Madame de Staël, *Lettres à Narbonne,* ed. Georges Solovieff (Paris, 1960), p. 113, n. 2.

36

du Pont de Nemours to Madame de Staël

1 May 1802

From a draft, WMSS 2/4

New York 1er may 1802

Mme de Stael de Holstein

Madame

Mon grand Enfant[1] qui n'a presque pas cessé de courir d'un bout a l'autre des Etats unis depuis qu'il y est arrivé ne m'a remis qu'avant hier votre livre[2] qui était demeuré dans ses ballots.

Je l'ai dévoré et j'ai besoin de savoir que vous avez de très beaux yeux la peau fort douce, le bras et la main superbes et beaucoup d'autres charmes qui même a quinze cent lieues me donnent de l'emotion pour me persuader que cet ouvrage soit d'une femme. Je n'en connais point de plus viril.

On peut compter les morceaux qui trahissent votre sexe, ils sont en très petit nombre mais ils sont d'un grand effet: Les pages 31 et 32 du discours preliminaire[3] l'article de Brutus et de Porcie[4] les réflexions qui le suivent la page 257 du 1er volume[5] le chapitre sur les femmes qui cultivent les lettres.[6]

Nous n'aurions pas fait aussi bien que vous ces morceaux là mais nul de nous n'eut mieux fait le reste ni pour les choses, ni pour le gout dans une[7] erudition, ni pour la pureté du stile et la noblesse.

Je vous demande une correction pour l'edition prochaine a la page 246. Ne supposons pas que personne puisse être en rien au dessus de Marc Aurele.[8] C'est le grand des grands. Nous n'avons de lui que quelques pages qu'il n'a point fait pour notre instruction mais pour lui même, comme de simples souvenirs qui exercaient sa noble raison et soulagaient sa grande ame au milieu des fatigues d'une guerre longue et perilleuse contre des barbares dans un Pays affreux.

Il a gouverné le monde connu avec une activité que le Roi de Prusse[9] a seul egalee et une sagesse parfaite que le Roi de Prusse plus semblable a julien[10] qu'a Marc Aurele n'avait pas toujours.

Il a êté un très grand militaire et a passe dix ans de sa vie dans les camps. Un Prince ordinaire qui eut fait la moitié seulement de ses belles campagnes serait celebre comme general.

La bonté, les lumieres, la douceur bienfaisante du Philosophe ont couvert l'empereur et le guerrier. Il est audessus d'Epictete par son livre plus qu'il ne l'etait par son rang. Et cependant Epictete a une bien honorable place parmi les philosophes vertueux.

J'ai pleuré avec vous à la page 30 du second volume sur le respectable remords d'avoir eu quelque part au 18 Fructidor.[11]

"Dieu fit du repentir la vertu des mortels." [12]

Ne craignez pas de ne point retrouver des amis partout où il y aura des hommes qui sauront reconnaitre dans votre tête et dans votre cœur l'amour du bien, et dans ce qu'on pourrait vous reprocher la preuve même de cette tendresse ou amitié qui peut seule vous causer quelque égarement.

Ce que vous risquez de ne trouver que bien peu d'hommes dignes d'être vos amis. Heureusement qu'il n'est pas besoin d'en avoir beaucoup.

Quant aux femmes ne comptez sur aucune non pas même sur Madame de Genlis[13] malgré le beau compliment que vous lui faites. Cela s'appelle *donner des chandelles au diable*. L'orgueileux et l'ingrat n'en trouve jamais assez. Quoiqu'elle ait beaucoup d'esprit, cette dame qui veut si absolument que nous la croyions catholique appotolique [*sic*] et romaine, et qui a eu et toujours eu principe qu'il ne faut aimer personne qu'avec la plus auguste froideur peut elle jamais avoir rien de commun avec une Philosophe sensible comme vous— Elle vous repondra des injures, si elle ne l'a fait.

Votre livre n'est pas de ceux qu'on ne lit qu'une fois. Je le relirai souvent la plume à la main. J'en barbouillerai de notes ses marges et puis je les mettrai à vos pieds avec mon tendre et profond respect.

TRANSLATION

New York, May 1, 1802

Madame de Staël de Holstein

Madame,

My oldest son,[1] who has scarcely stopped running from one end of the United States to the other since he arrived here, gave me your book, which had remained in his luggage, only the day before yesterday.

I devoured it, and I need to know that you have very beautiful eyes, very soft skin, superb arms and hands, and many other charms which, even at 1,500 leagues, arouse my emotions to convince myself that this work is by a woman. I do not know any more virile.

One can count the portions which betray your sex. They are very few, but they produce a great effect: pages 31 and 32 of the preface,[3] the part about Brutus and Portia,[4] the reflections which follow it, page 257 of the first volume,[5] the chapter about women who devote themselves to literature.[6]

We should not have done those portions as well as you, but not one of us would have done the rest better, neither for things nor for taste in[7] erudition, nor for the purity of style and nobility.

I request a correction for the next edition on page 246. Let us not suppose that anyone can be in any way superior to Marcus Aurelius.[8] He is the greatest of the great. We have from him only a few pages, which he did not write for our instruction, but for himself, as simple memories which exercised his noble reason and relieved his great soul in the midst of the fatigues of a long and perilous war against barbarians in a terrible country.

He governed the known world with an activity which the King of Prussia[9] alone equaled and a perfect wisdom which the King of Prussia, more similar to Julian[10] than to Marcus Aurelius, did not always have.

He was a great soldier and spent ten years of his life in camps. An ordinary prince who would have waged only half of his great campaigns would be famous as a general.

The goodness, enlightenment, and beneficent gentleness of the philosopher concealed the emperor and warrior. He is above Epictetus because of his book more than he was by his rank. And yet, Epictetus has a very honorable place among philosophers of virtue.

I wept with you at page 30 of the second volume about the respectable remorse at having had some part in the 18 Fructidor.[11]

"God made repentance the virtue of mortals." [12]

Do not fear that you will not encounter friends everywhere that there are men who can recognize in your mind and in your heart the love of good. Even that for which people might reproach you is the very proof of that tenderness or friendship which alone may cause you to go astray.

What you risk is finding only a very few men worthy of being your friends; fortunately, there is no need to have a great many.

As for women, do not count on any of them, not even on Mme. de Genlis,[13] in spite of the fine compliment that you pay her. That is called *giving candles to the devil*. The proud and ungrateful never find enough of them. Although she has much wit, can that lady, who wants so absolutely to have us believe that she is Catholic, Apostolic, and Roman, and who has always had as a principle that one must never love anyone except with the most august coldness, ever have anything in common with a sensitive philosopher like you? She will answer you with insults, if she has not done so already.

Your book is not one of those that one reads only once. I shall often read it again with a pen in my hand. I shall cover its margins with notes, and then I shall place them at your feet with my tender and profound respect.

NOTES

1 Victor du Pont, who had returned to the United States in February, 1802.

2 The second edition of Mme. de Staël's *De la littérature*.

3 After lamenting the excesses of the French Revolution, Mme. de Staël observes, on the pages mentioned by du Pont de Nemours:

> C'est sans doute un triste effort que de transporter son intérêt, de reposer son attente, à travers l'avenir, sur nos successeurs, sur les étrangers bien loin de nous, sur les inconnus, sur tous les hommes enfin dont le souvenir et l'image ne peuvent se retracer à notre esprit. Mais, hélas! si l'on en excepte quelques amis inaltérables, la plupart de ceux qu'on se rappelle après dix années de révolution, contristent votre cœur, étouffent vos mouvemens, en imposent à votre talent même, non par leur supériorité, mais par cette malveillance qui ne cause de la douleur qu'aux ames douces, et ne fait souffrir que ceux qui ne la méritent pas.
>
> Enfin relevons-nous sous le poids de l'existence, ne donnons pas à nos injustes ennemis, à nos amis ingrats, le triomphe d'avoir abattu nos facultés intellectuelles. Ils réduisent à chercher la gloire, ceux qui se seroient contentés des affections: eh bien! il faut l'atteindre. Ces essais ambitieux ne porteront point remède aux peines de l'ame; mais ils honoreront la vie. La consacrer à l'espoir toujours trompé du bonheur, c'est la rendre encore plus infortunée. Il vaut mieux réunir tous ses efforts pour descendre avec quelque noblesse, avec quelque réputation, la route qui conduit de la jeunesse à la mort."

(It is doubtless a sad effort to transport one's interest, to replace one's expectation, through the future, to our successors, to foreigners very distant from us, to strangers, to all the men, finally, whose memory and appearance cannot be recalled to our mind. But, alas, if one excepts a few loyal friends, the majority of those whom one remembers after ten years of revolution sadden your heart, stifle your impulses, make an impression on your talent itself, not by their superiority, but by that malevolence which causes sorrow only to gentle souls, and makes suffer only those who do not deserve to do so.

Finally, let us rise again under the weight of existence, let us not give to our unjust enemies, to our ungrateful friends, the triumph of having destroyed our intellectual faculties. They are driven to seeking glory, those who would have been content with affection: well! they must achieve it. These ambitious attempts will not provide a remedy for the sorrows of the soul; but they will honor life. To dedicate it to the always deceived hope for happiness is to make it still more unfortunate. It is better to concentrate all one's efforts on descending with some nobility, with some reputation, the road that leads from youth to death.)

4 The passage to which du Pont de Nemours refers appears on pages 177 to 179 of the second edition of *De la littérature*. There Mme. de Staël relates the following episode:

Plutarque, qui laisse de ce qu'il peint des souvenirs si animés, raconte que Brutus, prêt à s'embarquer pour quitter l'Italie, se promenant sur le bord de la mer avec Porcie, qu'il alloit quitter, entra avec elle dans un temple; ils y adressèrent ensemble leur prière aux dieux protecteurs. Un tableau qui représentoit les adieux d'Hector à Andromaque, frappa d'abord leurs regards. La fille de Caton, qui jusqu'alors avoit réprimé les expressions de sa douleur, en voyant ce tableau, ne put contenir l'excès de son émotion. Brutus, alors attendri lui-même, dit en s'approchant de quelques amis qui l'avoient accompagné: "Je vous confie cette femme, qui unit à toutes les vertus de son sexe le courage du nôtre"; et il s'éloigna.

Je ne sais si nos troubles civils, où tant d'adieux ont été les derniers, ajoutent à mon impression en lisant ce récit; mais il me semble qu'il en est peu de plus touchans. L'austerité romaine donne un grand caractère aux affections qu'elle permet. Le stoïcien Brutus, dont la farouche vertu n'avoit rien épargné, laissant voir un sentiment si tendre dans ces momens qui précèdent, et ses derniers efforts, et ses derniers jours, surprend le cœur par une émotion inattendue; et l'action terrible et la funeste destinée de ce dernier des Romains, entourent son image d'idées sombres, qui jettent sur Porcie l'intérêt le plus douloureux.

(Plutarch, who leaves such animated memories of what he describes, relates that Brutus, ready to sail from Italy, walking on the seashore with Portia, whom he was going to leave, entered a temple with her; there they both prayed to the protecting gods. A picture which showed the farewell of Hector to Andromache attracted their attention first. Cato's daughter, who had repressed the expression of her sorrow until then, on seeing this picture could not restrain the excess of her emotion. Brutus, then himself touched, said, approaching some friends who had accompanied him: "I entrust to you this woman, who joins with all the virtues of her sex the courage of ours"; and he went away.

I do not know whether our civil disturbances, where so many farewells

were the last ones, add to my impression on reading this account; but it seems
to me that there are few more touching ones. Roman austerity gives great
character to the affections that it permits. The stoic Brutus, whose grim
virtue had spared nothing, showing such tender feeling in these preceding
moments, and his last efforts, and his last days, surprises the heart with an
unexpected emotion; and the terrible action and the tragic destiny of this last
of the Romans surround his image with somber ideas, which give to Portia
the most sorrowful interest.)

5 In Chapter IX of *De la littérature* (2nd ed., Vol. I), "De l'Esprit général de la
Littérature chez les Modernes," p. 257, Mme. de Staël states:

> Les anciens savaient animer les argumens nécessaires à chaque circonstance;
> mais de nos jours les esprits sont tellement blasés, par la succession des siècles,
> sur les intérêts individuels des hommes, et peut-être même sur les intérêts
> instantanés des nations, que l'écrivain éloquent a besoin de remonter toujours
> plus haut, pour atteindre à la source des affections communes à tous les
> mortels.
>
> .   .   .   .
>
> Sans doute il faut frapper l'attention par le tableau présent et détaillé de
> l'objet pour lequel on veut émouvoir; mais l'appel à la pitié n'est irrésistible,
> que quand la mélancolie sait aussi bien généraliser que l'imagination a su
> peindre.
>
> Les modernes ont dû réunir à cette éloquence, qui n'a pour but que d'en-
> traîner, l'éloquence de la pensée, dont l'antiquité ne nous offre que Tacite
> pour modèle. Montesquieu, Pascal, Machiavel sont éloquens par une seule
> expression, par une épithète frappante, par une image rapidement tracée,
> dont le but est d'éclaircir l'idée, mais qui agrandit encore ce qu'elle explique.
> L'impression de ce genre de style pourroit se comparer à l'effet que produit
> la révélation d'un grand secret; il vous semble aussi que beaucoup de pensées
> ont précédé la pensée qu'on vous exprime, que chaque idée se rapporte à des
> méditations profondes, et qu'un mot vous permet, tout-à-coup, de porter vos
> regards dans les régions immenses que le génie a parcourues.

> (The Ancients knew how to vitalize the support necessary for each circum-
> stance; but in our time, minds are so satiated, by the succession of the cen-
> turies, about the individual interests of men, and perhaps even about the
> instantaneous interests of nations, that the eloquent writer needs to rise
> higher and higher to reach the source of affections common to all mortals.
>
> .   .   .   .
>
> Doubtless one must attract attention by the present and detailed picture of
> the object for which one wants to arouse emotion; but the appeal to pity is
> irresistible only when melancholy knows how to generalize as well as imagina-
> tion has known how to describe.
>
> The Moderns have had to join to this eloquence, which has as its goal only
> to incite, the eloquence of thought, of which antiquity offers us only Tacitus
> as a model. Montesquieu, Pascal, and Machiavelli are eloquent in a single
> expression, in a striking epithet, in a rapidly drawn image, whose purpose is
> to clarify the idea, but which also enlarges what it is explaining. The im-
> pression of this kind of style could be compared to the effect that the revela-
> tion of a great secret produces; it seems also to you that many thoughts have
> preceded the thought that is expressed to you, that each idea is related to

profound meditations, and that a word permits you, suddenly, to look into the immense regions which genius has passed through.)

6 Chapter IV, "Des Femmes qui cultivent les Lettres," appears in the second part of *De la littérature*. In this chapter, Mme. de Staël criticizes the inferior status of women and, particularly, the difficulties encountered by the woman of talent and genius.

7 An illegible word or phrase inserted between the lines. The following reading has been suggested: *dans une suspension d'erudition* ("in a suspension of erudition").

8 On page 246 of the first volume of *De la littérature,* Mme. de Staël observes: "S'il existe une distance infinie entre les derniers hommes célèbres de l'antiquité et les premiers, qui, parmi les modernes, se sont illustrés dans la carrière des sciences et des lettres; si Bacon, Machiavel et Montaigne ont des idées et des connoissances infiniment supérieures a celles de Pline, de Marc-Aurèle, &c. n'est-il pas évident que la raison humaine a fait des progrès pendant l'intervalle qui sépare la vie de ces grands?" ("If there exists an enormous distance between the last famous men of antiquity and the first who, among the moderns, have distinguished themselves in the career of science and letters; if Bacon, Machiavelli, and Montaigne have ideas and knowledge infinitely superior to those of Pliny, Marcus Aurelius, etc., is it not evident that human reason has made progress during the interval that separates the life of these great men?")

9 Frederick the Great.

10 Julian the Apostate.

11 The page cited by du Pont de Nemours contains the following statement:

Il suffit d'un jour où l'on ait pu prêter un appui par quelques pensées, par quelques discours, à des résolutions qui ont amené des cruautés et des souffrances, il suffit de ce jour pour tourmenter la vie, pour détruire au fond du cœur, et le calme, et cette bienveillance universelle que faisoit naître l'espoir de trouver des cœurs amis par-tout où l'on rencontroit des hommes. Ah! que les nations encore honnêtes, que les hommes doués de talens politiques, qui ne peuvent se faire aucun reproche, conservent précieusement un tel bonheur! et si leur révolution commence, qu'ils ne redoutent au milieu d'eux que les amis perfides qui leur conseilleront de persécuter les vaincus.

(It takes only one day when one may have given support by a few thoughts, a few speeches, to resolutions which brought on cruelty and suffering. This day is enough to torment one's life, to destroy, in the bottom of one's heart, both the calm and that universal benevolence which resulted from the hope of finding friendly hearts wherever one encountered men. Ah! let the nations which are still honest, the men endowed with political talents who cannot reproach themselves for anything, treasure such happiness! and if their revolution begins, let them fear among them only the treacherous friends who will advise them to persecute the vanquished.)

This passage appears at the end of Chapter XVII of the first part of *De la littérature,* entitled "De la Littérature allemande." Madame de Staël has just urged the Germans to remain faithful to principle and morality should they adopt republican ideals, and not to make the mistakes of the French in this respect.

The *coup d'état* of the 18 Fructidor (September 4, 1797) had been directed against the royalists, who had won the elections of the year V. Although Mme. de

Staël's role in the *coup* is somewhat uncertain, she had undoubtedly played a major part in effecting it.

12 I have been unable to identify the source of this quotation.

13 Stéphanie-Félicité, Comtesse de Brusbart de Genlis (1746–1830). In her younger years, she had been the governess of the children of Philippe-Egalité, Duc d'Orléans, and the latter's mistress. In later life, she tried to atone for her scandalous past by writing popular novels filled with religion, sentiment, and morality. Napoleon said that she spoke of virtue as if she had just made a discovery. Her jealousy toward Mme. de Staël was well known.

37

Madame de Staël to du Pont de Nemours

28 July 1802

WMSS 2/16

Coppet ce 28 juillet[1]

Vous ètes arrivé mon cher dupont.[2] C'est le mouvement de joye le plus vif que j'aye èprouvè depuis long-tems! Je vous reverrai donc cet hyver. Vous serez donc encor l'un des meilleurs amis de ma vie. Dites moi de vos nouvelles, de celles de mad. du pont. Un mot de vos projets qui vous fixent pour jamais je l'espère en france, un mot aussi du bonheur que vous y espèrez. Voulez vous ètre placè? Vous y oblige t on? Enfin songez que mon père et moi nous avons besoin des plus grands dètails sur tout ce qui vous touche.

Un de mes amis en voyage ici benj[amin][3] ne veut pas que je l'oublie auprès de vous.

[Sans signature]

On the reverse:

A Monsieur
dupont de Nemours
à paris
rue de montolon f[b] poissonnière[4]

TRANSLATION

Coppet, July 28[1]

You have arrived, my dear du Pont.[2] It is the strongest feeling of joy that I have had in a long time! So I shall see you again this winter. You will again be one of the best friends of my life. Give me news of yourself and of Mme. du Pont. A word about your plans, which fix you forever, I hope, in France. A word also about the happiness that you hope for there. Do you want a position? Are you obliged to have one? Finally, remember that my father and I need the greatest details about everything that concerns you.

One of my friends on a visit here, Benj[amin],[3] does not want me to forget to give you his regards.

[No signature]

On the reverse:

To Monsieur
dupont de Nemours
in Paris
rue de montholon faubourg poissonnière[4]

NOTES
1 The year 1802 has been added by another hand.
2 Du Pont de Nemours had returned to France at the end of June 1802 to direct the new Paris headquarters of his company, to try to raise money for it, and to attempt to collect the money due from the French government on the Santo Domingo drafts (see letter 53, note 9). Victor du Pont remained in New York, in charge of his own new company, which du Pont de Nemours, however, considered to be a branch of the original company (Ambrose Saricks, *Pierre Samuel Du Pont de Nemours* [Lawrence, Kans., 1965], pp. 292, 303).
3 Benjamin Constant.
4 The correct spelling of this street is Montholon. The rue de Montholon is in the ninth arrondissement of Paris.

38

Necker to du Pont de Nemours

16 August 1802

WMSS 2/16

Soyez le bien venu Monsieur dans notre Europe. C'est là votre place et puisque vous y paroissez encore en avant de l'esprit des autres, que devoit-ce etre en Amérique? Est-ce au Senat qu'on vous appellera. Les appointements y sont excellents.

"Je la crois galvanique"[1] le mot est parfait. Tout est artificiel tout est en effort en cela comme en d'autres choses. On n'a pas cru a la force du grand cabestan de la morale et de la raison ou l'on n'a pas sçu le manier. Voilà Mr de Pusy qui s'approche de nous.[2] J'en suis fort aise. Vous aurez ainsy [. . .][3] et le petit mot que vous me dites là dessus me fait grand plaisir.

Agreez les assurances de mon tendre interest et de mon invi[o]lable attachement.

[Sans signature]

16 aoust 1802

On the reverse:

a Mr. Dupont de Nemours
rüe montholon n° 301

TRANSLATION

Welcome, Sir, to our Europe. This is your place, and since you seem to be far ahead of the minds of others here, what must it be in America? Will you be called to the Senate? The salary there is excellent.

"I believe it to be galvanic."[1] The word is perfect. Everything is artificial. Everything is strained in that as in other things. People did not believe in the strength of the great capstan of morality and reason, or people did not know how to handle it. I see that M. de Pusy is moving close to us.[2] I am very happy about it. You will have thus [. . .][3] and the little remark that you make about it causes me great pleasure.

Accept the assurances of my tender interest and of my inviolable attachment.

[No signature]

August 16, 1802

On the reverse:

To M. Dupont de Nemours
301, rue de Montholon

NOTES

1 Edouard Chapuisat quotes from an unpublished letter in the Archives of Coppet from du Pont de Nemours to Necker written July 24, 1802. Du Pont wrote: "Vous faites contrepoids pour la religion chrétienne protestante, alliée de la philosophie,

contre la religion catholique, apostolique et romaine, alliée de la politique, dont la résurrection ne me paraît pas accompagnée d'une santé parfaite. Je la crois galvanique. J'ai cependant dîné avec des évêques en croix d'or et *monseigneurisés* et même à Rouen avec notre archevêque en habits pontificaux, mais la chaleur des fidèles ne me semble pas au niveau de l'éclat des titres et de la déclaration." ("You set off the Protestant Christian religion, in alliance with philosophy, against the Catholic, apostolic, and Roman religion, in alliance with politics, the resurrection of which does not seem to me to be accompanied by perfect health. I believe it to be galvanic. Even though I have dined with *monseigneurized* bishops in golden crosses and even at Rouen with our archbishop in pontifical attire, the zeal of the faithful does not seem to me on a level with the pomp of titles and declaration.") (Édouard Chapuisat, *Necker* [Paris, 1938], p. 263.)

2 Bureaux de Pusy was transferred to Lyons on August 30, 1802.

3 A word missing here.

39

Madame de Staël to du Pont de Nemours

5 November 1802

WMSS 2/16

ce 5 9bre 1

J'ai attendu avec impatience une occasion mon cher dupont, pour vous dire que je vous aime de toute mon ame, et que je souhaite que vous soyez tout ce que vous désirerez d'ètre; je ne sais pas comment on feroit du bien en france aujourd'hui dans toute autre place que celle de Bon[aparte] mais si ce moyen existe vous le trouverez. Du reste vous avez si bien combattu qu'il vous est permis de vous reposer, et le civil aussi a ses vétérans. Quand à moi que la vie tient encor dans toute sa force et dans toute la mienne je ferois peu de cas de mon caractère si je ne bravois pas pour conserver mes opinions quelques dangers, j'ai bravè pis que des dangers, lors que je les ai soutenue ces opinions malgrè ceux qui les déshonoroient, c'est alors que j'ai souffert. Maintenant la position est simple, je ne me mèle de rien, je n'ècrirai sur rien, je tacherai mème de ne parler sur rien. Mais jamais mon cœur et mon esprit n'ont été plus pénétrés et plus convaincus de l'amour de la liberté. Après cette profession ou cette confession de foi, laissez moi vous dire quel plaisir j'aurai à vous revoir! En vous quittant je craignois que ce bonheur ne me fut plus réservé que dans un de ces nuages amis que vous peignez si bien dans la philosophie de la nature,[2] je bènis le ciel de vous retrouver sur la terre, et je prie votre respectable compagne de me permettre d'avoir pour vous une tendresse filiale, et un gout qui tient à la coquetterie. Adieu encore mais adieu sur le mème continent et avec l'espoir très prochain de vous embrasser.

[Sans signature]

TRANSLATION

November 5[1]

   I have waited impatiently, my dear du Pont, for an opportunity to tell you that I love you with all my soul, and that I hope that you will be all that you wish to be. I do not know how anyone could do any good in France today in any position but Bon-[aparte's], but if there is a way, you will find it. Moreover, you have fought so well that you are entitled to rest, and the civil life also has its veterans. As for me, whom life still maintains in all its strength and mine, I should have little respect for my character if I did not face some dangers in order to keep my opinions. I have faced worse than dangers when I upheld those opinions in spite of those who dishonored them. That is when I suffered. Now the position is simple. I do not concern myself with anything, I shall not write about anything, I shall even try not to speak about any-thing. But never have my heart and my mind been more pene-trated with and earnest in the love of liberty. After that profession, or that confession, of faith, let me tell you what pleasure I shall have on seeing you again. On leaving you, I was afraid that that happiness was no longer reserved for me except in one of those friendly clouds that you describe so well in the philosophy of nature.[2] I thank Heaven at finding you again on earth, and I beg your respectable wife to permit me to have for you a filial affection and a fondness which borders on coquetry. Adieu again, but adieu on the same continent and with the hope of embracing you very soon.

[No signature]

NOTES
1 The date 1802 has been added in another hand.
2 An allusion to du Pont de Nemours' *Philosophie de l'univers*, published in 1796.

40

Necker to du Pont de Nemours

12 November 1802

WMSS 2/16

J'ai receu Monsieur votre lettre du 17 Vendemiaire[1] et la precedente. Vous m'envoyez une lettre de change de 2791 francs et 38 centimes pour les interests de mon depost chez votre maison echu le p[remie]r Juillet dernier mais vous ne me dites pas a quel prix vous avez reglé la piastre due en Amerique & sur quelle regle. Je vous prie d'agréer les assurances de mon inviolable attachement.

Necker

12 9bre 1802

On the reverse:

Au Citoyen Dupont
de Nemours à Paris

Postmark:

25 B^{re} An 11
99 Geneve

TRANSLATION

I have received, Sir, your letter of the 17 Vendémiaire[1] and the preceding one. You send me a bill of exchange for 2,791 francs and 38 centimes for the interest due last July 1 on my investment in your company, but you do not tell me at what price you paid for the piaster due in America and at what rate. I beg you to accept the assurances of my inviolable attachment.

Necker

November 12, 1802

On the reverse:

To the Citizen Dupont
de Nemours in Paris

Postmark:

25 Brumaire, year XI
99 Geneva

NOTE
1 This letter is in the Archives at Coppet and was not available for publication.

41

Necker de Germany to Jacques Roman

28 November 1802

WMSS 2/33

Je suis proprietaire Monsieur, d'une action dans la sociéte du commerce de Messieurs Dupont de Nemours & Cie à New York, d'une dite dans la manufacture de poudre sous la direction de Mr Irenée Dupont. La premiere doit me valoir un interet de 4 p[our] cent l'an. La 2de un interet de 6 p[our] cent. Il y a depuis quelques mois une année d'interet échuë sur l'une & sur l'autre. C'est à vous Monsieur, que je dois m'adresser pour en obtenir le payement. Je viens vous prier de me marquer quelle somme je puis tirer sur vous pour le montant de ces interets. Veuilliez me guider pour cette fois & m'indiquer si independamment de ma traite je dois envoyer quelque quittance particuliere et dans quelle forme elle doit être conçue.

Quant à l'etat de ces deux sociétés vous me feriez plaisir de me marquer si elles ont envoyé des bilans ou etats de situation faisant connoitre le nombre d'actions qui participent aux bénéfices & aux pertes les capitaux qui composent l'actif de cette sociéte leur emploi, les bénéfices ou les pertes resultant des opèrations qui ont èté faites jusqu'à ce jour: et cela d'une maniere aussi exacte et aussi claire que le seroit l'etat des affaires de votre maison de Paris et que doit l'être en général celui de toute maison bien réglée.

Je n'ai pris cet interet dans ces entreprises que par consideration pour M Dupont de Nemours & pour l'obliger. Veuilliez me rappeller à son souvenir et le prier de me donner quelque explication de la situation actuelle d'entreprises que ni lui ni Mr Bureau de Pusy ne dirigent plus & dont je n'ai que l'idèe la plus imparfaitte. Je vous prie d'agrèer Monsieur, ma tres parfaite consideration & mes salutations.

Necker de Germany

Geneve le 7 Frimaire[1] [an] 11

On the reverse:

A Monsieur Roman
chez Messieurs Gros & Davilliers
à Paris

Postmark:

13 [. . .][2] an 11
Geneve 99

TRANSLATION

I am the owner, Sir, of one share in the business firm of Messrs. Du Pont de Nemours & Cie. in New York, and of another in the powder factory under the direction of M. Irénée Dupont. The first is to bring me 4 per cent interest a year; the second, 6 per cent. For several months, a year's interest has been due on both of them. It is to you, Sir, that I am to address myself to obtain payment. I beg you to inform me what sum I can draw on you for the total of this interest. Please guide me for this time and indicate to me whether, independently of my draft, I must send some individual receipt and in what form it must be drawn up.

As to the condition of these two companies, you would please me by indicating to me whether they have sent any balance-sheets or statements revealing the number of shares which participate in the profits and losses, the capital which composes the assets of this company, its employment, the profits or losses resulting from the operations carried on to this time, and that in a manner as exact and as clear as the financial statement of your company in Paris would be and which must be, in general, that of any well-run company.

I took this interest in these enterprises only out of consideration for M. Dupont de Nemours and to oblige him. Please remember me to him and request him to give me some explanation of the present condition of the companies which neither he nor M.

Bureaux de Pusy any longer directs and of which I have only the most imperfect idea. I beg you to accept, Sir, my best regards and my greetings.

Necker de Germany

Geneva, 7 Frimaire[1] [year] XI

On the reverse:

To Monsieur Roman
in care of Messieurs Gros and Davilliers
in Paris

Postmark:

13 [. . .] [2] year XI
99 Geneva

NOTES

1 This word, written in another hand, is inserted between the lines; *Brumaire* is crossed out. *Repondue le 20 frimaire* appears at the beginning of the letter in another handwriting.

2 The name of the month is illegible.

42

Necker de Germany to du Pont de Nemours

26 December 1802

WMSS 2/16

Geneve 5 Nivose 11

Je vous remercie beaucoup Monsieur, des détails dans les quels vous avez la bonté d'entrer avec moi par votre lettre du 10 Frim[ai]re. Ce n'est gueres que depuis que je l'ai reçue que je commence à me former quelque idée un peu précise de ces deux sociétés aux quelles j'ai pris part sans les bien connoitre & par pure déférence pour vous basée sur vos lumieres et sur votre probité. Je conserverai avec soin les pré[cieux] renseignemens que vous me donnez et une lettre du meme genre chaque année continuera à me tenir au fait moi ou les miens. Il n'y a qu'un point qui est encore une enigme—pour moi c'est la maniere dont vous avez dressé votre bilan chaque année dont vous avez partagé les bénéfices ou fait supporter les pertes aux actionnaires qui sont entrés a diverses époques dans vos sociétés. C'est ce que vous me direz j'espere dans l'occasion. Une notte explicative de cette remise que vous me faites de f. 1046.87 cent sur Paris m'auroit aussi été agreable. Je comprends pourtant que c'est la valeur de deux cent dollars et j'en fais écriture sur ce pied là. J'ai bien remis votre incluse a sa destination. Agréez mes vœux pour votre bonheur, Monsieur, & mon cordial attachement.

Necker de Germany

On the reverse:

A Monsieur
Dupont de Nemours pere
fils & Comp^e
rue de Montholon N° 300
a Paris

TRANSLATION

Geneva, 5 Nivôse, year XI

I thank you very much, Sir, for the details which you had the kindness to explain to me in your letter of 10 Frimaire [December 1]. It is scarcely only since I received it that I have begun to form a rather clear idea about those two companies in which I invested without knowing them very well and out of pure deference to you, based on your enlightenment and probity. I shall preserve with care the priceless information that you give me, and a letter of the same kind each year will continue to keep me or my family informed. There is only one point that is still puzzling: for me, that is the manner in which you have set up your annual balance-sheet, in which you have divided the profits among or caused losses to the stockholders who invested at different times in your companies. I hope that you will explain at an opportune time. A note explaining that remittance of 1,046.87 francs on Paris that you send me would also have pleased me. I understand, however, that that is the equivalent of $200, and I enter it on that basis. I have delivered your enclosure to its destination. Accept my wishes for your happiness, Sir, and my cordial attachment.

Necker de Germany

On the reverse:

To Monsieur
Dupont de Nemours, Père
et Fils & Cie.
300, rue de Montholon
in Paris

43

Madame de Staël to du Pont de Nemours

7 March 1803

WMSS 2/17

ce 7 mars

J'ai reçu une très aimable lettre de vous mon cher du pont[1] et j'y rèponds par une occasion parce qu'il me semble que vous le prèfèrez. Je ne discuterai point mon roman[2] avec vous. Une prèface à la téte de la 2de èdition dira tout ce que je crois convenable de dire et je ne mèle point aux intérets de l'amitiè les intérets de l'amour propre littéraire. Je ne rèpondrai qu'à deux articles de votre lettre. Vous me dites que j'ai des ennemis parmi les femmes auteurs. Si j'ai quelque talent cela doit ètre mais ne dois-je pas espèrer que mes amis ne cèderont pas à mes ennemis? Je me charge des neutres. C'est au public impartial qu'il faut dèdier ce que l'on ècrit. Vous me conseillez ensuite un peu trop lègèrement de m'enterrer de mon vivant. Le sèjour de copet est un couvent et celui de genève ce que je connois au monde de plus opposè à mes gouts mes habitudes et mes idèes. J'aime mon père de toute mon ame mais il est le premier à sentir que cette vie là est odieuse pour moi et je vous dèclare qu'aucune puissance humaine ne parviendra à me la faire mener. Rèflèchissez un peu en vous mème si il y a 30 ans si à prèsent mème que vous ètes si jeune d'ame et d'esprit vous vous rèsigneriez à faire chaque jour un whisk pendant trois heures et à ne pouvoir causer du fond du cœur ni du fond de l'esprit avec personne hors de mon intimité. Daignez songer que depuis mon enfance j'ai vècu avec les hommes les plus

distingués et parlè des intérets les plus nobles et demandez vous ce
qu'il m'en coute pour entendre discuter du matin au soir si Mlle
une telle qui m'ennuye èpousera M^r un tel qui produit sur moi le
mème effet. On en a bien vite fait du sort des autres, dans une
seule ligne on leur conseille la retraite et l'exil mais pour exècuter
cette ligne il faut se dèvorer soi mème pendant tous les longs jours
d'une longue annèe. Mon cher du pont la vie est une si triste chose.
Sa perspective descendante avec une imagination qui auroit
besoin d'espèrance. Les hommes, l'ingratitude, la mort que sais-je
encor tant de souffr[ances] [3] diverses ne peuvent se supporter que
par la distraction et quand vous menez une vie qui vous met en
prèsence de vous mème tout le jour l'imagination devient tellement sombre que l'existence à ce prix seroit odieuse. Joignez au
dègout de ce pays un gout extreme pour la france pour l'esprit
françois une grande affection pour mes amis et ces souvenirs de
l'enfance qui vous rendent la patrie si chère. C'en est assez pour
vous faire concevoir que je mourrois ici si j'y ètois relèguèe. Ne
traitez donc pas si lègèrement l'idée de l'exil. Ovide[4] en mourut.
Cicèron[5] qui présenta sa tète sans crainte aux poignards ne pouvoit
supporter mème la grèce et je ne suis pas en grèce. Enfin tout ce qui
est nè sur ce sol fortuné de la france ne peut supporter la vie
ailleurs. Adieu cher du pont. Je suis malade et triste mais je n'ai
pas voulu que vous ignorassiez tout ce que je sens. N'oubliez pas
que je vous aime et que vous revoir sera pour moi le moment le
plus doux.

[Sans signature]

On the reverse:

A Monsieur
Monsieur Dupont de Nemours
a Paris
mercredi matin[6]

TRANSLATION

March 7

   I received a very kind letter from you, my dear du Pont,[1] and
I am answering it at an opportune time because it seems to me that
you would prefer it. I shall not discuss my novel [2] with you. A
preface at the beginning of the second edition will say everything

that I consider fitting to say, and I do not mix with the interests of friendship the interests of literary self-love. I shall answer only two points in your letter. You tell me that I have enemies among women writers. If I have some talent, that is bound to be so, but must I not hope that my friends will not yield to my enemies? I shall concern myself with those who are neutral. It is to the impartial public that one must dedicate what one writes. You advise me next, a bit too frivolously, to bury myself during my lifetime. Living at Coppet is like life in a convent, and living in Geneva is the one thing in the world most opposed to my tastes, habits, and ideas. I love my father with all my soul, but he is the first to feel that life there is odious to me, and I declare to you that no human power will succeed in making me lead it. Think a bit about it yourself, whether thirty years ago, or even at present when you are so young in soul and mind, you would resign yourself to playing a game of whist for three hours each day and to not being able to chat from the bottom of your heart or from the depths of your mind with anyone outside of my immediate circle. Just think that, since my childhood, I have lived with the most distinguished men and talked about the most noble interests, and ask yourself how it pains me to hear discussed from morning to evening whether Mlle. So-and-so, who bores me, will marry M. So-and-so, who produces the same effect on me. People quickly dispose of the fate of others. In a single line, they advise them to accept retirement and exile, but to follow that advice, one must consume oneself during all the long days of a long year. My dear du Pont, life is such a sad thing. Its declining years, with an imagination which would need hope. Men, ingratitude, death, and so many other things, so many different sufferings[3] cannot be borne except by amusements, and when you lead a life which leaves you with yourself all day long, the imagination becomes so gloomy that existence at that price would be odious. Add to the distaste for this country an extreme taste for France, for the French mind, a great affection for my friends and those childhood memories which make one's country so dear. That is enough to make you understand that I should die here if I were banished here. Do not treat so lightly the idea of exile. Ovid[4] died from it. Cicero,[5] who presented his head without fear to daggers, could not even stand Greece, and I am not in Greece. In a word, everyone who is born on that fortunate soil of France cannot bear life elsewhere. Adieu, dear du Pont. I am ill and sad, but I did not want you to remain ignorant of all that I feel. Do not forget that I love you and that seeing you again will be the sweetest moment for me.

[No signature]

On the reverse:

To Monsieur
du Pont de Nemours
in Paris
Wednesday morning[6]

NOTES
1 This letter seems to have been lost.
2 *Delphine.*
3 A tear in the paper. Mme. de Staël must, however, have written *souffrances.*
4 Ovid died in exile in what is now Rumania. The reason for his exile has remained a mystery.
5 Cicero was assassinated at Formia in Italy.
6 The address and notation on the reverse are in another handwriting.

44

du Pont de Nemours to Madame de Staël

17 March 1803

From a draft, WMSS 2/5

Paris 26 ventose An onze[1]

Je retrouve dans votre lettre un des biens de ma vie, votre constante amitié; mais j'y vois vos profonds ennuis et ils me donnent un chagrin dont vous seriez touchée. Je ne vous parlerai point d'autre chose.

Ils me peinent d'autant plus que je n'y sais aucun remede qui ne fût pire que le mal, et qui ne dût amener un plus grand mal.

Non Mon Amie ce n'est pas legerement que je vous ai conseillé de prendre comme vous pourriez patience au bord de votre lac. Je ne suis point de ces gens qui lâchent un conseil pour parler et se croient quittes. Je pense à votre bonheur ou à votre moindre tourment.

Vous vous ennuyez dans votre Helvetie soumise ou dans votre Genêve detruite,[2] et je n'ignore pas que l'ennui est comme le cauchemar dont le poids s'accroissant a chaque moment donne les plus mauvais rêves. Mais a Paris ce ne seraient pas de l'ennui et des reves que vous auriez. Ce serait de la réalité du malheur et de la douleur poignans à chaque minute, en supposant même qu'on vous y laissât rester: ce qui est plus que douteux.

Les circonstances, l'activité de votre caractere la liberté de vos discours, les affaires dont vous avez partagé le secret, dans lesquelles vous avez agi, ou été le point de ralliement de ceux qui agissaient ont fait de vous un Personnage public; très grand malheur pour un homme, beaucoup plus grand pour une femme. On vous croit et vous croirait conspiratrice tandis que vous n'êtes et ne seriez qu'une philosophe aimant la liberté de penser de parler et d'écrire cherchant dans des conversations fortes et variées à employer un peu de cette surabondance de vie qui vous rend la plus part des hommes insipides et qui fait que vous ne pouvez trouver presque aucun ami digne de votre durable intimité.

Sans cesse espionnée dans votre maison, calomniée pour les moindres choses que vous auriez dites et pour celles auxquelles vous n'auriez jamais pensé dechirée dans les journaux, houspillée par tous les hourets dont les jappemens ignorés de ceux même auxquels ils voudraient plaire, ne laisseraient pas de vous importuner. Chaque jour vous apporterait une ou plusieurs querelles au dessus desquelles votre sensibilite ne vous permettrait pas de vous mettre.

Les moustiques sont charmés d'avoir affaire a quelqu'un qui ait la peau tendre. Lorsque vous croyez les ecraser, ils s'envolent et rient du grand mouvement qu'à fait votre main.

Songez ce que serait d'avoir tous les matins a recevoir un coup d'epingle de la prude et haineuse Genlis,[3] de quelques autres qui valent mieux mais dont la rivalité ne pardonne rien, du plat et lâche Geoffroi[4] digne heritier de Trevoux[5] de des Fontaines,[6] et de tous les petits athées convertis, faisant maigre et mordant le prochain, devenus bons catholiques a la confession près parce qu'elle occuperait toute leur vie.

Dans cette anxiété, on vous seduirait aisement avec quelques mots de liberté, avec quelque petit interet. Votre société se composerait de tous les ambitieux entierement desappointés car les autres ne seraient pas si hardis a moins qu'ils ne fussent perfides. Vous repondriez de toutes leurs fautes. Tout ce qu'ils auraient dit ou fait de mal serait repété comme dit ou fait par vous même. Vous avez toujours été trop facile sur les gens que vous receviez chez vous. J'y ai vu vingt Jacobinets, réels comme Riouffe[7] ou soi disant tels comme Masclet,[8] qui me traitaient du haut en bas se pretendant bien meilleurs citoyens bien plus fiers Républicains que moi. Ils me reprocheraient aujourd'hui, avec la même amertume d'aimer encore la liberté du commerce et celle de la religion. Ceux qui vous viendraient a present seraient beaucoup pires et plus dangereux, et vous ne pourriez savoir si ceux qui parleraient le plus dans votre sens et paraitraient le plus vous admirer n'iraient pas en vous quittant vous accuser à la police des propres discours avec lesquels ils vous auraient tendu des pieges. Je ne connais rien d'insupportable comme de vivre ainsi en defiance perpetuelle et de regarder avec inquiétude dans les yeux des gens qui se disent vos amis quel mal ils peuvent ou veulent vous faire.

Le chef de l'empire est certainement un homme de genie et de talent, fils de ses œuvres et de grandes œuvres, le seul qui puisse et presque le seul qui veuille faire encore quelque bien. Il le veut pour sa gloire: l'amour de la gloire est un bel et utile amour. Mais il est susceptible, quelquefois irascible et plus qu'il ne conviendrait a un homme tel que lui. Il vous croit son ennemie, il vous sait du courage et sa devise est *parcere subjectis et debellare superbos*.[9] Nul moyen donc de vivre sous ses yeux, a moins que vous ne l'ayez convaincu que [vous] n'êtes opposée ni a lui ni a son gouvernement que vous mettez au contraire en lui l'esperance de ce qui peut rester a faire de bon pour la France et pour l'Europe. Et il ne vous en croirait pas a votre premier mot.

Que vois-je donc devant vous? Nos cailletes de Paris males et femelles sont contagieusement empoisonnées. Vos cailletes de Geneve ne sont qu'ennuyeuses et ne vous le paraitraient peut être pas si vous n'etiez pas d'avance ennuyée, car j'ai toujours aime les hommes et les femmes de votre pays, les premiers sont penseurs les secondes sont sensibles. Les uns et les autres sont instruits.

"Tel voudrait bien etre soldat a qui le soldat porte envie." [10] Vous desirez d'etre a Paris. J'ambitionnerais le bonheur de cultiver auprès de Geneve l'histoire naturelle cette interessante mere de toute philosophie dont je suis amant passionné et dont le tourbillon des affaires me separe.

Vous pleurez de ne pas causer ou je suis. Je pleure de ne pas être debarassé de toutes les causeries pour travailler ou vous êtes.

Et pourquoi n'y travailleriez vous point? Vous avez infiniment d'esprit vous êtes jeune vous avez deja beaucoup d'instruction et vous avez tout autour de vous la plus belle nature. La botanique peut adoucir les peines, parce qu'elle exige des promenades qui sont elles mêmes un bonheur. La Zoologie eleve l'ame et perfectionne l'entendement, elle est semée de plaisirs nobles et purs. Et vos voisins y ont fait de grands progrès. Haller[11] Bonnet [12] Trembley[13] ont laissé parmi eux de dignes successeurs.

La geologie a son trone sur les montagnes, d'où la vue embrasse le monde entier.

Je ne vous invite pas à la chimie quoique je l'estime et je l'aime, ses experiences sont trop sedentaires. Elle demande pour des details qui n'ont point assez de propreté pour une dame et dans lesquels il faut porter une attention trop soutenue trop minutieuse.

Avec ces belles sciences on vit dans la retraite sans aucun ennui, on laisse amortir les haines on deroute la jalousie et l'on reparait ensuite couronnée de fleurs de plumes de fourrures de pierres precieuses et la raison fortifiée par l'habitude de l'observation.

Si vous prenez ce parti, vous verrez combien nos lettres deviendront meilleures et combien les faits curieux que vous me communiquerez m'inspireront de reconnaissance, avec quel plaisir je vous conterai ceux que j'ai ou que j'aurai pu recueillir.

Et Dieu me preserve de renoncer au bonheur d'aller philosopher avec vous sur les œuvres de Dieu oubliant les folies et les petitesses des hommes.

J'espere bien passer quelques jours chez vous dès cette année et y presenter mon hommage a votre respectable Pere.

Salut, respect et tendresse pour la vie et par delà ma bien belle amie digne d'être plus forte qu'on ne le croirait si l'on vous jugeait d'après votre dégout pour l'helvetie et votre amour pour le cahos de Paris.

Madame du Pont vous dit mille choses. Elle vous aime et vous estime sincerement.

TRANSLATION

Paris, 26 Ventose, year XI [1]

I find again in your letter one of the good things of my life, your constant friendship, but I see in it your profound unhappiness, and it arouses a sorrow in me which would touch you. I shall not speak to you of anything else.

It pains me all the more since I do not know of any remedy for it which would not be worse than the disease, and which might not bring on a worse disease.

No, my friend, it is not frivolously that I advised you to be as patient as you could on the shore of your lake. I am not one of those people who give advice just to have something to say and then believe themselves excused. I think of your happiness or of your slightest torment.

You are bored in your subjected Switzerland or in your destroyed Geneva,[2] and I am not ignorant of the fact that boredom is like a nightmare whose weight, increasing at every moment, causes one to have the worst dreams. But in Paris it would not be boredom and dreams that you would have. It would be reality, poignant unhappiness and sorrow at every moment, even supposing that you were allowed to stay there, which is more than doubtful.

Circumstances, the activity of your character, the freedom of your speech, the affairs whose secrets you have known, and in which you have taken part or been the rallying-point of those who acted, have made you a public figure, a very great misfortune for a man, and a much greater one for a woman. People believe, and would continue to believe, that you are a conspirator, while you are, and would be, only a philosopher loving the freedom of thought, of speech, and of writing, seeking in lively and varied conversations to use a bit of that superabundance of life which makes the majority of men seem insipid to you and which makes it almost impossible for you to find any friend worthy of your lasting intimacy.

Unceasingly spied upon in your house, slandered because of the slightest things you might say and those which you never would have thought of, torn to bits in the newspapers, abused by all the curs whose yapping, which even those whom they would like to please would not know about, would not fail to bother you. Each day would bring you one or several quarrels which your sensitivity would not permit you to disregard.

Mosquitoes are delighted to deal with someone who has a tender skin. When you think that you are destroying them, they fly away and laugh at the great movement which your hand has made.

Just think what it would be to have to take a pinprick every morning from the prudish and hateful Genlis,[3] from some others who are better but whose rivalry pardons nothing, from the low and cowardly Geoffroy,[4] the worthy heir of Trévoux[5] and Desfontaines,[6] and from all the little converted atheists, fasting and biting their fellow-men, having become good Catholics except for confession because it would occupy their whole life.

In that anxiety, people would trap you easily with a few words about liberty, with some little interest. Your society would be composed of all the entirely disappointed ambitious people, for the others would not be so bold unless they were treacherous. You would answer for all their faults. Everything bad that they might have said or done would be repeated as said or done by you. You have always been too tolerant about the people that you received at your house. I have seen there twenty little Jacobins, real ones like Riouffe[7] or so-called ones like Masclet,[8] who treated me with contempt, claiming to be much better citizens, much prouder republicans than I. They would reproach me today, with the same bitterness, for still loving freedom of trade and of religion. Those who would come to see you at present would be much worse and more dangerous, and you could not know whether those who talked most like you and seemed most to admire you would not go, on leaving you, to denounce you to the police for the very conversations they had carried on in order to trap you. I know nothing as unbearable as living thus in perpetual distrust and watching uneasily the eyes of people who call themselves your friends to see what harm they can or want to do to you.

The leader of the Empire is certainly a man of genius and talent, a self-made man and a great one, the only one who can, and almost the only one who still wants to, do some good. He wants it for his glory. Love of glory is a fine and useful love. But he is touchy, sometimes irascible, and more so than is fitting for a man such as he. He thinks you are his enemy. He knows you have courage, and his motto is *parcere subjectis, debellare superbos.*[9] There is no way therefore to live in his presence, unless you have convinced him that you are not opposed either to him or to his government, that you place in him, on the contrary, your hope for what good may remain to be done for France and for Europe. And he would not believe you at your first word.

What do I see before you? Our frivolous Parisian gossips, male and female, are contagiously poisoned. Your gossips of Geneva are only boring and perhaps would not seem so to you if you were not bored in advance, for I have always loved the men and women of your country. The former are thinkers, and the latter are sensitive. Both are educated.

"He whom the soldier envies would like to be a soldier." [10] You want to be in Paris. I should like to have the happiness of studying natural history near Geneva, that interesting mother of all philosophy, which I love passionately and from which I am separated by the whirlwind of business.

You weep about not conversing where I am. I weep at not being free from all the conversations in order to work where you are.

And why should you not work on it? You have a great deal of wit. You are young, you are already very well educated, and you have around you nature at its most beautiful. Botany can sweeten sorrows, because it requires walks which are themselves a happiness. Zoology elevates the soul and perfects the understanding; it is scattered with noble and pure pleasures. And your neighbors have made great progress in it. Haller,[11] Bonnet,[12] and Trembley[13] have left worthy successors among them.

Geology has its throne on the mountains, from where the view embraces the whole world.

I do not recommend chemistry, although I respect it and love it, because its experiments are too sedentary. It requires details which are not clean enough for a lady and to which one must devote too long and careful attention.

With these fine sciences, one may live in retirement without any boredom, one may let hatreds die out, one turns away jealousy and one then reappears crowned with flowers, with feathers, with furs, with precious stones, one's reason strengthened by the habit of observation.

If you make this decision, you will see how much better our

letters will become and how much gratitude the curious facts that you will communicate to me will arouse, and with what pleasure I shall tell you those that I have or will have been able to gather.

And God keep me from renouncing the happiness of going to philosophize with you about the works of God, forgetting the follies and pettiness of men.

I hope, indeed, to spend a few days with you this year and present my homage to your respectable father.

Greetings, respect, and tenderness for life, and beyond, my very beautiful friend, worthy of being stronger than one would believe, if one judged you from your distaste for Switzerland and your love for the chaos of Paris.

Mme. du Pont sends all her regards. She loves you and sincerely esteems you.

NOTES

1 The date 1803 has been added in another handwriting.

2 Geneva had been annexed to France in 1798.

3 Mme. de Genlis. See Letter 36, note 13

4 Julien-Louis Geoffroy (1743–1814), the literary and dramatic critic of the *Journal des Débats*. He had a great knowledge of literature; but, extremely prejudiced in his views, he indulged in bitter invective in his comments on current literature.

5 The *Journal de Trévoux*, a literary journal founded by the Jesuits of Trévoux in 1701 which opposed the *philosophes* during the eighteenth century.

6 Pierre François Guyot Desfontaines (1685–1745), a Jesuit who left his order in 1715 to become a writer in Paris. Threatened with prison because of a morals charge, he was released through the efforts of Voltaire. Desfontaines, however, turned on his benefactor and attacked him in several works, to which Voltaire did not fail to reply.

7 Honoré Riouffe (1764–1813), baron of the Empire and close friend of Mme. de Staël. A Girondin during the Revolution, he was imprisoned in 1793. After his liberation, he wrote his *Mémoires d'un détenu,* which became part of his *Histoire de la tyrannie de Robespierre* (Paris, 1794–95). He became a member of the Tribunate in 1799 and was president of that group for a time. He served Napoleon faithfully and was prefect of Côte d'Or and la Meurthe (Philippe Godet, *Madame de Charrière et ses amis d'après de nombreux documents inédits* [Geneva, 1906], II, 208, n. 1).

8 The aide-de-camp of the duc d'Aiguillon. During the Revolution, he took refuge in England, where he worked as a journalist and attempted to obtain the release of Lafayette and his fellow prisoners held at Olmütz. Before his departure from France, he had been one of the editors of the *Mercure national.* See Madame de Staël, *Lettres à Narbonne,* ed. Georges Solovieff (Paris, 1960), p. 180, n. 3; and Madame de Staël, *Lettres inédites à Louis de Narbonne,* ed. Béatrice W. Jasinski (Paris, 1960), p. 94, n. 2.

The Eleutherian Mills Historical Library possesses a letter from Masclet to du Pont de Nemours dated 19 thermidor, year X (August 7, 1802), in which

Masclet welcomes du Pont back to France and predicts a prominent position
under the Napoleonic regime for this friend and disciple of Turgot.
9 "Spare those who submit and conquer the proud" (*Aeneid* VI.853).
10 I have been unable to identify the source of this quotation.
11 Albrecht von Haller (1708–77), Swiss physiologist and botanist.
12 Charles Bonnet (1720–93), Swiss naturalist and philosopher.
13 Abraham Trembley (1700–1784), Swiss naturalist, best known for his studies of
the fresh-water hydra.

45

Madame de Staël to du Pont de Nemours

4 April 1803

WMSS 2/17

coppet ce 4 avril
Eugènes[1] retournant en france je lui remets ce petit mot pour
vous mon cher dupont. Il sera de plainte uniquement. Vous me
donnez comme une raison de craindre la france les critiques im-
pertinentes de Mad. de genlis et de geoffroy. En vèrité je me crois
de force à pouvoir attacher très peu d'importance à tout cela. Vous
me conseillez la zoologie, l'ornitologie et la gèologie, pour me
consoler d'ètre sèparèe de mes amis et de mon pays. Je n'ai malheureusement ni gout ni talent pour toutes ces belles sciences mais
quand j'en aurois je trouverois un peu dur que l'on me donnat
ce conseil. Cela me rappelle le pauvre homme dont on disoit *il est
philosophe il quittera la vie sans regret.* Je prie qu'on ne soit pas
philosophe pour moi et je m'engage à ne jamais l'ètre pour les
autres. Vous ètes bon et très bon mais vous avez mal pris ma situation. Il me semble cependant qu'après vous avoir dit qu'elle étoit
malheureuse il falloit la prendre comme je la sentois. Vous me
faites un tableau très triste de ce qui rempliroit ma maison à paris.
On a pu vous dire que l'hyver prècèdent tout ce que les ètrangers
et les françois renfermoient d'hommes distinguès avoient la bonté
d'y venir sans cesse, et je crois en vèrité que ce seroit de mème et
cette annèe et toutes les autres. Pardon si je suis fat mais vous m'y
avez obligèe. Enfin je vous demande quel que soit votre avis de
souhaiter que je revienne la moitiè autant que j'ai souhaité de
vous revoir, de *parler* dans ce sens et de songer qu'il faut que les

amis ne tiennent pas le mème language [*sic*] que les ennemis. Or il n'est pas un de mes ennemis qui ne s'abonnat à ce que je me vouasse à l'histoire naturelle dussai-je y dècouvrir un insecte de plus. Ayez donc la bonté de me faire jouir de votre amitiè par des consolations plus douces, deux fois vos lettres ont aggravè mes peines, et je les aurois avec une espèrance toute contraire. Parlez moi comme matthieu[2] benj[amin][3] &.—enfin comme ceux qui m'aiment ou laissez moi espèrer qu'en vous revoyant je vous plairai assez pour que vous vous consoliez de la fin de mon exil.

　　Mes tendres hommages à Mad. du pont.

[Sans signature]

TRANSLATION

Coppet, April 4

Since Eugene[1] is returning to France, I am giving him this little note for you, my dear du Pont. It will be composed only of complaints. You give me, as a reason for fearing France, the impertinent criticisms of Mme. de Genlis and of Geoffroy. Truly, I believe I have enough strength to attach very little importance to all that. You advise me to study zoology, ornithology, and geology in order to console myself for being separated from my friends and my country. Unfortunately, I have neither taste nor talent for all those fine sciences; but, even if I had, I should find it a bit harsh to have that advice given to me. That recalls to me the poor man of whom it was said: *"He is a philosopher. He will leave life without regret."* I request that people not be philosophers for me, and I swear never to be one for others. You are kind, very kind, but you have misunderstood my situation. It seems to me, however, that after I had told you that it was unhappy, you were obliged to understand it as I felt it. You paint a very sad picture of what would fill my house in Paris. You may have heard that last winter all the most distinguished foreigners and Frenchmen had the kindness to come there unceasingly, and I believe, in truth, that it would be the same, both this year and all the others. Pardon me if I am conceited, but you forced me to it. Finally, I ask you, whatever your opinion may be, to hope that I return half as much as I have hoped to see you again, to *speak* in that sense, and to bear in mind that friends must not use the same language as enemies. Now, there is not one of my enemies who would not approve of my devoting myself to natural history, even if I discovered a new insect. Have the kindness then to let me enjoy your friendship by sweeter consolations. Twice your letters have aggravated my sorrows, and I should like to get them with a completely contrary hope. Talk to me like Mathieu,[2] Benjamin,[3] etc.—in short, like those who love me. Or else let me hope that on seeing you again, I shall please you enough so that you will console yourself for the end of my exile.

My tender respect to Mme. du Pont.

[No signature]

NOTES

1 Joseph Uginet, called Eugène, Mme. de Staël's confidential business agent for many years.
2 Mathieu Félicité de Montmorency, Duc de Laval (1767–1826), a diplomat during the Restoration and a close friend of Mme. de Staël for many years.
3 Benjamin Constant.

46

du Pont de Nemours to Madame de Staël

17 April 1803

From a draft, WMSS 2/5

Paris 27 germinal 11

Je reçois seulement aujourd'hui, mon excellente amie, votre lettre du 4 avril.

Elle m'afflige beaucoup.

Comment n'avez vous pas vu dans les avertissemens que j'ai cru necessaire de vous donner sur un Pays que vous ne connaissez plus, un effort de ma bien tendre amitié qui parlait contre mon propre interêt?

Faire de la peine à quelqu'un me serait toujours triste; mais à une dame, à une belle dame, à une dame que j'aime beaucoup, qui m'a toujours temoigné de l'amitie, et de que [sic] j'ai la presomption d'esperer un attachement durable parce que celui que j'ai pour elle est très vif et ne peut être alteré. Cela ne saurait entrer dans mon cœur.

Venez dès que vous le pourrez, puisque cela vous fait tant de plaisir. Je ne serai certainement pas dans les gens qui auront peur de vous: bien moins encore dans ceux dont vous devrez avoir peur.

Mais ayez peur. Car vous serez perpetuellement espionnée, surveillee, trahie, calomniée, traduite en mille façons absurdes, ridicules, perfides pour tout ce que vous direz ou ne direz point et compromise dans toutes les conspirations et conjurations, ou rèelles, ou imaginaires, ou imaginées, ou imaginables. Cela n'est ni agréable, ni sur; et l'indignation que vous en concevrez augmentera les dégouts et les dangers.

C'est précisement parce que les hommes distingués de tout pays se réuniront chez vous, et parce que ceux qui voudront vous ruiner s'y permettront tout *par ordre,* que vous serez classée comme bureau ouvert de révolte et que tous ces beaux esprits tous ces hommes eminens vous attireront une multitude de peines. Vous me direz cent fois, cent fois au moins ah! combien tu avais raison.

Les données à cet égard sont beaucoup plus fortes qu'elles ne l'êtaient quand je suis arrivé, infiniment plus que lorsque vous êtiez ici. Elles peuvent s'étendre du Temple[1] a Madagascar.

S'il vous était possible de vous borner a un petit nombre d'amis et de ne vous mêler de rien, vous seriez en paix, même à Paris.

Mais il vous faut de l'éclat, du bruit, de la foule, une celebrité toujours entretenue; vous trouverez en même tems des pieges affreux et vous éprouverez des horreurs.

Comment pouvez vous aimer cent personnes? ou même cinquante? ou même douze? Pauvre cœur sensible! il vaudrait bien mieux n'en aimer qu'un, et l'aimer passionnement d'amour;

    deux d'amitié

    trois de bienveillance

    quelle intimité peut aller jusqu'à six?

C'est la distraction que vous cherchez. La distraction est ce qu'il y a de plus loin de la félicité.

Son besoin prouve le malheur.

Je voudrais bien concourir à l'adoucissement de votre malheur; vous m'êtes extrêmement chere.

Mais puisque vous êtes si bonne et que vous daignez me compter parmi vos richesses ou comme une assez grosse pierre de taille au milieu des moellons de toute figure et des petits cailloux dont vous voulez bâtir votre maison, je vous supplie, mon amie, changez en le local. Ne me faites point venir dans le sallon où Turgot m'a donné de si doux momens, dans le cabinet où j'ai tant travaillé avec lui, dans la chambre où après l'avoir veillé quatre vingt nuits, je l'ai tenu quinze heures expirant entre mes bras.[2]

Ma reconnaissance et mon amitié pour ce grand homme sont mes deux sentimens les plus profonds.

N'allez pas croire pour cela que ceux qui me lient à vous soient faibles ou legers. Je n'aime pas faiblement et vous ne pouvez pas être faiblement aimee.

Je baise votre main. Je mets mon tendre attachement à vos pieds.

Presentez mon respect à M\r votre Pere.

TRANSLATION

Paris, 27 Germinal, year XI

I received only today, my excellent friend, your letter of April 4. It grieves me very much.

How did you not see in the warnings that I thought necessary to give you about a country that you no longer know, an effort of my very tender friendship, speaking against my own interest?

To hurt someone would always be sad for me; but a lady, a beautiful lady, a lady whom I love very much, who has always shown me friendship, and from whom I presume to hope for a lasting attachment because the one I have for her is very strong and cannot be changed—all that could not enter my heart.

Come as soon as you can, since that will give you so much pleasure. I certainly shall not be one of the people who will be afraid of you, still less one of those of whom you will have to be afraid.

But be afraid, for you will be perpetually spied on, watched, betrayed, slandered, interpreted in a thousand absurd, ridiculous, treacherous ways in all that you say or do not say, and compromised in all the conspiracies and plots, whether real, or imaginary, or imagined, or imaginable. That is neither pleasant nor safe, and the indignation that you will feel because of it will increase the displeasures and the dangers.

It is precisely because the distinguished men of every country will gather at your house, and because those who will want to ruin you will take liberties there, *on orders,* that you will be considered an open office of revolution and that all those fine wits, all those eminent men will attract a multitude of troubles for you. You will tell me a hundred times, a hundred times at least: "Ah! How right you were!"

The data in that regard are much more extensive than they were when I arrived, infinitely more than when you were here. They can stretch from the Temple[1] to Madagascar.

If it were possible for you to limit yourself to a small number of friends and not to become involved in anything, you would be in peace, even in Paris.

But you must have sparkle, noise, crowds, constantly maintained celebrity; you will find at the same time frightful traps and will experience horrors.

How can you love one hundred persons? or even fifty? or even twelve? Poor sensitive heart! It would be better to love only one, and really love him;

> two in friendship
>
> three in benevolence
>
> what intimacy can go up to six?

It is amusement which you seek. Amusement is the farthest thing from happiness.

Its need proves unhappiness.

I should like to cooperate in the relieving of your unhappiness; you are extremely dear to me.

But since you are so good and since you deign to count me among your riches, or as a rather large freestone in the midst of the varied quarry-stones and the pebbles with which you want to build your house, I beg you, my friend, change its location. Do not make me come to the salon where Turgot gave me so many pleasant moments, to the study where I worked so much with him, to the bedroom where, after having watched over him for eighty nights, I held him dying in my arms for fifteen hours.[2]

My gratitude and friendship for this great man are my two most profound feelings.

Do not believe, because of that, that those which tie me to you are weak or frivolous. I do not love weakly and you cannot be weakly loved.

I kiss your hand. I place my tender attachment at your feet.

Present my respects to your father.

NOTES
1 Du Pont de Nemours is referring, presumably, to the Temple in Paris, which was razed in 1811.
2 Turgot had bought the house at 121, rue de Lille in 1779. He died there in 1781. It was rented in 1803 to Mme. de Staël, who was able to stay there only a short time (Jacques Hillairet, *Dictionnaire historique des rues de Paris* [Paris, n.d.], II, 576–77).

47

Madame de Staël to du Pont de Nemours

September or October 1803

WMSS 2/17

Ce n'est point à paris mais à une campagne à sept lieux de paris que je suis mon cher du pont, j'y vais passer la fin de l'automne. J'espère que vous trouverez un moment pour me donner le plaisir de vous voir. Mon adresse est à mafliers[1] par baumont sur oise dep. de seine et oise. Mais quand on m'ècrit dans ma maison à paris les lettres me parviennent par occasion et point par la poste. Mille amitiès. Oui en vérité j'abdique non les regrets mais les espèrances qui feroient ècrire ou parler. Et je n'ai plus une idée sur tout ce qui m'a occupé dans les belles illusions de ma jeunesse, une rèsignation parfaite ne suffit elle pas? C'est ce que je puis offrir. Mais pour vous je vis encor et mon amitié est restée toute entiére. Adieu.

[Sans signature]

On the reverse:

a Monsieur
Dupont de Nemours
rue de Montolon
N° 301 où 103

TRANSLATION
I am not in Paris, but at a country house seven leagues from Paris, my dear du Pont. I am going to spend the last days of autumn here. I hope that you will find a moment to give me the pleasure of seeing you. My address is at Mafliers,[1] near Beaumont-

sur-Oise in the department of Seine-et-Oise. But letters addressed
to me at my house in Paris reach me when there is an opportunity
and not at all through the post office. A thousand friendships. Yes,
I really abdicate, not regrets, but hopes which would make me
write or speak. And I no longer have a single idea about all that
occupied me in the fine illusions of my youth. Is not a perfect
resignation sufficient? That is what I can offer. But for you I still
live, and my friendship has remained complete. Adieu.

[No signature]

On the reverse:

To Monsieur
du Pont de Nemours
rue de Montholon
No. 301 or 103

NOTE

1 Although this letter is undated, the mention of Maffliers makes it possible to
assign it a date. On September 16, 1803, Mme. de Staël left Coppet, accompanied
by Mathieu de Montmorency (see Letter 45, note 2), with the intention of living
in a house she had rented at Maffliers. She arrived there on September 26. Early
in October, she humbly wrote to Napoleon, assuring him of her intention to live
quietly and peacefully at Maffliers. Napoleon angrily refused her request to
remain there and gave her five days in which to prepare to withdraw to forty
leagues from Paris. The attempts of Mme. de Staël and her friends to reverse his
decision did not succeed, and on October 15, an officer came to Maffliers to escort
her away. She left for Metz on October 19 and from there went on to Germany
(André Lang, *Une Vie d'orages, Germaine de Staël,* 2nd ed. [Paris, 1958], pp.
39–42).

48

du Pont de Nemours to Madame de Staël

9 October 1803

From a draft, WMSS 2/5

16 Vendemiaire 12

Que devez vous dire de moi, ma très belle et bonne amie?
Ne vous avoir pas été chercher! Ne vous avoir pas même écrit!

C'est parce que de moment en moment je comptais aller passer deux heures avec vous que j'ai toujours reculé de vous écrire.

Je mene une vie plus qu'occupée, harassée, accablée. L'amitié et une sorte de point d'honneur m'ont entrainé dans l'arrangement des affaires de la banque territoriale.[1] Les créanciers m'ont nommé leur Président, et depuis quatre mois ils sont contens de ma gestion.

Comme j'ai tâché de rendre cette gestion aussi douce qu'équitable et qu'active. Les actionnaires de la banque ont eté contens de leur côté jusqu'a la semaine derniere.

Mais il faut conclure: et se decider sur le parti à prendre pour l'interet de tous.

J'ai fait un plan: il a eprouvé des objections. J'en ai refait un second, il en a essuyé du [sic] plus fortes car le premier etait meilleur. J'en ai refait un troisieme, un quatrieme, on m'a refusé: j'ai répondu; et je fais le cinquieme.

Les creanciers se sont divisés en deux partis, les actionnaires en deux autres. Les gens de loi se sont jettés à travers la mêlée. Je ne sais plus auquel entendre ni comment me faire entendre: et cependant mon opiniatre caractere n'y renonce pas.

Voila huit jours qu'ils me font parler depuis le matin jusqu'au soir et écrire depuis le soir jusqu'au matin a deux ou trois heures près.

Je gemis d'epuiser mes forces à ce métier, qui au fond ne me convient pas du tout, a ce genre d'affaires qui sont haissables et que pourtant il faut que je fasse avec distinction. Car, que veut-on mal faire?

Une compagnie formée en partie de creanciers unis, en partie d'interessés à la banque suspendue veut relever l'affaire, et veut absolument m'avoir pour chef; mais ne veut suivre aucune de mes idées, et ne veut pas davantage me donner mon congé.

Je les ai crus un moment d'accord, et je me disais avec satisfaction

> À pres de soixante et quatre ans
> dans mon age climaterique
> j'institue une République
> de financiers et de marchands
> qui seront pour tous honnêtes gens

secourables et bienfaisans:
mon pouvoir est presque magique!
    quand j'aurai soixante et dix ans,
dans les déserts de l'amerique
d'une plus noble politique
je poserai les fondemens;
et sur la vertu domestique,
sur le travail, sur les talens,
sur les bonnes mœurs des Parens,
sur les progrès de leurs enfans,
de la Félicitè publique
j'etablirai les elemens,
la Théorie et la pratique.

Je crains aujourd'hui de ne reussir à former ni l'une ni l'autre de mes deux Républiques: car il n'y a que les magistrats despotiques qui se fassent obéir, et la raison; ni même l'interêt bien entendu n'ont que très peu de pouvoir sur les hommes.

Pendant que je combats ainsi contre des moulins a vent et des girouettes, vous êtes à Mafliers. Qu'est-ce que Mafliers? Vous devez vous y ennuyer autant et plus qu'à Genêve.

Chez qui êtes vous?

J'ai entendu dire au troisieme écho que vous y faisiez dans cette retraite une préface apologetique pour la seconde édition de Delphine.

Vous êtes bien bonne de vous défendre. Laissez dire les gens qui ne parlent que par esprit de parti. Et faites plus tot un nouvel ouvrage, si vous n'aimez pas mieux ne rien faire, metier si doux, tresor si precieux qu'on en fit autrefois le partage des dieux.

Je vous ai déja invitée a cultiver les sciences naturelles que j'aime passionnement. Vous m'avez repousse avec perte. Je crois que vous avez eu tort. Votre prodigieuse facilité y ferait de grands progrês et elles vous serviraient pour l'instruction de votre fils. De toute mon éducation rien ne m'a profité que ce qui m'a été enseigné par ma mere.

Vous avez des amis. Il n'en faut pas une multitude, et sans doute vous en avez a *Mafliers*.

Vous les aimez fortement. Ils vous aiment donc beaucoup. Ce sont des consolations.

Si j'étais un beau jeune homme, et si je n'avais pas peur que vous vous moquassiez de moi, je vous proposerais mieux.

Mais je dois me borner a vous dire que je vous suis tendrement et respectueusement attaché.

Madame du Pont vous dit mille choses et je baise vos belles mains.

TRANSLATION

16 Vendémiaire, year XII

What must you be saying about me, my very beautiful and good friend?

Not to have gone to see you! Not even to have written to you!

It is because I expected momentarily to go spend a couple of hours with you that I kept delaying writing to you.

I am leading a life that is more than busy, harassed, and over-burdened. Friendship and a kind of point of honor dragged me into the settlement of the affairs of the Banque Territoriale.[1] The creditors appointed me as their president, and for four months they have been pleased with my administration.

As I have tried to make that administration as mild as equitable and active, the stockholders of the bank have been pleased for their part until last week.

But we must conclude this matter and decide what course to follow for the interest of everybody.

I made a plan. It encountered objections. I made a second one. It encountered stronger objections, for the first one was better. I made a third one, a fourth one. I was turned down. I replied and am making the fifth one.

The creditors have divided into two groups, the stockholders into two others. The lawyers have become involved in the quarrel. I no longer know which one to listen to or how to make myself heard; but my stubborn character does not give up.

For a week they have had me talking from morning until evening, and writing from evening until morning, to around two or three o'clock.

I moan about exhausting my strength in this job, which, on the whole, does not suit me at all, in this kind of business which is hateful and which, even so, I must do with distinction. For what does one want to do badly?

A company, formed in part of united creditors, in part of persons interested in the closed bank, wants to take over the affair, and wants absolutely to have me as head, but does not want to follow any of my ideas and does not want to dismiss me either.

I thought for a moment that they were in agreement, and I said to myself with satisfaction:

> At the age of almost sixty-four years
> In my climacteric year
> I set up a republic
> Of financiers and merchants
> Who will be for everyone honest men,
> Helpful and beneficent:
> My power is almost magic!
>   When I am seventy,
> In the deserts of America,
> Of a more noble politics
> I shall lay the foundations;
> And on domestic virtue,
> On work, on talents,
> On the good morals of parents,
> On the progress of their children,
> I shall establish the elements,
> The theory, and the practice
> Of public felicity.

Today, I am afraid of not succeeding in forming either one of my republics, for only despotic magistrates make themselves obeyed, and reason, or even self-interest, of course, has very little power over men.

While I am fighting thus against windmills and weathervanes, you are at Maffliers. What is Maffliers? You must be as bored there as in Geneva, if not more so.

At whose house are you?

I have heard a rumor that you were writing in that retreat a defensive preface for the second edition of *Delphine*.

You are quite right to defend yourself. Let the people who speak only by party spirit talk. And write a new work, unless you prefer idleness, such a sweet job, such a precious treasure that it was formerly the portion of the gods.

I have already urged you to cultivate the natural sciences, which I love passionately. You rejected my suggestion with loss to yourself. I believe that you were wrong. Your prodigious ability would make great progress in them, and they would serve you for the education of your son. Of all my education nothing has profited except what my mother taught me.

You have friends. You do not need a multitude of them, and doubtless you have some at *Maffliers*.

You love them very much. Thus, they love you very much. Those are consolations.

If I were a handsome young man, and if I were not afraid that you would make fun of me, I should propose something better to you.

But I must limit myself to saying that I am tenderly and respectfully attached to you.

Madame du Pont sends her regards to you, and I kiss your beautiful hands.

NOTE

1 After the financial chaos of the Revolution and the collapse of the assignats, a group of sixteen persons, in the year VII (1798–99), formed the Banque Territoriale to lend money on real property. Several of the founders proceeded to borrow sums of money from the bank on collateral too highly appraised or already heavily mortgaged. In the year X (1801–2), the bank was robbed of 400,000 francs, and although the thieves were captured, only 200,000 francs were recovered. This episode damaged the credit of the bank. Then the Law of the 24 Germinal year XI (April 14, 1803), which suppressed all banknotes issued by private banks, forced the Banque Territoriale to withdraw its notes. It could not redeem all those presented and was soon forced to suspend payment (*Affaire de la Banque territoriale*, *Précis* [Paris, 1808], pp. 2–8).

49

Necker to du Pont de Nemours

25 October 1803

WMSS 2/17

Votre maison de Newyork me doit Monsieur au premier de juillet dernier l'interest d'un an sur 8889.60/100 dollars et l'interest de deux ans sur 295 1/100 dollars. Dans l'attente que vous me previendriez a cet egard je ne vous ai point ecrit. Je vous prie de vouloir bien m'envoyer votre mandat pour cet objet ou de m'indi- quer quelque autre mode de payement qui vous seroit plus agre- able. Agreez Monsieur les assurances de mon inviolable attache- ment.

Necker

25 octobre 1803

On the reverse:

Monsieur Dupont
de Nemours Chez M^rs
Gros Davelier & Comp^e
a Paris

Postmark:

7 B^re An 12
Geneve 99

TRANSLATION

Your New York firm owes me, Sir, from last July 1 the interest for one year on $8,889.60 and the interest for two years on $295.01. With the expectation that you would inform me about this matter, I did not write to you. I beg you to be so kind as to send me your order for this purpose or to indicate to me some other means of payment which would suit you better. Accept, Sir, the assurances of my inviolable attachment.

Necker

October 25, 1803

On the reverse:

Monsieur Dupont
de Nemours in care of Messrs.
Gros, Davillier and Co.
in Paris

Postmark:

7 Brumaire, year XII
Geneva 99

50

Necker to du Pont de Nemours

10 November 1803

WMSS 2/17

Conformement a votre lettre Monsieur du 10 Brumaire je charge Mʳˢ Hentsch et C[ⁱ]ᵉ de Geneve[1] de tirer sur vous—2925 francs et 42 centimes, a un jour de datte selon l'avis qu'ils vous en donneront.

Toujours avec le plus parfait attachement.

Necker

10 Novembre 1803

TRANSLATION

In conformity with your letter, Sir, of the 10 Brumaire, I am ordering Messrs. Hentsch and Co. of Geneva[1] to draw on you 2,925 francs and 42 centimes, at one day from this date according to the information that they will give you.

Always with the most perfect attachment.

Necker

November 10, 1803

NOTE

1 A Swiss banking firm. Henri Hentsch (1761–1835) established banks in Geneva, Lyon, and Paris. At his home near Geneva, he entertained such distinguished guests as the Empress Josephine, Queen Hortense, Byron, and Mme. de Staël (*Journaux intimes,* p. 510, n. 1 [to p. 288 of text]).

51

Necker to du Pont de Nemours

15 November 1803

WMSS 2/17

J'ai receu Monsieur la lettre que vous m'avez fait l'honneur de m'écrire le 10 Brumaire. On vous employe donc toujours tant que l'on peut pour les choses publiques et de preference pour celles qui exigent un travail desinteresse. J'ai vu dans les papiers publics que vous aviez èté mis a la tete de la banque territoriale.¹ Ne prenez de tout cela je vous prie que l'indispensable.

J'ai autorisé Mrs Hentsch & c[ie] de tirer sur vous a un jour de datte 2925 francs & 42 centimes; mais il y a erreur ce me semble dans le calcul puisqu'il faut joindre a la somme d'interest que vous m'avez payée l'annèe dernier l'interest a 6 p[our] c[ent] pour deux ans soit 12 pour cent sur 295 piastres. Ce qui feroit 35 piastres et quelques centimes et a 5 f[rancs] 6 s[ols] environ 185£. Revoyez cela a votre loisir.

Nous aurons le tems de nous entendre d'icy au p[remi]er juillet prochain pour le remboursement qui m'est du a cette epoque.

J'ai execute votre comission auprès de mon frere. Agreez je vous prie les assurances de mon inviolable attachement.

Necker

15 Novembre 1803

On the reverse:

M. Dupont de Nemours
recomandé
a Mrs Gros Davelier et C
a Paris

Postmark:

29 B^{re} an 12

TRANSLATION
I have received, Sir, the letter that you honored me by writing the 10 Brumaire. You are still employed as much as possible in public affairs and, by preference, in those which require disinterested work. I have seen in the papers that you had been placed at the head of the Banque Territoriale.¹ Do only what is essential in all that, I beg you.

I have authorized Messrs. Hentsch and Co. to draw on you at one day from this date the sum of 2,925 francs and 42 centimes. However, it seems to me that there is an error in the figures, since one must add to the interest that you paid me last year, the interest at 6 per cent for two years, or 12 per cent on 295 piastres, which would make 35 piastres and a few centimes, and at 5 francs 6 sous, about £185. Check that at your leisure.

We shall have time to come to an agreement before next July 1 for the payment of what is due me then.

I have transmitted your message to my brother. Accept, I beg you, the assurances of my inviolable attachment.

Necker

November 15, 1803

On the reverse:

M. du Pont de Nemours
registered
at Messrs. Gros, Davillier and Co.
in Paris

Postmark:

29 Brumaire, year XII

N O T E
1 See Letter 48.

52

Necker de Germany to du Pont de Nemours

23 November 1803

WMSS 2/17

En consequence Monsieur, de la lettre que vous m'avez fait l'honneur de m'écrire le 10 Brumaire je viens de tirer sur vous fr. 1060 a un jour de datte valeur des interets qui me sont dus et à l'ordre de Grivel.[1] Je suis bien aise que vous ayez de bonnes nouvelles d'amérique. J'aimerois bien aussi scavoir quelque chose de plus précis des deux sociétés dans lesquelles j'y suis interessé sous la direction de messieurs vos fils. Je n'ai jamais scu si le fond capital de l'une et de l'autre en etoit definitivement affecté et à combien d'actions de 2000 dollars chacune il s'elevoit, quels en etoient les gérans solidaires: si vous & Mr Bureau de Puzy avez pu cesser de l'etre avant la fin de la societe, si la société ci-devant à New York a son siege à Paris conformément aux derniers arrangemens si vous en êtes le seul gérant en Europe si la maison pour la frabrique de la poudre a fait ses établissemens: si elle travaille, si elle a des succes &c &c. J'avoue que malgré mon entieree confiance en messieurs vos fils & vous, cette maniere d'ignorer les choses les plus simples de ne pas entendre parler de bilans ni de resultat de bilans, qui ne ressemble en rien à ce qui se pratique dans les autres sociétés n'est rien moins que satisfaisante ou du moins merite d'etre motivée et expliquée. Un mot je vous prie sur tout cela, et vous obligerez votre dévoué serviteur.

Necker de Germany

Geneve le 23 9bre 1803

On the reverse:

A Monsieur
Dupont de Nemours
à Paris

TRANSLATION

As a result, Sir, of the letter that you honored me by writing the 10 Brumaire, I have just drawn on your account 1,060 francs at one day from this date, the value of the interest which is due to me and to the order of Grivel.[1] I am very happy that you have some good news from America. I should like also to know something more exact about the two companies in which I am interested and which are under the direction of your two sons. I have never known whether the capital fund of either company was definitely appropriated and of how many shares at $2,000 it consisted, who its responsible managers were, if you and M. Bureaux de Pusy could cease to be so before the end of the company, if the company formerly in New York has its office in Paris in conformity with the latest arrangements, whether you are its sole manager in Europe, whether the company for making gunpowder has been established, whether it is operating, whether it has any success, etc. I confess that, in spite of my complete confidence in your sons and you, this manner of not knowing the simplest things, of not hearing about balance-sheets or the result of balance-sheets, which resembles in no way what is done in other companies, is anything but satisfactory, or at least, deserves to be justified and explained. A word, I beg you, about all that, and you will oblige your devoted servant.

Necker de Germany

Geneva, November 23, 1803

On the reverse:

To Monsieur
du Pont de Nemours
in Paris

NOTE

1 Probably Louis Grivel, a native of the canton of Vaud, who was the partner of Etienne Delessert from 1778 to 1788, and apparently, at this time, director of Grivel et Compagnie, the Swiss banking firm (Herbert Lüthy, *La Banque protestante en France de la Révocation de l'Edit de Nantes à la Révolution* [Paris, 1959], II, 622, n. 50; 684, n. 131; 712, n. 21).

53

du Pont de Nemours to Necker de Germany

4 December 1803

From a draft, WMSS 2/5

Paris 12 Frimaire 12

A Mr Necker de Germany.

Vos demandes sont très justes, Monsieur, et je n'aurais pas du les attendre. Mais je me trouve a Paris plus de travail et moins de santé que je ne désirerais.[1]

Cependant jusqu'à present je suffis a tout.

Notre principale compagnie n'a plus pour Administrateurs que mon fils ainé[2] et moi.

Le plus jeune[3] en se cantonnant au fonds des bois dans son moulin à poudre a du abandonner les affaires générales et en donner sa demission. Et Mr de Pusy ne pouvait certainement administrer en même tems une Prefecture en France et une grande affaire en amerique. Il a donné sa demission dès qu'il a eu accepté la Préfecture de Moulins.

Je l'avais envoyé en Europe pour y tenir notre maison centrale de correspondance dont je me suis chargé après lui; et pour terminer avec la Cour d'Espagne une affaire de Piastres sur laquelle nous avions de tres belles données mais que la Paix a rendue sans objet, et dont la prosperite ne peut avoir lieu dans la guerre presente tant que l'Espagne gardera sa neutralité.[4]

Revenant à vos autres questions, je vous parlerai d'abord de la société principale puis de celle de la Poudre à feu.

Notre premiere société dont vous avez vu la naissance avait êté formée sur un très grand plan; et avait eu pour trois millions deux cent mille livres de souscriptions.

Mais les divers evenemens qui ont eu lieu en France en Holland et en Suisse entre le 18 fructidor An 5 et le 18 brumaire An 8 ont mis la plus grande partie des soumissionnaires hors d'etat de faire ou de completter leurs fonds, il n'y avait de réalisé lors de notre depart que 397,500 F. sur lesquels nous perdîmes la premiere année 30,200 francs dans la faillite de Corsange.[5]

Les administrateurs n'ont donc eu à leur disposition que 367300 et même que 361500, car les 5800 francs qu'on a retiré de Corsange sur 36,000 qu'il avait eu entre les mains n'ont ete touchés que l'année derniere et c'est dans les deux dernieres qu'ont eté realisées votre mise et celle de Mr du Quesnoy[6] [montant en comble?] a 42,400.

A la somme fournie en argent par les sociétaires doit être ajoutée la valeur des terres du Kentucky que Mr Bidermann a mises dans la société, pour ce qu'elles sont ou seront.[7] Nous les estimons a 80,000 aujourd'hui comme alors. Elles ne procureront de dividende qu'a compter du jour où elles seront vendues, elles coutent des impositions et un agent il est vrai très médiocrement payé. Mais cependant elles sont une richesse. Il y a cinquante six mille acres dont seize mille ne sont pas contestés. J'ai donné ordre de racheter le procès de celles qui sont en contestation.

L'actif actuel y compris ces mêmes terres est de	609,000
et le passif de	69,000
reste net	540,000
d'ou deduisant les terres du Kentucky	80,000
il y a en autres biens fonds ou produits de commerce	460,000
d'ou retranchant encore la rentrée et une de Corsange vos fonds et ceux de Mr du Quesnoy nouvellement reçus	48,200
nous trouvons	411,800
provenans de 361500.	

Le capital après avoir payé tous les frais d'etablissement et de voyage est donc accru de 50,500,[8] ou de quatorze pour cent du fonds primitif. Ce benefice le payement de 98,000 fr. d'interets et le remplacement de tous les frais n'est le fruit que des deux dernieres années, la prudence avait voulu que nous hasardassions très peu dans les trois premieres et la necessité que nous dépenssassions beaucoup.

Une operation heureuse à St Domingue et la relache d'une escadre a New York dont nous avons ete bien payés nous ont conduit a ce résultat.[9]

Nous avons quelque risque à courir sur des traites du Gouvernement. Mes amis auprès de lui m'assurent cependant qu'elles seront payées et j'ai tout lieu de l'esperer. J'ai les preuves exigées pour le payement.

Nous avons une suite d'affaires à la Guadeloupe qui ne sont pas dangereuses parce que les retours se font en caffé et qui sont profitables.[10]

Ce n'avait pas du tout été mon plan de faire la moindre affaire de commerce, mais n'ayant point assez de fonds pour de grandes operations de culture, et les terres etant en baisse continue pendant mon sejour en amerique comme je l'ai dans le tems exposé a Mr votre frere et a vous Monsieur j'ai été obligé de me résoudre a suspendre l'execution de mes propres idées jusqu'à ce que nous fussions plus riches que les operations terriennes fussent meilleures, et que notre maison mieux connue aux Etats unis eut acquis la renommée qui nous dispenserait de les faire toutes en argent effectif.

Je reviendrai à la terre et fuirai la mer le plus tot que je le pourrai.

J'ai racheté pour la compagnie l'interet de Mr Abbema.[11] Il avait souscrit pour cinq actions. Il n'en avait payé qu'une et demie. Au lieu de disputer avec ses creanciers pour nous faire payer les trois autres et demie, dont ils n'auraient fait les fonds que successivement et qu'au marc la livre des autres payemens supposé qu'ils y eussent été condamnés, j'ai cru mieux faire de retirer l'action et demie pour 14,000 francs qu'ils ont acceptés.

Je ne l'aurais pourtant pas fait si j'eusse alors prévu l'acquisition que les Etats unis ont fait de la Louisianne. C'est là que les operations territoriales sont dans leur plus heureux germe, et que le commerce interieur par l'Ohio et le Mississipi ne comporte aucune danger. C'est la que tendront à present les canadiens qui ne peuvent souffrir les anglais et n'aimaient pas mieux les Espagnols. C'est là que viendront les hollandais, les suisses, et ceux des Français qui ont le gout de la colonisation.

Toute espece de capital versé à la Louisiane doit y quintupler dans le tems qui reste à courir de notre société et je suis très disposé à m'y rendre moi même, si un certain nombre de nouveaux actionnaires ou les benefices des autres parties de nos affaires m'y donnent le moyen d'y operer sur une echelle un peu etendue. Une augmentation dans le nombre des actionnaires serait à present de la plus haute importance pour ceux qui le sont deja.

Quant à notre seconde société dont je fais encore plus de cas que de la premiere parce que j'aime mieux un métier assuré qu'une speculation quelconque, vous savez que la premiere y est la plus forte interessée.

Vous savez encore que trois parts avaient été reservées sans faire fonds pour un personnage[12] qui sous le precedent gouvernement des Etats unis pouvait nous procurer une infiniment utile protection. Mon fils a céde ces trois parts pour une mise réelle de trois actions dont les fonds etaient necessaires car les frais d'etablissement sont toujours un peu plus forts qu'on n'a pu les calculer, et sous le gouvernement de l'excellent Mr Jefferson, il ne faut d'autre protection que l'utilité même de son travail.

Toutes les constructions sont finies, la fabrication de la poudre commence et continuera sans autre interruption que celle que peuvent necessiter les glaces.

Le ministre de la guerre[13] est venu visiter la manufacture. Il en a été parfaitement satisfait et en a rendu au Président le compte le plus avantageux. Il a promis de nous donner tout le salpêtre de l'etat a rafiner et toutes ses poudres à rebattre.

Cette portion de notre entreprise ne peut nous donner moins de trente pour cent de benefice l'année prochaine, de quarante la suivante et de cinquante celles d'après.

Je souhaite Monsieur que ces renseignemens remplissent vos vues.

Salut et attachement respectueux.

Paris, 12 Frimaire, year XII

To M. Necker de Germany.

Your questions are very just, Sir, and I ought not to have waited for them. But I find myself in Paris with more work and less health than I should like.[1]

However, up to the present time I have been handling everything.

Our main company now has as its only administrators my older son[2] and me.

The younger one,[3] by withdrawing to the depths of the woods to his powder mill, had to abandon general business affairs and resign. And M. de Pusy certainly could not administer at the same time a prefecture in France and a large business in America. He resigned as soon as he had accepted the Prefecture of Moulins.

I had sent him to Europe to direct our central correspondence office, which I took charge of after him, and to conclude with the Spanish Court a matter concerning piastres about which we had very good information but which the peace has rendered purposeless and which cannot prosper in the present war as long as Spain maintains its neutrality.[4]

Returning to your other questions, I shall speak to you first about the main company and then about the powder company.

Our first company, which you saw born, had been formed on a very large scale, and had had 3,200,000 livres subscribed.

But the various events which took place in France, in Holland, and in Switzerland between the 18 Fructidor, year V [September 4, 1791] and the 18 Brumaire, year VIII [November 9, 1799] made the largest number of the tenderers incapable of investing or of completing the investment of their funds. At the time of our departure, we had collected only 397,500 francs, from which we lost, in the first year, 30,200 francs in Corsange's[5] bankruptcy.

The administrators had, therefore, at their disposal only 367,300 francs and really only 361,500 francs, for the 5,800 francs which we got from Corsange of the 36,000 that he had had in his hands were drawn only last year, and it has been in the last two years that we obtained your investment and that of M. du Quesnoy,[6] amounting to 42,400.

To the sum the stockholders furnished in cash must be added

the value of the land in Kentucky which M. Bidermann invested in the company, for its present or future worth.[7] We appraise it at 80,000 francs today, as we did earlier. It will not bring any dividend until the day it is sold. We have to pay taxes and an agent, who is very poorly paid, it is true. But it is still a form of wealth. There are 56,000 acres, 16,000 of which are not contested. I have given an order to settle out of court the law-suit of the land which is contested.

The present assets, including this land are	609,000 fr.
and the liabilities	69,000
net balance	540,000
from which, deducting the Kentucky land	80,000
There is in other real estate or commercial products	460,000
from which, deducting the money from Corsange, your funds and those of M. du Quesnoy newly received	48,200
we find	411,800 fr.
coming from	361,500 fr.

The capital, after we had paid all the expenses of establishment and the trip, has increased by 50,500[8] francs, or 14 per cent of the original fund. This profit, the payment of 98,000 francs interest, and the repayment of all the expenses is only the result of the last two years. Prudence had required us to gamble very little during the first three and necessity required us to spend a great deal.

A fortunate operation in Santo Domingo and the call of a naval squadron at New York, for which we were well paid, have brought us this result.[9]

We have to run some risk on some drafts of the government. My friends in it assure me, however, that they will be paid, and I have every reason to hope for it. I have the proof required for payment.

We have a continuing business with Guadeloupe which is not dangerous because the returns are made in coffee, which is profitable.[10]

It had not been my plan to engage in commerce at all; but since I did not have enough funds for big farming operations and since land has continually decreased in value during my stay in America, as I have formerly revealed to your brother and you, Sir, I was obliged to suspend the execution of my own plans until we were richer, land development was in a better condition, and our company, better known in the United States, had acquired the reputation that would free us from paying for land in cash.

I shall return to the land and leave the sea as soon as I can.

I repurchased for the company the investment of M. Abbema.[11] He had subscribed for five shares. He had paid for only one and a half. Instead of disputing with his creditors to be paid for the other three and a half, for which they would have acquired the funds only successively and at the rate of one mark per livre from the other payments, supposing that they had been forced to pay, I considered it better to withdraw the share and a half for 14,000 francs, which they accepted.

I should not have done it, however, if I had then foreseen the acquisition that the United States made of Louisiana. It is there that land operations are in their most fortunate germ and that internal commerce by the Ohio and the Mississippi presents no danger. It is there that the Canadians who cannot stand the English and did not like the Spanish any better will tend to go. It is there that the Dutch, the Swiss, and those of the French who have a taste for colonization will come.

Any kind of capital invested in Louisiana must quintuple during the time that our company will last, and I am very much inclined to go there myself, if a certain number of new stockholders or the profits from the other parts of our business give me the means of operating there on a rather extensive scale. An increase in the number of stockholders would be, at present, of the greatest importance for those who are already stockholders.

As for our second company, to which I attach still more importance than the first because I prefer an assured job to any kind of speculation, you know that the first one is the most involved in it.

You know also that three shares had been reserved without payment for a person[12] who, under the preceding government of the United States, could obtain for us an infinitely useful protection. My son yielded these three shares for a real payment for three shares of stock whose funds were necessary, because the expenses of starting business are always a bit higher than one can calculate them; and under the government of the excellent Mr. Jefferson, one needs no other protection than the usefulness of one's work.

All the buildings are finished, the manufacture of the powder is beginning and will continue without any other interruption than that which the ice may necessitate.

The Secretary of War[13] has come to visit the factory. He was completely satisfied with it and gave the President the most favorable report about it. He promised to give us all the government's saltpeter to refine and all its powder to remake.

That part of our enterprise cannot give us less than 30 per cent profit next year, 40 the following year, and 50 those after that.

I hope, Sir, that this information will bring you to date.

Greetings and respectful attachment.

NOTES

1 In a letter to Victor du Pont dated 18 Nivôse, year XII (January 9, 1804; WMSS 2/5), du Pont de Nemours writes: "Je suis malade. Je l'ai été de la poitrine un vessicatoire m'en a tiré. Je le suis de nouveau de la goute dans l'estomac et les entrailles avec des douleurs cruelles." ("I am ill. I had an infection in the chest; a vesicatory pulled me out of it. I am ill again from gout in the stomach and entrails, with cruel pains.")

2 Victor du Pont.

3 Eleuthère-Irénée du Pont.

4 See Letter 33 and note 1 to that letter.

5 A Paris banker, in whose bank du Pont de Nemours had deposited, in 1798, about 36,000 francs for safekeeping. The bankruptcy of a certain Haraneder caused the collapse of Corsange's bank that same year. Du Pont tried to recover all his funds, since they were merely on deposit and drew no interest. A legal decision reached on April 4, 1799, stated that his money should be returned to him in its entirety. But as he says, he was unable to recover the whole amount. For an account of this episode and the judges' decisions, see the *Mémoires à consulter et Consultations, sur les dépots en banque*, which consists of three *consultations* and a *résumé général et conclusion*. The first *consultation* is signed by Cambacérès, Emmery, La Cretelle aîné, and Bigot-Préameneu, and is dated 23 Pluviose, year VII; the second, by Redon and Le Brun and dated 26 Ventose, year VII; the third, by Muraire and Siméon and dated 1 Germinal, year VII; the final part, by J.-B. Sirey and dated 15 Germinal, year VII.

6 Adrien Cyprien Duquesnoy (1759–1808). A member of the States General and Constituent Assembly, he was placed in the prison of La Force, during the Terror because of his moderate views. He and du Pont de Nemours, who had also been imprisoned there, became close friends at this time. Duquesnoy later invested in the du Pont enterprises (*E. I. du Pont*, II, 337, *et passim*). Bonaparte, on his rise to power, appointed him to several government positions, and Duquesnoy remained a prominent figure until 1805, when he fell out of favor with the Emperor.

Victor du Pont notes on March 14, 1801: "I dined with Duquesnoy who is now very rich and living *à la mode du jour*, that is at a very great expence. There is not a more active man than he; he is mayor of one of the sections of Paris, Director general of the salt pits; he belongs to all the Commissions for the administration of the hospitals and establishments for the poor and he finds time to write pamphlets and translate books. He is very much attached to our family" (*1801 Journey*, p. 49).

7 See Letter 18 and note 13 to that letter.

8 In a copy made by Gustave Schelle of the final version of this letter in the Archives at Coppet, this figure reads *60,100*.

9 In 1801 a French expedition under General Leclerc was sent to Haiti, then called Saint-Domingue or Santo Domingo, to overthrow Toussaint L'Ouverture, who had revolted against French rule, and to restore slavery on the island. Obviously, the French frigates and transports could be supplied more easily from the United States than from France. In 1802, Victor du Pont made arrangements through Louis André Pichon, the French Consul General in Washington, to send supplies to the French troops, and three ships were dispatched.

At the end of 1803, four French naval vessels arrived in New York from the colonies. They were in a desperate situation, badly in need of food, clothing, and money. Their efforts to obtain help from General Rey, the French Consul, from Pichon, and from various commercial firms met with little or no success, because of distrust of the French government. Various persons tried to convince Victor du Pont that if he advanced the needed supplies, he would be reimbursed without difficulty, thanks to his father's presence in France. The French naval commanders appealed also to his patriotism. Consequently, in spite of his own rather precarious financial position, Victor du Pont arranged to come to the assistance of his compatriots (B. G. du Pont, *Lives of Victor and Josephine du Pont* [Newark, Del., 1930], 147–48).

Because of his suspicion of irregularities in the drafts, and also of Pichon himself, Napoleon refused to pay anything to settle the accounts of either of these unfortunate business ventures. Victor du Pont was eventually ruined financially. He left New York City to settle at Angelica, New York, before ultimately joining his brother in Wilmington.

In Paris, du Pont de Nemours made every effort to collect these bills but failed to do so. Thus ended the hopes of a fortune to be made from the newly formed company and began the series of financial woes revealed in this correspondence.

10 Ambrose Saricks notes: "Five of the seven projects which he [du Pont de Nemours] had elaborated concerned various services which his company could perform for the French government. These covered such matters as marketing sugar from Guadeloupe and French Guiana during the period of warfare between France and Britain" (*Pierre Samuel Du Pont de Nemours* [Lawrence, Kans., 1965], p. 283).

11 Balthasar Elias Abbema (1739–1805), a Dutch banker. One of the leaders of the Dutch republicans, Abbema left the Netherlands after the defeat of that group and settled in Paris in 1787. There, he entered the banking business and served for a time as administrator of the Compagnie des Indes and of the Caisse d'Escompte. In 1795, he became minister of the Batavian Republic in Hamburg (Herbert Lüthy, *La Banque protestante en France de la Révocation de l'Edit de Nantes à la Revolution* (Paris, 1959), II, 623–24, n. 55.

In Victor du Pont's Letter Book, there are copies of three letters written to Abbema's son in 1801. They reveal that the Abbemas had lost interest in providing all the capital they had promised for the new company.

12 Colonel Tousard. See Letter 28, note 3.
13 General Henry Dearborn.

54

Necker to du Pont de Nemours

21 January 1804

WMSS 2/22

Vous aurez surement receu Monsieur ma derniere lettre où je vous prevenois de la disposition que je faisois sur vous pour les interests qui m'etoient dus & où je relevois une erreur de calcul a mon desavantage faite dans la supputation de ces interests.

Vous scavez Monsieur qu'au premier Juillet de l'année actuelle le capital est exigible et ce n'est pas trop tôst pour y songer si je dois faire recevoir cet argent en Amerique et donner des directions a cet egard. Je n'ai aucun éloignement pour être payé en france mais le change de 5 f[rancs], 6 sols me seroit trop onereux et dans une affaire qui m'a causé par hasard un grand prejudice je dois y prendre garde. Je crois que cinq francs & huit sols par piastre seroit le tau raisonable. Enfin Monsieur il convient que nous en-tendions à l'avance sur tout cela.

Je vous renouvelle avec empressement Monsieur, les assurances de mon inviolable attachement.

[Sans signature]

Geneve, le 21 janvier 1804

TRANSLATION

You will certainly have received my last letter, in which I in-formed you of the arrangement which I was making where you were concerned for the interest which was due me and in which I pointed out an error in arithmetic to my disadvantage made in the computation of that interest.

You know, Sir, that the capital is payable on July 1 of the pres-ent year, and it is not too soon to be thinking about whether I am to be paid this money in America and to be giving orders for that purpose. I have no objection to being paid in France, but the rate of exchange at five francs, six sous would be too unfavorable for me, and in an affair which has caused me, by accident, a great loss, I must be careful. I believe that five francs and eight sous per piastre would be a reasonable rate. In any case, Sir, we should come to an agreement in advance about all that.

I repeat earnestly, Sir, the assurances of my inviolable attachment.

[No signature]

Geneva, January 21, 1804

NOTE

The text of this letter is taken from the original manuscript at the Eleutherian Mills Historical Library. The place, date, and last paragraph, however, are missing in that letter and have been taken from a typed copy which Gustave Schelle made of a duplicate at the château of Coppet and presented to the late Colonel Henry A. du Pont. Schelle attributes this letter to Necker de Germany, but the letter at the Eleutherian Mills Historical Library is unmistakably in Jacques Necker's handwriting, and it is unlikely that the two men would have written identical letters; moreover, the first paragraph of the letter seems clearly to refer to Jacques Necker's letter of November 15, 1803 (Letter 51).

In a letter to Victor du Pont preserved in the Eleutherian Mills Historical Library and dated 18 Nivôse, year XII (January 9, 1804), du Pont de Nemours writes: "J'espere me soutenir jusqu'en Prairial: quoique les embarras augmentent tous les jours. Mais à cette époque je ne me vois point de fonds pour payer les interets de mes actions, bien moins pour rembourser Mr Necker et pas même pour aller vous rejoindre." ("I hope to hold on until Prairial, although troubles increase every day. But at this time, I do not see any funds to pay the interest on my shares of stock, much less to reimburse M. Necker, and not even to go join you.")

In another letter to Victor du Pont written 8 Pluviôse, year XII (January 29, 1804; WMSS 2/5), du Pont states that Van Merbeck (see Letter 57, note 11) wants 4,000,000 francs, that there is no possibility of collecting the money due them from the government (see Letter 53, note 9), and that his position is in danger. He writes:

Mon existence physique devient ici d'une extrême difficulté. Mon existence morale commence à être insupportable; et elle empirera.

J'ai encore de la consideration dans le commerce; et elle est très embarrassante à soutenir sans fortune.

J'en ai chez les gens de lettres et dans les sociétés du second ordre. Ailleurs depuis quelque tems je n'ai que des dégouts.

Les traites de St. Domingue m'ont entierement perdu.

(My physical existence here is becoming extremely difficult. My state of mind is beginning to be unbearable, and it will get worse.

I still have some respect in the world of business, and it is very difficult to uphold without any money.

I have some among men of letters and in second-rate associations. Elsewhere, for some time I have been having only unpleasantness.

The Santo Domingo drafts have completely ruined me.)

A postscript of 22 Ventôse (March 13) adds:

Ma situation personnelle est chaque jour plus desagréable. Je suis réduit à la plus necessaire economie, et à essuyer des airs protecteurs de la part d'un tas de petits personnages qui n'ont ni le pouvoir ni l'envie de me proteger, et qui me faisaient la cour il y a un an.

. . . .

Mᵣ Necker me demande le remboursement des cinquante mille francs que nous avons à lui payer le 1ᵉʳ Juillet. Nous sommes là dessus dans une belle correspondance dont j'ignore quel sera le résultat.

. . . .

Je voudrais pouvoir retourner embrasser mes chers petits enfans; et cela même je ne le puis.

(My personal situation is more disagreeable each day. I am reduced to the strictest economy and to putting up with patronizing airs from a group of people of no consequence who have neither the power nor the desire to help me, and who were paying court to me a year ago.

. . . .

M. Necker is asking me for the repayment of the 50,000 francs that we owe him on July 1. We are having a fine correspondence about that, and I do not know what the result will be.

. . . .

I should like to be able to return to embrace my dear grandchildren, and I cannot even do that.)

55

Necker de Germany to du Pont de Nemours

23 February 1804

WMSS 2/17

Je vous dois, Monsieur, beaucoup de reconnoissance des détails dans lesquels vous avez eu la complaisance d'entrer avec moi par votre lettre du 13 Frimaire. Quoiqu'elle contienne a peu pres tout le nécessaire, cependant il est une derniere importunité dont je ne puis quoiqu'avec regret me dispenser, c'est de vous prier de me dire de *combien d'actions* ayant part en ce moment aux bénefices & aux pertes la société est composée soit celle qui travaille à New-York soit la manufacture de poudres afin que je sache quelle aliquote mon interêt represente un 20ᵉ un 30ᵉ un 40ᵉ enfin quoi, et dans quelle proportion j'ai part aux pertes & aux benefices. 2° s'il y a eu des pertes essuyées dans la société de New York, ou des bénéfices acquis, avant que j'y dusse [*sic*] part & s'il y a eu des moyens pris pour les connoitre [. . .]¹ les réserver ou les faire supporter a qui de droit. Les noms des actionnaires ne sont pas absolument necessaires. Cependant je mettrois quelque prix a les connoitre. A mesure que l'on avance en age et que les infirmites arrivent on met plus d'importance à donner aux affaires toute la regularite dont elles sont susceptibles et qui au surplus est usitée dans toutes les sociétés.

Vous comprenez, Monsieur, que je ne veux prendre qu'un quart d'heure de votre tems et que je n'attends qu'une reponse très courte, peut etre Monsʳ Roman voudra bien vous en épargner l'embarras.

Vous connoissez mieux que personne l'amérique et M. Jefferson. Avez vous des moyens de justifier le rapport du comité sur les Florides? Il me suffit de scavoir que oui pour que sans autre detail je me separe de ceux qui s'en scandalisent en apparence avec juste raison.²

Agréez, Monsieur, les sinceres assurances de ma haute considération.

Necker de Germany

Genève le 3 ventose an 12

On the reverse:

a Monsieur Dupont
de Nemours
à Paris

Postmark:

7 [Ventôse] an 12 99 Genève

TRANSLATION

I owe you, Sir, much gratitude for the details which you had the kindness to go into in your letter of the 13 Frimaire. Although it contains almost everything necessary, there is still one last bothersome detail which, regretfully, I cannot do without: that is to ask you to tell me *how many shares* now participate in the profits and losses of the company, either the one in business in New York or the powder factory, so that I may know what aliquot my interest represents, one twentieth, one thirtieth, one fortieth—in short, what share have I in the losses and profits and in what proportion?

Secondly, whether there were any losses suffered or profits gained in the New York company before I had a share, and whether action was taken to account [. . .] [1] for them, reserve them, or have them borne by those concerned. The names of the shareholders are not absolutely necessary. However, I should attach some importance to knowing them. As one grows older and infirmities arrive, one attaches more importance to giving to business matters all the orderliness possible, which, moreover, is customary in all companies.

You understand, Sir, that I wish to take only a quarter of an hour of your time, and I expect only a very brief answer. Perhaps M. Roman will be willing to spare you the trouble.

You know America and Mr. Jefferson better than anyone else. Have you any way of justifying the report of the Florida committee? It is enough for me to know that you do, without any other detail, to separate myself from those who are shocked by it and apparently with good reason.[2]

Accept, Sir, the sincere assurances of my high consideration.

Necker de Germany

Geneva, 3 Ventôse, year XII

On the reverse:

to Monsieur du Pont
de Nemours
in Paris

Postmark:

7 [Ventôse], year XII 99 Geneva

NOTES

1 An illegible word.

2 An allusion to the controversy over the Floridas. The Treaty of San Ildefonso, which returned Louisiana to France, did not settle the boundaries of that colony in the east or in the west. They were defined only as those that the colony had under Spain and previously under France, which were not identical. With the Louisiana Purchase in 1803, the United States became involved in a dispute over these boundaries. There existed a possibility of warfare for some time until the French conquest of Spain put an end to these colonial problems. Jefferson had been determined to round out the boundaries of the United States and claimed that the two Floridas had been included in the Louisiana Purchase.

56

du Pont de Nemours to Necker

27 February 1804

From a copy by Gustave Schelle, wmss 8/108

A Monsieur Necker, à Coppet, par Genève

Paris, 7 Ventose 12

Monsieur,

Je n'ai point encore renoncé à effectuer votre remboursement à l'époque indiquée. C'est pour que vous n'eussiez pas à me reprocher de vous avoir induit en erreur à cet égard que je me suis cru dans l'obligation rigoureuse, et qui m'a été très pénible, de vous faire part de mon inquiétude sur l'èvènement qui peut m'en ôter la possibilité, supposé que je ne trouve pas un autre moyen d'y pourvoir d'ici là.

Le plus simple de tous serait véritablement une augmentation de capital par l'union à notre Société de Gens qui sentiront quel beau théatre présente la Louisiane, et qui concevraient combien peuvent etre utiles les lumières que j'ai acquises dans le pays, tant sur les suites de cette acquisition faite par les Etats-Unis et que je prévoyais, que sur les moyens d'attendre pour la revente l'accroissement de la valeur des terres qu'on aurait acquises, en tirant sans danger de très grands profits du commerce intérieur par l'Ohio, la Kentucky, la Cumberland et la Tenessée, versant tous quatre au Mississipi.

Je vous enverrai à ce sujet un mémoire.

Le Gouvernement américain m'accorde toute amitié.

Je ne ferais aucun tort à ma société en prenant sur ses nouveaux fonds le remboursement de ce qu'elle doit sur les anciens.

Elle n'a pas d'autres dettes.

Vous pourriez entrer dans cette addition de société pour le tout ou partie de votre créance.

Votre capital, puisque c'est lui que vous soignez, ne court dans aucun cas aucun risque.

J'avais songé à l'hypothéquer sur *Good Stay*. Mais *Good-Stay* n'étant qu'une maison avec un bien de campagne, j'ai préféré de l'asseoir sur le terrain occupé par notre manufacture de Poudre à feu dont la valeur augmente et augmentera dans une progression bien plus rapide. Et j'en ai chargé mon second fils qui est la délicatesse et la probité mêmes.

Vous voudriez une autre sureté en France. Je vais travailler à vous la procurer; et j'en ai plusieurs espérances.

L'exigeance précipitée sur la manufacture de Poudre nous serait aussi funeste que sur l'une ou l'autre des maisons de commerce. On ne peut briser un anneau d'une chaine.

Ainsi votre revenu sera régulièrement payé dans tous les cas. Et s'il arrivait que votre capital ne put pas être remboursé à l'époque que nous désirons tous deux, il continuera du moins d'être en parfaite sureté.

Ne prenez donc point les soucis, que vous dites qui ne vous vont plus.

Ce n'est pas moi qui voudrais augmenter les vôtres. Ne savez vous pas combien je vous suis dévoué.

Salut et respect.

Du Pont (de Nemours)

TRANSLATION
To M. Necker, at Coppet, near Geneva

Paris, 7 Ventôse, year XII

Sir,

I have not yet given up the idea of paying you at the indicated time. It is so that you would not have to reproach me for having deceived you in that regard that I believed myself to have the strict and painful obligation to inform you of my uneasiness about the event which may render me unable to, supposing that I do not find another means of providing for it before then.

The simplest of all would really be an increase in capital by the addition to our company of people who feel what a fine theater Louisiana presents and understand how useful the knowledge that I acquired in the country can be, both about the results of this acquisition by the United States, which I foresaw, and about the ways of awaiting the increase in the value of the land that we would have acquired for resale, while making, without danger, large profits from the interior commerce on the Ohio, the Kentucky, the Cumberland, and the Tennessee, all four emptying into the Mississippi.

I shall send you a memoir on that subject.

The American Government accords me complete friendship.

I should not harm my company by taking from these new funds the payment of what it owes on the old ones.

It has no other debts.

You could enter this new activity of the company for all or part of your credit.

Your capital, since it is that you are concerned with, runs no risk in any case.

I had thought of mortgaging *Good Stay*. But *Good Stay* being only a house with some surrounding land, I preferred to mortgage the land occupied by our powder factory, whose value is increasing and will increase in a much more rapid progression. And I have instructed my second son, who is the soul of delicacy and probity, to do so.

You would like another guarantee in France. I shall endeavor to obtain it for you, and I have several hopes of it.

A hasty demand on the powder factory would be as disastrous for us as on either one of the business houses. One cannot break a link of a chain.

Thus, your payments will be made regularly in any case. And if it happened that your capital could not be repaid at the time that we both wish, it will continue, at least, to be in perfect safety.

Do not assume worries, therefore, which you say are no longer suitable for you.

It is not I who would like to increase yours. Do you not know how much I am devoted to you?

Greetings and respect.

Du Pont (de Nemours)

NOTE

The text of this letter is taken from a copy made by Gustave Schelle of the original manuscript at the château of Coppet.

57

du Pont de Nemours to Necker de Germany

28 February 1804

From a copy by Gustave Schelle, WMSS 8/108

A Monsieur Necker de Germany

Paris 8 Ventose an 12

Monsieur,

Vous me demandez par votre lettre du 3 de ce mois, combien d'actions ont part aux bénéfices ou aux pertes dans l'une et dans l'autre de nos deux sociétés; et vous désirez aussi savoir le nom des Actionnaires.

En voici le catalogue:

Actionnaires de la Société principale:	Actions	
M. *Bidermann,* sous son nom	8 actions	
et sous celui de M. Roman		13
ou Demorest[1]	5 actions	

Il a, en outre, cédé à la société 56.000 acres de terre dans le Kentucky, dont 40.000 sont sujets à contestation, et dont la propriété sur les 16.000 autres, heureusement situés dans la partie la plus fertile du *Tract,* est assurée. M. Bidermann ne touche aucun intéret pour cette cession. Mais, à mesure que les terres seront vendues et que l'argent en sera reçu, il sera crédité d'autant d'actions que cette rentrée de fonds en pourra payer.

En attendant, les frais généraux sont chargés pour cette partie de l'actif de la société de 60 dollars pour les impositions, et pour le traitement d'un agent de 100. Cet agent est le fils de M. *Mentelle* le géographe.[2] Nous lui avons promis, s'il prend l'engagement de les défricher, de lui donner 200 acres qui commenceront un établissement de culture pour la concession.

C'est dans cette espérance qu'il se contente d'un si faible traitement.

Mon fils est en marché avec trois familles Suisses pour leur vendre à chacune 200 acres, sous la condition que leurs fermes ne

Madame de Staël

From a miniature in the Wallace Collection, Manchester Square,
London. Reproduced by permission of the Trustees of the
Wallace Collection.

Pierre Samuel du Pont de Nemours

From an oil portrait by Rembrandt Peale. The original is now in the
possession of Pierre Samuel du Pont III and is reproduced by his permission.

Jacques Necker

From a Wedgwood medallion made about 1789. The original is now in the
possession of M. Mellanay Delhom of Chicago and is reproduced by her
permission.

J'ai reçu Monsieur la lettre que vous m'avez fait l'amitié de m'écrire le 21 aoust. Toutes vos paroles sont douces et vont a mon cœur. Je souhaite plus que je ne puis vous l'exprimer que vous conserviez longtems tous les biens dont vous pouvez pas une heureuse association par des fils estimables et par la serenité de votre ame... Je ne suis point allé a Paris; la paix est une epoque qui devroit me decider mais je suis encore déchiré entre le desir bien vif d'un rapprochement durable avec mon

First page of a letter from Jacques Necker
to du Pont de Nemours, 29 October 1801

From the Henry Francis du Pont Collection of Winterthur Manuscripts,
Papers of P. S. du Pont de Nemours, Group 2, Box 15. Reproduced
by permission of the Eleutherian Mills Historical Library.

First page of a letter from du Pont de Nemours
to Madame de Staël, 1 May 1802

From the Henry Francis du Pont Collection of Winterthur Manuscripts,
Papers of P. S. du Pont de Nemours, Group 2, Box 4. Reproduced
by permission of the Eleutherian Mills Historical Library.

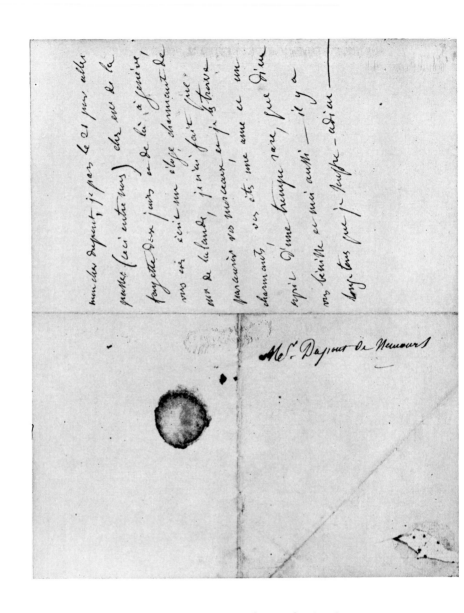

Letter from Madame de Staël
to du Pont de Nemours, April 1807

From the Henry Francis du Pont Collection of Winterthur Manuscripts,
Papers of P. S. du Pont de Nemours, Group 2, Box 19. Reproduced
by permission of the Eleutherian Mills Historical Library.

soient pas contigues; mais laissant entre elles au moins la place d'une autre ferme. Elles devront payer leurs 600 acres en six ans.

	Actions
M. Johannot	5
Du Pont (de Nemours)	6
Mme Du Pont (de Nemours)	1
M. Bureaux de Pusy	5
M. de Crillon	1½
M. Hom[3]	½
M. Ochs,[4] pour lequel on a consenti de mettre cette action au porteur	1
M. Wischer,[5] pour lequel on a consenti de mettre cette action au porteur	1
M. Forcart-Weiss[6]	1
M. Necker de Germany	1
M. Du Quesnoy	3
La société pour rachat par elle fait de l'intérêt de M. Abbema	1½
Total des actions réalisées	40½
Total des actions existantes	39

Vous etes donc intéressé pour $\frac{1}{39}$ dans la Société principale.

Actionnaires de la seconde société.	
M. Bidermann	1
M. Du Quesnoy	1
MM. Bauduit Frères[7]	8
La société principale	10
M. Necker de Germany	1
Total	21

Vous êtes en conséquence intéressé dans cette seconde société pour la manufacture de Poudre à Feu: 1° d'un vingt-unième et 2° du trente neuvième de dix vingt-unièmes; ou un total d'environ $\frac{1}{16}$.

Il n'y a point eu de pertes avant votre entrée dans la société que celle de 32.200 francs, qui a eu lieu par la faillite de Corsange.

On n'a pas cru devoir la regarder, non plus que les frais

d'établissement comme particulière à ceux qui étaient alors actionnaires. Il a paru que les survenans prenaient part à la chose telle qu'elle se poursuivait et comportait. Et le même principe sera observé pour les souscripteurs que l'attrait des terres de la Louisiane et du commerce intérieur dont elle sera le débouché appellera dans notre compagnie.

Ce sont deux opérations, dont la première devient de la plus grande importance depuis l'acquisition de ce nouveau territoire par les Etats-Unis; et dont j'avais préparé la 2de dans tous les détails avant mon départ de l'Amérique.

Il nous est facile d'obtenir à choix, et aux meilleures conditions les Terres qui nous conviendront à la Louisiane. Et sous la sage direction de M. Jefferson, les concessions ne seront pas litigieuses comme celles du Kentucky et de la Virginie. La plus grande partie des Canadiens, qui, depuis plus de 40 ans, n'ont pas su s'accoutumer aux Anglais, et n'ont pas voulu apprendre un mot de leur langue, viendra s'y établir; beaucoup de Hollandais, de Suisses, et de gens de quelques autres nations, y passeront eux-mêmes attirés comme ils le sont par la fécondité du sol. Le décuplement de la valeur du capital y est assuré en très peu de temps.

Quant au commerce intérieur, en fournissant par la maison de New-York à un certain nombre de Stores des différentes vallées, de l'Ohio des rivières y affluentes, les marchandises de leur débit, du sucre, du café, du thé, de l'eau de vie, de la bonneterie, de la toile blanche et peinte, des chapeaux, des draps communs en commission; et les faisant vendre aux Fermiers par compte courant à solder après les récoltes en Farine, planches, potasse, etc. on aura ces marchandises à trente pour cent meilleur marché qu'en argent. On les fera descendre à la nouvelle Orléans avec beaucoup d'économie.

Les Teneurs de Stores gagnant une double commission, et n'étant obligés à aucune avance, soigneront bien nos intérêts de peur de voir manquer leur approvisionnement, ou d'être obligés de le payer en argent dont ils sont dénués.

Il y a déjà exemple de cette façon d'opérer, mais sur trop petite échelle. Il suffit pour la conduire, de deux voyageurs qui aillent tous les ans régler les comptes; et d'une maison d'entrepôt à la nouvelle Orléans. Ce commerce est sûr. Il est peu cultivé. Il ne craint ni révolutions, ni corsaires.

Ces deux perspectives me rendent extrêmement amère la suspension du payement des Traites de St Domingue.[8] Suspension qui a presque entièrement épuisé ce que ma maison de Paris avait de fonds, et qui gêne celle de New-York dans l'établissement du commerce par l'Ohio.

Nous sommes porteurs de 281.017 francs de ces Traites, lesquelles proviennent de fournitures que nous avons faites de compte à demi avec M. Ogden.[9] Ainsi cela nous tient cent quarante mille cinq cent huit francs.

Nous avons de M. Daure,[10] ancien Préfet colonial, les certificats de cette fourniture, et du Garde magasin l'attestation sous serment qu'elle a été effectuée pour le compte et à la décharge de MM. Vanmeerbeke, Granié et Kien,[11] fournisseurs généraux qui nous ont transmis les traites avec lesquelles on les a payés, et qui sont eux-mêmes des Commis associés de M. Guérard.[12]

Il est vrai que nous n'aurons pas à y perdre, attendu qu'il est du quatre millions à MM. Vanmeerbeke, Granié et Kien au delà des Traites qui leur ont été données, et à M. Guérard leur commettant dix huit mille francs de traites qu'il n'a point négociées. De sorte que si le gouvernement trouve leurs comptes sujets à réduction, elle portera d'abord sur les 4.000.000 frs. par eux réclamés, et ensuite sur les Traites qui appartiennent à M. Guérard.

En s'opposant donc à ce que celles-ci soient payées à M. Guérard qui nous doit garantie de son fait et de celui de son commis, il devient aussi impossible qu'il serait injuste que la réduction dont on les frapperait nous atteigne, nous sous-fournisseurs qui avons effectué l'approvisionnement.

Mais la rentrée sera longue, et son retard, comme le grand avantage d'étendre autant qu'il nous sera possible les acquisitions à la Louisiane et le commerce de l'Ohio, nous rend extrêmement important de multiplier nos actionnaires et d'augmenter notre capital.

Revenant à vos questions, Monsieur, je sais qu'on a parlé dans quelques Gazettes anglaises, traduites peut-être par d'autres gazettes, d'un prétendu projet du Gouvernement des Etats-Unis pour s'emparer des Florides par la force. C'est une calomnie britannique.

M. Jefferson qui a résisté à la nation entière et a risqué toute sa popularité, qui s'est exposé à n'être pas réélu, en refusant de s'emparer de la Louisiane, pays presque sans limites et dont le territoire est excellent, ne changera certainement pas de principes après le succès de sa négociation pacifique, et pour les Florides qui n'ont que peu d'étendue, dont le sol n'est qu'un sable stérile, et qui n'importent à la Confédération américaine que par les débouchés que peuvent offrir quelques rivières.

Il les aura sans doute; mais à prix d'argent, comme il vient d'avoir la Louisiane. Et le grand excès de Revenu public des Etats-Unis sur leur dépense lui rendra l'opération facile.

Salut et respectueux attachement.

Du Pont (de Nemours)

Je ne finis que le 16 Ventose cette lettre commencée le 8, et j'y joins duplicata corrigé de la précédente laquelle renfermait une erreur de dix mille francs.

TRANSLATION

To M. Necker de Germany

Paris, 8 Ventôse, year XII

Sir,

You ask me in your letter of the third of this month how many shares have a part in the profits and losses in each of our two companies, and you wish also to know the names of the stockholders.

Here is the list of them:

Stockholders of the main company:	Shares	
M. *Bidermann,* under his own name	8 shares	
and under that of M. Roman		13
or Demorest [1]	5 shares	

In addition, he has transferred to the company 56,000 acres of land in Kentucky, of which 40,000 are in dispute; the ownership of the other 16,000, fortunately situated in the most fertile part of the *Tract,* is assured. M. Bidermann receives no interest on this transfer. But as the land is sold and the money is received for it, he will be credited with as many shares as those funds will pay for.

Meanwhile, the general expenses for that part of the assets of the company are burdened with $60 for taxes and $100 for the salary of an agent. This agent is the son of M. *Mentelle,* the geographer.[2] We promised to give him 200 acres, if he agrees to clear them, which will begin a farming operation for the concession.

It is because of this hope that he is content with such a low salary.

My son is negotiating with three Swiss families to sell 200 acres to each of them, on condition that their farms will not be contiguous, but will leave between them at least the space for another farm. They will have to pay for their 600 acres in six years.

	Shares
M. Johannot	5
Du Pont (de Nemours)	6
Mme. du Pont (de Nemours)	1
M. Bureaux de Pusy	5
M. de Crillon	1½
M. Hom[3]	½
M. Ochs,[4] for whom we agreed to mark this share "to the bearer"	1
M. Wischer,[5] for whom we agreed to mark this share "to the bearer"	1
M. Forcart-Weiss[6]	1
M. Necker de Germany	1
M. Du Quesnoy	3
The company, for the repurchase it made of the interest of M. Abbema	1½
Total shares sold	40½
Total existing shares	39

You have therefore a $\frac{1}{39}$ share in the main company.

Stockholders of the second company.	
M. Bidermann	1
M. Du Quesnoy	1
The Bauduy brothers[7]	8
The main company	10
M. Necker de Germany	1
Total	21

Consequently, your share in this second company for the manufacture of gunpowder amounts to, first, a $\frac{1}{21}$ share, and second, $\frac{1}{39}$ of $\frac{10}{21}$, or a total of about $\frac{1}{16}$.

There were not any losses before your investing in the company except that of 32,000 francs, which resulted from the bankruptcy of Corsange.

We did not believe we should consider the loss, or the expenses of establishing the company, as peculiar to those who were then stockholders. It seemed that the chance comers participated in the thing such as it was carried on and was required. And the same principle will be observed for the subscribers that the appeal of the land in Louisiana, and the internal trade of which it will be the outlet, will attract to our company.

These are two operations, the first of which becomes of the greatest importance, since the acquisition of this new territory by the United States, and the second of which I had prepared in all its details before leaving America.

It is easy for us to obtain at our choice, and on the best conditions, the land which will suit us in Louisiana. And under the wise direction of Mr. Jefferson, the concessions will not be subject to litigation like those of Kentucky and Virginia. The majority of the Canadians, who, for more than forty years, have not been able to accustom themselves to the English and have refused to learn a word of their language, will come and establish themselves there. Many Dutch, Swiss, and people of some other countries will go there themselves, attracted as they are by the fertility of the land. A tenfold increase in the value of the capital is assured there in very little time.

As for internal trade, by supplying from the New York company a certain number of stores of the different valleys of the Ohio and its tributaries with merchandise for retail sale—sugar, coffee, tea, brandy, knit goods, white and printed cloth, hats, and cheap cloth on commission—and having them sold to the farmers on a current account to be settled after the harvests with flour, lumber, potash, etc., we will have this merchandise 30 per cent cheaper than with cash. We shall send it down to New Orleans with great economy.

The storekeepers, earning a double commission, and not being obliged to make any advance, will take good care of our interests for fear of seeing their supplies disappear, or of being obliged to pay for them in cash, which they do not have.

There is already an example of this way of carrying on business, but on too small a scale. To conduct it, two travelers who will go every year to settle the accounts, along with a warehouse in New Orleans, are enough. This business is safe. It is little cultivated. It is subject to neither revolutions nor privateers.

These two prospects make extremely bitter for me the suspension of payment on the Santo Domingo drafts.[8] This suspension has almost entirely exhausted the funds that my Paris office had and hinders the New York office in the establishment of the business along the Ohio.

We have 281,017 francs in these drafts, which result from supplies that we provided in half partnership with Mr. Ogden.[9] So, that amounts to 140,508 francs for us.

We have received from M. d'Aure,[10] the former colonial prefect, the receipts for these supplies, and from the warehouseman the statement under oath that it was effected for the account and for the release of Messrs. Van Merbeck, Granié and Kien,[11] general suppliers, who delivered to us these drafts with which they were paid, and who are themselves representatives associated with M. Guérard.[12]

It is true that we shall not lose in it, considering that four million is due Messrs. Van Merbeck, Granié and Kien beyond the drafts which were given to them and to M. Guérard, their principal, 18,000 francs in drafts which he has not negotiated; so that if the government finds their accounts subject to a reduction, it will bear first on the 4,000,000 francs claimed by them, and then on the drafts which belong to M. Guérard.

By opposing the payment of the latter to M. Guérard, who owes us a warranty on his account and that of his representative, it becomes as impossible as it would be unjust for the reduction which they would suffer to reach us, we the subcontractors who provided the supplies.

But the payment will take a long time, and this delay, like the great advantage of extending, as much as is possible for us, acquisitions in Louisiana and commerce on the Ohio, makes it extremely important for us to increase the number of our stockholders and enlarge our capital.

Returning to your questions, Sir, I know that there has been mention in a few English newspapers, translated perhaps by other papers, of a so-called project of the United States government to seize the Floridas by force. That is a British slander.

Mr. Jefferson, who resisted the whole country and risked all his popularity, who ran the risk of not being reelected by refusing to seize Louisiana, an almost limitless country whose land is excellent, will certainly not change his principles after the success of his peaceful negotiation, and for the Floridas, which have only a small area, whose soil is only a sterile sand, and which have no importance for the American confederation except for the outlets which a few rivers can offer.

He will get them doubtlessly, but for money, as he has just obtained Louisiana. And the great surplus of the public revenue of the United States over expenses will make the operation easy for him.

Greetings and respectful attachment.

Du Pont (de Nemours)

I am finishing only on the 16 Ventôse this letter begun on the eighth, and I am adding to it a corrected duplicate of the preceding one, which contained an error of 10,000 francs.

NOTES

1 The last two words inserted in the margin.

2 Edme Mentelle (1730–1815), the French geographer and historian. He attracted attention with his work *Eléments de géographie* (1783) and was subsequently appointed to the chair of geography and history at the *École Militaire*. At the time of the organization of the *écoles centrales,* he was named professor of geography at the *École normale*. He became a member of the Institut de France upon its creation in 1795 and must have known du Pont de Nemours through that organization.

His son Waldemar acted as the agent for the du Pont company and its holdings near Lexington, Kentucky. Discussions of the younger Mentelle's apparently capable business dealings on behalf of du Pont de Nemours in Kentucky, as well as interesting accounts of frontier life, are found in eleven letters in the Eleutherian Mills Historical Library dated 1801 from Mentelle to du Pont.

According to another letter in the Eleutherian Mills Historical Library from Edme Mentelle to Waldemar Mentelle, dated July 26, 1806, the younger Mentelle had an almost complete break with his father in 1806. In this letter the father reproaches his son in a hostile tone for his ignorance, for his poor scholastic record, and for his having an illegitimate child, born to a Mlle. Leclerc, before his marriage to her. Evidently, Waldemar Mentelle had written his father about a legacy from the estate of his mother, who had died in the year XIII (1804–5); his father's letter indicates that he can expect nothing from his mother's estate, although he had been named her sole heir. Waldemar Mentelle was still living in Kentucky at this time.

3 Gilbert Hom, whose name appears frequently in documents preserved at the Eleutherian Mills Historical Library. Little is known about him, however; see *1801 Journey*, p. 100, n. 27.

4 Peter Ochs, a banker in Basel. In Victor du Pont's Letter Book, there is a copy of a letter written to Ochs on 3 Complementaire, year IX (September 20, 1801) concerning the arrangements for payment of interest due Ochs.

5 J. J. Wischer, another banker in Basel (*E. I. du Pont*, VIII, 59, 305; IX, 239).

6 Forcart-Weiss, or Fourcard-Weiss, another banker in Basel. (See *ibid.*, vols. V, VIII, IX, X.) As late as 1819, he is mentioned as a stockholder in the powder company (*ibid.*, X, 317).

7 This name is usually spelled Bauduy.

For the purposes of this correspondence, the most important of the brothers was Pierre (later anglicized to Peter) Bauduy (1769–1833). A friend of Bureaux de Pusy, he was associated with E. I. du Pont in the early days of the powder company. This relationship was often far from cordial, and many quarrels and problems resulted from it (see vol. II of B. G. du Pont, *Du Pont de Nemours, 1739–1817* [Newark, Del., 1933]; and also *E. I. du Pont*). Peter Bauduy eventually started his own rival powder mill at Eden Park near Wilmington. In 1830 he went to Cuba, where he died.

Another brother, Louis-Alexandre-Amélie Bauduy (1773–1827) was born at Port-au-Prince. He served as an officer with the French troops stationed there and was wounded several times in the Negro uprisings. He was in Wilmington in 1801 and 1802 (*E. I. du Pont*, V, 295, *et passim*). He returned to Haiti later (*ibid.*, VI, 154–55, 188–89) and to France in 1804 (*ibid.*, VI, 306).

There seems to have been a third brother, Eugene Bauduy, of whom little is known (*ibid.*, VI, 107).

8 Napoleon refused to honor these drafts, in spite of du Pont de Nemours' efforts to collect the money due the company; see Letter 53, note 9.

9 Samuel G. Ogden (1746–1810), the American iron founder and land speculator. He invested heavily in land in northern New York, and the town of Ogdensburg, N. Y. owes its name to him. His wife was the sister of Gouverneur Morris.

The Eleutherian Mills Historical Library has a letter written by him from Washington on October 19, 1803, in which he describes his efforts to obtain payment for the supplies sent to Santo Domingo. He attempted to connect the funds due on these drafts with the Louisiana purchase, which was then being negotiated in the Senate.

10 Jean-Pierre-Paulin-Hector, Comte d'Aure (1774–1846). After serving as an officer in the French army in Syria and Egypt, he accompanied General Leclerc to Santo Domingo as chief finance officer. When the government suspended payment of bills incurred in connection with this expedition, d'Aure found himself in an unpleasant situation. He was recalled to France and ordered to appear in court by the Council of State. Napoleon, however, prevented this. See *Dictionnaire de biographie française*.

11 Van Merbeck is mentioned as a Paris banker in a letter preserved at the Eleutherian Mills Historical Library which Victor du Pont wrote to E. I. du Pont on May 16, 1804, and is mentioned frequently in the letters of du Pont de Nemours to Victor.

12 Perhaps the Baron Antoine Guérard de Rouilly (1777–1832), a French government official. In a letter written to Victor du Pont on 18 Nivôse, year XII (Jan-

uary 9, 1804; WMSS 2/5), du Pont de Nemours states that Guérard is "en banqueroute . . . pour dix huit cent mille francs de pareilles traites qui leur sont dues. Tu m'as marqué que pour la partie qui ne nous appartient pas tu avais une garantie sur Guerard. Tu vois ce qu'elle vaut." ("Bankrupt to the amount of 1,800,000 francs of such drafts as are owed to them. You wrote that you had a guarantee from Guérard for the part that does not belong to us. You see what it is worth.") (Unpubl. MS, Eleutherian Mills Historical Library.) The difference in tone between du Pont's comment to his son and his comments to Necker de Germany is obvious.

58

Necker to du Pont de Nemours

22 March 1804

WMSS 2/17

J'ai receu Monsieur votre lettre du 7 ventos. Je veux bien esperer avec vous que vous me rembourserez a l'epoque fixée mais ne regrettez pas de m'avoir confié votre situation car j'aurois pu selon mon droit tirer sur votre maison a New york ce qui auroit ouvert là peut-être une explication et des debats dont vous auriez été faché.

Je lirai avec attention le memoire que vous vous proposez de m'envoyer sur la Guyanne[1] mais mon interest a recommander vos vues ne peut et ne doit avoir aucun rapport a ma creance car il me sufiroit de croire a un motif particulier de ma part pour me considerer moi mème comme suspect et me tenir a l'ecart. Vos relations d'intimité avec Mr Jefferson quand elles seront connues seront un moyen propre à accroitre la confiance dans vos speculations. Je ne serois point eloigné d'y prendre un modique interest si la chose est bien organisée mais pour des embarras et des correspondances je ne vaux plus grand chose.

Vous me dites trop facilement que je ne cours aucun risque car d'après votre propre compte a mon frere votre creance sur le tresor est l'equivalent a peu près de votre capital non compris votre interest dans la manufacture des poudres. Qui est ce Mr Ogden dont vous me parlez? Il me semble qu'avec sa signature et celle de votre maison vous pourriez emprunter sur le depost des [stocks] [2] tirés de St Domingue. Je vous ai offert de prolonger ma creance avec une sureté parfaite. Je consens aujourd'huy a la prolonger d'un an sur votre seule parole en m'en payant la moitié. Je vous demande un patronage actif. Vous m'aviez mandé que vous m'aviez mis en sureté parfaite par une hypothèque. Vous m'ecrivez aujourd'huy que cela n'a pas èté fait. Je ne puis comprendre que vous m'offrez en place une hypotheque sur le terrein borné d'une manufacture de poudre située peut etre dans les bois & dont la valeur ne peut avoir aucune proportion avec ma creance. Il vaudroit mieux me demander de solder ce qui vous manqueroit en argent par deux actions de cette manufacture et je ne les voudrois pas en mon nom mais au porteur. Je crois que toutes les actions de votre societe et les actionaires seroient responsables selon les loix d'Amerique au moins pour ma creance faite sous la direction de dupont par Pusy et avant le changement posterieur.

Mon frere me prie de vous demande[r] si Mr Biderman est libre ou non de prendre les actions qu'il doit payer en terres. Agreez je vous prie les assurances de mon inviolable attachement.

[Sans signature]

Geneve le 22 Mars 1804

TRANSLATION

I have received, Sir, your letter of 7 Ventôse. I am willing to hope, with you, that you will reimburse me at the date agreed upon; but do not regret having confided your situation to me, for according to my right, I could have drawn upon your firm in New York, which would perhaps have started explanations and discussions there which would have annoyed you.

I shall read attentively the memoir that you propose to send me about Guyenne;[1] but my interest in recommending your opinions cannot and must not have any relation to my credit, for it would be enough for me to believe in a special motive on my part to consider myself as suspect and stand aside. Your friendly relations with Mr. Jefferson, when they are known, will be a proper means of increasing confidence in your speculations. I should not be averse to taking a slight interest in it if the matter is well organized; but as for difficulties and correspondence, I am no longer worth much.

You tell me too casually that I run no risk, for according to your own account to my brother, your credit on the Treasury is almost the equivalent of your capital, not including your interest in the powder factory. Who is this Mr. Ogden of whom you speak? It seems to me that, with his signature and that of your company, you could borrow on the deposit of the merchandise brought from Santo Domingo. I offered to extend my credit with a good guarantee on your part. I consent now to extend it for a year simply on your promise to pay me half of it. I ask you for an active direction. You had told me that you had guaranteed me by a mortgage. You now write me that that was not done. I cannot understand your offering me instead a mortgage on the limited area of a powder factory located perhaps in the woods whose value cannot have any relationship to my credit. It would be better to ask me to settle what you lack in cash with two shares in that factory, and I should not want them in my name but "to the bearer." I believe that all the shares in your company and the stockholders would be responsible according to American law at least for my credit made by Pusy under the direction of du Pont before the subsequent change.

My brother requests me to ask you whether or not M. Bidermann is free to take the shares that he is to pay for with land. Please accept the assurances of my inviolable attachment.

[No signature]

Geneva, March 22, 1804

NOTES

1 In 1764, du Pont de Nemours had published *Lettre sur la cherté du blé en Guyenne,* in which he proved that the recent high price of grain in that province had not been due to freedom of export, as some economists had claimed, but to poor harvests. When, in July, 1764, greater freedom of trade in grain was announced, Necker had made his fortune by speculating in this commodity (Gustave Schelle, *Du Pont de Nemours et l'école physiocratique* [Paris, 1888], p. 28).

It is difficult to understand why du Pont should send Necker a copy of a work written forty years earlier. Perhaps he wished to show that a great deal of money could be made from the free trade in the Mississippi Valley. He may also have planned a new treatise on Guyenne, which was not completed or has been lost.

2 This word is almost illegible; *stocks* seems to be the only logical reading.

59

du Pont de Nemours to Necker

8 April 1804

From a copy by Gustave Schelle, WMSS 8/108

Paris 18 Germinal 12

A Monsieur Necker

Monsieur,

J'ai reçu un peu tard votre lettre du 22 Mars, 1er Germinal. Il vaudrait mieux me les adresser directement, Rue de Montholon N° 300.

Vous me donnez une grande facilité en me laissant le choix, ou de vous procurer une nouvelle garantie sur le tout; ou d'acquitter la moitié, et quant à l'autre de rester *in statu quo*, ou de vous céder deux actions dans la fabrique de poudre.

Je me crois sûr de pouvoir prendre un de ces arrangements.

Ma pensée y est constamment tendue.

Je vais répondre à quelques autres articles de votre lettre.

Il s'en faut beaucoup que notre capital soit près d'être absorbé par la somme que nous doit la Trésorerie et par notre intérêt dans la fabrique de poudre.

Vous avez pu voir, dans le compte que j'ai rendu à M. Votre Frère de votre situation, que c'est, *votre Créance acquittée,* et les terres

du Kentucky mises à part, que nous avons	411.800 Frs
dont nous n'avons mis dans la Poudrière que	106.000 Frs
Reste donc a la disposition de la 1re société	305.800
Nous ne sommes intéressés que pour moitié dans les 281.000 Frs qui nous sont dus par la Marine	140.500
Il nous reste donc outre le capital de votre créance et celui que nous avons mis dans la Poudrière	165.300
Et nous avons de plus 1° Votre capital qui répond de lui-même	50.000
2° Notre part de la Poudrière	106.000
3° Les terres du Kentucky au moins	80.000
Total	401.300

pour répondre de 50.000 Frs, quand meme les Traites de St Domingue ne seraient pas payées du tout.

Mais certainement le gouvernement en payera quelque chose. Il nous payera meme le tout, parce que nous nous opposons à ce qu'il acquitte rien à ses Fournisseurs généraux, auxquels il redoit six millions, avant l'acquittement des Traites par eux remises à nous autres sous fournisseurs.

Il nous est parvenu à ce sujet, depuis ma dernière lettre, un évènement améliorateur. M. Vanmeerbeke, de qui M. Ogden et nous tenons les Traites, nous fait remettre pour couverture des pertes possibles 204.000 Francs de Traites semblables, qu'il autorise M. Ogden et nous à garder jusqu'à concurrence de ce que nous pourrions avoir à perdre en cas de liquidation affaiblie par les 281.000 Frs qui nous sont dus: si mieux nous n'aimons remettre ces nouvelles Traites de 204.000 Frs dans le courant d'Août prochain, à son correspondant, contre 28.000 frs en écus. Et M. Ogden a consenti à n'être couvert qu'après nous.

Ainsi le risque sur nos 140.500 Frs est diminué au moins de 28.000 frs ou de ce que pourront produire 204.000 Frs de nouvelles traites; et il est encore garanti par nos mesures conservatoires contre les Fournisseurs généraux.

M. Ogden est un négociant de New-York, dont mon fils a cru devoir employer le nom plus anglais que le nôtre, dans l'expédition faite avec lui de compte à demi à St Domingue bloqué, de laquelle nos traites sont le résultat. Nous ne pourrions lui proposer une circulation toujours dangereuse, et surtout en Amérique. Il est comme nous un peu gêné par la suspension du payement de ses Traites de St Domingue. Et dans un tel cas, une circulation pourrait perdre les deux maisons qui s'y livreraient, pour peu qu'une des deux inspirât la moindre inquiétude.

Une hypothèque sur la Poudrière vaut mieux que sur Good-Stay. J'ai déjà eu l'honneur de vous dire que Good-Stay n'était qu'une maison avec une petite ferme de vingt acres. Cela est fort joli: mais son *maximum* de valeur n'excède pas 12.000 dollars, et ne peut augmenter beaucoup.

Le terrain de la manufacture est plus que triple. Il a couté 8.000 dollars; et vous jugez combien il est augmenté de valeur par la construction de nos moulins. Cette valeur continuera de s'accroitre tant que la manufacture fera des progrès; car on ne peut plus séparer la fabrique du sol.

Vous avez raison de croire que toute notre société est responsable de votre capital, qui d'ailleurs est la seule dette.

Quant aux terres du Kentucky, sur lesquelles M. Votre Frère nous fait une question, elles sont cédées à la société; elles sont sa propriété, administrée, régie payant les impositions sous son nom.

La société n'en doit compte à M. Bidermann que par la délivrance des actions dont elles fourniront la valeur, à fur et mesure de leur vente successive.

M. Bidermann en nous cédant les terres ne s'en est pas réservé d'autre prix. Il ne peut les retraire.

Elles vous sont donc engagées comme tous les autres biens de la société. Vous aurais-je dit que votre sureté était parfaite, si elle ne l'eut pas été?

J'aurai l'honneur de vous envoyer le plus tot que je pourrai le développement de mes idées sur la Louisiane et le commerce de l'Ohio.

Agréez mon respectueux et inviolable attachement.

Du Pont (de Nemours)

TRANSLATION
Paris, 18 Germinal, year XII

To M. Necker

Sir,

I received your letter of March 22, 1 Germinal, a bit late. It would be better to send letters to me directly, 300, Rue de Montholon.

You give me a great facility by leaving to me the choice, either of getting a new guarantee on the entire amount, or of paying half of it and letting the other half remain *in the status quo,* or of turning over to you two shares in the powder factory.

I believe that I can certainly make one of these arrangements.

I think about it constantly.

I am going to answer some other points in your letter.

It is far from true that our capital is almost absorbed by the sum that the Treasury owes us and by our interest in the powder factory.

You could see, in the account that I made to your brother about your situation that, *your credit paid off* and the Kentucky land omitted, we have   411,800 fr.
of which we put into the powder mill only   106,000
There remains therefore at the disposal
of the first company   305,800
We are interested only in one half of the
281,000 francs which are owed to us by
the Navy   140,500
There remains for us, besides the capital
of your credit and that which we put into the
powder mill   165,300
And we have, in addition, (1) your capital,
which answers for itself   50,000
(2) Our share in the powder mill   106,000
(3) The Kentucky land, worth at least   80,000

Total   401,300 fr.

to answer for 50,000 francs, even if the Santo Domingo drafts were not paid at all.

But certainly the government will pay something. It will even pay us everything, because we are opposed to its paying anything to its general suppliers, to whom it still owes 6,000,000, before the settlement of the drafts given by them to us, the subcontractors.

Since my last letter, there has been an improvement in this matter. M. Van Merbeck, from whom Mr. Ogden and our company got the drafts, is sending us, to cover possible losses, 204,000 francs in similar drafts; these drafts, he authorizes Mr. Ogden and us to keep to the amount of what we might have to lose in case of a reduced liquidation of the 281,000 francs owed us, if we do not prefer to remit the new drafts for 204,000 francs next August to his correspondent for 28,000 francs in écus. And Mr. Ogden has agreed to be covered only after us.

Thus the risk on our 140,500 francs is diminished at least by 28,000 francs or by what 204,000 francs in new drafts may produce, and it is still guaranteed by our protective measures against the general suppliers.

Mr. Ogden is a businessman in New York, whose name, more English than ours, my son thought he should use in the shipment made with him on mutual account to blockaded Santo Domingo, from which our drafts resulted. We could not propose to him a circulation of the drafts, always dangerous, and especially so in America. Like us, he is a bit in difficulty because of the suspension in payment of his Santo Domingo drafts. And in such a case, circulating the drafts could ruin the two companies that might do so, if even one of the two should inspire the slightest uneasiness.

A mortgage on the powder factory is better than one on Good Stay. I have already had the honor of telling you that Good Stay was only a house with a little farm of twenty acres. It is very pretty, but its maximum value does not exceed $12,000 and cannot increase much.

The factory land is worth more than three times as much. It cost $8,000, and you can imagine how it has increased in value by the construction of our mills. This value will continue to increase as long as the factory makes progress, for one can no longer separate the factory from the land.

You are right to believe that our whole company is responsible for your capital, which is, moreover, its only debt.

As for the Kentucky land which your brother asks about, it has been turned over to the company. It is the company's property, administered, managed, and taxed under the company's name.

The company owes no account to M. Bidermann except for the delivery of the shares for which it will provide payment in proportion to their successive sales.

On turning the land over to us, M. Bidermann did not reserve any other price. He cannot withdraw it.

It is committed to you like all the other property of the company. Would I have told you that your guarantee was complete if it had not been so?

I shall have the honor of sending you, as soon as I can, the development of my ideas about Louisiana and trade on the Ohio.

Accept my respectful and inviolable attachment.

Du Pont (de Nemours)

60

du Pont de Nemours to Madame de Staël

18 April 1804

From a copy by Gustave Schelle, WMSS 8/108

A Madame de Stael de Holstein à Coppet

Paris, 28 Germinal 12

Je pleure avec vous, mon excellente amie, votre illustre Père, si remarquable par l'étendue de ses vues, l'éclat de son Ministère, la bienvaillance de son cœur, et l'élévation de son style.[1]

Nos opinions politiques ont souvent été différentes: un sentiment de vertu, l'amour du bien public, l'injustice des Français envers lui pendant la révolution nous avaient réunis.

Il a été content de moi dans cette circonstance orageuse; et n'a cessé depuis de me témoigner de la bonté, de se[2] complaire à mon respect.

Dans ma nouvelle carrière pour laquelle il avait une capacité si haute, mon travail, mes plans, ma conduite ont eu son approbation. Il m'a aidé de ses conseils et de son argent.

Je lui dois près de cinquante mille Francs.[3] Vous trouverez à cet égard notre correspondance et nous en parlerons une autre fois.

Ce que je vous dois aujourd'hui, ce que j'ai besoin de vous exprimer, ce dont vous ne doutez point, est la part bien vive que je prends à tout ce qui vous intéresse. Vous n'avez pas une peine, ni une consolation qui ne retentisse à mon cœur. Et ce qui m'afflige beaucoup est que vous etes plus susceptible de l'une que de l'autre.

Achille n'était vulnérable qu'au talon, et ne le montrait guère. Vous pouvez être aisément blessée dans l'esprit et dans le cœur; et vous le montrez sans cesse presque malgré vous.

Tâchez de retrancher au moins de vos dangers tout ce qui tient aux affaires publiques. Donnez-en votre démission. Si mon exemple pouvait etre de quelque poids auprès de vous, je vous dirais que j'en ai complètement donné la mienne; quoique le désir d'y influer ait été pendant plus de quarante ans une de mes passions dominantes, dévorantes même.

Ce n'est plus à cette passion là qu'il faut être fidèle. Il en est de plus douces, de plus aimables, de plus généralement utiles.

Vous êtes amie, Mère et Femme de lettres. Aucune façon d'aimer ni de travailler ne vous est étrangère. Aimez et travaillez.[4]

Marquez-moi si vous résiderez quelque temps à Coppet, ou à Genève? Je suis capable de vous y aller voir.

Ou si vous retournerez dans le Nord? Je ne pourrais vous y suivre. Mon premier et mon dernier grand voyage seront au delà des mers.

En quelque lieu que je vive, vous aurez un Ami très dévoué.

Agréez son attachement et son respect.

Du Pont (de Nemours)

TRANSLATION

To Madame de Staël de Holstein at Coppet

Paris, 28 Germinal, year XII

I mourn with you, my excellent friend, your illustrious father, so remarkable for the extent of his knowledge, the brilliance of his ministry, the benevolence of his heart, and the elevation of his style.[1]

Our political opinions were often different. A feeling of virtue, love of the public good, and the injustice of the French to him during the Revolution had brought us together.

He was pleased with me during that stormy event and did not cease afterwards to show me kindness, to take pleasure in my respect.

In my new career, for which he had so great a capacity, my work, my plans, my conduct had his approval. He helped me with his advice and his money.

I owe him nearly 50,000 francs.[3] You will find our correspondence in that regard, and we shall speak of it another time.

What I owe you today, what I need to express to you, what you do not doubt at all, is the very strong interest that I take in everything that concerns you. You have no pain or consolation which does not resound in my heart. And what afflicts me very much is that you are more susceptible to the one than to the other.

Achilles was vulnerable only in the heel and scarcely showed it. You can easily be wounded in the mind and the heart, and you show it unceasingly almost in spite of yourself.

Try to eliminate, at least, from the dangers that face you every-thing concerned with public affairs. Resign from them. If my example could be of some weight with you, I should tell you that I have resigned completely, although the desire to influence pub-lic affairs was one of my dominant, even devouring, passions for more than forty years.

It is no longer to that passion that we must be true. There are sweeter, more pleasing, and more generally useful ones.

You are a friend, mother, and woman of letters. No way of loving or working is foreign to you. Love and work.[4]

Tell me whether you will reside for some time at Coppet, or in Geneva? I may possibly go see you there.

Or whether you will return to the North? I could not follow you there. My first and my last great trip will be beyond the seas.

In whatever place I live, you will have a very devoted friend.

Accept his attachment and his respect.

Du Pont (de Nemours)

NOTES

1 Jacques Necker died on April 10, 1804, at Coppet.

2 Gustave Schelle wrote le, which must be an error.

3 Du Pont de Nemours discusses his financial problems in a letter to Victor (WMSS 2/5) which he started on 1 Floréal, year XII (April 21, 1804) and finished on 5 Floréal (April 25):

> Voici d'autres inquiétudes. M. Necker m'a demandé de lui rembourser au 1er juillet les 50,000 F que nous lui devons. Je l'ai prévenu que si je n'obtenais pas un à compte du Gouvernement, il me serait très difficile, peut-être impos-sible de faire ce remboursement. Il m'a demandé alors de lui donner une nouvelle et double sureté en biens fonds: (ce que je ne puis, le Bois des Fossés étant déjá engagé à Mme Lavoisier). Ou bien de lui payer moitié, moyennant quoi il accorderait délay pour le reste, ou consentirait à prendre sur cette autre moitié deux actions de la Poudriere que je ne puis pas donner davantage, car il n'y en [a] déja que trop de cédées.
>
> La chose en était là quand Mr Necker est mort. Si c'est son Frere qui suit ses affaires, je doute que je puisse en obtenir plus de facilité. Si c'est sa Fille j'ai plus d'espérance. Je voudrais qu'elle consentit à recevoir en payement cinq actions de la Société principale. Mais le voudra-t-elle? Son Oncle ne l'en empêchera-t-il point? Pourra-t-elle venir à Coppet soigner ses affaires? Ne les abandonnera-t-elle point ou à cet Oncle qui n'est point facile en négociation, [ou] à des gens d'affaires dont j'éprouverais encore moins de facilité? J'ignore tout cela.

> (Here are other worries. M. Necker has asked me to repay him on July 1 the 50,000 francs that we owe him. I have informed him that, if I did not obtain a partial payment from the Government, it would be very difficult for me,

perhaps impossible, to make this payment. He then asked me to give him a new, double guarantee in real estate (which I cannot do since le Bois-des-Fossés is already pledged to Mme. Lavoisier). Or else to pay him half, in consideration of which he would grant a delay for the remainder, or would consent to take for this other half two shares in the powder mill, which I cannot give either, for there are too many already surrendered.

Things were at that point when M. Necker died. If it is his brother who continues with his business affairs, I doubt that I can obtain more favorable terms. If it is his daughter, I have more hope. I should like her to agree to receive in payment five shares in the main company. But will she be willing? Will not her uncle prevent her from doing so? Will she be able to come to Coppet to take care of her business affairs? Will she not turn them over to that uncle, who is not at all easy to deal with, or to business agents, with whom I should have still more difficulty? All this I do not know.)

Lavoisier had lent du Pont money to establish a printshop in 1791 and had accepted Bois-des-Fossés, du Pont's property in the country, as security for the mortgage. Mme. Lavoisier had become increasingly dissatisfied with this arrangement.

4 This advice recalls du Pont de Nemours' motto: *Aimer et connaître.*

61

Madame de Staël to du Pont de Nemours

22 May 1804

WMSS 2/17

coppet ce 22 may

Mon cher du pont ce n'est pas du malheur c'est la destruction de toute la vie. Je n'agis plus pour moi. Que parlez vous de donner la démission des intérets politiques? Je l'ai donnèe de tout intéret personnel sur la terre. Je suis obligèe de transmettre sa fortune à ses enfants et d'exècuter son testament. Voila ce qui fait que je ne passe pas le jour à rèver sur cette idèe qui dèvoie tant la mort. Parmi les lettres de mon père j'ai vu la vôtre. Il vous offroit de payer la moitié au 4 juillet ou de donner une garantie bonne pour le tout, ou de lui faire avoir deux actions dans la poudrière. Le 1er moyen m'est presque indispensable parce qu'il m'a laissé 35 mille livres à payer sous 4 mois et que je n'ai pas trouvé d'autre argent disponible. Quand à la poudrière je n'en veux pas. Il falloit le génie de mon père pour comprendre les affaires èloignèes. Quand à moi je ne dois avoir qu'un but conserver et transmettre car il faut que de la fortune qu'il a si noblement acquise et perdue il reste de quoi vivre honorablement pour mes trois enfants. Ayez la bonté mon cher du pont de me rèpondre et d'arranger cette affaire si cela se peut comme j'en ai besoin. Nous prorogerons l'autre moitiè de la somme à l'annèe suivante et vous m'indiquerez quelle est la manière la plus avantageuse à nous deux avec laquelle je dois tirer ces 25 mille livres. Ah mon cher du pont quelles occupations pour une personne qui avoit toujours vècu protégèe mais enfin le tems de l'avenir est passè. Il faut lutter avec le présent sans guides qu'une raison affaiblie par la douleur. Adieu.[1]

N[ecker] Stael de H[olstein]

Je reste ici. Il seroit doux de vous y voir.

TRANSLATION

Coppet, May 22

My dear du Pont, it is not misfortune. It is the destruction of my whole life. I no longer act for myself. What do you mean by resigning from political interests? I have done so for every personal interest on earth. I am obliged to transmit his fortune to his children and to execute his last will and testament. That is what causes me not to spend my days in thinking about that idea which turns death away so much. Among my father's letters I saw yours. He offered to have you pay half on July 4, or give a guarantee good for the whole amount, or give two shares in the powder mill. The first choice is almost indispensable to me, because he left me 35,000 francs to be paid in four months, and I have not found any other money available. As for the powder mill, I do not want any part of it. It took my father's genius to understand distant affairs. As for me, I must have only one purpose, to keep and transmit, for it is necessary that, from the fortune which he so nobly acquired and lost, there remain something on which to live honorably for my three children. Be good enough, my dear du Pont, to answer me and to settle this matter, if possible, in the way I need to have it settled. We shall extend the other half of the amount till next year, and you will indicate to me the manner most advantageous to both of us for me to draw those 25,000 francs. Ah, my dear du Pont, what occupations for a person who had always lived protected; but finally the time of the future has passed. It is necessary to struggle with the present without any guides except a reason weakened by sorrow. Adieu.[1]

Necker Staël de Holstein

I am remaining here. It would be pleasant to see you here.

NOTE

1 In a letter written to Victor du Pont on 10 Prairial, year XII (May 30, 1804; WMSS 2/5), du Pont de Nemours observes:

Mr Necker est mort.

Mme de Stael persiste comme lui à vouloir un a compte de moitié sur le capital.

Je lui ai envoyé mille ecus pour les interets, et j'irai la voir à Genêve pour savoir si je ne négocierai pas plus heureusement en personne que par lettres. Ce voyage acheverait de me perdre a la cour [*the preceding three words written in code*] si je n'y êtais pas deja tout perdu. Mais un crédit d'un an de plus pour ce capital nous est si important que je sacrifierais bien davantage pour n'être pas encore forcé au remboursement.

(M. Necker has died.

Mme. de Staël persists, as he did, in wanting a part payment of half of the capital.

I have sent her 1,000 écus for the interest, and I shall go see her in Geneva in order to learn whether or not I can negotiate more favorably in person than by letter. This trip would finish my ruin at the Court if I were not already ruined completely there. But a credit of one more year for this capital is so important for us that I should sacrifice much more in order not to be forced to repay yet.)

62

du Pont de Nemours to Madame de Staël

22 May 1804

From a copy by Gustave Schelle, WMSS 8/108

Madame de Stael

Paris 2 Prairial an 12

Mon excellente amie.

J'espère que vous avez reçu la première expression de la douleur que m'a causé la perte de M. Votre Père et que je vous ai fait passer à Genève.

Vous n'avez jamais douté de mon cœur, ni d'aucun de vos droits sur lui.

J'ai à vous parler aujourd'hui des affaires que cet homme respectable me laisse avec vous.

Il m'a prêté un contrat sur les Etats-Unis, *au cours* qu'ils avaient le 1er Juillet 1801, *neuf cent mille huit cent trente trois dollars soixante et six cents.*[1]

Ce cours était à 90½. Ainsi les 9.833,66 valaient   8.889,65 dollars[2]
qui faisaient alors en France 47.115 frs 25.

Il y avait en outre pour des intérets échus
que nous n'avons touchés qu'un an après   295   dollars[2]

Total   en   dollars   9.184,66
et en francs 48.678 frs 75.

C'est de cette somme dont je vous dois au 1er Juillet prochain l'intérêt à six pour cent, pour quoi je joins ici le mandat sur nous-memes que vous placerez à Genève aisément.

Mais je lui devais bien autre chose. C'était le remboursement du capital à la même époque. Il ne nous l'avait prêté que pour trois ans.

Nous comptions mes enfants et moi pour effectuer ce remboursement sur celui que le gouvernement devait nous faire des derniers secours que nous avions donnés à l'armée de St Domingue. Il avait jusqu'a présent très bien payé ses fournisseurs. Mais la colonie perdue, il a suspendu les payements.

Quand il ne devrait pas les reprendre, notre perte ne serait pas aussi considérable que je l'avais craint d'abord, parce que mes enfants avaient fait l'opération en société avec un autre négociant[3] et n'y sont intéressés que pour moitié.

Il n'en résulte pas moins, à ma très grande douleur, que je ne puis vous rembourser ni actuellement, ni au 1er Juillet.

M. Votre Père avait consenti à m'accorder une prolongation, soit en lui donnant une nouvelle sureté, soit en lui remboursant moitié et dans ce dernier cas il consentait meme à placer l'autre moitié en actions de ma société.

Si je puis obtenir du Gouvernement ou le Payement ou à un compte[4] notable, il ne m'en coutera pas plus de rembourser le tout que la moitié. Mais si je n'en obtiens rien, l'un me serait pour le moment presque aussi difficile que l'autre.

J'ai montré à M. Necker, par la dernière lettre que j'ai eu l'honneur de lui écrire, et que vous avez du recevoir, que relativement à la *sureté,* elle est entière; et quant à l'*utilité* le placement en actions de ma société est beaucoup plus avantageux que le prêt.

La situation de l'Europe et l'acquisition de la Louisiane par les Etats-Unis rendent bien préférable un emploi de capitaux dans ce pays, à un remboursement dans quelque partie que ce soit de l'ancien monde.

Si vous séjournez à Coppet ou à Genève, j'irai y passer quelques jours avec vous; et je crois que vous serez de mon avis.

Mais je n'ai pas voulu attendre ce moment pour vous parler de l'affaire privée que nous avons ensemble.

Je ne veux point que vous regardiez votre fidèle ami comme un mauvais comptable.

Salut, respect, tendre et inviolable attachement.

Du Pont (de Nemours)

Ma femme qui vous aime comme vous le méritez, se rappelle à votre souvenir.

TRANSLATION
Madame de Staël

Paris, 2 Prairial, year XII

My excellent friend,

I hope that you have received my first expression of sorrow over the loss of your father, which I sent to you in Geneva.

You have never doubted my heart nor any of your rights over it.

I have to speak to you today about the business which that respectable man leaves me with you.

He lent me a contract on the United States, *at the rate* which was in effect on July 1, 1801, for *$9,833.66*.[1]

This rate was 90½. Thus the $9,833.66 was worth $8,889.65[2] which was then the equivalent of 47,115.25 francs in France.

In addition, for interest due, which we received only a year later, there was $ 295   [2]

Total in dollars $9,184.66

and in francs 48,678.75.

It is that sum on which I owe you interest at 6 per cent next

July 1, for which I am enclosing the money order on our company; you can cash it easily in Geneva.

But I owed him something else. That was the reimbursement of the capital at the same time. He had lent it to us for only three years.

In order to make this reimbursement, my children and I were counting on the one that the government was to make to us for our latest assistance to the army of Santo Domingo. It had paid its suppliers very well up to now. But with the colony lost, it stopped payments.

Even if it should not resume them, our loss would not be as considerable as I had feared at first, because my children had operated together with another businessman[3] and are involved only for one half.

It is nevertheless true, to my great regret, that I cannot reimburse you either at the present time or on July 1.

Your father had agreed to grant an extension, either by giving him a new guarantee or by paying him one half, and in the latter case, he even consented to invest the other half in stock of my company.

If I can obtain from the government either the payment or a considerable installment, it will cost me no more to repay the entire amount than the half. But if I obtain nothing, the one would be, at the moment, almost as difficult as the other.

In the last letter that I had the honor of writing to him, which you must have received, I showed M. Necker that in regard to *safety*, it is complete; and as for *utility*, the investment in stock of my company is much more advantageous than the loan.

The situation in Europe and the acquisition of Louisiana by the United States make a use of capital in that country much preferable to a reimbursement in any part at all of the Old World.

If you are staying at Coppet or at Geneva, I shall go spend a few days there with you, and I believe that you will be of my opinion.

But I did not want to wait for that moment to speak to you about the private affair that we have together.

I do not want you to consider your faithful friend a bad accountant.

Greetings, respect, tender and inviolable attachment.

Du Pont (de Nemours)

My wife, who loves you as you deserve to be, asks to be remembered to you.

NOTES

1 The figure in the French is an error, either in the original or in the copy. The amount was $9,833.66, as is shown in the next paragraph of the text; see also Letter 31.
2 In his copy, Gustave Schelle wrote *francs*. This is obviously an error and has been corrected to read *dollars*.
3 Samuel G. Ogden. See Letter 57, note 9.
4 This seems to be an error on the part of Gustave Schelle. Du Pont probably wrote *un à compte*.

63

Madame de Staël to du Pont de Nemours

5 June 1804

WMSS 2/17

Coppet le 5 juin 1804

Mon cher du pont, je ne connais rien de plus triste que de traiter des affaires entre des amis mais il faut pourtant que je me conforme aux respectables instructions que j'ai reçues. Et si vous ne pouvez pas payer à l'èchèance il faut que je vous prie de me renvoyer un billet à un an de datte avec la garantie de quelqu'un que vous me nommerez. *Mon père dit dans ses papiers qu'il a perdu dans l'affaire avec vous assez pour se croire le droit de vous demander ce qui lui convient.* Je ne sais rien du passè mais pour l'avenir je vous demande positivement une garantie parce que vous ou moi nous pouvons mourir moi surtout. Et que nous avons des enfants. Rèpondez moi donc sur ce point. Ou bien aimez vous mieux que je charge fourcault[1] mon notaire de suivre cette affaire? J'attends votre rèponse pour l'en charger car je ne veux pas faire un pas sans votre consentement. J'ai reçu la lettre de change de 2900 francs pour les intérets et je vais la passer à l'ordre de Mrs Hentsch de Genève. Je reste ici ou à Genève tout l'èté au moins. Je serois bien heureuse de vous y voir. Je prie madame du pont de m'aimer et de me plaindre.

Il me faut un nouveau billet de vous à mon ordre à moi, et je vous renverrai le vòtre ou le déclarerai nul. C'est sur ce billet qu'il faudra mettre la garantie du negociant que vous m'offrirez d'abord par lettres. C'est ainsi que mon père l'a mis dans ses nottes. C'est ainsi qu'il faut que cela soit fait.[2]

[Sans signature]

On the reverse:

A Monsieur
Monsieur Dupont de Nemours
Rue Montolon N° 301
à Paris[3]

Postmark:

21 p[al] an 12

TRANSLATION

Coppet, June 5, 1804

My dear du Pont, I know nothing sadder than having business affairs between friends, but I must nevertheless conform to the respectable instructions which I received. And if you cannot pay on the due date, I must ask you to send me a note for a year from this date with the guarantee of someone that you will name. *My father says in his papers that he lost enough in his business with you to believe himself within his rights in asking you for what suits him.* I know nothing of the past, but for the future, I ask you explicitly for a guarantee, because you or I, especially, may die, and we have children. Answer me then on that point. Or do you prefer to have me let Fourcault,[1] my notary, handle this matter? I am waiting for your reply before giving it to him, for I do not want to take a step without your consent. I received the bill of 2,900 francs for the interest, and I am going to endorse it to Messrs. Hentsch of Geneva. I am staying here or in Geneva all summer at least. I should be very happy to see you here. I beg Mme. du Pont to love and pity me.

I must have a new note from you made out to me, and I shall return yours to you or declare it null. It is on this note that you will have to put the guarantee of the businessman whom you will propose to me first by letter. It is in this way that my father put it in his notes. It is in this way that it must be done.[2]

[No signature]

On the reverse:

To Monsieur
M. du Pont de Nemours
301, rue Montholon
in Paris[3]

Postmark:

21 Prairial, year XII

NOTES
1 Pierre Fourcault de Pavant, a notary in Paris since 1783. His office was located at 343, rue Saint-Honoré (*Journaux intimes*, p. 475, n. 2 [to p. 42]).
2 In a letter written to Victor du Pont on 5 Messidor, year XII (June 24, 1804; WMSS 2/5), du Pont de Nemours observes:

Je reste dans un grand embarras vis-a-vis Madame de Stael qui veut son remboursement au moins pour moitié ou caution pour le tout avec obligation de rembourser dans un an.
J'avais esperé que Bidermann pourrait et voudrait lui donner cette garantie. Cette esperance est évanouie comme les autres.
J'aurais affaire a Geneve pour traiter en personne avec elle au risque d'achever de me perdre a la cour [*the preceding three words written in code*].

. . . .

Si Madame de Stael persiste à vouloir une caution et si Bidermann continue de ne vouloir pas la donner, nous serons poursuivis à Paris et aux Etats Unis.
Ce ne sont pas là des roses. Ce sont de cuisantes épines.

(I remain in a very embarrassing position with Mme. de Staël, who wants repayment of at least half or else a guarantee for the entire amount, with an obligation to repay in one year.
I had hoped that Bidermann could and would give her that guarantee. That hope has vanished like the others.
I should deal personally with her in Geneva, at the risk of ruining myself completely at the court.

. . . .

If Mme. de Staël persists in wanting a guarantee and if Bidermann continues to refuse to give it, we shall be prosecuted in Paris and in the United States.
This is no bed of roses. It is a bed of sharp thorns.)

3 The address is in another handwriting.

❀

64

du Pont de Nemours to Madame de Staël

16 June 1804

From a copy by Gustave Schelle, WMSS 8/108

27 Prairial [1] 12

à Madame de Stael

Mon excellente amie,

M. Votre père n'a rien perdu avec ma maison, et ne peut avoir laissé sans méprise une note qui l'indiquat à moins qu'il n'ait voulu dire qu'il aurait pu faire de ses fonds un emploi plus avantageux; ou que le cours des effets qu'il nous a transmis s'est trouvé moins favorable qu'il ne le pensait, ce qui est possible. Mais ni lui ni nous ne faisions le cours et nous étions convenus de le suivre.

Il a cédé à ma maison le 20 Juillet 1801 des contrats américains de *neuf mille huit cent trente trois dollars soixante six cents,* valeur nominale, sur le pieds du cours qu'ils auraient eu en Amérique le premier du meme mois.

Ce cours était le 1ᵉʳ Juillet à 90½, ce qui a fixé la valeur des contrats à *huit mille huit cents quatre vingt neuf dollars soixante et cinq cents.*

Les contrats ne nous sont parvenus que le 30 Novembre suivant.

Sa convention avec mon fils a été que nous en tiendrions la valeur à sa disposition le 1ᵉʳ Juillet 1804; et que nous en payerions les intérets à six pour cent à compter de ce 1ᵉʳ Juillet 1801,[2] antérieur de vingt jours à notre Traité, de cinq mois à notre jouissance.

Il nous a cédé en outre *deux cent quatre vingt quinze dollars un cent* d'intérets échus, dont le titre pour les toucher ne nous est parvenu qu'un an après.

Nous lui devons donc en tout *neuf cent mille cent quatre vingt quatre dollars soixante six cents*[3] de capital, faisant au change moyen établi entre nous *quarante huit mille six cent soixante dix huit frs cinquante cinq centimes.*

Nous lui en avons payé les intérets exactement, et vous avez notre effet que j'acquitterai pour l'année courante le jour où elle échoira.

Ni lui, ni vous, mon amie, n'avez donc rien perdu à cette transaction.

Mais il est vrai que je lui dois, que je vous dois au 1ᵉʳ Juillet *quarante huit mille six cent soixante dix huit francs cinquante cinq centimes.*

J'avais pour y satisfaire *cent quarante mille cinq cent francs à* prendre sur *deux cent quatre vingt un mille* dus par le Gouvernement Français à M. Ogden et à nous pour des farines que nous avons fournies en société à l'armée de St Domingue.

Le Gouvernement a suspendu ce payement. J'ai prévenu M. Votre Père de l'embarras qui en résultait pour notre maison. Il a compati. Je ne désespère cependant pas encore d'obtenir un accompte de la Trésorerie; et c'est ce qui me retient en France. Les premiers fonds sont à vous.

Vous avez pour sureté notre société toute entière qui n'a pas d'autre créancier que vous; nos terres du Kentucky de cinquante six mille acres suivant les titres, dont *seize mille* qui ne sont pas contestés valent au moins cent soixante mille francs; la manufacture de poudre de notre Irénée que j'ai chargé de vous l'hypothéquer spécialement.

Il n'y a point d'intérets mieux servis, ni de capital plus assuré.

Je ne sais meme si votre bon esprit capable de juger l'Europe, ne doit pas trouver que des fonds aux Etats Unis y sont avec plus de sécurité qu'en aucun autre pays du monde.

M. Votre Père m'a demandé:

ou une nouvelle sureté en Europe;

ou la moitié comptant, et deux actions qui feraient *vingt un mille deux cent francs* sur le reste, sans autre sureté.

Je me conformerai à l'une ou à l'autre proposition, puisque c'est sa volonté que vous et moi voulons suivre. Je n'aurai pas condition plus dure avec une femme aimable qu'avec un grand homme, tous deux bienveillants.

Si je puis donc trouver l'argent, je vous donnerai promptment 24.340 Frs et pour les 24.338 frs 55 restants.

D'abord deux actions faisant		21.200	
puis un billet à un an de		3.326,85	
Savoir pour solde du capital	3.138,55		
et pour les intérets de			3.326,85
cette portion	188,30		

Si je ne puis pas sous un court délai vous donner 24.340, j'espère pouvoir engager mon ami M. Bidermann à m'accorder auprès de vous la caution dont je ne devrais pas avoir besoin, puisque la chose se cautionne d'elle même; et je continuerai de vous payer les intérets.

Nous conviendrons, si vous y consentez, de partager la remboursement en plusieurs époques, à moins que le payement de la France ne me fournisse le moyen de me dégager comme il le devait.

Je vous prie de continuer à traiter cela directement avec moi. Ne valons nous pas mieux que des Notaires?

Je me flatte toujours que je pourrai vous aller voir, et j'en ai bien besoin.

Ne connaissez vous pas mon inviolable et tendre et respectueux attachement.[4]

Du Pont (de Nemours)

Madame Du Pont est bien sensible à votre souvenir. Elle vous dit mille choses, et sera très affligée de ne pouvoir m'accompagner dans ma course rapide à Genève.

Que le ciel vous rende heureuse!

TRANSLATION

27 Prairial,[1] year XII

To Madame de Staël

My excellent friend,

Your father lost nothing with my company and cannot have left, except by mistake, a note which would indicate it, unless he meant that he could have used his capital more advantageously, or that the rate of the stocks he transferred to us was less favorable than he thought, which is possible. But neither he nor we set the rate, and we had agreed to follow it.

He turned over to my company on July 20, 1801, some American contracts for $9,833.66 face value, at the rate they would have had in America on the first of the same month.

On July 1, this rate was at 90½, which made the value of the contracts $8,889.65.

The contracts reached us only on the following November 30.

His agreement with my son was that we would hold the amount

at his disposition on July 1, 1804, and that we would pay the interest at 6 per cent starting from this July 1, 1801,[2] twenty days before our agreement, with five months for our benefit.

In addition, he turned over to us *$295.01* in interest due, for which authority to draw it reached us only a year later.

We owe him therefore altogether $9,184.66[3] as capital, making, at the rate of exchange settled between us, *48,678.55* francs.

We paid the interest to him at the exact time, and you have our bill, which I shall settle for the present year on the day it falls due.

Neither he nor you, my friend, have lost anything in this transaction.

But it is true that I owe him, that I owe you on July 1, *48,678.55* francs.

I had, in order to pay it, *140,500* francs to draw from *200,810* which the French government owed Mr. Ogden and us for flour which we supplied together to the army of Santo Domingo.

The government suspended this payment. I informed your father about the critical situation which resulted from it for our company. He sympathized. I do not yet despair, however, of obtaining an installment from the Treasury, and that is what keeps me in France. The first funds belong to you.

You have as a guarantee our whole company, which has no other creditor but you; our Kentucky land of *56,000* acres according to the deeds, of which *16,000* are uncontested and are worth at least 160,000 francs; and the powder factory of our Irénée, whom I ordered to mortgage it to you especially.

There are no interests better served, or capital more insured.

I do not know even whether your good mind, which is so capable of judging Europe, ought not to find that funds in the United States are more secure there than in any other country in the world.

Your father asked me for either a new guarantee in Europe; or half in cash, and two shares of stock which would make *21,200* francs on the remainder, without any other guarantee.

I shall agree to one proposal or the other, since it is his will that you and I want to follow. I shall not have a harsher condition with a charming woman than with a great man, both benevolent.

If I can find the money, I shall give you promptly 24,340 francs, and for the remaining 24,338.55 francs:

At first, two shares, making		21,200 fr.;
then a note for a year for		3,326.85 fr.
That is, for the balance		
of the capital	3,138.55	
and for the interest on that		3,326.85 fr.
portion	188.30	

If I cannot soon give you 24,340 francs, I hope I can engage my friend M. Bidermann to grant me for your sake the guarantee which I ought not to need, since the matter guarantees itself, and I shall continue to pay you the interest.

We shall agree, if you consent, to divide the reimbursement into several periods, unless payment from the French government provides me with the means of extricating myself as it should.

I beg you to continue to deal directly with me. Are we not better than notaries?

I still fancy that I shall be able to go see you, and I need to do so.

Do you not know my inviolable, tender, and respectful attachment? [4]

Du Pont (de Nemours)

Madame du Pont appreciates your remembrance of her. She sends her best regards and will be sorry not to be able to accompany me on my hasty trip to Geneva.

May Heaven make you happy!

NOTES

1 On the Schelle copy, the date is given as 27 Floréal. Le Marois, however, quotes from this letter (*Cahiers*, pp. 508–9) and gives the date as 27 Prairial. I have chosen the latter date as the correct one, since it fits better into the context of the correspondence.

2 In the Schelle copy, this date is erroneously given as 1808.

3 Another error in the amount, probably made by the copyist. It is obvious that the correct sum is $9,184.66.

4 In a letter du Pont de Nemours wrote to Victor du Pont on July 4, 1804 (WMSS 2/5), he states: "Je crains plus que je ne te puis dire d'avoir trop promis à Madame de Stael." ("I fear more than I can tell you that I have promised too much to Mme. de Staël.")

All the letters written by du Pont to Victor at this time reveal du Pont's desperation and worry about financial matters.

65

Necker de Germany to du Pont de Nemours

20 June 1804

WMSS 2/17

J'ai reçu Monsieur, votre lettre du 3 Prairial [1] renfermant une remise sur votre maison de fr. 1272 valeur des interets d'une année à 6 p[our] cent sur 2 actions de Dollars 2000. Chacune d[oll]ar 240 a f. 5.30—f 1272. J'en credite votre maison.

J'ai parlé a Mad de Stael de la créance que son Père lui a laissé sur votre maison et qui échoit au 1er du mois prochain, et je lui ai communiqué ce que vous m'avez marqué de relatif à la gene passagère où vous mettoit le non payement des traites sur le Thresor public dont vous êtes porteur, gêne qui laisse cependant à vos créanciers des motifs de confiance sur la bonté de leur créance. Elle m'a paru les sentir comme son Pere, et disposée à s'y preter en partie: ainsi elle vous a demandé de recevoir pour le prèsent la moitie et d'attendre quelque tems pour le reste. Elle vous a meme proposé de lui donner une garantie nouvelle pour le tout et de fixer des termes à une distance moderée pour le remboursement total, en cela elle respecte ce qu'elle connoit des intentions où etoit son pere et il est difficile de croire que vous ne puissiez pas faire usage de l'un ou l'autre de ces moyens. Il me semble que sur l'hypotheque que vous donnass[i]ez a quelqu'un sur ces memes traites protestées vous devriez trouver à Paris un pret ou tout au moins une caution suffisante et si pour y parvenir il falloit faire quelque sacrifice en augmentation d'interets ou autrement il est assez d'usage qu'un debiteur jaloux de remplir ses engagemens s'y soumette s'il ne peut faire autrement.

Je vous conjure donc, Monsieur, de vous en occuper très sérieusement et le plus promtement possible. Agréez l'expression sincere de ma parfaite considération & de mon dévouement.

Necker de Germany

Geneve le 20 juin 1804

On the reverse:

A Monsieur
Dupont de Nemours
à Paris

Postmark:

7 M^{or} an 12
99 Genève

TRANSLATION

I have received, Sir, your letter of 3 Prairial [May 23] [1] enclosing a remittance from your company for 1,272 francs, the value of the interest for one year at 6 per cent on two shares of stock worth $2,000 each, or $240 at a rate of 5.30 francs to a dollar amounting to 1,272 francs. I am crediting your company with it.

I have spoken to Mme. de Staël about the credit which her father left her in your company and which falls due on the first of next month, and I informed her of what you indicated to me concerning the temporary financial embarrassment in which you are placed by the nonpayment of the drafts on the public treasury of which you are the bearer, an embarrassment, however, which gives your creditors reason to lack confidence in the safety of their claims. She seemed to me to feel about it as her father did and to be disposed to adapt herself to it in part. So she asked you to pay half for the present and agreed to wait some time for the rest. She even proposed to you to give her a new guarantee for the entire amount and to settle on a moderately distant date for the complete reimbursement. She thereby respects what she knows of her father's intentions, and it is difficult to believe that you cannot use one or the other of these means. It seems to me that on the mortgage which you might give to someone on these same protested drafts, you ought to find in Paris a loan or at least a sufficient guarantee; and if, in order to succeed in doing so, it were necessary to make some sacrifice by increasing the interest or otherwise, it is rather common usage for a debtor eager to fulfill his obligations to submit to it if he cannot do otherwise.

I beseech you, therefore, Sir, to concern yourself with it very seriously and as promptly as possible. Accept the sincere expression of my perfect consideration and my devotion.

Necker de Germany

Geneva, June 20, 1804

On the reverse:

To Monsieur
du Pont de Nemours
in Paris

Postmark:

7 Messidor, year XII
99 Geneva

N O T E
1 This letter is not in the Eleutherian Mills Historical Library nor in the Archives at Coppet. It may be still in the possession of the heirs of Necker de Germany.

66

Madame de Staël to du Pont de Nemours

28 June 1804

WMSS 2/22

ce 28 juin[1]

Non assurèment mon cher dupont, je ne voudrois pas vous *traiter mal.* Ainsi j'accepterai la caution de M^r bidermann quand vous me la donnerez et avec cette caution nous prendrons des termes *mais une caution en europe m'est absolument nécessaire,* et je vous demande de finir cette affaire le plutot possible. Dans la lettre que mon père vous a ècrit vous savez qu'il insistoit positivement sur cette caution. Je n'y puis renoncer. Je ne prendrai point de notaire puisque vous aimez mieux le direct, mais c'est que je dèteste les affaires avec vous. Finissez donc celle là le plutot possible. Et venez vite à genève. Je suis bien aise que vous pensiez à y venir et bien tentée d'ètre mauvaise pour hàter votre arrivèe.

Adieu. Je finis parce que ma tète est si foible que je ne puis ècrire sans éblouissements. Adieu. Je voudrois bien mourir.

[Sans signature]

TRANSLATION

June 28[1]

No, certainly, I should not like to *treat you badly.* So I shall accept the guarantee of M. Bidermann when you give it to me and with that guarantee we shall decide on terms, *but a guarantee in Europe is absolutely necessary for me,* and I ask you to settle this matter as soon as possible. In the letter that my father wrote to you, you know that he positively insisted on that guarantee. I cannot give it up. I shall not involve any notary in this since you prefer to deal directly, but the fact is that I detest business relations with you. End this one then as soon as possible. And come quickly to Geneva. I am very happy that you are thinking about coming here and quite tempted to be unpleasant in order to hasten your arrival. Adieu. I am closing because my head is so weak that I cannot write without dizziness. Adieu. I should like very much to die.

[No signature]

NOTE

1 The year "1806," written in another hand, precedes this date in the manuscript, but the correct date must be 1804, if one judges from the context of the letter.

67

du Pont de Nemours to Madame de Staël

2 July 1804

From a draft, WMSS 2/5

Paris 2 juillet 1804

Madame de Stael

Mon excellente Amie,

Je prends des mesures que je crois certaines pour vous rembourser dans le courant d'Aoust la moitié du capital que je devais à Mr Votre Pere.[1]

Mais je ne saurai positivement si la rentrée que j'espere sera sure que le premier d'Aoust.

Je vous l'écrirai le deux, à un mois de ce jour.

J'ignore de même si je pourrai vous aller voir: ce dont mon cœur et mon esprit ont également besoin.[2]

Monsieur de la Vallette[3] a pour les belles lettres un gout si décidé, que, quoique j'aie l'honneur d'être précisement de l'Académie des belles lettres je ne puis plus me déterminer à en écrire ni à en recevoir.[4]

J'aime a me flatter que vous ne douterez jamais qu'en silence ou non je vous suis devoué pour la vie.

Salut et respect.

du Pont (de Nemours)

Que Dieu bénisse vos enfans et vous!

TRANSLATION

Paris, July 2, 1804

Madame de Staël

My excellent friend,

I am taking measures which I believe certain to reimburse you during August for half of the capital which I owed your father.[1]

But I shall not know positively whether the collection that I am hoping for will be certain until August 1.

I shall write you about it on the second, one month from this day.

I do not know either whether I shall be able to go see you, something which my heart and mind both need.[2]

M. de La Valette[3] has such a decided taste for belles lettres that, although I have the honor of belonging to the Academy of Belles Lettres, I can no longer force myself to write any or receive any.[4]

I like to flatter myself that you will never doubt that, in silence or not, I am devoted to you for life.

Greetings and respect.

du Pont (de Nemours)

God bless your children and you!

NOTES

1 See Letter 70.

2 It is obvious from du Pont de Nemours' letters to Victor du Pont at this time that he was, in reality, trying to avoid Mme. de Staël.

3 Antoine-Maris Chamans, Comte de La Valette (1769–1830). A great admirer of Napoleon, he had married Emilie-Louise de Beauharnais, Josephine's niece by her first marriage. After the 18 Brumaire, he was placed in charge of the postal service. Du Pont de Nemours was clearly afraid that his correspondence was being read by the postal authorities.

4 In a copy of the original made by Gustave Schelle at the château of Coppet, the last four words do not appear.

68

du Pont de Nemours to Necker de Germany

2 July 1804

From a copy by Gustave Schelle, WMSS 8/108

à Monsieur Necker de Germany à Genève

Paris, 13 Messidor 12
2 Juillet 1804

Monsieur,

J'ai reçu la lettre dont vous m'avez honoré le vingt Juin.

J'ai la plus grande espérance de pouvoir dans le courant d'Aout payer à Madame votre nièce la moitié de ce que lui doit ma maison.

Mais je ne le saurai avec certitude que le premier d'Août.

Je me hâterai alors de l'en instruire et vous aussi.

Et dans le cas où ce payement ne pourrait pas être réalisé je me conformerai à l'autre condition que Monsieur Necker m'avait imposée.

Soyez convaincu, Monsieur, du zèle que je mettrai toujours à mériter et à entretenir la bienveillance que vous et votre famille n'avez cessé de m'accorder.

Salut et attachment respectueux.

Du Pont (de Nemours)

TRANSLATION

To M. Necker de Germany in Geneva

Paris, 13 Messidor, year XII
July 2, 1804

Sir,

I have received the letter with which you honored me on June 20.

I have the greatest hope of being able to pay your niece half of what my company owes her during the month of August.

But I shall not know with certainty until August 1.

I shall hasten then to inform her about it, and you also.

And in the event that this payment cannot be made, I shall conform to the other condition that M. Necker had imposed.

Be assured, Sir, of the zeal that I shall always show in deserving and keeping the benevolence that you and your family have not ceased according me.

Greetings and respectful attachment.

Du Pont (de Nemours)

69

Madame de Staël to du Pont de Nemours

15 August 1804

WMSS 2/17

coppet ce 15 aoüst

Vous avez pourtant tort mon cher du pont d'avoir peur de m'ècrire sur de simples affaires. Il me semble qu'il est interdit de parler sur tout ce que dèfend figaro[1] mais sur des lettres de change! Ce genre de lettres n'est il pas permis? Vous m'avez ècrit que le 2 aoüst vous me manderiez votre rèsolution relativement à notre crèance. Vous n'avez pas eu la bontè de m'ècrire sur ce sujet. Je vous observe cependant que prète à partir pour l'italie[2] il faut absolument que cette affaire soit règlèe avant mon dèpart. Vous m'avez promis ou la moitiè du payement ou la garantie pour le tout. Je vous prie de tenir cet engagement. Mon pauve oncle qui nous servoit d'intermèdiaire n'existe plus.[3] Oh! je suis isolèe de tous les liens paternels. Il faut que je menne seule le sort de trois enfants, et vous devez me pardonner si cette responsabilité me rend plus règulière. Ayez la bontè de me rèpondre le plutot possible sur notre affaire. M[r] de la valette ne peut pas le trouver mauvais. N'ètiez vous pas d'ailleurs autrefois accoutumé?[4] Mais je ne veux pas vous rappeller votre jeunesse d'il y a peu d'annèes. Conservez en toujours un peu pour m'aimer.

N[ecker] Stael de H[olstein]

Vous ne m'avez pas dit mon cher du pont si M^r bureau de puzi est garant de la somme que nous vous avons prètèe. Vous ne m'avez pas renvoyè un billet à mon ordre de la somme due? Vous me traitez un peu en poète pour les affaires d'argent.

Rappellez moi au souvenir de Madame du pont.

On the reverse:

A Monsieur
Monsieur Dupont de Nemours
rue de Montaulon N° 301
a Paris

TRANSLATION

Coppet, August 15

You are wrong, my dear du Pont, to be afraid to write to me about simple business matters. It seems to me that it is forbidden to speak about everything that Figaro[1] forbids, but about bills! Is not that kind of letter allowed? You wrote to me that on August 2, you would send me your decision concerning our credit. You did not have the kindness to write about that subject. I point out to you, however, that, ready to leave for Italy,[2] it is absolutely necessary that this matter be settled before my departure. You promised me either half of the payment or a guarantee for the whole amount. I beg you to hold to this obligation. My poor uncle, who acted as intermediary for us, is no longer living.[3] Ah, I am isolated from all paternal connections. I must direct alone the fate of three children, and you must pardon me if that responsibility makes me more orderly. Have the kindness to answer me as soon as possible about our business. M. de La Valette cannot find that bad. Were you not once accustomed to it, moreover?[4] But I do not want to recall to you your youth of a few years ago. Keep a little of it always in order to love me.

Necker Staël de Holstein

You did not tell me, my dear du Pont, whether M. Bureaux de Pusy is the guarantor of the sum that we lent you. Did you not send me a note payable to me for the amount due? You act a bit like a poet with me in money matters.

Remember me to Mme. du Pont.

On the reverse:

To Monsieur
M. du Pont de Nemours
301, rue de Montholon
in Paris

NOTES
1 An allusion to the famous monologue by Figaro in Beaumarchais's *Marriage of Figaro*, V, iii:

> On me dit que, pendant ma retraite économique, il s'est introduit dans Madrid un système de liberté sur la vente des productions, qui s'étend jusqu'à celles de la presse; et pourvu que je ne parle en mes écrits, ni de l'autorité, ni du culte, ni de la politique, ni de la morale, ni des gens en place, ni des corps en crédit, ni de l'Opéra, ni des autres spectacles, ni des personnes qui tiennent à quelque chose, je puis tout imprimer sous l'inspection néanmoins de deux ou trois censeurs.

> (I am told that during my economic retreat [stay in prison], there has been introduced in Madrid a system of liberty in the sale of productions, which extends even to those of the press; and that provided I do not speak in my writings about authority, religion, politics, morals, people in prominent positions, respected organizations, the Opera, other theatrical performances, or people who are attached to something, I can print anything under the inspection, nevertheless, of two or three censors.)

2 Mme. de Staël did not leave for Italy until December 11 (*Journaux intimes*, p. 175).
3 Louis Necker de Germany died July 31, 1804.
4 Probably an allusion to du Pont de Nemours' difficulties during the Revolution.

70

du Pont de Nemours to Madame de Staël

21 August 1804

From a copy by Gustave Schelle, WMSS 8/108

à Madame de Stael à Coppet

Paris 3 Fructidor 12

Mon excellente amie.

Je ne vous écris point en Poëte, quoique vous méritiez certainement qu'on fasse de beaux vers à votre louange.

Je vous envoie *dix mille francs* en vile et bonne prose.

Je ferai successivement le reste des *vingt quatre mille trois cent quarante.*

J'attendais le 1er Aout pour savoir si je serais autorisé à vendre des traites de St Domingue que j'ai pour sureté de ce que me doit Vanmeerbek.

Je vois que vous savez très bien la chronologie, et je sais qu'elle est importante en affaires. Mais il a fallu plus de temps pour avoir cette autorisation complète.

La vente ne peut aller aussi vite que je voudrais.

Elle se fait à grande perte pour Vanmeerbek et pour moi.

Mais elle se fait, et c'est à raison de celà que j'ai cet accompte à vous donner.

M. de Pusy n'a plus, depuis son retour en France, de part à notre administration; et celà ne diminue pas votre sureté, attendu qu'il n'a aucune autre fortune que son intéret dans notre société, et que la Préfecture ne l'enrichit nullement.

Nous avons pour garant la société toute entière dont les principaux membres sont: Mon ami Bidermann, mon ami et le votre Johannot, Pusy et moi. Les autres n'ont que de petits intérets. J'ai envoyé leur catalogue à feu M. Votre oncle, qui était lui-même pour *vingt un mille deux cent francs* notre associé, et par conséquent votre débiteur.

Nul de nous ne peut toucher un sol de son capital avant que vous soyez payée en entier.

Les six banquiers de la Cour ne vous donneraient pas une sureté aussi grande. Je ne céderais point notre Fabrique de poudre pour tout ce qu'ils auront de net dans trois ans.

Il n'a pas été nécessaire jusqu'à présent que je vous envoyasse un nouvel engagement. Sa forme et sa qualité dépendent des payements que je vous fais.

Le premier n'étant pas soldé conserve sa force, et notre correspondance, tant avec vous qu'avec M. Votre Père suffit pour constater nos délais.

Si vous voulez un titre nouvel et négociable, je vous le donnerai volontiers, comme l'acquit de l'ancien.

Je désirerais dans ce cas, qu'il fut divisé en trois époques pour chacune desquelles nous pourrions joindre les intérets au capital.

La première en l'an 13, la seconde en 14, et la solde en l'an 15.

Je comptais régler le tout avec vous à Coppet, et je l'espère encore. Mais il m'a fallu rester ici pour ces arrangements meme.

J'ai appris avec bien de la douleur la perte que vous avez faite de Monsieur votre Oncle, vous ne pouvez avoir aucun chagrin que je ne partage vivement.

Nous en avons plusieurs communs.

Permettez-moi de croire que vous entrez aussi dans les miens. Je baise vos mains avec tendresse et respect.

Du Pont (de Nemours)

Madame Du Pont vous dit mille choses.

TRANSLATION

To Madame de Staël at Coppet

Paris, 3 Fructidor, year XII

My excellent friend,

I am not writing to you as a poet, although you certainly deserve to have someone write beautiful verses in praise of you.

I am sending you *10,000 francs* in vile and good prose.

I shall send successively the rest of the *24,340*.

I was waiting for August 1 in order to learn whether I should be authorized to sell some Santo Domingo drafts which I have as a guarantee for what van Merbeck owes me.

I see that you know chronology very well, and I know that it is important in business. But more time was required to get the complete authorization.

The sale cannot go as fast as I should like.

It is being made at a great loss for van Merbeck and me.

But it is being made, and it is because of that that I have this installment to give you.

Since his return to France, M. de Pusy no longer has had any part in our administration; but that does not diminish your guarantee, considering that he has no other wealth than his interest in our company and that his position as prefect does not enrich him at all.

We have as a guarantee the entire company, whose principal members are my friend Bidermann, my friend and yours Johannot, Pusy, and me. The others have only small interests. I sent the list of them to your late uncle, who had invested *21,200 francs* in our company, and was consequently your debtor.

Not one of us can touch a sou of his capital before you are completely paid.

The six bankers of the Court would not give you as large a guarantee. I would not give up our powder factory for all that they will have clear in three years.

It was not necessary up to now for me to send you a new pledge. Its form and quality depend on the payments that I am making to you.

The first one, not being settled, keeps its force, and our correspondence, both with you and your father, suffices to record our delays.

If you want a new and negotiable certificate, I shall gladly give it to you, as the receipt for the former one.

I should like it, in this case, to be divided into three periods, for each of which we could add the interest to the capital.

The first one in the year XIII, the second in XIV, and the remainder in the year XV.

I expected to settle the whole thing with you at Coppet, and I still hope to do so. But it was necessary for me to remain here for these very arrangements.

I learned with great sorrow of the loss of your uncle. You cannot have any sorrow that I do not share strongly.

We have several common ones.

Permit me to think that you share mine also.

I kiss your hands with tenderness and respect.

Du Pont (de Nemours)

Mme. du Pont sends her regards to you.

71

Madame de Staël to du Pont de Nemours

31 August 1804

WMSS 2/17

ce 31 aoust 1804

J'ai reçu mon cher du pont les dix mille livres que vous m'avez envoyè. J'accepte votre proposition de solder par trois lettres de change mais je dèsire que le tout en trois payements ègaux d'intéret et de capital soit, le 1ᵉʳ, le 1ᵉʳ de 9ᵇʳᵉ de cette annèe, le second un an après, et le 3ᵉᵐᵉ six mois après le second. J'ai besoin de savoir avant deux ans de toute manière ce que je deviendrai. Si vous ètiez venu ici je n'aurois jamais fait que ce que vous auriez voulu mais par lettres je suis sevére. Croyez aux sentiments qui vous sont conservés dans mon cœur tout dévasté qu'il est. Envoyez moi ces engagements à mon ordre. Recevez pour Mad. du pont et pour vous mes plus tendres amitiès.

[Sans signature]

On the reverse:

A Monsieur
Monsieur Dupont de Nemours

TRANSLATION

August 31, 1804

I received, my dear du Pont, the 10,000 francs that you sent me. I accept your proposition to settle with three bills of exchange, but I want the entire thing in three equal payments of interest and capital; the first one, on November 1 of this year; the second one, a year later; and the third one, six months after the second. I need to know before two years have passed, in any case, what will become of me. If you had come here, I should have done only what you wanted, but when we correspond by letter, I am severe. Believe in the feelings which are kept for you in my heart, broken though it is. Send these pledges payable to me. Receive for Mme. du Pont and yourself my most tender, friendly greetings.

[No signature]

On the reverse:

To Monsieur
M. du Pont de Nemours

72

du Pont de Nemours to Madame de Staël

2 October 1804

From a copy by Gustave Schelle, WMSS 8/108

à Madame de Stael à Coppet, Genève

Paris 10 Vendémiaire 13

Mon excellente amie

Je vous enverrai sous huit à dix jours l'appoint de la première moitié de ce que je vous dois, qui avec les intérets depuis Juillet se montera à environ 14.800 frs. que je ferai en sorte de rendre payable à Genève pour votre plus grande commodité, et j'y joindrai trois effets de ma maison payables le 1er de 9.570 frs 68 au 1er Juillet, 12 Messidor prochain; le second de 9.092 frs 19 à la même époque de l'année suivante; et le dernier pour solde de 8.599 frs 29 au 12 messidor an 15. Les intérets se trouveront ainsi compris dans chaque payement avec le tiers du capital.

Je n'ai pu faire tomber les échéances en Novembre comme vous le désiriez en dernier lieu, puisque c'est tout près de novembre que je vous remettrai le second payement pour acquit de la première moitié.

Je chargerai mon Beau-frère[1] de vous remettre ces différents effets et je vous prierai alors de vouloir bien lui remettre en échange l'engagement que mon Fils avait contracté avec M. Votre père en notre nom.

Quand je dis que je chargerai mon Beau-frère de cette opération, c'est en supposant que je ne puisse pas être moi-meme le commissionnaire, et je tâcherai bien de lui en épargner la peine.

Je suis loin d'avoir renoncé à vous aller voir; et vous ajoutez beaucoup à mon désir en me parlant des avantages de la Présence réelle, que je n'ignore pas, quoique né calviniste et devenu philosophe.

Je mettrais un prix extreme à quelques heures de conversation intime avec vous.

Vous écrivez la vie de M. Votre Père, et publiez quelques uns de ses manuscrits.[2] J'espère que ce monument de piété filiale vous empechera d'aller si vite en Italie; Pays où il n'y a plus de beau que les sites et le climat, et où la nation, quoique pleine d'esprit a toujours été sans morale.

Si dans la décade qui suivra la réception de ma lettre vous n'aviez pas encore de mes nouvelles, vous seriez sure que je suis en route, parti comme un éclair dès que j'aurais eu votre argent dans mes poches, ou que je l'aurais fait passer dans les votres.

Je suis persuadé que si je vous avais vue, je vous en aurais indiqué le meilleur usage. Mais le premier point était de le recueillir et n'ayant pu vous communiquer que par lettres, j'ai du me conformer à vos ordres autant qu'ils ont été à portée de ma possibilité.

Je baise vos très belles mains avec respect et tendresse.[3]

Du Pont (de Nemours)

Soyez assez bonne pour me mander de suite combien vous serez encore de temps à Coppet ou à Genève.

TRANSLATION

To Madame de Staël at Coppet, Geneva

Paris, 10 Vendémiaire, year XIII

My excellent friend,

I shall send you in eight or ten days the balance of the first half of what I owe you, which, with the interest since July, will amount to about 14,800 francs, which I shall arrange so that it will be payable in Geneva for your greater convenience, and I shall add to it three bills on my company, the first one payable for 9,570.68 francs on July 1, next 12 Messidor; the second one for 9,092.19 francs at the same time the following year; and the last one settling the account for 8,599.29 francs on 12 Messidor, year XV. The interest will be thus included in each payment with the third of the capital.

I could not set the term in November, as was your last request, since it is quite close to November that I shall send you the second payment for the acquittance of the first half.

I shall request my brother-in-law[1] to give you these different bills, and I shall ask you then to be so kind as to give him, in exchange, the pledge that my son had made with your father in our name.

When I say that I shall ask my brother-in-law to handle this matter, it is supposing that I cannot be the agent myself, and I shall try indeed to spare him the trouble.

I have far from given up the idea of going to see you, and you add much to my desire by speaking to me of the advantages of the real presence, which I am not ignorant of, although born a Calvinist and having become a philosopher.

I should value highly a few hours of intimate conversation with you.

You are writing a biography of your father, and are publishing some of his manuscripts.[2] I hope that this monument of filial piety will prevent you from going so soon to Italy, a country where there is no longer anything beautiful but the landscapes and the climate, and where the nation, although full of wit, has always been without morality.

If, in the ten days that follow the receipt of my letter, you do not have news of me, you can be sure that I am on my way, having left like a flash as soon as I had your money in my pockets or had it passed to yours.

I am convinced that if I had seen you, I should have indicated the best use for it. But the first point was to collect it; and having been able to communicate with you only by letter, I had to agree to your orders as much as was possible.

I kiss your very beautiful hands with respect and tenderness.[3]

Du Pont (de Nemours)

Be so kind as to inform me at once how much longer you will be in Coppet or in Geneva.

NOTES

1 Philibert Boullée, the husband of Mme. du Pont's sister and director of the registry in Bourg, a town near Geneva.

2 The *Manuscrits de Mr Necker publiés par sa fille* (Geneva, XIII).

3 In a letter written to Victor du Pont on 17 Vendémiaire, year XIII (October 9,

1804; WMSS 2/5), du Pont de Nemours notes: "Je conclus avec Madame de Stael en lui donnant 24340 F et les interets jusqu'à la fin d'octobre et trois billets de moi, l'un de 9571 F^{es} au 1er juillet prochain, l'autre de 9093 F a la même epoque de l'année suivante, le dernier de 8600 F au premier juillet 1807." ("I have settled with Mme. de Staël by giving her 24,340 francs and the interest to the end of October and three bills on myself, one for 9,571 francs due next July 1, the second for 9,093 francs due the same time the following year, [and] the last for 8,600 francs due July 1, 1807.")

73

Madame de Staël to du Pont de Nemours

10 October 1804

WMSS 2/17

Mon cher dupont je reste ici jusqu'au 15 9bre précisément et je trouve que vous devriez venir avant ce tems. Ne vous gènez pas pour me faire toucher l'argent à genève. Cela m'est tout à fait ègal à genève ou à paris. J'aime mieux même qu'il soit dècidè dès à prèsent que vous le remettrez à M^{rs} de lessert.[1] Mandez moi seulement quand vous l'aurez fait ou plutot ne me le mandez pas: venez me le dire. Que j'aurois de plaisir à vous voir!

[Sans signature]

ce 10 8bre 1804

On the reverse:

pour M^r dupont de Nemours
rue montolon N° 301

TRANSLATION

My dear du Pont, I am staying here until exactly November 15, and I believe that you ought to come before that time. Do not bother to arrange to have me receive the money in Geneva. It is all the same to me, in Geneva or in Paris. I even prefer to have it decided right now that you will deposit it at Messrs. Delessert.[1] Inform me only when you have done so, or rather do not inform me: come tell me. What pleasure I should have in seeing you!

[No signature]

October 8, 1804

On the reverse:

for M. du Pont de Nemours
301, rue de Montholon

NOTE
1 See Letter 14, note 5.

74

Madame de Staël to du Pont de Nemours

[October 1804?]

WMSS 2/22

My dear friend,[1]

J'ai fait d'eugenes mon homme d'affaires. Il va à paris pour quelques jours. Dites lui si je puis compter sur le plaisir de vous voir ou si devant y renoncer avec tristesse je puis ètre certaine que vous avez terminé notre affaire avec M^rs de lessert. Donnez lui les lettres de change. Il me les rapportera. Mille amitiès. Je ne sais rien vous dire mais si vous savez quelque chose qui m'intéresse vous pouvez me mander tout en sureté par eugènes.

[Sans signature]

On the reverse:

A Monsieur Dupont de Nemours

TRANSLATION
My dear friend,

I have made Eugene my business agent. He is going to Paris for a few days. Tell him whether I can count on the pleasure of seeing you or whether, having to abandon it with sadness, I can be certain that you have settled our affair with Messrs. Delessert. Give him the bills. He will bring them back to me. A thousand friendly greetings. I know nothing to tell you; but, if you know something that interests me, you can inform me of everything in safety through Eugene.

[No signature]

On the reverse:

To M. du Pont de Nemours

NOTES

The date 1807 appears on this letter. It is in another handwriting, and judging from the context of the letter, does not seem logical. Mme. de Staël's desire to see du Pont de Nemours, and the mention of Delessert and the payments to be made, seem to place the letter about October 1804. Moreover, Eugene (Joseph Uginet) was on a trip in October and November 1804, returning to Coppet on November 10 (*Journaux intimes,* pp. 155, 160, 161).

1 This salutation is one of two instances of Mme. de Staël's using English in this correspondence: the other occurs in the first sentence of Letter 119.

75

Madame de Staël to du Pont de Nemours

5 November 1804

WMSS 2/17

Mon cher dupont, si au reçu de cette lettre vous ne venez pas je ne serai plus ici. J'espère bien que vous n'attendrez pas d'avoir mon argent pour venir me voir. Mon dieu je serai si triste si vous partez pour l'amèrique sans que je vous aye vu. Adieu. Je pars le 20 9ᵇʳᵉ pour proffiter du passage du pape sur le mont cenis qui doit ètre tout balayè pour lui faciliter la route.¹

[Sans signature]

ce 5 9ᵇʳᵉ

On the reverse:

A Monsieur

Monsieur Dupont de Nemours

TRANSLATION

My dear du Pont, if, on the receipt of this letter, you do not come, I shall no longer be here. I hope, indeed, that you will not wait to have my money to come see me. My word, I shall be so sad if you leave for America without my having seen you. Adieu. I leave on November 20 in order to take advantage of the Pope's passage over Mont Cenis, which is to be swept clean to make the road easy for him to pass along.¹

[No signature]

November 5

On the reverse:

To Monsieur
M. du Pont de Nemours

NOTE
1 An allusion to Pope Pius VII's trip to France to crown Napoleon on December 2, 1804.

76

du Pont de Nemours to Madame de Staël

12 November 1804

From a copy by Gustave Schelle, WMSS 8/108

à Madame de Stael

Paris 21 Brumaire 13[1]

Il est très vrai, mon excellente amie, que le désir de terminer avec vous nos affaires d'argent avant d'aller vous voir a contribué à retarder mon voyage; et vrai encore que je n'en toucherai les fonds que le 29 brumaire (20 Novembre), jour même de votre départ.

Mais une autre affaire extrêmement importante pour des Amis que j'ai en Amérique m'aurait de meme retenu.[2] Ils ont déposé près de onze cent mille francs entre les mains du général Hedouville[3] pour retirer un navire que revenait de l'Inde et qu'un corsaire Français avait pris injustement, illégalement. Il s'agissait de savoir:

1° Si le corsaire avait raison ou tort: j'ai gagné ce procès, le conseil des prises a jugé contre lui.

2° Si les fonds seraient payés par les Etats-Unis en accompte de la Louisiane ou par la France en bons de deux tiers et un tiers consolidé. J'ai encore obtenu que ce soient les Etats-Unis qui payent. Mais il reste à savoir s'ils payeront les onze cent mille francs ou s'ils n'en payeront que neuf cent cinquante mille et je ne puis quitter la présence réelle aux discussions avant d'avoir sauvé encore ces cinquante mille écus à mes amis.

Cependant, il m'est plus amère que je ne puis vous dire de ne vous avoir pas vue et si je n'ai pas ce bonheur avant de retourner dans mon nouveau monde, j'y emporterai une profonde affliction.

Vous allez en Italie, croyez-vous qu'elle vaille mieux que la France ou la Suisse? Non pas meme pour le climat, si ce n'est à Naples où tout le reste est si détestable.

Milan, Florence et Boulogne méritent chacun un séjour de quelques semaines.

Rome n'a d'intérêt que pour un élève de l'Académie de Peinture, de sculpture et d'architecture, encore est-il beaucoup baissé; et pour un membre de ma classe à l'Institut.

C'est l'europe toute entière qui ne vaut rien; et qui doit constamment empirer.

Mais renfermons-nous en nous-mêmes. Je ne veux ni sacrifier à l'opinion, ni la changer. L'un est au-dessous de moi, l'autre au-dessus. Je m'en éloigne.

Je ne le puis, ni ne le veux, sans avoir réglé tous mes comptes.

Je remettrai à M. Fourcault de Pavant, selon vos ordres, l'appoint du vôtre et mes billets pour les années suivantes qui sont faits depuis longtemps. Veuillez lui faire passer le billet de mon fils en notre nom commercial qui est votre titre actuel, ou pouvoir d'expédier quittance dont il garderait minute, afin qu'il n'exige pas double titre, et double droit pour vos enfants en cas de malheur.

Je crains parce que m'a dit Eugène que vous n'ayiez égaré le billet de mon fils. Si vous ne pouvez pas le retrouver, il deviendra nécessaire que vous ayiez la bonté de donner un pouvoir bien détaillé pour

moyennant le payement fait le 27 fructidor de	5.000
celui fait le 2 Vendémiaire de	3.000
celui fait le 5 Vendémiaire de	2.000
celui fait le 7 Brumaire de	10.000
celui qui sera fait le 30 Brumaire de	4.770
et la remise de trois billets de ma maison	
l'un au 12 Messidor an 13 de	9.570,68
l'autre au 12 Messidor an 14[4] de	9.092,19
le troisième au 12 Messidor an 15 de	8.599,29
Total	50.032,16

donner quittance du billet de neuf mille huit cent trente trois dollars soixante et dix cents souscrit par Victor Du Pont le vingt

Juillet 1801 au nom de ma maison pour pareille valeur en stocks américains au cours qu'ils avaient en Amérique le premier Juillet précédent, lequel s'est trouvé de 9.184,66 valant en francs 48.678 frs.

Je n'ai que le temps de clorre cette lettre et de baiser vos belles mains.

Du Pont (de Nemours)

Madame Du Pont se recommande à votre constante amitié.

TRANSLATION

To Madame de Staël

Paris, 21 Brumaire, year XIII [1]

It is very true, my excellent friend, that the desire to conclude with you our financial affairs before going to see you contributed to the delay of my trip, and true also that I shall not receive the funds until the 29 Brumaire (November 20), the very day of your departure.

But an extremely important affair for some friends in America would have detained me likewise.[2] They placed nearly 1,100,000 francs with General Hédouville[3] in order to recover a ship returning from India which a French privateer had seized unjustly, illegally. It was a question of learning:

1. Whether the privateer was right or wrong. I won this suit; the Council of Prizes ruled against it.

2. Whether the funds would be paid by the United States as part of the payment for Louisiana or by France with two thirds in bonds and one third consolidated. I succeeded in arranging for the United States to pay. But whether it will pay the 1,100,000 francs or whether it will pay only 950,000 remains to be seen, and I cannot remove the real presence from the discussions before having saved these 50,000 écus for my friends.

However, it is more bitter for me than I can tell you not to have seen you, and if I do not have that pleasure before returning to my New World, I shall carry back a deep affliction.

You are going to Italy. Do you believe that it is better than France or Switzerland? Not even for the climate, unless it is in Naples, where everything else is so detestable.

Milan, Florence, and Bologna are each worth a visit of a few weeks.

Rome has interest only for a student of the Academy of Painting, Sculpture, and Architecture (moreover, it has declined greatly) and for a member of my class in the Institut.

The whole of Europe is worth nothing and must get constantly worse.

But let us withdraw into ourselves. I want neither to make a sacrifice to opinion nor to change it. One is beneath me, the other beyond me. I am leaving it.

I cannot leave, and do not wish to, without settling all my accounts.

I shall give to M. Fourcault de Pavant, according to your orders, the balance of your account and my notes for the following years, which have been made out for a long time. Please give him my son's note in the name of our company, which is your present certificate, or power to send a receipt, of which he would keep a copy, so that he may not demand a double certificate, and a double fee from your children in case of misfortune.

I am afraid because Eugene told me that you have misplaced my son's note. If you cannot locate it, you will have to be kind enough to give a very detailed authorization

in return for the payment made on 27 Fructidor of	5,000	fr.
the one made on 2 Vendémiaire of	3,000	
the one made on 5 Vendémiaire of	2,000	
the one made on 7 Brumaire of	10,000	
the one that will be made on 30 Brumaire of	4,770	
and the delivery of three notes from my company,		
the one on 12 Messidor, year XIII of	9,570.68	
the other on 12 Messidor, year XIV [4] of	9,092.19	
the third on 12 Messidor, year XV of	8,599.29	
Total	50,032.16 fr.	

in order to give a receipt for the note of $9,833.70 signed by Victor du Pont on July 20, 1801, in the name of my company for said amount in American stocks at the rate of exchange which they had in America the preceding July 1, which was $9,184.66, or 48,678 francs.

I have only the time to end this letter and to kiss your beautiful hands.

Du Pont (de Nemours)

Mme. du Pont wishes to be remembered to you.

NOTES

1 The Schelle copy erroneously gives the year as XII.

2 The affair in question concerned the American ship, the *New Jersey*, belonging to two men named Nicklin and Griffith. The vessel had been captured in Puerto Rico by the French, who required the owners to pay 203,000 piastres gourdes to General Hédouville in Santo Domingo. The French claimed that the owners were English and that the ship had been insured by an English company. This was eventually shown to be false. Nicklin and Griffith were finally repaid by the United States government as part of the price of the Louisiana Purchase.

Du Pont de Nemours acted as the authorized agent for the owners in this matter, along with a certain attorney, de La Grange.

A history of the episode appears in the five following memoirs by du Pont de Nemours and de La Grange, all published in Paris with no date:

Observations sommaires et preuves sur le navire le New Jersey, et ses propriétaires;

Dernières observations sur le navire le New-Jersey;

Doutes et préventions relativement à la restitution à faire aux propriétaires américains du navire le New-Jersey. Réponses à ces doutes, réfutation de ces préventions;

[with J. B. Sirey], *Nouvelles Questions proposées par M. le Directeur de la quatrième division de la Liquidation générale, membre du Conseil de Liquidation, et de la part de ce Conseil. Aux fondés de pouvoirs et défenseurs des Propriétaires du navire le New-Jersey, et de leurs co-intéressés. Réponses à ces questions;*

A Leurs Excellences Les Ministres plénipotentiaires Français et Américain, chargés de prononcer sur les Réclamations des Citoyens des Etats-Unis, qui ont droit de prendre part aux Avantages stipulés entre les deux Nations, par les deux Nations, par les Traités du 8 Vendémiaire An IX, et du 10 Floréal An XI.

3 Gabriel-Théodore-Joseph, Comte d'Hédouville (1755–1825), a general in the Revolutionary and Napoleonic armies. Because of his success in putting down the insurrections in Brittany, the Directory sent him to Santo Domingo in 1797 in an effort to reconcile that island with France. Unable to counteract the influence of Toussaint L'Ouverture, he was forced to return to France in 1799. In his copy of this letter, Gustave Schelle incorrectly spelled the name as Hédonville.

4 On the copy made by Gustave Schelle, the year XV appears: this is an obvious error and has been corrected.

77

Madame de Staël to du Pont de Nemours

13 November 1804

WMSS 2/18

geneve ce 13 9ᵇʳᵉ

J'ai vu une lettre de vous à Mʳ fourcault mon cher dupont qui mérite un reproche doux mais nécessaire. Je ne discute point s'il ne devoit pas vous suffire de ma déclaration en suisse, sans exiger les frais assez considérables de la france. Je ne discute pas, si vous, jugeant à propos de ne pas me payer à l'échéance du billet je n'ètois pas tout à fait en droit d'exiger en le prolongeant un acte dont les frais auroient toujours regardè le dèbiteur. *Je passe condemnation sur ces frais,* mais il est un article de votre lettre sur lequel aucune puissance humaine ne me feroit passer condemnation. Vous dites, *je crois en ma conscience que Mʳ Necker a voulu anèantir le billet de mon fils.* Si je croyois cela le moins du monde je ne recevrois pas un sol de cette dette mais 1° je vous demanderai quel seroit le motif de mon père pour vous faire prèsent de 50 mille livres quand il n'a pas laissè au de là de 3 mille livres à ses parents et amis les plus proches? Je ne sais pas s'il y a une fortune en france qui permit une telle libéralité à un ètranger. Ce n'est pas du moins celle d'un homme qui laisse à sa fille et à ses trois enfants trois mille louis de revenu. 2° de plus vous avez des lettres de mon père qui montrent de la sollicitude sur votre mode de payement, et dans les propositions que vous m'avez faites vous vous appuyez, et avec raison, de ces mèmes propositions que j'ai acceptées à cause de ces mèmes lettres. 3° dans le billan de mon père il y a votre dette inscrite de sa main et cela le 1ᵉʳ janvier 1804 trois mois avant sa perte. Enfin et ceci n'est plus qu'une preuve morale mon père m'a souvent parlè de cette relation avec vous mon cher du pont, et il l'a prise par estime pour votre caractére. Mais avec l'examen de vos affaires! Pardonnez moi la vivacitè que je mets sur ce sujet, ma religion sur cette terre c'est la mèmoire de mon père et je ne sais rien du moins je l'espère que je ne sacrifiasse à une ligne ècrite de sa main, ou à une parole authentique de lui. Vous avez donc

touchè par votre lettre à M^r fourcault au point qui me ranimeroit
mourante et je suis trés en vie. Adieu mon cher dupont. Ceci ne
change rien au fond de nos affaires, mais vous m'offenseriez mor-
tellement si vous conserviez une pensèe, qui supposeroit une folie
dans mon père et dans moi un manque de respect pour ses intentions. À la fin de tout cela je vous dis comme toujours mille amitiès.

[Sans signature]

TRANSLATION

Geneva, November 13

I have seen a letter from you to M. Fourcault, my dear du Pont,
which calls for a gentle but necessary rebuke. I do not argue
whether it should not suffice for you to have my statement in
Switzerland, without requiring the rather considerable expenses
of France; I do not argue whether, since you consider it fitting not
to pay me on the due date of the note, I had not every right to
demand, in extending it, a deed whose expenses would still have
been the debtor's concern: *I am willing to disregard these expenses,*
but there is one article in your letter which no human power could
make me disregard. You say, *"I believe, in my conscience, that M.
Necker wanted to destroy my son's note."* If I believed that the
least bit, I would not accept a sou of that debt; but (1), I ask you
what my father's motive would be in making you a gift of 50,000
francs when he did not leave more than 3,000 francs to his closest
relatives and friends? I do not know whether there is a fortune in
France which would allow such generosity to a stranger. It is not,
at least, that of a man who leaves to his daughter and to her three
children an income of 60,000 francs. (2) Moreover, you have letters
from my father which show concern about your manner of payment; and in the proposals that you have made to me, you depend,
and with reason, on these same proposals, which I accepted because of these same letters. (3) In my father's balance-sheet, your
debt is entered in his handwriting, and that on January 1, 1804,
three months before his death. Finally—and this is nothing more
than a moral proof—my father spoke often to me about this relationship with you, my dear du Pont, and he assumed it through
esteem for your character. But with the examination of your
business affairs! Pardon me for the vehemence that I show about
this matter. My religion in this world is the memory of my father,

and I know nothing, at least, so I hope, that I would not sacrifice to a line written in his handwriting or to an authentic word from him. You have touched, by your letter to M. Fourcault, the spot that would revive me while dying, and I am very much alive. Adieu, my dear du Pont. This changes nothing, after all, in our business, but you would mortally offend me if you entertained one thought which would suppose anything foolish in my father and, in me, a lack of respect for his intentions. After all that, I send you, as always, very friendly greetings.

[No signature]

78

Madame de Staël to du Pont de Nemours

24 November 1804

WMSS 2/17

J'ai donnè l'ordre à M[r] fourcault pavant notaire mon cher dupont de terminer avec vous. Comme vous me l'ècrivez vous lui remettrez les billets et il vous remettra ma quittance. Ne partez pas pour l'amérique avant le mois de juin prochain et venez me voir alors. Vous me ferez tant de plaisir. Envoyez moi votre règponse si vous m'ècrivez chez mon valet de chambre[1] à paris. Je ne sais ce que je deviendrai cet hyver. J'ai peur de l'italie à cause de mes enfants. Voila benjamin qui est obligè de me quitter[2] et ce pays où j'ai perdu mon père m'est affreux. Plaignez moi. La terre ne me porte plus et chaque jour de ma vie est un effort. Si je vous vois au mois de juin ces jours là me seront doux.

[Sans signature]

ce 24 9bre

On the reverse:

A Monsieur
Monsieur Dupont de Nemours
Rue Montolon N° 301
a Paris

Postmark:

10 F^{re} an 13, Genève

TRANSLATION

I have ordered M. Fourcault Pavant, a notary, to finish my business with you, my dear du Pont. As you indicate in your letters, you will give him the notes, and he will give you my receipt. Do not leave for America before next June, and come see me then. You will give me so much pleasure. Send me your answer, if you write to me, in care of my valet[1] in Paris. I do not know what will become of me this winter. I am afraid of Italy because of my children. Now Benjamin is obliged to leave me,[2] and this country where I lost my father is horrible for me. Pity me. The world is no longer bearable for me, and each day of my life is an effort. If I see you in June, those days will be sweet for me.

[No signature]

November 24

On the reverse:

To Monsieur
M. du Pont de Nemours
301, rue de Montholon
in Paris

Postmark:

10 Frimaire, year XIII, Geneva

NOTES

1 Undoubtedly Joseph Uginet; see Letter 45, note 1.
2 Benjamin Constant left the following day, November 25, in order to examine his father's affairs at Brévans. From there, he went on to Lyon and to Paris, where he arrived on December 22 (*Journaux intimes*, p. 260).

In his *Journaux intimes*, p. 167, Constant notes on 2 Frimaire (November 23):

J'éprouve beaucoup de peine de celle que Minette [Mme. de Staël] ressent de notre séparation. . . . J'ai pris son parti hier contre un homme qui lui fait des difficultés d'argent. Comme j'ai eu un mouvement très vif, je l'en ai vue si heureuse que j'en ai été profondément touché. Une des choses qui m'intéressent le plus à elle, c'est l'idée qu'on la croit aujourd'hui plus dénuée de protection qu'autrefois et que chacun espère en tirer parti. Ce calcul de la bassesse et de l'avidité humaine suffirait pour m'attacher à elle et pour me rendre tout mon ancien dévouement.

(I feel great sorrow for the unhappiness that Mme. de Staël shows at our separation. . . . I took her side yesterday against a man who is causing her financial difficulties. I had a very ardent reaction and saw her so happy about it that I was profoundly touched. One of the things that interests me most about her is the idea that people believe that today she has less protection than formerly and that everyone hopes to take advantage of it. This scheming founded on baseness and human greed would be enough to attach me to her and revive all my former devotion.)

It seems logical to suspect that the man mentioned in this passage was du Pont de Nemours.

79

Fourcault de Pavant to du Pont de Nemours

19 December 1804

WMSS 2/17

Fourcault Pavant notaire a l'honneur de presenter ses respects à Monsieur Dupont de Nemours, et de l'informer que Madame de Stael ne lui a point envoyé l'engagement contracté par sa maison envers M. Necker, mais seulement une note que Fourcault Pavant est bien aise de comparer avec celle qu'il prie Monsieur Dupont de Nemours de vouloir lui envoyer, pour pouvoir sur les notes rediger la quittance notariée qui suppleera à la restitution de l'engagement.

Fourcault Pavant sera à la disposition de Monsieur Dupont de Nemours samedi matin, s'il veut se donner la peine de passer chez lui pour causer de cette affaire.

[Sans signature]

le 28 frimaire [an 13]

On the reverse:

A Monsieur
Monsieur Dupont de Nemours
rue Montholon N° 300
à Paris

Postmark:

28 F^{re} an 13

TRANSLATION

Fourcault Pavant, notary, has the honor of presenting his respects to M. du Pont de Nemours, and of informing him that Mme. de Staël has not sent him the agreement contracted by his company with M. Necker, but only a note that Fourcault Pavant is very happy to compare with the one that he requests M. du Pont de Nemours to send him, in order to be able, on the notes, to compose the notarized receipt which will be substituted for the return of the agreement.

Fourcault Pavant will be at the disposal of M. du Pont de Nemours Saturday morning, if he will take the trouble to come to his office to discuss this matter.

[No signature]

28 Frimaire [year XIII]

On the reverse:

To Monsieur
M. du Pont de Nemours
300, rue de Montholon
in Paris

Postmark:

28 Frimaire, year XIII

❀

80

Necker de Saussure to du Pont de Nemours & Cie.

27 December 1804

WMSS 2/17

Geneve le 27 X^{bre} 1804

Messieurs Du Pont de Nemours et Cie

J'ai l'honneur de vous prevenir que j'ai remis ce jour a M^r J[ea]n L[oui]s Grivel [1] un mandat sur vous de f 1272 qui doit etre le montant des interets a 6% des 2 actions que mon Pere avait dans vos maisons d'Amerique. Vous voudrez bien y faire l'accueil & nous en debiter. Je dis nous car j'ecris tant en mon nom qu'en celui de Mad. Rilliet [2] ma sœur. Nos arrangements d'hoirie nous faisant desirer de liquider autant qu'il est possible les creances de notre Pere nous vous prions de nous marquer en reponse si vous pourriez nous negocier au moins une de nos actions & quel prix nous pouvons en esperer. Recevez Messieurs mes salutations empressées.

J. Necker de Saussure

On the reverse:

A Messieurs
Du Pont de Nemours et Cie
Paris

Postmark:

12 N[se] an 13
Genève 99

TRANSLATION

Geneva, December 27, 1804

Messieurs du Pont de Nemours and Co.,

I have the honor of informing you that I have given today to M. Jean Louis Grivel [1] an order on your account for 1,272 francs, which must be the amount of the interest at 6 per cent on the two shares of stock which my father had in your American companies. Be so kind as to accept it and debit it to us. I say "us," for I am writing both in my name and in that of my sister, Madame Rilliet.[2] Since the settling of our inheritance causes us to want to liquidate as much as possible the credits of our father, we beg you to indicate to us in reply whether you could redeem at least one of our shares and what price we can hope to receive for it. Receive, Sir, my attentive greetings.

J. Necker de Saussure

On the reverse:

To Messieurs
du Pont de Nemours and Co.
Paris

Postmark:

12 Nivôse, year XIII
Genève 99

NOTES

Jacques Necker de Saussure (1757–1825) was the son of Louis Necker de Germany. He had married Albertine de Saussure, the daughter of the Swiss geologist and physicist Horace Bénédict de Saussure. A mediocre man, he allowed his wife to prepare his lectures and do all his work, while he occupied a position as professor of mineralogy at the University of Geneva.

Benjamin Constant states that, at the time of his father's death, Jacques Necker de Saussure could scarcely conceal his satisfaction at inheriting his father's fortune (*Journaux intimes*, pp. 117–18).

1 See Letter 52, note 1.

2 Jeanne-Marie Necker (1753–1816). She had married Horace-Bénédict Rilliet, a member of the Council of the Two Hundred of Geneva.

81

Necker de Saussure to du Pont de Nemours & Cie.

16 January 1805

WMSS 2/18

Geneve le 16 J^r 1805

Messieurs,

D'après la lettre que vous m'avez adressée le 8 du C[ouran]t [1] j'ai verifie moi meme sur les livres de mon Pere les payements que lui avoient ete fait jusqu'a present par votre maison & j'ai vu en effet qu'il avoit recu trois années & que par concequent il ne nous sera du qu'une année en vendémiaire prochain. Comme je n'avois pas les livres au moment ou j'ai tiré sur vous j'ai pu etre induit en erreur d'après les nottes qu'on m'avoit fournie. Il nous est absolument indifferent de recevoir en messidor ou plus tard & nous entrerons volontiers dans vos convenances. Si nous n'avions pas nous memes des objets a liquider & des remboursements à faire nous ne penserions pas à nous defaire de ces deux actions mais nous y sommes forcés par la nature des autres placements. Ce sera donc nous rendre service Messieurs de nous les placer au pair.

Vous voudrez bien nous avertir dans le moment ou cela vous sera possible. Recevez Messieurs mes salutations les plus empressées.

J. Necker de Saussure

On the reverse:

A Messieurs
Dupont de Nemours Pere
Fils & Cie
Paris

Postmark:

2 P^{se} an 13
99 Genève

TRANSLATION

Geneva, January 16, 1805

Gentlemen,

   After the letter that you sent me on the eighth of this month,[1] I myself checked in my father's books for the payments that your company had made up to the present time, and I saw indeed that he had received three years interest and that consequently only one year of interest will be owed to us next Vendémiaire. As I did not have the books at the time I drew upon your company, I may have made an error because of the notes that I had been given. It does not matter at all to us whether we are paid in Messidor or later, and we shall gladly do whatever suits you. If we ourselves did not have some things to liquidate and payments to make, we should not think of getting rid of these two shares, but we are forced to it by the nature of other investments. You will be doing us a favor, gentlemen, if you redeem them at par. Please be so kind as to inform us when that will be possible for you. Receive, gentlemen, my most attentive greetings.

J. Necker de Saussure

On the reverse:

To Messieurs
Du Pont de Nemours, Père
et Fils & Cie.
Paris

Postmark:

2 Pluviôse, year XIII
99 Geneva

NOTE
1 This letter has apparently been lost.

❁

82

du Pont de Nemours to Madame de Staël

26 February 1805

From a copy by Gustave Schelle, WMSS 8/108

à Madame de Stael

Paris 7 Ventose 13

Je vous remercie, mon excellente amie, de ce que vous avez recueilli des manuscrits de M. Votre Père, et de l'envoi que vous m'en avez fait.[1]

J'ai dévoré le volume de suite, quoiqu'il me soit arrivé dans un temps où j'étais accablé du plus pressant travail.

J'ai applaudi à votre sensible cœur, à la chaleur de votre âme, à la vigueur de votre talent, à la beauté du Tableau. Cependant, vous ne devez vous attendre pour cette partie de l'ouvrage qui vous appartient qu'à un succès modéré.

Il y a mille raisons pour que vous ne soyez pas *à la mode;* et celle d'aimer les Portraits de Famille n'a jamais existé.

Quant au travail même de M. Votre Père, je n'ai pas lu d'un œil sec l'article *des larmes.*[2] Et à l'inverse, les *on,*[3] *la mode,*[4] les *Gènevois,*[5] *les usages de Paris en 1786,*[6] m'ont paru pleins de grâce et du meilleur ton. J'avais déjà lu *le bonheur des sots,*[7] dans les Archives littéraires.[8]

Vous me pardonnerez de n'etre pas de son avis sur ce qui concerne le commerce des grains.[9] Je sens autant que lui les avantages de l'abondance et du peu de variation des prix. Mais je suis entièrement convaincu qu'il ne peut y avoir aucun autre garant de l'abondance que les succès de l'agriculture; et que l'agriculture ne saurait etre encouragée que par la liberté du débit.

On ne cultive que pour vendre; et personne ne veut, ne peut vouloir cultiver pour perdre. Si l'on n'est pas certain de pouvoir vendre hors du pays, on ne cultive que bien juste ce qu'il faut pour la consommation moyenne; et, si l'intempérie des saisons nuit aux récoltes, on a la Famine, que les précautions du gouvernement aggravent en répandant l'effroi; et qu'elles ne peuvent adoucir par les plus grands sacrifices.

Quand on cultive au contraire pour vendre au dehors, il en reste toujours assez, meme dans les mauvaises années, pour manger.

L'opinion de M. Necker à cet égard a causé les plus amères peines de sa vie. Elle allait directement contre son objet. Elle a fortement contribué [au mal] [10] dont il gémissait, qu'il voulait empêcher.

Laissons l'économie politique. Venons à son Roman,[11] dont les pathétique et le coloris sont vraiment étonnants pour un homme de son âge. Il m'a causé la plus vive émotion. J'avoue cependant que j'ai été tout à fait *scandalisé,* et prêt à etre refroidi, en voyant deux amants, deux époux, comme Elisa et Henri, loger séparément chacun dans une aile du chateau, et s'eloigner l'un de l'autre même dans leur dernière nuit. Celà n'est ni vrai, ni vraisemblable. Delphine[12] avait bien plus de raison et de sentiment. Elle fut passer la nuit dans la prison de Léonce, et se garda bien d'y etre aussi sage que vous l'avez dit. Eh! que voulez-vous donc qu'on fasse la veille de sa mort, quand on n'a point de lâcheté et ne tombe pas de faiblesse? Tout ce que l'on peut de plus chaud, de plus tendre, de plus unissant. Dieu me préserve de mourir autrement!

Vous courez donc l'Italie, pays de ruines! vous désirez la France qui ne vaut guère mieux. Je conviens qu'il n'y a plus de Suisse. Et je regrette que l'Amérique, admirable pour moi, soit trop paisible et trop uniforme pour votre cœur agité, et qui n'a pas encore gouté le plaisir du repos. Au reste, je ne nie pas que l'Amérique me présente un attrait qu'elle ne peut vous offrir. J'y ai fait et fait approuver par Jefferson et par Madison, qui me les avaient demandés, tous les Plans de l'Education nationale,[13] et, quand j'y serai de retour, nous les exécuterons. L'usage n'y permet pas aux femmes de se mêler d'affaires publiques ni même d'en parler fréquement. Les beaux arts y sont peu cultivés. Il n'y a de gens de lettres que des géometres, des Physiciens, des Avocats et des Théologiens; vous pourriez vous y ennuyer à mort. Mais c'est la seule place où je puisse etre encore utile au monde et finir ma carrière comme je l'ai commencée. L'Amérique est nécessaire à *l'unité* de ma vie. Ce sera, je vous assure, avec beaucoup d'amertume que je m'éloignerai de vous encore une fois et pour toujours.

Je n'ai pu finir avec M. Fourcault de Pavant. Il n'avait pas les pouvoirs nécessaires pour me donner quittance, le titre étant égaré et ne pouvant m'etre rendu, mais pouvant se retrouver un jour quand vous n'y seriez plus pour certifier le payement, quand, ce qui est bien plus prochain, je n'y serai plus moi-même et pourrai avoir perdu une quittance fugitive. Il faut donc la faire avec minute notariée.

Que le ciel vous bénisse et vous rende la calme! à moins qu'il ne vous rende l'amour, et ne le rende heureux et durable!

Je baise vos belles mains avec tendresse et respect.

Madame Du Pont me charge de vous dire mille choses.

[Sans signature]

TRANSLATION

To Madame de Staël

Paris, 7 Ventôse, year XIII

I thank you, my excellent friend, for your collection of your father's manuscripts and for sending a copy to me.[1]

I devoured the volume at once, although it reached me at a time when I was overwhelmed by the most pressing work.

I applauded your sensitive heart, the warmth of your soul, the vigor of your talent, and the beauty of the tableau. However, you must expect only moderate success for that part of the work which belongs to you.

There are a thousand reasons why you are not *in style,* and that of liking family portraits has never existed.

As for your father's work, I did not read with a dry eye the article *on tears.*[2] And on the other hand, the articles on *One,*[3] *Style,*[4] the *Genevese,*[5] and *Customs of Paris in 1786*[6] seemed to me graceful and in the best taste. I had already read *The Happiness of Fools*[7] in the *Archives littéraires.*[8]

You will pardon me for not sharing his views concerning the grain trade.[9] I feel as much as he the advantages of abundance and of a minimum variation in prices. But I am completely convinced that there can be no other guarantee of abundance than the success of agriculture and that agriculture cannot be encouraged except by freedom of trade.

One cultivates only to sell, and no one wants, no one can want, to cultivate in order to lose. If farmers are not certain of being able to sell abroad, they cultivate only what is necessary for average consumption. And if bad weather harms the harvests, the result is famine, which the precautions of the government aggravate by spreading fear, and which they cannot alleviate by the greatest sacrifices.

When one cultivates, on the contrary, in order to sell abroad, there is always enough left to eat, even in bad years.

M. Necker's opinion in that regard caused the bitterest sorrows of his life. It went directly against his purpose. It contributed greatly [to the evil] [10] of which he complained, that he wished to prevent.

Let us leave political economy. Let us come to his novel,[11] whose pathos and coloring are really astonishing for a man of his age. It aroused the strongest emotion in me. I admit, however, that I was completely *scandalized,* and almost put off, on seeing two lovers, husband and wife like Elisa and Henri, each living separately in a wing of the chateau and even separating from each other on their last night. That is neither true nor probable. Delphine[12] had much more judgment and feeling. She went to spend the night in Léonce's prison and was careful not to be as good there as you said. Ah! what do you expect one to do on the eve of one's death, when one is not a coward and has not fallen from weakness? Everything as warm, as tender, as uniting as possible. God save me from dying in another way!

You are roaming through Italy, a country of ruins! You long for France, which is scarcely any better. I admit that there is no longer any Switzerland. And I regret that America, admirable where I am concerned, is too peaceful and too uniform for your agitated heart, which has not yet tasted the pleasure of repose. Moreover, I do not deny that America presents an attraction to me that it cannot offer you. There I have made, and had approved by Jefferson and Madison, both of whom had asked me for them, all the plans for national education;[13] and when I return, we shall carry them out. Custom does not permit women to mix in public affairs or even to talk about them frequently. The fine arts are not much cultivated there. Among men of letters there are only mathematicians, physicists, lawyers, and theologians; you might be bored to death there. But it is the only place where I can still be useful to the world and end my career as I began it. America is necessary to *the unity* of my life. It will be, I assure you, with much bitterness that I shall go so far away from you, once again and forever.

I was not able to finish with M. Fourcault de Pavant. He did not have the necessary powers to give me a receipt, the note being misplaced and impossible to return to me. But the note may be found again some day when you will no longer be here to certify payment and when—what is much closer—I shall no longer be here myself and may have lost a fleeting receipt. We must, therefore, make out a receipt with a notarized record.

May Heaven bless you and return calm to you, unless it returns love to you and makes it happy and durable!

I kiss your beautiful hands with tenderness and respect.

Mme. du Pont requests me to send you her regards.

[No signature]

NOTES

1 The *Manuscrits de Mr Necker publiés par sa fille*.

2 In this passage (pp. 102–5), which shows the influence of Rousseau, Necker speaks of the various kinds of tears. "Larmes d'orgueil . . . larmes d'amour propre," he says, "ne me touchent point." But "les larmes qui doivent nous toucher—celles qui nous touchent en effet, [sont] celles qui échappent à l'infortune presque à son insu, et dont il auroit honte de faire un art." He will attempt to prevent tears, but "lorsque des idées malheureuses . . . viennent nous assaillir, lorsqu'elles nous avertissent de la fragilité de la vie et de son inégale durée, ne cherchons point à échapper aux sentimens qui nous émeuvent, et cédons à ces douces larmes d'une origine céleste, à ces larmes pieuses qu'on secret instinct nous encourage à présenter au Souverain régulateur de notre destinée. C'est lui qui, par un des mystères de sa puissance, a mis nos pleurs en rapport avec sa bonté. Oui, dans cet état de tristesse et d'humilité, nous nous sentons plus près de notre Dieu." ("Tears of pride . . . tears of self-love . . . do not touch me at all. . . . the tears which must touch us—those which indeed do touch us—[are] those which come forth from misfortune almost unknowingly and of which it would be shameful to make an art. . . . when unhappy ideas . . . come to assail us, when they warn us of the fragility of life and of its unequal duration, let us not seek at all to avoid the sentiments that move us, and let us yield to those sweet tears of a celestial origin, to those pious tears which a secret instinct encourages us to present to the Sovereign Regulator of our destiny. It is He who, by one of the mysteries of His power, has placed our tears in harmony with His goodness. Yes, in that state of sadness and humility, we feel nearer our God.")

3 Necker comments as follows on the importance of the word *on* (pp. 112–13):

Quel est donc ce roi *On*, dont l'autorité est si souvent proclamée? C'est un roi sans apparat, sans pompe, sans trône visible, et à sa voix néanmoins chacun obéit, chacun tremble.

On, Roi si puissant, qu'il est doux de vous narguer! mais pour oser le faire, il faut vivre dans la solitude! *On*, Roi si puissant, tenez sans interruption vos Assises en France, c'est là que vous trouverez toujours à recruter cette milice qui fait votre force, l'immense légion des imitateurs.

(Who therefore is this king *One*, whose authority is so often proclaimed? He is a king without display, without pomp, without a visible throne; and nevertheless everyone obeys and trembles at his voice.

One, a King so powerful that it is sweet to make fun of you! but to dare to do so, we must live in solitude! *One*, King so powerful, continue to hold your court in France. There, you will always be able to recruit that militia which creates your strength, the immense legion of imitators.)

4 Necker states that "c'est une autorité singulière que l'autorité de la mode." Those who do not obey are subject to ridicule, but "la mode est obéie, quoiqu'elle soit un maître dont les opinions et les goûts changent à tout moment, et la mode encore est un souverain universellement respecté, quoiqu'il soit de bon ton de s'en narguer sans cesse." ("The authority of fashion is a strange authority. . . . fashion is obeyed, although it is a master whose opinions and tastes change at every moment, and yet fashion is a universally respected sovereign, even though it is in good taste to make fun of it unceasingly.") (Pp. 181–82.)

5 According to Necker (pp. 185–86), "les Genevois sont bien moins superficiels que les François, et pourtant je me sens moins d'encouragement à leur parler. On s'aperçoit à peine de l'impression qu'on leur fait. . . . [Ils] raisonnent mieux que les François, mais les François raisonnent davantage." ("The Genevese are considerably less superficial than the French, and yet I feel less encouragement in talking with them. One scarcely notices the impression that one makes on them. . . . [They] reason better than the French, but the French reason more.") Necker points out the distinction still made between the Genevese and the French, in spite of the annexation of Geneva to France. This distinction will doubtless disappear, he says, but there is honor in resistance and the memory of past greatness. According to the newspapers, the Genevese had been delighted to become French, at the time of the loss of their independence. Necker did not believe this to be true.

6 Necker states that, in 1786, opinion had ruled everything in France. He comments on nuances and their importance in French society, as well as vanity, its importance and subtle nature. Two years later, a great change had taken place in French society. He mentions, in particular, the coarseness of language (pp. 116–28).

7 The passage to which du Pont de Nemours refers is found on pp. 84–99 of the *Manuscrits*. To be happy, one must be a fool, Necker says. He cites the tale of Adam and Eve and their unhappiness after eating the apple from the Tree of Knowledge. Other men compare themselves with their peers and become unhappy, but nothing can disturb the serenity of a fool, since he knows neither envy nor jealousy. The distinctive characteristic of *folly* is the inability to notice, for it takes its restricted outlook as the limit of all that exists. Necker advises, "loin de mépriser les Sots que vous rencontrez, admirez leur bonheur, et recon-

noissez qu'il ne leur manque, pour prétendre au titre d'hommes de génie, que d'avoir été Sots par leur propre choix." ("Rather than scorn the fools you meet, admire their happiness and recognize that in order to claim to be men of genius, they would need only to have been fools by their own choice.")

8 The *Archives littéraires de l'Europe, ou Mélanges de littérature, d'histoire et de philosophie* published from 1804 to 1808, at first in Paris and later in Tubingen.

9 Du Pont de Nemours refers to an article in the *Manuscrits* entitled "Sur la législation et le commerce des grains." Necker opposes fluctuations in grain prices because of the burden placed on workers if prices rise. He suggests that exports be limited or curtailed in case of a shortage of grain and subsequent high prices.

10 Gustave Schelle made the following note on his copy of this letter: "Du Pont a sauté des mots; il faut probablement: 'au mal.' "

11 In the *Manuscrits* there is a novel by Necker entitled "Suites funestes d'une seule faute" ("Fatal Consequences of a Single Mistake"). It is the story of a very happily married couple, Elisa and Henri. Unfortunately, the husband is not knowledgeable about financial matters, begins to dip into his capital, and falls into the clutches of an unscrupulous man named John Foster. The latter speculates with Henri's money, gambling "dans les fonds publics," with the result that Henri is disgraced and ruined financially. Threatened with prison, he retires to a room to seek a solution to his problems, while Elisa goes to a room in another wing of the chateau. A piece of cloth will indicate Henri's decision to his wife. He decides on suicide, as does his wife.

   This is the sort of novel one might expect from a banker, with its emphasis on sound financial knowledge, and correct business procedures. It seems clear that du Pont de Nemours understood the implications of the tale as they applied to him.

12 Necker wrote the following "Avertissement de l'auteur" (*Manuscrits,* pp. 225–26) to his novel: "Dans une conversation, dont le roman de Delphine fut le sujet, on soutint que les seules affections domestiques pouvoient amener, aussi naturellement qu'un autre amour, les situations les plus tragiques; cette opinion fut contestée, et par une sorte de défi, on provoqua l'écrit suivant, dont le fond est véritable." ("In a conversation, of which the novel *Delphine* was the subject, it was maintained that even domestic affections could bring about, as naturally as another love, the most tragic situations; this opinion was disputed, and a sort of challenge provoked the following work, whose basis is true.")

   Mme. de Staël added the following statement:

> Cet avertissement est de mon père; il avoit consenti à laisser publier cette Nouvelle l'année dernière dans un Journal, mais, à la réflexion, il y renonça. Moi j'ai pensé que ce seroit presque laisser sa réputation incomplette que de ne pas faire connoître un ouvrage si admirable en lui-même, si extraordinaire aussi par le nom de l'Auteur.

> Il me conviendroit bien peu certainement de faire ressortir la morale d'un ouvrage de M^r. NECKER; cependant il me semble que les suites terribles du désordre dans les affaires sont montrées dans cet Ecrit avec une force qui n'existe nulle part, et dont l'application est d'une importance habituelle.

> (This preface is by my father; he had consented to let this short novel be published last year in a newspaper, but after further thought, he decided not to do so. I thought that it would be almost leaving his reputation incomplete

not to make known a work so admirable in itself, and so extraordinary also because of the author's name.

It would hardly be fitting for me to point out the moral of a work by M. NECKER; however, it seems to me that the results of disorder in business matters are shown in this work with a force that exists nowhere else, and its application is of universal importance.)

13 In 1800, soon after du Pont de Nemours' arrival in the United States, Jefferson requested him to submit a plan for a university. Instead of the memoir that Jefferson had expected, du Pont wrote an entire book, his *Sur l'éducation nationale dans les Etats-Unis d'Amérique* (Philadelphia, 1800), describing a complete educational system that might be established in the United States. For an account of this episode, see Gilbert Chinard, *The Correspondence of Jefferson and du Pont de Nemours* (Baltimore, 1931).

83

Rilliet to du Pont de Nemours & Cie.

7 March 1805

WMSS 2/18

a MM. Du Pont de Nemours pere fils et C[i]e

Geneve 7 mars 1805

Messieurs,

Mr Necker mon beau frere[1] m'a communiqué la corespondance qui a eu lieu entre vous et lui au sujet d'une action que Mr de Germany mon beau pere avoit dans votre compagnie generale et d'une autre dans votre manufacture de poudres. Par votre lettre du 8 Janvier dernier[2] vous nous donniez l'esperance du remboursement de ces 2 actions, ce que nous desirerions qui put s'effectuer afin de pouvoir hâter par là la liquidation de l'Hoirie de mon beau pere.

Comme on nous a dit que le Chef de votre maison se disposoit a retourner en Amerique, et que nous ignorons a qui nous aurions dans ce cas la a nous adresser en Europe pour suivre a nos interets, j'ai cru devoir m'adresser aussi a vous Messieurs comme administrateur des biens de ma femme, pour vous confirmer que je suis du même avis que mon beau frere, et pour vous prier de me marquer en reponse si, et quand, vous croyez pouvoir realiser le remboursement de ces 2 actions; que nous ne desirons que pour notre liquidation; n'estimant pas qu'elles puissent se diviser, ni qu'il nous convienne de le faire.

Je pense que mon beau frere vous aura répondu concernant l'echeance des interets, objet d'ailleur, qui s'ajoutteroit au Capital si le remboursement ne tardoit pas a se faire.

Agreez Messieurs l'assurance de mes sentiments pour vous.

Horace Benedict Rilliet

On the reverse:

Messieurs
Du Pont de Nemours pere fils et C[1]e
a Paris

Postmark:

22 V^{se} an 13
Geneve 99

TRANSLATION
To Messrs. du Pont de Nemours, Père et Fils & Cie.

Geneva, March 7, 1805

Gentlemen,

M. Necker, my brother-in-law,[1] has given me the correspondence which took place between you and him about a share of stock which M. de Germany, my father-in-law, had in your general company and about another in your powder factory. In your letter of last January 8,[2] you gave us the hope of reimbursement for these two shares, which we should like to have made in order to be able to hasten in that way the settlement of the inheritance from my father-in-law.

As we have been told that the director of your company was getting ready to return to America, and as we do not know, in that event, to whom we should write in Europe in order to pursue our interests, I thought I, as administrator of my wife's property, should write also to you, gentlemen, to assure you that I share the opinion of my brother-in-law and to request you to indicate to me in reply whether and when you believe you can effect the reimbursement of these two shares, which we desire only for our settlement, not considering that they can be divided nor that it suits us to do so.

I think that my brother-in-law has already answered you about the due date of the interest, a matter, moreover, which would be added to the capital if the reimbursement were not delayed.

Accept, gentlemen, the assurance of my sentiments for you.

Horace Benedict Rilliet

On the reverse:

Messieurs
du Pont de Nemours, Père et Fils & Cie.
in Paris

Postmark:

22 Ventôse, year XIII
Geneva 99

NOTES
1 Jacques Necker de Saussure.
2 This letter has apparently been lost.

84

Madame de Staël to du Pont de Nemours

7 June 1805

WMSS 2/18

Milan ce 7 juin

Faites moi le plaisir mon cher du pont de terminer nos affaires avec M^r fourcault, parce que nous devons règler nos affaires ensemble au moment de mon arrivèe à coppet, et qu'il doit payer pour moi mille ècus dus depuis long-tems au valet de chambre de mon père.[1] Ne viendrez vous donc pas à coppet cette annèe? Mad[ame] Recamier[2] y sera j'espère; les belles les spirituelles et par dessus tout celles qui vous aiment n'auront elles pas d'empire sur vous? J'ai plutot été contente d'ètre venue ici. Depuis trois jours que j'y suis l'emp[ereur][3] m'a accordèe [*sic*] vingt lieux de paris et il a renvoyè mon affaire au ministre des finances.[4] Voila pauvre moi, mon cher du pont ce que j'appelle du bonheur. Il a ajoutè d'ailleurs, "je suis si peu mal pour elle, que si on avoit voulu l'arrèter à naples j'aurois fait marcher vingt mille hommes pour la dèlivrer." En tout je suis avec lui comme cet officier qui rèpondoit sur la demande de la vie, "demandez moi toute autre chose. La vie pour moi c'est exister avec mes amis. Vous savez cher du pont si je vous mets au premier rang. Mais venez donc à coppet. Prony[5] y viendra peut être d'autres encor et enfin je vous y attends les bras ouverts.

[Sans signature]

TRANSLATION

Milan, June 7

Do me the pleasure, my dear du Pont, of ending our business with M. Fourcault, because we must settle our business together when I arrive at Coppet and because he must pay 1,000 écus for me which have been long due to my father's valet.[1] Will you not come to Coppet this year? Mme. Récamier[2] will be there, I hope. The beautiful, the witty, and above all, those women who love you, have they no power over you? I have been rather happy about having come here. In the three days that I have been here, the Emperor[3] has granted me twenty leagues from Paris, and he has referred my business to the Minister of Finance.[4] That is what— poor me—I call happiness, my dear du Pont. He added, moreover, "I am well enough disposed toward her that, if they had tried to arrest her in Naples, I should have sent 20,000 men to free her." In everything, I am with him like that officer who answered to the demand for his life, "Ask me for anything else at all." Life, for me, is living among my friends. You know, dear du Pont, whether I place you in the first rank of them. But do come to Coppet. Prony[5] will come perhaps, and still others, and finally, I await you there with open arms.

[No signature]

NOTES

1 On June 29, 1805, Mme. de Staël, in a letter to Le Ray de Chaumont, made the following inquiry: "Dites-moi confidentiellement ce que vous pensez de Dupont de Nemours, et si je dois être inquiète de ce qu'il me doit. . . ." ("Tell me confidentially what you think of du Pont de Nemours, and whether I should be uneasy about what he owes me. . . .") (Quoted in Richmond Laurin Hawkins, *Madame de Staël and the United States* [Cambridge, Mass., 1930], p. 31.)

2 The celebrated beauty and wit, Juliette Récamier, one of Mme. de Staël's most faithful friends.

3 Napoleon. He had been crowned King of Italy in Milan on May 26.

4 Martin Michel Charles Gaudin, Duc de Gaëte (1756–1841) was the Minister of Finance during the Consulate and the Empire. The business in question was the repayment of the 2,000,000 francs which Necker had lent to the government in 1778 and which Mme. de Staël was attempting to recover.

5 Probably Gaspard-Clair-François-Marie Riche de Prony (1755–1839), the French engineer and mathematician. In 1798 he became director of the Ecole des Ponts et Chaussées. He was also a professor at the Ecole Polytechnique and a member of the Institut, where he must have known du Pont de Nemours. Napoleon sent him to Italy in 1805 in connection with various engineering projects, and it is likely that Mme. de Staël met him there. She planned, at this time, to send her older son, Auguste de Staël, to the Ecole Polytechnique, believing, evidently, that this might open the gates of Paris to her once more.

85

du Pont de Nemours to Madame de Staël

30 June 1805

From a copy by Gustave Schelle, WMSS 8/108

à Madame de Stael

11 Messidor an 13, Paris

Mon excellente Amie,

M. de Pavant a malheureusement oublié deux choses: La première de vous envoyer il y a huit mois la lettre ci-jointe, qu'il vient de me rendre et que je vous restitue. La seconde de vous faire passer le modèle de la procuration spéciale que vous avez à lui donner pour opérer quittance certaine de ce que je devais à M. Votre Père puisqu'il n'a pas conservé le Billet de mon Fils.

Il avait encore ce billet sous les yeux en m'écrivant le 22 mars 1804. Ne l'a-t-il qu'égaré? L'a-t-il détruit volontairement? N'est-ce que par accident que vous ne l'avez pas trouvé? C'est ce que nous ignorons. Mais ce qui nous met dans la nécessité de donner à la quittance de cette dette, dont vous ne pouvez pas rendre le titre, toute la sureté possible; et partant de la faire notariée avec minute, afin que si le Billet se retrouvait un jour il ne puisse s'élever une contestation, ou donner lieu à une injustice entre nos enfants et nos petits enfants. L'amitié doit etre durable jusqu'à la millième génération.

M. Votre Père nous avait prêté *quarante huit mille six cent soixante dix huit francs cinquante cinq centimes,* dont j'ai payé à lui *et à vous* les intérets, à six pour cent selon notre convention jusqu'au 12 messidor de l'an 12 (1804 1er juillet).

Pour le remboursement, dans la lettre du 22 Mars 1804, dernier monument que nous ayions de sa volonté, il me laissait le choix ou de me prolonger la totalité du crédit en lui donnant une nouvelle sureté en France; ou, en lui payant la moitié, de lui donner, sans autre sureté pour la seconde moitié, deux actions au Porteur de ma société valant ensemble vingt un mille deux cent francs et pour l'appoint mon billet à un an.

Ce serait cet arrangement dont je désirerais le plus l'exécution; j'en ai rempli la première condition en payant *la moitié.*

Les affaires de ma société sont bien montées et marchent avec succès. Mais le gouvernement de France nous a vendu chèrement une très sage leçon; celle de ne lui faire à aucun prix aucune fourniture. En ne payant pas les Traites des Agents qu'il avait chargés d'administrer St Domingue, où nous lui avions rendu les plus grands et les plus nobles services, celles de son consul général en Amérique, il nous a fait perdre tout ce que nous avions gagné en six ans d'un travail habile et heureux.

De sorte que notre capital réduit à ce qu'il avait au commencement de notre entreprise, il nous importe beaucoup pour soutenir l'avantageuse étendue déjà donnée à nos opérations, de n'en détacher maintenant que le moins de fonds qu'il soit possible.

Si vous acceptiez les deux actions que M. Votre Père acceptait, les 21.200 frs de leur valeur vous revaudraient jusqu'au 12 Messidor an 15 six pour cent par an comme ils font aujourd'hui; et pendant les quatre années suivantes huit pour cent chaque année. Après quoi vous seriez remboursée en l'an 19 et toucheriez de plus votre portion des bénéfices sociaux. Or comme nous ne les laisserons plus dévorer par aucun gouvernement, ils doivent etre au moins aussi considérables que ceux dont la grandeur du notre nous a dépouillés. Ils le seront d'autant plus que notre commerce et notre manufacture sont en pleine activité, et que nos terres commencent à être en débit: au lieu que nos premières années ont dû se passer en préparatifs.

Si dans l'intervalle vous aviez besoin d'argent, les actions étant *au Porteur* vous trouveriez toujours à les réaliser. Mais dans votre position et dans celle de l'Europe, n'est-ce pas un avantage que d'avoir une portion de propriété en Amérique?

A votre place, je la voudrais plus forte.

Cependant, il est clair que c'est avec votre volonté que vous devez vouloir et selon votre jugement que vous devez juger.

Ainsi, supposé que l'autre arrangement dont nous étions à peu près convenus pour vous rembourser en trois ans, continue de vous plaire davantage, je n'ai point d'objection que la plus grande gene, qui en résultera pour moi.

Je vous ai payé

Le 27 Fructidor de l'année dernière	5.000 frs
Le 2 Vendémiaire de celle-ci	3.000
Le 5 du meme mois	2.000
Le 7 Brumaire	10.000
Et le 2 Messidor selon vos ordres à	
M. de Pavant	5.000
Total	25.000

Mais, comme les intérets y sont compris, celà ne m'acquitte que de 22.966 frs 60 et je vous reste redevable de 25.711 frs 95.

Si donc vous acceptez, comme M. Votre Père y consentait, mes deux actions au Porteur valant 21.200 frs dont les intérets vous seront exactement payés aux deux taux que je viens d'indiquer, je n'aurai plus à vous donner qu'un billet à ordre de 4.782,75.

Si vous les refusez, il faudra que je vous donne payables au 12 Messidor an 14 8.255,75.

Ce n'est que 3.472 frs de plus en prompt payement que par l'autre arrangement, et cette légère difference ne peut vous importer beaucoup: elle sera bien plus que compensée par les intérets plus forts et par le bénéfice sur le capital.

au 12 Messidor an 15	10.140
au 12 Messidor an 16	10.600

Dans tous ces payements, les intérets sont compris, comme vous le verrez par le tableau ci-joint, que je ne fais pas dans la forme commerciale de *doit* et *avoir* afin de vous rendre la chose plus intelligible.

Voilà l'étendue de ma possibilité.

Mais je désire que ce soit la forme adoptée par M. Votre Père qui ait la préférence.

Certainement, j'ai la plus grande envie d'aller passer quelques jours à Coppet, que je trouve tout aussi près de Paris que les vingt lieues qu'on vous accorde, qu'on nous accorde.

Mandez-moi si vous y restez, ou si ce rayon de vingt lieues vous touche au point de vous faire chercher un domicile inconnu où vous n'auriez pas vos livres?

Je vais porter cette lettre chez Eugène et, s'il part demain, je la lui donnerai sans le tableau n'ayant pas aujourd'hui dimanche de commis pour l'expédier.

S'il reste un jour de plus je rapporterai la lettre et le tableau y sera demain.

Salut, tendresse et respect, inviolable attachement.

Du Pont (de Nemours)

Madame Du Pont, bien sensible à votre souvenir, me charge de vous dire combien elle vous aime.

Elle a des affaires dans le Département de l'Ain[1] et il serait possible qu'elle vous rendit visite meme avant moi.

Comme c'est Eugène qui porte le paquet, j'y joins quelques brochurettes de votre vieux ami.

Letter 85 contains the following enclosure, also copied by Schelle:

Liquidation et Solde de ce Surplus

Suivant le plan consenti par M. Necker le 22 Mars 1804.

1° En deux actions de la société d'Amérique sous la raison de Du Pont (de Nemours) Père et fils et Compagnie, portant intérêt à six pour cent par an jusqu'au Messidor an 15, et à 8% pendant les quatre années suivantes: remboursable en l'an 19, avec leurs portions dans les bénéfices de la société   21.200 frs
   dont les dividendes réguliers
   produiront durant les deux
   premieres années   2.544⎫
   et durant les quatres   ⎬ 9.328
   autres   6.784⎭

2° En un billet payable le 12 Messidor an 14 de   4.782,75
      pour les intérets   270,80
      pour la solde du capital   4511,95
   Intérets fixes   9.598,80 ⎫
   Capital avec expectative   ⎬ 35.311,75
   de bénéfice   25.711,95 ⎭

Suivant celui qui a été indiqué par Mme de Stael

En trois Billets.

l'un au 12 Messidor		⌈ pour intéret	1.542,80
an 14 de	8.255 frs 75	⎨ En acquit du	
		⌊ capital	6.712,95
l'autre au 12 Messidor		⌈ pour intéret	1.140
an 15 de	10.140	⎨ En acquit du	
		⌊ capital	9.000
le dernier au		⌈ pour intéret	600
12 Messidor		⎨ Et solde du	
an 16 de	10.600	⌊ capital	10.000

Intéret	3.282,	80 ⎫	
Capital	25.711,	95 ⎭	28.993,75

TRANSLATION

To Madame de Staël

11 Messidor, year XIII, Paris

My excellent friend,

M. de Pavant has, unfortunately, forgotten two things: first, to send you eight months ago the enclosed letter, which he has just returned to me and which I am sending to you; secondly, to send you the draft of the special power of attorney which you have to give him to make a safe receipt for what I owed your father, since he did not keep my son's note.

He still had that note in front of him when he wrote to me on March 22, 1804. Did he only misplace it? Did he destroy it intentionally? Is it only by accident that you have not found it? That is what we do not know. But that is what makes it necessary for us to give all possible security to the receipt for that debt, whose note you cannot return, and consequently to have it notarized with a copy, so that if the note were found again some day, it could not give rise to any dispute, nor be the occasion for an injustice between our children and our grandchildren. Friendship must endure to the thousandth generation.

Your father had lent us *48,678.55 francs,* of which I paid him, *and you,* the interest at 6 per cent, according to our agreement, until 12 Messidor, year XII [July 1, 1804].

For the reimbursement, in his letter of March 22, 1804, the last record that we have of his wishes, he left me the choice of either extending the entire amount of the credit by giving him a new guarantee in France; or of paying him half and giving him, without any other security for the second half, two shares of stock in my company made out "to the bearer," with a combined value of 21,200 francs plus my note for one year for the balance.

It would be this arrangement which I should like most to have carried out; I have fulfilled the first condition by paying *half.*

The business of my company is well organized and is going along successfully. But the government of France taught us a very wise lesson at a high price, to wit, not to provide it with any supplies at any price. By not paying the drafts of the agents whom it had ordered to administer Santo Domingo, where we rendered it the greatest and noblest services, those of its consul general in America, it caused us to lose all that we had gained in six years of skillful and fortunate work.

So that with our capital reduced to what it was at the beginning of our operations, it is very important for us to release now only the smallest possible amount of our capital fund in order to maintain the advantageous scope already given to our operations.

If you accepted the two shares that your father accepted, the 21,200 francs of their value would pay you 6 per cent until 12 Messidor, year XV [July 1, 1807], as they do today, and 8 per cent each year during the following four years. After that, you would be reimbursed in the year XIX and would receive, in addition, your portion of the company's profits. Now, as we shall no longer let them be devoured by any government, they must be at least as considerable as those of which the greatness of our government has robbed us. They will be so all the more, since our business and our factory are in full operation, and our land is beginning to be in demand, whereas our first years had to be spent in making preparations.

If, in the interval, you needed money, you could always redeem the shares, as they are made out "to the bearer." But in your position, and in that of Europe, is it not an advantage to have a portion of one's property in America?

In your place, I would want it to be larger.

Clearly, however, it is with your wishes that you must decide, and according to your judgment that you must judge.

So, supposing that the other arrangement on which we had almost reached an agreement, to reimburse you in three years, continues to please you more, I have no objection, except the greater financial embarrassment which will result for me.

I have paid you

On 27 Fructidor of last year	5,000 fr.
On 2 Vendémiaire of this one	3,000
On the 5th of the same month	2,000
On 7 Brumaire	10,000
And on 2 Messidor, according to your orders, to M. de Pavant	5,000
Total	25,000 fr.

But, as the interest is included in it, that pays off only 22,966.60 francs, and I remain indebted to you for 25,711.95 francs.

If you accept, therefore, as your father agreed to do, my two shares made out "to the bearer" being worth 21,200 francs, whose interest will be paid promptly to you at the two rates that I have just indicated, I shall have nothing more to give you but a promissory note for 4,782.75 francs.

If you refuse them, I shall have to give you, payable on 12 Messidor, year XIV, 8,255.75 francs.

That is only 3,472 francs more in prompt payment than by the other arrangement, and that slight difference cannot matter much to you. It will be more than compensated for by the higher interest and by the profit on the capital:

on 12 Messidor, year XV	10,140 fr.
on 12 Messidor, year XVI	10,600 fr.

In all these payments, the interest is included, as you will see by the enclosed chart, which I am not making in the commercial form of *debtor* and *creditor,* so that the matter will be more intelligible for you.

That is the extent of my possibilities.

But I want the form adopted by your father to have the preference.

Certainly, I have the greatest desire to go spend a few days at Coppet, which I find just as near Paris as the twenty leagues granted to you, and to us.

Inform me whether you are staying there, or if this radius of twenty leagues affects you to the point of making you seek an unknown house where you would not have your books?

I am going to take this letter to Eugene's house, and if he is leaving tomorrow, I shall give it to him without the chart, not having any clerk to send it today, Sunday.

If he stays another day, I shall bring back the letter, and the chart will be there tomorrow.

Greetings, tenderness and respect, inviolable attachment.

Du Pont (de Nemours)

Mme. du Pont, touched by your greetings, requests me to tell you how much she loves you.

She has some business in the Department of Ain,[1] and it could be that she would visit you even before I do.

As it is Eugene who is taking the package, I am enclosing in it a few little pamphlets by your old friend.

Letter 85 contains the following enclosure, also copied by Schelle:

Liquidation and Balance of This Surplus

According to the plan agreed to by M. Necker on March 22, 1804:

1. In two shares of the American company under the name of du Pont (de Nemours), Père et Fils & Cie., bearing interest at 6 per cent per year until 15 Messidor, year XV, and at 8 per cent during the following four years, repayable in the year XIX, with their parts in the profits of the company   21,200 fr.
    whose regular dividends
    will produce during the
    first two years   2,544 ⎫
    and during the other   ⎬ 9,328 fr.
    four   6,784 ⎭
2. In a note payable on 12 Messidor,
    year XIV for   4,782.75 fr.
        for the interest   270.80
        for the balance of the capital   4,511.95
    Fixed interest   9,598.80 ⎫
    Capital with expectancy   ⎬ 35,311.75 fr.
    of profit   25,711.95 ⎭

According to that which was indicated by Mme. de Staël:

In three notes

one on 12 Messidor, year XIV for	8,255.75 fr.	for interest	1,542.80 fr.
		in payment of	
		the capital	6,712.95
another on 12 Messidor, year XV for	10,140	for interest	1,140
		in payment of	
		the capital	9,000
the last on 12 Messidor, year XVI for	10,600	for interest	600
		and balance of	
		the capital	10,000

Interest	3,282.80	28,993.75 fr.
Capital	25,711.95	

NOTE
1 Mme. du Pont's sister, Mme. Boullée, lived at Bourg, in the Department of Ain.

86

Madame de Staël to du Pont de Nemours

14 July 1805

WMSS 2/18

Coppet ce 14 juillet
Si vous voulez bien arranger les choses de manière que ce soit dans une maison de banque à paris que je sois payèe des intérets et du capital aux diffèrentes èpoques que vous me dèsignez, je consens à votre proposition. J'accepterai les deux actions remboursables en l'an 19 avec la part dans les bènèfices de la sociètè, le billet de 4,782 francs payable à paris le 12 messidor an 14, et pour les intérets de 9328 francs. Je vous prie de les diviser de manière que j'en touche chaque annèe une portion jusques à l'an 19 le tout en assignations de vous sur paris. Le tout ainsi convenu, faites moi

envoyer une procuration par M^r pavant que je signe selon les termes qu'il vous convient. Faites la moi envoyer tout de suite parce que mon fils[1] que j'envoye à paris le 1er d'aöust dans la pension thurot, vous la rapportera. Je reste ici jusqu'au 1er d'8bre. Ainsi vous avez bien le tems de venir m'y voir. Je vais aux vingt lieues[2] parce que je puis de là terminer mes affaires d'argent et que je ne le puis pas d'ici vu la longueur des lettres etc parce que mon fils ètant à paris il me convient de pouvoir le voir quelquefois, parce que de ces vingt lieues j'espère arriver une fois à paris mème, et que pour l'èducation de mes enfants comme pour mes gouts je veux une grande ville. Ce pays çi me dèplait et je ne connois guères que vous autres parisiens qui vous amusant beaucoup à paris trouviez tout simple que les autres s'ennuyent ailleurs. Je ne tiens plus autant à paris qu'autrefois mais j'ai beaucoup trop de mèlancolie dans le caractére pour pouvoir supporter la solitude, et si vous permettez que je vous le dise je suis beaucoup trop aimable pour n'avoir pas envie de l'ètre avec ceux qui en jouissent. Vous me dites que je ne suis pas *à la mode* à paris. Je le suis en europe, et cela finira par arriver à paris, ou paris pourroit bien avoir perdu par une certaine quantité de raisons le droit de l'arrogance. Je voudrois fort vous voir ici ou tout au moins à mes vingt lieues car indépendement du plaisir que j'aurois à vous voir, s'il est vrai que vous retournez en amèrique je voudrois vous prier d'y regarder mes terres.[3] Vos brochures ont toujours votre caractére d'originalité de sagacité et d'indépendance, si comme je l'espère vous me donnez bientot quelques moments à passer librement avec vous mon cher du pont, nous parlerons de cela et de tout.

[Sans signature]

On the reverse:

Monsieur
Monsieur Dupont de Nemours
Rue Montolon N° 301
A Paris[4]

Postmark:

1 T^{or} an 13
99 Genève

TRANSLATION

Coppet, July 14

If you wish to arrange things so that I shall be paid the interest and capital at a bank in Paris at the different periods that you indicate to me, I agree to your proposal. I shall accept the two shares repayable in the year XIX with the share in the profits of the company, the note for 4,782 francs payable in Paris on 12 Messidor, year XIV, and that for the interest of 9,328 francs. I beg you to divide the interest so that I shall receive a portion each year until the year XIX, all of it in assignments from you on Paris. Once everything is agreed on in this way, have a power of attorney sent me by M. de Pavant, and I shall sign it according to the terms that suit you. Have it sent to me immediately because my son,[1] whom I am sending to the Thurot pension in Paris on August 1, will bring it back to you. I am staying here until October 1. Thus, you have time indeed to come see me here. I am going to the twenty leagues[2] granted me because I can terminate my financial affairs from there, and I cannot do so from here, considering the slowness of letters, etc.; because, with my son in Paris, it suits me to be able to see him sometimes; because, from those twenty leagues, I hope to arrive finally in Paris itself; and because, for the education of my children, as well as for my tastes, I desire a large city. This country displeases me, and I scarcely know anyone but you Parisians, who, amusing yourselves in Paris, find it quite obvious that others should be bored elsewhere. I no longer insist as much on Paris as formerly, but I have much too much melancholy in my character to be able to stand solitude, and if you permit me to say so, I am much too amiable not to wish to be so to those who enjoy my company. You tell me that I am not *in style* in Paris. I am in style in Europe, and that will finally reach Paris, or Paris might well have lost, for a certain number of reasons, the right to be arrogant. I should like very much to see you here, or at least at my twenty leagues, for aside from the pleasure that I should have in seeing you, if it is true that you are returning to America, I should like to ask you to look at my land there.[3] Your pamphlets always have your character of originality, of sagacity, and of independence. If, as I hope, you soon give me a few moments to spend freely with you, my dear du Pont, we shall talk about that and about everything.

[No signature]

On the reverse:

Monsieur
M. du Pont de Nemours
301, rue de Montholon
in Paris[4]

Postmark:

1 Thermidor, year XIII
99 Geneva

NOTES
1 Auguste de Staël.
2 The twenty leagues from Paris which Napoleon had supposedly granted Mme. de Staël as a condition for her stay in France: see Letter 84.
3 Mme. de Staël had extensive property in the state of New York.
4 The address is in another handwriting. Computations in still another handwriting, probably du Pont de Nemours', appear also on the reverse.

87

Fourcault de Pavant to du Pont de Nemours

2 August 1805

WMSS 2/18

Paris 14 thermidor an 13

Monsieur,

Il me paroit extrêmement juste que Mad[am]e de Stael vous donne une décharge authentique de l'engagement que vous avez consenti à M Necker et qui ne se retrouve pas, et qu'elle acquitte tous les frais auxquels cette quittance donnera lieu; mais je crois qu'il y a moyen d'assurer votre décharge sans suivre *littéralement* votre projet de procuration.

L'enoncè que vous y faites de *la Cession de Contrats* sur les etats unis, donneroit lieu a plus de 1.100ᶠ d'enregistrement.

Je pense qu'on peut le supprimer et se borner à quittancer votre engagement sans en rappeller les causes, et vous donner une decharge générale de toutes les opérations que vous avez pu faire pour M Necker.

Au surplus, on pourroit dans un écrit particulier rappeller les causes de cet engagement: mais je crois cette precaution inutile d'apres la forme de la procuration que je propose et que je charge mon principal clerc de vous communiquer.

Agreez, monsieur, l'hommage de ma respectueuse considération.

Fourcault Pavant
no[tai]re Rue St Martin N° 19

P.S. Comme j'ecris aujourd'huy a Mad[am]e de Stael, je desirerois bien lui adresser ce modele de procuration qu'elle me renverroit sous 10 jours par son fils.

TRANSLATION

Paris, 14 Thermidor, year XIII

Sir,

It seems extremely just to me that Mme. de Staël give you an authentic release from the engagement you made with M. Necker which cannot be found, and that she pay all the expenses which will result from this receipt; but I believe that there is a way of assuring your release without following *literally* your plan of a power of attorney.

The wording that you use in it, the *Transfer of Contracts* on the United States, would occasion more than 1,100 francs in registration fees.

I think that we can omit it and limit ourselves to giving a receipt for your engagement without recalling the causes of it, and give you a general release from all the operations that you have been able to perform for M. Necker.

Moreover, we could recall the causes of that engagement in a private note, but I believe this precaution to be unnecessary according to the form of the power of attorney that I am proposing and which I am having my first clerk send you.

Accept, Sir, the homage of my respectful consideration.

Fourcault Pavant
Notary, 19, rue Saint-Martin

P.S. As I am writing today to Mme. de Staël, I should like to send her this draft of a power of attorney, which she would send back to me in ten days by her son.

88

Fourcault de Pavant to du Pont de Nemours

4 August 1805

WMSS 2/18

ce 16 thermidor an 13

J'ai l'honneur de présenter mes devoirs a monsieur Dupont et de lui faire passer la lettre de Mad[am]e de Stael qu'il avoit bien voulu me communiquer.[1]

J'ai envoyé le modele de procuration a Mad[am]e de Stael.

Fourcault Pavant

On the reverse:

A Monsieur
Monsieur Dupont (de Nemours)
Rue Montholon N° 60
pres la Barriere
Paris

Postmark:

16 T^{or} an 13

TRANSLATION

16 Thermidor, year XIII

I have the honor of presenting my respects to M. du Pont and of sending him the letter from Mme. de Staël which he had kindly sent to me.[1]

I have sent the draft of the power of attorney to Mme. de Staël.

Fourcault Pavant

On the reverse:

To Monsieur
M. du Pont (de Nemours)
60, rue de Montholon
near the Barrière
Paris

Postmark:

16 Thermidor, year XIII

NOTE
1 Her letter of July 14, 1805 (Letter 86).

89

Necker de Saussure to du Pont de Nemours & Cie

21 August 1805

WMSS 2/18

Geneve le 21 Aoust 1805

Messieurs,

Nous avions espere d'apres votre lettre du 8 Janv[ie]r de cette année[1] que vous nous feriez payer en messidor ainsi que cela paroissoit vous convenir 9 mois echus alors de notre interet dans vos deux etablissements. Apparemment que vous avez prefere que ces interets fussent payes seulement en vendemiaire pour la totalité de l'année. Je vous prie en consequence de me marquer en reponse si je dois fournir ma suite sur vous pour le p[remie]r Vendemiaire prochain ou plutot ce qui est difficile puisque nous sommes près de ce terme. Vous nous aviez aussi Messieurs fait esperer de vous charger de nos titres ce qui nous auroit ete infiniment agreable parce que nous avons besoin de fonds pour operer la liquidation de notre hoirie. Je sais que depuis peu vous en avez placé & nous aurions ete reconnoissans si vous aviez pris cette caution pour nous servir suivant nos desirs. Nous vous prions de ne point perdre de vue votre promesse à cet egard.

Recevez Messieurs mes salutations empressées.

J. Necker de Saussure

On the reverse:

A Messieurs
Dupont de Nemours Pere
fils & Ce
A Paris

Postmark:

9 F^{or} an 13
99 Genève

TRANSLATION

Geneva, August 21, 1805

Gentlemen,

We had hoped, according to your letter of January 8 of this year,[1] that in Messidor you would pay us nine months of our interest then due in your two establishments, as seemed to suit you. Apparently you preferred that this interest be paid only in Vendémiaire for the entire year. I beg you, consequently, to reply to me whether I am to draw on you for the remainder on the next 1 Vendémiaire or sooner, which is difficult because we are near that time limit. You had also caused us to hope, gentlemen, that you would attend to our stocks, which would have been extremely agreeable to us, because we need money in order to effect the settlement of our inheritance. I know that recently you negotiated some stock, and we should have been grateful if you had taken that deposit to serve us according to our wishes. We beg you not to forget your promise in this regard.

Receive, gentlemen, my attentive greetings.

J. Necker de Saussure

On the reverse:

To Messieurs
du Pont de Nemours, Père et
Fils & Cie.
in Paris

Postmark:

9 Fructidor, year XIII
99 Geneva

NOTE
1 This letter seems to have been lost.

90

Fourcault de Pavant to du Pont de Nemours

20 September 1805

WMSS 2/18

Monsieur.

On demande une somme considérable à Mad[am]e de Stael pour enrigistrer à Geneve la procuration, dont je lui ai fait passer le modèle, elle repugne à la donner, et elle vous propose de lui éviter de faire des frais inutiles.

Voici quel en seroit le moyen:

Ce seroit de faire sous seing privé à Paris l'acte tel qu'il est prévu et indiqué par la procuration; cet acte une fois redigé, Mad[am]e de Stael le déposeroit chez un notaire de Suisse, l'approuveroit et le ratifieroit, et vous en procureroit une expedition en forme dé-livrée par ce notaire.

Par là vous auriez une décharge complette et authentique, et vous seriez certain d'avoir à volonté une nouvelle expedition, si la premiere étoit égarée.

Dans le cas où cet arrangement vous conviendroit, comme je le presume, veuillez me le mander par un mot au pied de cette lettre.

Agreez, Monsieur, l'assurance de ma respectueuse consideration.

Fourcault Pavant

ce 3 Comp^re [an XIII]

On the reverse:

A Monsieur
Monsieur Dupont de Nemours
rue de Montholon N° 301
près la Barriere Cadet à droite
à Paris

TRANSLATION

Sir,

A considerable sum is being asked of Mme. de Staël to register the power of attorney, of which I sent her the draft, in Geneva. She is reluctant to pay it, and she proposes that you avoid unnecessary fees for her.

Here would be the means of doing so: to prepare under private contract in Paris the deed such as it is foreseen and indicated by the power of attorney. Once this deed has been drawn up, Mme. de Staël would deposit it with a notary in Switzerland, would approve it and ratify it, and would obtain a copy of it for you in the form issued by this notary.

In that way, you would have a complete and authentic release, and you would be certain of having a new copy at will if the first were misplaced.

If this arrangement suits you, as I presume, please so indicate to me by a note at the bottom of this letter.

Accept, Sir, the assurance of my respectful consideration.

Fourcault Pavant

3 Complémentaire[1] [year XIII]

On the reverse:

To Monsieur
M. du Pont de Nemours
301, rue de Montholon
near the Barrière Cadet on the right
in Paris

NOTES

This letter may have been written on September 19 and misdated by Fourcault de Pavant, since Pacout's letter of September 20 (Letter 92) refers to it as "the letter that he wrote . . . yesterday." It is equally possible, however, that Pacout's letter was written on September 21 and misdated.

1 The five days at the end of the French Republican calendar, also called *Sansculottides*.

91

du Pont de Nemours to Fourcault de Pavant

[19–21 September 1805]

WMSS 2/18

Monsieur, il me semble qu'on ne peut pas faire à Paris même sous seing prive un acte entre Madame de Stael et moi sans procuration de sa part.

Ni en Suisse sans procuration de la mienne, pour laquelle on demanderait les mêmes frais à Paris qu'à Genêve.

Comment surmonter cette difficulté? A combien se monteront ces frais?

Coppet est en Suisse. Une procuration donnee en Suisse n'est elle pas valable en France?

Est-elle pour en user en France soumise au même enregistrement?

Salut et respectueuse considération.

[Sans signature]

Ne peut-on pas donner une procuration pour compter transiger solder ou recevoir sans specifier les sommes?

TRANSLATION

Sir, it seems to me that one cannot draw up, even under private contract, a deed between Mme. de Staël and me in Paris without a power of attorney on her part.

Nor in Switzerland without a power of attorney on mine, for which the same fees would be required in Paris as in Geneva.

How can we overcome this difficulty? What will the fees amount to?

Coppet is in Switzerland. Is not a power of attorney given in Switzerland valid in France?

Is it subject to the same registration fee in France in order to use it?

Greetings and respectful consideration.

[No signature]

Can one not give a power of attorney in order to pay, come to an agreement, settle, or receive without specifying the amounts?

NOTE

This reply to Fourcault de Pavant's letter of September 20, 1805, is written on that letter. Although du Pont de Nemours' reply is undated, it must have been written between September 19 and 21, since Pacout's reply to du Pont (Letter 92) was written either September 20 or 21 (see the note to Letter 90).

92

Pacout to du Pont de Nemours

20 September 1805

WMSS 2/18

Monsieur

M. Fourcault Pavant en partant ce matin pour la campagne, où il a été appellé pour affaires, m'avoit chargé de recevoir la réponse que vous deviez faire à la lettre qu'il vous a écrite hier,[1] et d'en faire part à Mad[am]e de Stael pour la quelle j'ai un paquet à mettre à la poste.

Je reçois à l'instant votre reponse et je vois que vous faites quelques objections sur l'acte proposé par M. Pavant. Vous avez raison de dire que cet acte, si on vouloit le faire definitif, ne pourroit etre passé à Paris sans une procuration de Mad[am]e de Stael, mais le projet de M. Pavant est de faire representer cette dame par une personne qui agira comme ayant charge et pouvoir d'elle, l'obligera à ratifier en en faisant le depot en Suisse, et cette ratification rendra l'acte aussi parfait que si Mad[am]e de Stael l'eut signé elle même ou par un fondé de pouvoir ad hoc.

Si cette explication vous tranquilise, Monsieur, et que vous croyiez pouvoir donner votre consentement à l'arrangement proposé, je vous reitere la priere de M. Pavant de vouloir bien donner ce consentement au pied de la lettre qui vous a été remise de sa part ce matin.

J'ai l'honneur, Monsieur, de vous présenter l'assurance de mon respect.

Pacout p[rinci]pal clerc de M. [Pavant]

Paris, ce 3 comp^re [an XIII]

On the reverse:

A Monsieur
Monsieur Dupont de Nemours
rue Montholon N° 301
près la Barriere Cadet
à Paris

TRANSLATION
Sir,

M. Fourcault Pavant, on leaving this morning for the country, where he was called on business, had directed me to receive your reply to the letter that he wrote you yesterday,[1] and to inform Mme. de Staël, for whom I have a package to mail, about it.

I have just now received your reply, and I see that you raise some objections to the deed proposed by M. Pavant. You are right to say that if one wanted to make it definitive, this deed could not be drawn up in Paris without a power of attorney from Mme. de Staël; but M. Pavant's plan is to have this lady represented by a person who will act as having authority and power from her, which will oblige her to ratify it by having it deposited in Switzerland; and that ratification will make the deed as perfect as if Mme. de Staël had signed it herself or by a special proxy.

If this explanation sets your mind at ease, Sir, and you believe you can give your consent to the proposed arrangement, I repeat M. Pavant's request to please give this consent at the bottom of his letter which was given to you this morning.

I am honored, Sir, to present you with the assurance of my respect.

                                        Pacout, first clerk of M. [Pavant]
Paris, 3 Complémentaire [year XIII]

On the reverse:

To Monsieur
M. du Pont de Nemours
301, rue de Montholon
near the Barrière Cadet
in Paris

NOTE
1 Letter 90. Pacout's letter may have been written on September 21 and misdated.

93

Pacout to du Pont de Nemours

24 September 1805

WMSS 2/18

Monsieur,

Je reçois à l'instant une lettre de M. Fourcault Pavant qui me charge de vous demander si vous acceptez la proposition qu'il vous a faite de passer à Paris sous signatures privées l'acte qui doit avoir lieu entre Mad[am]e de Stael et vous; ainsi que j'ai eu l'honneur de vous le mander Mad[am]e de Stael sera representée par une personne qui declarera avoir charge et pouvoir d'elle, et qui l'obligera à ratifier. Cette forme s'employe très souvent, quand on est sur de l'adhesion et du consentement de celui pour lequel on stipule.

Vous connoissez le moyen que M. Pavant compte employer pour donner au sous seing privé toute la force qu'il auroit s'il etoit passé à Paris devant notaires et par une personne qui auroit un pouvoir spécial c'est de le faire deposer par Mad[am]e de Stael, après qu'elle l'auroit ratifié, à un notaire de Suisse, qui en delivreroit une expedition, ainsi que de la ratification, pour vous etre remise.

M. Pavant qui arrive demain de la campagne desire connoitre votre reponse, pour écrire sur le champ à Mad[am]e de Stael et lui demander le projet de procuration qui serviroit à la redaction du sous seing privé.

J'ai l'honneur, Monsieur, de vous présenter l'assurance de mon respect.

Pacout p[rinci]pal clerc de M. Pavant

ce 2 vend[re] an 14[1]

TRANSLATION

Sir,

I have received just now a letter from M. Fourcault Pavant which directs me to ask you whether you accept his proposition of drawing up in Paris under private signatures the deed which is to be made between Mme. de Staël and you. As I have had the honor of informing you, Mme. de Staël will be represented by a person who will declare that he has authority and power from her, and who will oblige her to approve it. This form is used very often when one is sure of the acceptance and the consent of the person in whose name one acts.

You know how M. Pavant expects to give to the private agreement all the force that it would have if it were drawn up in Paris before notaries by a person who would have special authority: that is, to have Mme. de Staël, after she had approved it, deposit it with a Swiss notary, who would deliver a copy, as well as the approval, for you.

M. Pavant, who arrives tomorrow from the country, wishes to know your reply so that he may write at once to Madame de Staël and ask her for the power of attorney which would serve for drawing up the private agreement.

I am honored, Sir, to present you with the assurance of my respect.

Pacout, first clerk of M. Pavant

2 Vendémiaire, year XIV [1]

NOTE

1 The date 1806, obviously an error, appears at the head of this letter. It is not in the handwriting of Pacout or of du Pont de Nemours, and seems to have been added later.

94

du Pont de Nemours to Pacout

[24–25 September 1805]

WMSS 2/18

Il m'est très pénible de paraitre hesiter à faire quoi que ce soit qui puisse être agréable à Madame de Stael.

Mais puisque le billet de mon fils en notre nom social, effet de commerce exigible, qui devrait etre rendu lors du payement avec l'*acquit au dos* a êté détruit ou égaré par Monsieur Necker, qui l'avait encore quinze jours avant que nous eussions le malheur de

le perdre; et comme rien ne peut être prouvé quant à la non-exist-
ence, de ce billet, comme il est possible qu'il soit un jour retrouvé,
lorsque nous n'y serions plus; comme c'est à nous à pourvoir à ce
qu'il n'en résulte aucune contestation entre nos enfans, Madame
de Stael et Monsieur de Pavant pensent ainsi que moi qu'il faut
donner à la quittance toute la certitude la plus approchante que
l'on pourra de celle que l'acquit au dos et la restitution du titre
auraient complettement assurée. En un tel cas, l'enregistrement
me semble une petite consideration.

Les minutes des notaires de Paris et les régistres de l'enregistrement subsisteront: car Paris ne sera certainement point le theatre
de la guerre: on ne peut en dire autant des actes passés chez les
notaires de Suisse. Car la Suisse sera théatre de la guerre tres certainement, et par sa position politique actuelle très fréquemment.

La question est donc de savoir si la ratification donnée en Suisse
entrainera les mêmes droits lorsqu'on voudra la déposer à Paris
que ferait la quittance donnée à Paris même.

Et si en reconnaissant le payement de vingt cinq mille francs
déja effectué, l'enregistrement doit s'etendre à la somme entiere
qui êtait due ou être borné a celle qui reste à fournir pour l'àpoint.

Quoique ce ne soit certainement pas ma faute si l'on ne peut me
rendre le billet de ma maison acquitté, ou si le titre de la dette
n'existe plus, j'aimerais mieux contribuer à l'enregistrement que
de ne pas terminer cette affaire avant mon retour en Amérique.[1]

[Sans signature]

TRANSLATION

It is very painful for me to seem to hesitate to do anything that
may please Mme. de Staël.

But since my son's note in the name of our company, a payable
commercial bill which should be returned at the time of payment
with the *receipt on the back,* was destroyed or misplaced by
M. Necker, who still had it two weeks before we had the misfortune of losing him; and since nothing can be proved as to the non-
existence of this note; since it is possible that it may be rediscov-
ered some day when we are no longer alive; and since it is up to us
to see that no controversy about it may result among our children,
Mme. de Staël and M. de Pavant think, as do I, that we must make
the receipt as nearly secure as the receipt on the back and the re-

turn of the note would have been. In such a case, the registration fee seems to me a small consideration.

The minutes of the notaries of Paris and the registers of the registration will remain, for Paris will certainly not be a theater of war. One cannot say as much about deeds drawn up by the notaries of Switzerland, for Switzerland will very certainly be a theater of war, and because of its present political position, very frequently so.

The question then is to find out whether ratification given in Switzerland will entail the same fees when one wants to deposit it in Paris as the receipt given in Paris itself would cause.

And whether, in recognizing the payment of 25,000 francs already made, the registration must be extended to the entire sum which was due or be limited to that which remains to be provided for the balance.

Although it is certainly not my fault if the receipted bill of my company cannot be returned, or if the statement of the debt no longer exists, I should prefer to contribute to the registration than not to finish this business before my return to America.[1]

[No signature]

NOTES

This reply to Pacout's letter of September 24, 1805, is written on that letter. Although du Pont de Nemours' letter is undated, it must have been written on September 24 or 25, since Fourcault de Pavant answered it on September 25 (Letter 95).

1 In a letter written to Victor du Pont on September 2, 1805 (WMSS 2/5), du Pont de Nemours states: "J'ai payé Madame de Stael avec deux actions de la société générale, vingt cinq mille francs argent, six mille francs de billets au 12 messidor de l'année prochaine, et des billets pour les interêts dont mention sur les actions, pour qu'on ne puisse les demander deux fois, ainsi l'emprunt de Necker est soldé. Nous ne devons rien en Europe que les interets de l'année prochaine, mais il en faudra faire les fonds, et il faudra que je vive d'ici là." ("I have paid Mme. de Staël with two shares of stock in the general company, 25,000 francs in cash, 6,000 francs in notes due on 12 Messidor of next year, and some notes for the interest with a mention of the shares of stock, so that it may not be asked for twice. Thus the loan from Necker is paid. We owe nothing in Europe except the interest for next year, but it will be necessary to obtain the funds, and it will be necessary for me to live until then.")

95

Fourcault de Pavant to du Pont de Nemours

25 September 1805

WMSS 2/18

Paris 3 vendemiaire an 14

Monsieur,

Je ne peux vous dissimuler que l'expedition de l'acte passé ou deposé en Suisse sera assujettie au droit d'enregistrement, si l'on veut en faire usage à Paris, et la deposer à un notaire.

On prendra un droit de quittance sur les vingt cinq mille francs déja payés, c'est un objet d'un demi pour cent; le droit sur ce qui reste dû sera d'un pour cent.

Puisque vous avez des craintes sur le sort d'un acte qui seroit deposé en Suisse, je vais faire part à Mad[am]e de Stael de votre offre de contribuer aux droits d'enregistrement et l'engager à m'envoyer sa procuration pour terminer avec vous à Paris.

J'ai l'honneur Monsieur de vous présenter l'assurance de ma respectueuse consideration.

Fourcault Pavant

On the reverse:

A Monsieur
Monsieur Dupont de Nemours
rue Montholon N° 301 ancien
près la Barriere cadet
à Paris

TRANSLATION

Paris, 3 Vandémiaire, year XIV

Sir,

I cannot conceal from you that the copy of a deed drawn up or deposited in Switzerland will be subject to a registration fee if one wants to use it in Paris and deposit it with a notary.

A receipt fee on the 25,000 francs already paid will be imposed.

This is a matter of one-half per cent. The fee on what remains due will be one per cent.

Since you have fears about the fate of a deed deposited in Switzerland, I am going to inform Mme. de Staël of your offer to contribute to the registration fees and request her to send me her power of attorney in order to end this matter with you in Paris.

I am honored, Sir, to present you with the assurance of my respectful consideration.

Fourcault Pavant

On the reverse:

To Monsieur
M. du Pont de Nemours
formerly 301, rue de Montholon
near the Barrière Cadet
in Paris

96

Fourcault de Pavant to du Pont de Nemours

2 November 1805
WMSS 2/18

ce 11 Brumaire an 14

J'ai l'honneur de présenter mes devoirs à monsieur Dupont et de lui annoncer que Mad[am]e de Stael a perdu, ou egaré le projet de procuration que je lui avois envoyé; ainsi j'ai recours à monsieur Dupont pour avoir en communication son premier projet qui lui étoit resté: je promets de le lui faire remettre au bout de 24 heures.

Fourcault Pavant

On the reverse:

A Monsieur
Monsieur Dupont de Nemours
rue Montholon

TRANSLATION

11 Brumaire, year XIV

I have the honor of presenting my respects to M. du Pont and of informing him that Mme. de Staël has lost, or misplaced, the draft of a power of attorney which I had sent her. So, I request M. du Pont to send me his first draft which has remained with him. I promise to return it to him in twenty-four hours.

Fourcault Pavant

On the reverse:

To Monsieur
M. du Pont de Nemours
rue de Montholon

NOTE

In a letter written to Victor du Pont on November 10, 1805 (WMSS 2/5), du Pont de Nemours states:

> Un autre mal est qu'il devient douteux que Madame de Staël veuille accepter pour solde les deux actions qu'elle était convenue de prendre; et j'ai l'engagement de lui payer en outre six mille francs en messidor prochain.
> Je ferai pour le mieux. Je ne serai point audessous de mon courage.
> Je supporterai les privations et ce qui est pire qu'elles quoiqu'il n'y ait pas de ma faute.

> (Another misfortune is that it is becoming doubtful that Mme. de Staël will accept in settlement the two shares of stock that she had agreed to take, and I am obliged to pay her, in addition, 6,000 francs next Messidor.
> I shall do the best I can. I shall not be unequal to my courage.
> I shall put up with privations, and even worse, although I am not at fault.)

By this time, Victor du Pont's business in New York had failed, and in September 1805 he had left for Western New York to examine newly opened lands. In the following year, he and his family settled at Angelica, New York.

97

Fourcault de Pavant to du Pont de Nemours

26 November 1805

WMSS 2/18

Monsieur,

J'ai l'honneur de vous informer que j'ai reçu la procuration de Mad[am]e de Stael pour l'arrangement convenu entr'elle et vous;

je me suis occupé de suite de rediger le projet d'acte qui doit opérer votre libération, je vous l'envoye en communication, s'il vous paroit convenable, et remplir le but desiré, ayez la complaisance de me le renvoyer, en m'indiquant le jour où vous pourrez venir signer.

La remise que vous faites à Mad[am]e de Stael d'actions et de billet de votre Société, en meme tems qu'elle vous libere du montant du billet perdu, vous oblige au payement des sommes portées dans les nouveaux effets remis, aussi le receveur de l'enregistrement percevra-t-il un droit proportionnel sur cette remise, qui sera de deux pour cent sur les actions, si votre société est toute mobiliaire, il seroit de quatre pour cent si votre société etoit en partie mobiliaire et en partie immobiliaire, je vous prie donc de vouloir bien me dire quelle est la nature de cette société, afin que Mad[am]e de Stael ne paye que ce qu'elle devra payer.

Je joins une lettre que Mad[am]e de Stael m'a adressée pour vous.[1]

J'ai l'honneur, Monsieur, de vous presenter l'assurance de ma respectueuse considération.

Fourcault Pavant

ce 5 frimaire an 14

P.S. Je vous serai obligé, Monsieur, de vouloir bien m'envoyer la copie des deux actions et du billet que vous devez remettre à Mad[am]e de Stael afin que je les enonce dans l'acte.

TRANSLATION
Sir,

I have the honor of informing you that I have received the power of attorney from Mme. de Staël for the arrangement agreed upon between her and you. I immediately started to work to draw up the proposed deed which is to effect your release. I am sending it to you. If it seems to you to be proper and to fulfill the desired purpose, kindly return it to me, indicating the day when you can come sign it.

The transfer that you make to Mme. de Staël of shares of stock and a note of your company, at the same time that it releases you from the amount of the lost note, obliges you to pay the amounts stated in the new bills transferred. So, the receiver of registry fees will impose a proportional fee on this transfer, which will be 2 per cent on the shares if your company is entirely in stocks and shares. It would be 4 per cent if your company were part in stocks and shares and part in real estate. I beg you, therefore, to be so kind as to tell me what the nature of that company is, so that Mme. de Staël will pay only what she ought to pay.

I am enclosing a letter which Mme. de Staël sent me for you.[1]

I am honored, Sir, to present you with the assurance of my respectful consideration.

Fourcault Pavant

5 Frimaire, year XIV

P.S. I shall be obliged to you, Sir, if you will kindly send me the copy of the two shares and the note which you are to turn over to Mme. de Staël so that I can describe them in the deed.

NOTE
1 This letter seems to have been lost.

98

Madame de Staël to du Pont de Nemours

26 March 1806

WMSS 2/18

ce 26 mars genève

Je vous remercie mon cher dupont et de votre souvenir et de votre bonne intention comme dèbiteur. Je voudrois que vous missiez quand vous voudrez ce que vous voulez me payer chez votre excellent ami M^r bidermann, en le priant de me le faire tenir à auxerre.[1] Quand j'y serai, je voudrois (*ceci bien entre nous*) aller voir là (distance qui m'est permise) mon fils et matthieu,[2] et c'est là que j'aurois besoin d'argent. Je n'ose pas demander à M^r bid[ermann] de me louer la maison qu'il a là. J'en serois pourtant bien aise parce qu'il y a surement des livres et que j'y serai seule tout à fait pendant le peu de tems que j'y passerai. Je veux aussi essayer si je n'obtiendrai pas un sauf conduit de trois semaines pour aller à paris m'expliquer sur ma liquidation, savez vous qu'on me refuse tout même le tiers pour le dèpot de mon père sous prètexte qu'il a ètè inscrit sur la liste des èmigrès une fois bien que rayè depuis 8 ans.[3] On m'assure que l'emp[ereur] ne sait pas cette rèponse inouie de M[r] de ferment![4] Qu'en dites vous, et qu'en dit on? Car cela me paroit plus fort que le probable. Il est vrai que dans cet hyver si pènible à tant d'egards pour moi j'ai essayè un talent que j'ai assez remarquable pour jouer la tragèdie, mais quoi que vous en puissiez dire mes amis excepté j'aurois prèfèrè votre seule mine un peu doguine pour spectateur à tout ce que nous avions là. Mais ceci entre nous. Je reviens à mon affaire. Si je ne puis aller plaider moi même ma cause à paris je ferai et j'imprimerai un mèmoire que je distribuerai à tous les membres du gouvernement, et j'aurai du moins le bonheur de raconter l'histoire de ce dèpot qui est celle de la vie publique de mon père. Adieu cher du pont, je vous embrasse d'ici.

[Sans signature]

TRANSLATION

March 26, Geneva

I thank you, my dear du Pont, both for your remembrance and your good intention as a debtor. I should like you, when you wish, to give what you want to pay me to your excellent friend, M. Bidermann, requesting him to keep it for me at Auxerre.[1] When I am there, I should like (*this is strictly between us*) to go see (a distance which is granted me) my son and Mathieu,[2] and it is there that I should need money. I do not dare ask M. Bidermann to rent me the house that he has there. I should be very happy with it, however, because there are surely books, and I shall be completely alone during the little time that I shall spend there. I want also to try to obtain a safe-conduct for three weeks in order to go to Paris to have an explanation about my liquidation. Do you know that they refuse me everything, even a third on the deposit of my father, on the pretext that he was placed on the list of *émigrés* once, although he was removed eight years ago.[3] People assure me that the Emperor does not know about that unheard-of reply from M. Defermon![4] What do you say about it, and what are people saying about it? That seems to me more outrageous than is probable. It is true that during this winter,

so painful for me in so many respects, I have tried a rather remarkable talent I have for playing in tragedies; but whatever you
may say, except for my friends, I should have preferred only your
pug-dog face as a spectator to all that we put on. But this is between us. I return to my business. If I cannot go plead my case
myself, I shall write and print a memoir which I shall distribute
to all the members of the government, and I shall at least have the
pleasure of telling the story of this deposit, which is that of my
father's public life. Adieu, dear du Pont. I embrace you from
here.

[No signature]

NOTES
1 Mme. de Staël was to go to the town of Auxerre in April.
2 Mathieu de Montmorency. See Letter 45, note 2.
3 Mme. de Staël refers here to the two million francs which Necker lent to the
French government and which she was trying to recover.
4 Joseph Jacques, Comte Defermon des Chapellières (1752–1831), a prominent
figure during the Revolutionary and Napoleonic era. In 1802 he was appointed
director general of the liquidation of the public debt. He used every means
possible, often unscrupulous ones, in carrying out his duties.
  Benjamin Constant notes on March 2, 1806: "Lettre de Fermont. Quelles gens
et quelle jurisprudence." ("Letter from Defermon. What people and what jurisprudence.") The editors of Constant's *Journaux intimes* interpret this entry as a
reference to the Necker credit (*Journaux intimes*, p. 281).

99

du Pont de Nemours to Madame de Staël

11 May 1806

From a copy by Gustave Schelle, WMSS 8/108

à Madame de Stael de Holstein, à Auxerre

11 mai 1806

J'ai toujours voulu, mon excellente amie, m'abonner avec la
Sainte-Providence pour faire la moitié de ce que je dois, et le tiers
de ce que je veux; mais elle a trouvé que j'avais trop d'ambition.
Je n'ai pu répondre plus tôt qu'aujourd'hui à votre lettre du 26

Mars, et depuis ce temps je garde *inutile votre argent à votre disposition.*

Je le remettrai, ou chez mon digne ami Bidermann, c'est à dire chez MM. Gros et d'Avilliers, ses associés, car il est à la campagne, ou chez qui vous plaira.

Mais il faut pour celà que vous ayiez la bonté d'y envoyer mes *deux billets acquittés* qui doivent *m'être rendus en les payant:* la chose sera faite *dès que vous le voudrez.*

Je ne sais pas officiellement le lieu de votre séjour, où je voudrais bien me trouver auprès de vous. On me dit que vous vous y ennuyez déjà. Vous êtes une dame à laquelle il faudrait un monde. "Il ne vous suffit pas de regner sur un cœur," [1] ni sur mille.

Je ne puis vous exprimer combien je désire que la négociation que vous avez entamée ait du succès:[2] premièrement parce que la chose serait bonne en soi: et aussi parce que tout succès en amène un autre. Mais je suis si accoutumé à me tromper lorsque j'espère, que je n'ose espérer sur rien. Ne connaissant ni la langue, ni les mœurs, ni les Personnes, je ne saurais même rien conjecturer.

Autrefois je jugeais les hommes, et surtout les femmes, d'après mon cœur. Celles-ci ont répondu quelquefois, jamais assez long-temps: Et pour les hommes, j'ai eu raison trois ou quatre fois dans ma vie; encore vois-je aujourd'hui que c'est que je suis né heureux.

Qu'ai-je appris de cette longue expérience? à ne me point cour-roucer, à ne pas vouloir que les choses soient autrement que ne le comporte leur nature, et à aimer d'autant ceux chez qui je trouve quelque amitié et une générale envie de bien faire.

A ce double titre, vous avez de grands droits sur mon cœur. Je voudrais néanmoins, et dans mon tendre attachement pour vous, que vous ne fussiez pas si active, qu'avec tant de valeur, d'esprit, de vertus et meme au besoin de raison, vous sussiez et pussiez vous rendre plus heureuse.

Votre ame est dans l'embarras des richesses: une médiocrité douce et dorée vous ferait plus de bien.

Je baise vos mains superbes; je voudrais qu'il me fut permis et donné d'en faire autant à vos beaux yeux; je chéris et révère cette ame excellente que je plains.[3]

Du Pont (de Nemours)

To Madame de Staël de Holstein, at Auxerre

May 11, 1806

I have always wanted, my excellent friend, to subscribe with Holy Providence to do half of what I must and a third of what I want, but it found that I had too much ambition.

I could not answer sooner than today your letter of March 26, and since that time I have been keeping *your money useless at your disposal.*

I shall deliver it, either to my worthy friend Bidermann, that is, to Messieurs Gros and Davilliers, his associates, for he is in the country, or to whomever you wish.

But in order for me to do that, you must have the kindness to send there my *two receipted notes,* which must be *returned to me, on paying them.* The thing will be done *as soon as you wish.*

I do not know officially where you are staying, where I should like to be near you. I am told that you are already bored there. You are a lady who would need a whole world.

"It is not enough for you to reign over one heart," [1] or over a thousand.

I cannot tell you how much I wish that the negotiation you have started should be successful,[2] first of all, because the thing would be good in itself, and also because any success brings on another. But I am so accustomed to being deceived when I hope, that I dare not hope about anything. Not knowing either the language, the customs, or the persons, I could not even make any guesses about the matter.

Formerly, I judged men, and especially women, by my heart. The women came up to expectation sometimes, but never for long enough: and as for the men, I was right three or four times in my life. Yet I see today that it is because I was born fortunate.

What have I learned from this long experience? Not to become angry, not to want things to be different from what their nature allows, and to love in proportion those in whom I find some friendship and a general desire to do good.

In both of these respects, you have great rights to my heart. Nevertheless, in my tender attachment for you, I should like you not to be so active, when with so much worth, wit, virtue, and even reason when needed, you could learn how and be able to make yourself happier.

Your soul has too much wealth. A gentle and gilded mediocrity would do you more good.

I kiss your superb hands. I should like it if I were allowed to do the same to your beautiful eyes. I cherish and revere this excellent soul which I pity.[3]

Du Pont (de Nemours)

NOTES

1 I have been unable to identify the source of this quotation.

2 Undoubtedly an allusion to Mme. de Staël's efforts to obtain from the government reimbursement of the money Necker had advanced before the Revolution. See Letter 98.

3 Gustave Schelle made the following notation on his copy of this letter:

> (*Au dos de la lettre,* d'une autre main probablement que celle de Du Pont)
>   L 300. Le 9 Avril
>   288.   8 Mai
>   600 qui ont été fournis par mon compte à Mme de Stael
>
>   je paierai demain intérets sous déduction de l'escompte
>   Si les effets que je lui ai remis en paiement ont été encaissés.

> ([*on the back of the letter,* probably in a different hand from du Pont's]
>   300 fr. on April 9
>   288   May 8
>   600 which were provided by my account to Mme. de Staël.

> Tomorrow I shall pay the interest after deduction of the discount if the bills that I have sent her in payment have been collected.)

100

Madame de Staël to du Pont de Nemours

21 June 1806

WMSS 2/18

venselles[1] auxerre
ce 21 juin

J'ai lu mon cher dupont, des brochures de vous charmantes un extrait de Mad. de genlis singulièrement piquant,[2] un morceau sur la liberté plein de force,[3] un jugement sur le B[ar]on de besenval au quel je m'associe,[4] un traité sur la banque dont vous savez bien ce que je pense,[5] enfin quelques pages sur l'amour toutes aimables toutes jeunes comme vous.[6] Est il vrai que vous allez en amérique? Si cela ètoit ne devriez vous pas venir me voir ici, avec ou sans Mr Bidermann? J'aurois à vous charger de quelques affaires et surtout il me seroit bien pènible de vous voir partir sans vous dire encore une fois—adieu.

[Sans signature]

On the reverse:

A Monsieur
Monsieur Dupont de Nemours
Rue de Montolon
a Paris

Postmark:

23 juin 1806

TRANSLATION

Vincelles,[1] Auxerre
June 21

I have read, my dear du Pont, some charming pamphlets by you: a singularly biting review of Mme. de Genlis,[2] a forceful item about liberty,[3] a judgment about the Baron de Besenval with which I agree,[4] a treatise on the Bank about which you know very well what I think,[5] and finally, a few pages about love, quite engaging and quite young like you.[6] Is it true that you are going to America? If that is so, should you not come see me here, with or without M. Bidermann? I should have a few business affairs to entrust to you; and above all, it would be painful for me to see you leave without saying to you once more, Adieu.

[No signature]

On the reverse:

To Monsieur
M. du Pont de Nemours
rue de Montholon
in Paris

Postmark:

June 23, 1806

NOTES

1 Mme. de Staël had rented the château of Vincelles near Auxerre in April, 1806. The years "1807 or 08" appear in the dateline, probably in the handwriting of Mrs. S. F. du Pont. The correct date, 1806, is in still another hand.

2 Mme. de Genlis published two works in 1806: *Alphonsine, ou la Tendresse maternelle* and *Madame de Maintenon, pour servir de suite à l'Histoire de la duchesse de la Vallière.* Du Pont de Nemours wrote reviews of both works, which appeared in the *Bibliothèque Française.*

His review of *Alphonsine* ridicules the absurd love affair of dona Elvire with a young page which is described there, in which, after four years, the page suddenly learns by accident that she is 55 years old, has false teeth and hair, and is suffering from gout, and that her supposed pregnancy, what she had described as "le fruit précieux de son amour," is really only dropsy. Du Pont states that Mme. de Genlis wishes to establish the fact that a reasonable woman must not love anyone, and especially not her husband, but that it is good that such a cold woman be loved passionately, because she will exercise more authority in this way. According to him, Mme. de Genlis believes that the woman must always rule and that children must have as little education as possible: their religious faith will thus be blinder and more meritorious, and girls will obey their mothers more readily. Furthermore, paradise is reserved for the "pauvres d'esprit," a maxim which, du Pont comments, the authoress "n'a certainement pas intérêt de répandre" ("certainly has no interest in spreading abroad"). See *Extrait de la Bibliothèque Française,* V, no. 5.

Du Pont de Nemours wrote another sarcastic review of Mme. de Genlis' *Madame de Maintenon.* He observes that this will probably be the last work with which she will have enriched French literature, for where else could she find the opportunity to compose one so appropriate to her talent? Mme. de Genlis identifies herself with Mme. de Maintenon and regrets her inability to discover some slight defects in Mme. de Maintenon in order to give some variety to this portrayal of the most admirable character a woman can have. Du Pont comments acidly that every woman is pleased with herself when she looks in a mirror. See *Extrait de la Bibliothèque Française,* V, no. 8.

3 This may be du Pont de Nemours' review of a work by J.-J. Leuliette read before the class of moral and political sciences of the Institut de France, entitled "Discours sur cette question: Comment l'abolition progressive de la servitude en Europe a-t-elle influé sur le développement des lumières et des richesses des nations?" See *Extrait de la Bibliothèque Française,* V, no. 7.

It is more likely, however, that the work in question is du Pont's "Sur la liberté morale. Lu à la classe des sciences morales et politiques de l'Institut national, dans la séance du 30 nivose an XI," published in 1805 in the *Archives littéraires de l'Europe, ou Mélanges de littérature, d'Histoire et de Philosophie,* VII (Paris), 145–59. At the beginning of this work, du Pont observes: "Se déterminer *sans motifs,* serait agir sans intelligence; se déterminer contre les motifs, serait *folie*" (p. 145). He states that "la liberté cesse dès que la folie vient" (p. 151) and that "la liberté consiste dans le pouvoir de conformer ses actions à sa volonté, dirigée elle-même par l'intelligence et le raisonnement, non par une autorité étrangère" (p. 155). He concludes with the observation that "DIEU, le plus libre des êtres, puisqu'il est le seul dont la volonté ne puisse rencontrer aucun obstacle, est le seul aussi qui ne tombe jamais dans l'erreur; le seul dont chaque action soit toujours un bienfait" (p. 159). (. . . "To make a decision *without motives* would be to act without intelligence; to make a decision against motives would be madness. . . . liberty ceases as soon as madness comes . . . liberty consists in the power of making one's actions conform to one's will, itself directed by intelligence and reason, not by a foreign authority. . . . GOD, the freest of beings, since He is the only one whose will cannot encounter any obstacle, is also the only one who never falls into error; the only one whose every action is always a benefit.")

4 Pierre-Victor, Baron de Besenval (1722–91), a Swiss general in the French army, was better known for his *Mémoires,* published in 1805 and 1807 by the executor of his estate, than for his military or political career. The memoirs reveal, in a caustic and scandalous manner, the weaknesses, absurdities, and vices of the persons he had known.

In a review of the *Mémoires* (*Extrait de la Bibliothèque française,* V, no. 2), du Pont de Nemours criticizes them for their indiscretions. He wrote: "Rien de plus méprisable que d'écrire de tels souvenirs. Il parle mal de M. de Malesherbes et de M. Turgot, qui auroient été bien affligés de ses éloges. Il convient qu'il doit la vie à M. Necker; et il dit que cela lui ferme la bouche sur les mauvaises intentions qu'il lui suppose. . . . les trois volumes pourroient être intitulés: *Satyre amère contre M. de Besenval, écrite par lui-même.*" ("There is nothing more contemptible than writing such memoirs. He speaks ill of M. de Malesherbes and of M. Turgot, who would both have been very grieved by his praise. He admits that he owes his life to M. Necker; and he says that that closes his mouth about the bad intentions that he suspects in him. . . . the three volumes might well be entitled: *A Bitter Satire against M. de Besenval, written by Himself.*")

5 In 1806, du Pont de Nemours published *Sur la Banque de France, les causes de la crise qu'elle a éprouvée, les tristes effets qui en sont résultés et les moyens d'en prévenir le retour; avec une théorie des banques.* In this work he defended the principle of the freedom of banks and their independence from the state. Napoleon immediately suppressed the book.

6 Mme. de Staël is once more thinking of du Pont de Nemours' irritation at being described as an old man, when, so she claimed, she and Chénier had saved him from deportation at the time of the *coup d'état* of 18 Fructidor in 1797.

It is difficult to identify the work in question. In 1779 du Pont had published a poem entitled "L'Amour et l'amitié" in his *Poésies diverses,* but it seems unlikely that he would send Mme. de Staël a copy of this poem after so long an interval. The *Mercure de France* published another poem entitled "L'Amitié, l'amour, les amours" in its issue of April 18, 1812. Perhaps du Pont sent Mme. de Staël a manuscript copy of this poem.

101

Madame de Staël to du Pont de Nemours

8 December 1806

Pennsylvania Historical Society

On me dit mon cher du pont que vous pensez à aller en amérique. Je pense à y envoyer de l'argent peut etre à y faire voyager mon fils.[1] Je voudrois pour tout cela causer avec vous. Et il me semble qu'il ne vous seroit pas difficile de venir à St. Germain où vous trouveriez mes chevaux si vous m'ècriviez un mot. Je voudrois que M[r] biedermann eut envie de venir recevoir mes remerciments. Sa campagne est tout près d'ici. Mille amities.

ce 8 X[bre]

N[ecker] Stael de H[olstein]
aubergenville par meulan[2]

On the reverse:

pour M[r] dupont de Nemours
hotel montholon
boulevard Montmartre

TRANSLATION

I am told, my dear du Pont, that you are thinking of going to America. I am thinking of sending some money there, perhaps of having my son travel there.[1] I should like to chat with you about all that. And it seems to me that it would not be difficult for you to come to Saint Germain where you would find my horses if you wrote me a note. I should like it if M. Bidermann were willing to come and receive my thanks. His country house is quite near here. A thousand friendly greetings.

December 8

Necker Staël de Holstein
Aubergenville near Meulan[2]

On the reverse:

For M. du Pont de Nemours
Hotel Montholon
Boulevard Montmartre

NOTES
The original of this letter is in the collections of the Historical Society of Pennsylvania and is reproduced by the Society's permission.
1 Auguste de Staël.
2 On November 29, 1806, Mme. de Staël moved into the château of Acosta at Aubergenville. The château belonged to the Comte Boniface de Castellane.

102

du Pont de Nemours to Madame de Staël

16 December 1806

From a copy by Le Marois

A Madame de Stael

16 X^bre 1806

Dieu soit béni, qui dans les négociations de couronne à couronne, entre votre grande puissance et les plus augustes des autres grandes puissances a permis que vous puissiez, mon excellente amie, prendre *une position* à moindre distance de la cidevant capitale de notre Empire, et qui permette à vos amis d'aller vous baiser la main.

Je tâcherai de me faire mener par Mr Bidermann à Becheville, que l'on dit fort près d'Aubergenville.

Sinon, je vous prie de me faire savoir comment on vous prévient du jour où vous pouvez avec certitude avoir la bonté d'envoyer vos chevaux à Saint Germain.

Mon impatience de vous voir est extrême. Votre lettre a été me chercher de porte en porte.

C'est *Rue Martel n° 11* que je loge à présent.

Il n'est pas sur que je retourne en Amérique: du moins cette année. Les motifs qui m'y décideraient sont encore incertains. Je voulais partir à la fin de septembre. Nos enfans me croient en route. J'avais demandé congé à l'Institut. De semaine en semaine, j'ai été retenu, et je puis l'être plus longtems.

Je ne fais pas plus de comparaison entre le nouveau monde et l'ancien qu'entre une dame de dix huit ans et une de soixante.

Mais cet ancien a cependant des consolations, dont votre amitié n'est pas une des moindres.

Je mets mon respect à vos pieds, et si vous le permettez mes levres sur votre main.

Du Pont de Nemours

On the reverse:

A Madame
de Stael de Holstein
à Aubergenville près Meulan

TRANSLATION
To Madame de Staël

December 16, 1806

God be praised, who in the negotiations between crowns, between your great power and the most august of other great powers, has permitted you to be able, my excellent friend, to take *a position* closer to the former capital of our Empire, which permits your friends to go kiss your hand.

I shall try to have M. Bidermann take me to Bêcheville, which, I am told, is quite near Aubergenville.

If not, I beg you to let me know how to inform you of the day when you can, with certainty, have the kindness to send your horses to Saint-Germain.

My impatience to see you is extreme. Your letter went from door to door to seek me.

I now live at *No. 11, rue Martel.*

It is not certain that I shall return to America, at least this year. The motives that would make up my mind to do so are still uncertain. I wanted to leave at the end of September. Our children think I am on my way. I had asked for a leave from the Institut. From week to week, I have been detained, and I may be detained still longer.

I make no more comparison between the New World and the Old than between a lady eighteen years old and one sixty years old.

But this old one has consolations, of which your friendship is not one of the least.

I place my respect at your feet, and if you permit it, my lips on your hand.

Du Pont de Nemours

On the reverse:

To Madame
de Staël de Holstein
at Aubergenville near Meulan

NOTE
The text of this letter is taken from a copy made by the Comte Le Marois and presented to Mr. Lammot du Pont Copeland. It is reproduced by the former's permission. The copy is now in the possession of the Eleutherian Mills Historical Library (Acc. 360).

103

Madame de Staël to du Pont de Nemours

26 December 1806

WMSS 2/18

J'ai reçu des vers charmants[1] dont j'ètois fière et que je voulois montrer à mes amis. Je les ai placès sur ma cheminée pour les porter au dèjeuner et ma stupide femme de chambre les a jettés au feu. Je demande à genoux qu'on me les renvoye. Il seroit encor plus aimable de me les rapporter. Je n'avois pas passè depuis longtems une journèe aussi doucement originale. J'ai écrit a fourcault. Je vous ferai passer sa rèponse.

[Sans signature]

ce vendredi [26 décembre 1806]

On the reverse:

A Monsieur
Monsieur Dupont de Nemours
Rue Martel N° 11
à Paris

Postmark:

29 Décembre 1806
72 Meulan

TRANSLATION

I received some charming verses[1] of which I was proud and which I wanted to show to my friends. I put them on my mantel to take them to lunch, and my stupid maid threw them in the fire. I ask you, on bended knee, to send them to me again. It would be still nicer if you brought them to me. I had not spent such a charmingly unusual day for a long time. I have written to Fourcault. I shall send you his reply.

[No signature]

Friday [December 26, 1806]

On the reverse:

To Monsieur
M. du Pont de Nemours
11, rue Martel
in Paris

Postmark:

December 29, 1806
72 Meulan

NOTE
1 I am unable to identify these verses. They may have been part of the translation of Ariosto's *Orlando furioso* on which du Pont worked for many years.

104

Madame de Staël to du Pont de Nemours

10 January 1807

WMSS 2/19

ce 10 j^{er}
aubergenville par Meulan
dep. de seine et oise

J'ai enfin retrouvé mes jolis vers dont je regrettois tant la perte. Les compagnons s'en tireront comme ils pourront. Ce n'est qu'ulysse qui m'intéressoit dans cette affaire. En m'ècrivant deux jours d'avance vous aurez toujours ma voiture au grand cerf à St Germain. Et je serai vous le savez ravie de vous voir. Si j'ètois payèe par le gouvernement[1] je serois votre notaire dans cette affaire au lieu de fourcault. Je regarderois comme le deuil de tout ce qu'il reste d'esprits et d'amis votre dèpart pour l'amèrique. Amitiè et dèvouement inaltèrable.

[Sans signature]

TRANSLATION

January 10
Aubergenville near Meulan
Department of Seine-et-Oise

I have finally recovered my pretty verses whose loss I regretted so much. The companions will get along as best they can. It is only Ulysses who interested me in this matter. By writing to me two days in advance, you will always have my carriage at the Grand Cerf in Saint-Germain. And I shall be, you know, delighted to see you. If I were paid by the government,[1] I should be your notary in this affair, instead of Fourcault. I should consider your departure for America as cause for mourning by all remaining minds and friends. Friendly greetings and undying devotion.

[No signature]

NOTE
1 An allusion to the two million francs advanced by Necker which Mme. de Staël was trying to recover.

105

Madame de Staël to du Pont de Nemours

15 February 1807

WMSS 2/19

Vous devriez en preux chevalier mon cher du pont, venir mardi à St Germain au grand cerf. Vous y trouveriez ma voiture et peut être une belle dame, le tout à 2 h. et vous viendriez ici. Jeudi cette mème voiture y sera si hochet[1] vient comme je le crois. Enfin il fait beau et je me suis rèveillèe ce matin avec le dèsir de causer avec vous. Le partagez vous? Venez mardi.

[Sans signature]

ce dimanche [15 février 1807]
accosta

Ma voiture vous remennera.

On the reverse:

A Monsieur
Monsieur Dupont de Nemours
Rue Martel N° 11
fb. poissonnière a Paris

Postmark:

16 Février 1807
72 Meulan

TRANSLATION

You should, like a gallant knight, my dear du Pont, come Tuesday to Saint-Germain to the Grand Cerf. You would find my carriage there, and perhaps a beautiful lady, both at two o'clock; and you would then come here. Thursday, this same carriage will be there if Hochet[1] comes, as I believe he will. In a word, the weather is fine, and I awoke this morning with a desire to chat with you. Do you share it? Come on Tuesday.

[No signature]

Sunday [February 15, 1807]
Acosta

My carriage will take you back.

On the reverse:

To Monsieur
M. du Pont de Nemours
11, rue Martel
Faubourg Poissonière in Paris

Postmark:

February 16, 1807
72 Meulan

NOTE

1 Claude Hochet (1773–1857), a collaborator on the *Journal des Débats* and the *Publiciste* and official of the Council of State. He was a friend of Mme. de Staël, Madame Récamier, and Benjamin Constant. The letters Hochet received from Mme. de Staël and Constant have been published by Jean Mistler under the title *Lettres à un ami* (Neuchâtel, 1949).

106

du Pont de Nemours to Madame de Staël

22 February 1807

From a draft, wmss 2/6

Paris 22 Fevrier 1807

a Madame de Stael

Mon excellente amie,

Gardez vous de croire que je ne sois pas très serieusement occupé de tout ce qui vous interesse.

J'ai trouvé le moyen d'empêcher de naitre l'objection commune contre votre nouvel ouvrage, et le sentiment qui pourrait y donner lieu.

Le tout dépend du titre.

Si vous gardez celui d'*Oswald,* ou de *Corinne et de l'Italie,* ce pays sera subordonné au roman avec des avantages pour l'un et pour l'autre, le lecteur, et surtout cette nombreuse portion de lecteurs [et] de lectrices qui n'ouvrent que des Romans, allechés d'ailleurs par le commencement de celui-ci qui a beaucoup de charme, éprouveront quelque *desappointement* comme je l'ai fait moi meme aussitôt qu'ils arriveront aux descriptions quelque art que vous ayiez mis à lier les deux sujets. Tous deux y perdront et l'accident serait arrivé à l'abbé Barthelemy[1] si son titre n'eut pas été voyages d'*Anacharsis,* et s'il eut employe celui d'*Anacharsis* ou seul ou comme idée premiere et principale: par exemple s'il eut dit anacharsis *en Grece* ou anacharsis *et* la Grece.

Ne donnez donc aucun Roman à esperer. Qu'on le trouve en surcroit, comme un cadre heureux a l'ouvrage qu'on aura eu l'intention de lire. D'abord vous jouirez de l'avantage qui n'est pas petit d'avoir une meilleure classe de lecteur et nul d'eux n'aura été trompé, ils ne se plaindront pas d'un mecompte, ils vous sauront gré du talent avec lequel vous aurez animé votre tableau et diminué la monotonie presque inevitable des meilleures descriptions quand elles sont repetées ou multipliées.

Que votre titre soit L'ITALIE. Rien de plus.

Et votre Préface, à peu près ceci:

"Je n'ai d'autre dessein dans cet ouvrage que celui de donner une idée générale de l'Italie, son climat, ses monumens, ses arts, le caractere même de ses habitans qui des circonstances plus heureuses releveraient bientôt au niveau de leur esprit, font une impression à laquelle voudraient en vain resister les âmes les plus fortement préoccupées.

"Celle de Lord Sydney[2] êtait, comme la mienne, lorsque je l'y rencontrai, presque accablée sous de profonds chagrins, remplie de souvenirs amers et douleureux.

"En exprimant l'effet de ses émotions successives, je peindrai mes propres sensations et l'adoucissement qu'elles ont données a mes durables peines.

"Peut-être en résultera-t-il que quelque autre de ceux qui auront à pleurer de grandes pertes, qui seront fatigués d'une longue suite d'effrayantes secousses iront à leur tour chercher en Italie le calme reconnaissant que l'aspect des plus beaux efforts du génie et les temoins muets des plus grandes vicissitudes fait involontairement eprouver aux caracteres doués de quelque élevation, aux cœurs dont la sensibilité n'est pas perdue, aux esprits reflechissans.

"J'aurai payé une partie de mes dettes à ce beau pays et rendu service aux affligés qui après moi seront soulagés par sa magique influence."

Ensuite entrez en matiere comme vous voudrez; prenez la route qui vous plaira peignez les sites, les edifices, les choses, les arts, les hommes, et vos personnages, Corinne Oswald, ornez votre sujet par les inquietudes ou les plaisirs de ces deux amans comme le Poussin mettait des bergers dans ses nobles paysages.[3] Personne ne dira que vous avez refroidi votre roman que vous aurez suspendu sa marche, parce que vous n'aurez promis de Roman à personne, ni appellé l'interêt de personne sur un Roman. Le Public est comme les autres creanciers, il ne demande l'execution que des engagemens qu'on a pris, et comme eux il recoit volontiers ce qu'on lui donne de bon au dela.

Je baise avec respect et tendresse vos très belles mains.

TRANSLATION

Paris, February 22, 1807

To Madame de Staël

My excellent friend,

Take good care not to think that I am not seriously concerned with everything that interests you.

I have found the means of preventing the common objection against your new work, and the feeling that could give rise to it, from springing up.

Everything depends on the title.

If you keep that of *Oswald,* or of *Corinne and Italy,* that country will be subordinate to the novel, with advantages for both. The reader, and especially that numerous group of readers of both sexes who open only novels, enticed, moreover, by the quite charming beginning of this one, will experience some *disappointment,* as I did myself, as soon as they reach the descriptions, whatever skill you have shown in tying together the two subjects. Both will lose in it, and the mishap would have happened to the Abbé Barthélemy[1] if his title had not been TRAVELS *of Anacharsis,* and if he had employed *Anacharsis,* either alone or as the main and principal idea; for example, if he had said ANACHARSIS *in Greece,* or ANACHARSIS *and* GREECE.

Do not give any expectation of a novel. Let the reader find it as a bonus, like a happy frame for the work that he intended to read. First of all, you will enjoy the advantage, which is not small, of having a better class of reader, and not one of them will have been deceived. They will not complain about a disappointment. They will be grateful to you for the talent with which you have animated your tableau and diminished the almost inevitable monotony of the best descriptions when they are repeated or multiplied.

Let your title be ITALY. Nothing more.

And your preface, something like this:

"I have no other purpose in this work than that of giving a general idea of Italy, its climate, its monuments, its arts, the very character of its inhabitants, who, in happier circumstances, would soon rise again to their former level of intellect and make an impression which even the most greatly preoccupied souls would resist in vain.

"That of Lord Sydney[2] was, like mine when I met him there, almost overwhelmed by profound sorrows, filled with bitter and painful memories.

"By expressing the effect of his successive emotions, I shall depict my own sensations and the relief that they gave to my lasting sorrows.

"Perhaps the result will be that others of those who have great losses to mourn, who are weary of a long series of frightful upsets, will go, in their turn, to seek calm in Italy, recognizing that the sight of the finest efforts of genius and the silent witnesses of the greatest vicissitudes causes characters endowed with some loftiness, hearts whose sensitivity is not lost, and thinking minds to feel involuntarily.

"I shall have paid a part of my debt to that beautiful country and rendered a service to the afflicted ones who, after me, will be relieved by its magic influence."

Then proceed with your text as you wish; take the course that pleases you; describe landscapes, buildings, things, art, men, and your characters, Corinne, Oswald; decorate your subject with the worries or the pleasures of those two lovers, as Poussin put shepherds in his noble landscapes.[3] No one will say that you have chilled your novel, that you have stopped its movement, because you will not have promised a novel to anyone or attracted the interest of anyone to a novel. The public is like other creditors. It asks only for the execution of the pledges that one has made; and like them, it gladly receives whatever good is given beyond that.

I kiss with respect and tenderness your very beautiful hands.

NOTES

1 The Abbé Jean-Jacques Barthélemy (1716–95), an archaeologist and the author of the *Voyage du jeune Anacharsis en Grèce,* published in 1788. He spent thirty years writing this work, in which he attempted to portray the life and genius of ancient Greece. Although it appeared at an unfavorable time, on the eve of the Revolution, the *Voyage* was greatly successful.

2 The original name for Lord Nelvil in *Corinne.* The change may have been made to avoid confusion with Sidney Smith. See Geneviève Gennari, *Le Premier Voyage de Madame de Staël en Italie et la Genèse de Corinne* (Paris, 1947), p. 149.

Benjamin Constant states that the printing of *Corinne* began on February 13,

1807 (*Journaux intimes*, p. 318). Du Pont de Nemours had obviously read, or heard read, a manuscript copy of the novel.

3 Du Pont must have been thinking of Poussin's famous painting "Et in Arcadia ego," which depicts four shepherds contemplating a tomb in an idyllic, pastoral setting.

❀

107

Madame de Staël to du Pont de Nemours

26 February 1807

WMSS 2/19

Ce 26 fèvrier

Je suis vraiment touchée, mon cher dupont, de tant de bonté et dans le but je prendrois la prèface *mot pour mot,* mais je suis persuadée que quand vous aurez lu l'ouvrage en entier il ne vous sera pas possible de persister dans votre avis. Je vous demande donc de venir me voir dès que je vous donnerai avis que j'ai fait mon nid,[1] et comme le titre et la prèface sont la dernière feuille nous en causerons. Quand rousseau a fait èmile ou de l'èducation la mème double attente existoit. Avec toute humilité j'espère pour moi la mème chose, mais encor une fois quel sentiment aimable vous a inspiré cette pensée. Corinne m'a dèja beaucoup valu de bonheur, et mème d'honneur. Je garderai votre lettre.

[Sans signature]

On the reverse:

A Monsieur
Monsieur Dupont de Nemours
Rue Martel N° 11
à Paris

Postmark:

28 Février 1807
72 Meulan

TRANSLATION

February 26

I am really touched, my dear du Pont, by so much kindness, and with that in mind, I should take the preface *word for word;* but I am convinced that when you have read the work in its entirety, it will not be possible for you to persist in your opinion. I ask you, therefore, to come see me as soon as I inform you that I have made my nest;[1] and as the title and the preface are the last sheet, we shall chat about them. When Rousseau wrote *Emile, or Education,* the same double expectation existed. With all humility, I hope for the same thing for me, but once more, what a kind feeling inspired this thought in you! *Corinne* has already brought me much happiness, and even honor. I shall keep your letter.

[No signature]

On the reverse:

To Monsieur
M. du Pont de Nemours
11, rue Martel
in Paris

Postmark:

February 28, 1807
72 Meulan

NOTE

1 Mme. de Staël was still residing at the château of Acosta. About this time, however, she bought the château of Cernay with the intention of moving there. Napoleon frustrated her plans by ordering her to return to Switzerland in April.

108

Madame de Staël to du Pont de Nemours

8 March 1807

WMSS 2/19

Je ne puis encor aller à Cernay (que j'ai acheté). Des ouvriers dans la maison &c m'en empecheront encor pendant un mois. Ainsi donc mon cher du pont quand vous aurez un jour à me donner ècrivez moi pour que j'envoye mes chevaux à St germain. Et à tout hasard je vous dis qu'ils ramenneront matthieu[1] mercredi mais ils sont comme leur maitresse tous les jours à vos ordres. Mille amitiès.

[Sans signature]

ce 8 mars dimanche

On the reverse:

A Monsieur
Monsieur Dupont de Nemours
Rue Martel N° 11
à Paris

Postmark:

72 Meulan

TRANSLATION

I cannot yet go to Cernay (which I bought). Workmen in the house, etc., will prevent me from doing so for another month. Thus, my dear du Pont, when you have a day to give me, write to me so that I may send my horses to Saint-Germain. And, on the off chance, I tell you that they will bring back Mathieu[1] on Wednesday, but they are like their mistress, every day at your command. A thousand friendly greetings.

[No signature]

Sunday, March 8

On the reverse:

To Monsieur
M. du Pont de Nemours
11, rue Martel
in Paris

Postmark:

72 Meulan

NOTE
1 Mathieu de Montmorency.

109

Madame de Staël to du Pont de Nemours

11 April 1807

WMSS 2/19

Ce 11 avril Meulan
dep. de seine et oise.

J'ai vu mon cher dupont que vous n'ètiez pas nommé.[1] Il y a un genre de distinction piquant et naturelle, puissante et dèsarmèe, qui obtient plutot l'applaudissement que les places. Je vous crois celle là. C'est celle que j'aurois si j'ètois homme. Donnez moi des nouvelles de Mad. biedermann. Je m'en inquiette de cœur. Dites le je vous prie à son mari.[2] Si elle est mieux ne vous verrai-je pas avant que je parte d'ici, c'est à dire avant le 25? Je vais d'abord à Rouen et de là à Coppet. Et mon pauvre Cernay que je n'ai pas même vu.[3] Voulez vous que je le prète à Madame du pont cet èté?

[Sans signature]

On the reverse:

A Monsieur
Monsieur Dupont de Nemours
Membre de l'Institut rue Martel
N° 11 f ᵇ poissonniere
a Paris

Postmark:

12 avril 1807
72 Meulan

TRANSLATION

April 11, Meulan
Department of Seine-et-Oise

I have seen, my dear du Pont, that you were not appointed.[1] There is a kind of distinction, piquant and natural, powerful and disarmed, which obtains applause rather than positions. I believe you have that. It is what I should have if I were a man. Give me

some news of Mme. Bidermann. I am quite worried about her.
Please tell her husband.[2] If she is better, shall I not see you before
I leave here, that is to say, before the twenty-fifth? I am going first
to Rouen and from there to Coppet. And my poor Cernay, which
I have not even seen![3] Do you want me to lend it to Mme. du
Pont this summer?

[No signature]

On the reverse:

To Monsieur
M. du Pont de Nemours
Member of the Institut
11, rue Martel
Faubourg Poissonière
in Paris

Postmark:

April 12, 1807
72 Meulan

NOTES

1 Du Pont de Nemours had hoped to be appointed to the Sénat conservateur.
2 In a letter to Victor du Pont on March 30, 1807 (WMSS 2/6), du Pont de
Nemours wrote:

> Je suis toujours dans les mêmes incertitudes sur ce que sont devenues tes
> affaires, sur ce qu'auront retiré tes creanciers, sur le destin des terres de
> M^r. Bidermann que nous n'avions qu'en simple confiance, et outre sa mise
> de cent trente six mille francs dans ma société.
> Mes peines avec cet excellent ami sont ameres.

> (I am still in the same uncertainty about what has become of your busi-
> ness, about what your creditors may have withdrawn, about the fate of
> M. Bidermann's land which we have only in trust, and further, his investment
> of 136,000 francs in my company.
> My troubles with this excellent friend are bitter.)

3 See Letter 107, note 1.

110

Madame de Staël to du Pont de Nemours

April 1807

WMSS 2/19

Mon cher dupont, je pars le 21 pour aller passer (ceci entre nous) chez M^r de la fayette deux jours[1] et de là à genève. Vous avez écrit un èloge charmant de M^r de la lande.[2] Je n'ai fait que parcourir vos morceaux,[3] et je les trouve charmants. Vous êtes une ame et un esprit d'une trempe rare. Que dieu vous bènisse et moi aussi. Il y a long-tems que je souffre. Adieu.

[Sans signature]

On the reverse:

Mr Dupont de Nemours

TRANSLATION

My dear du Pont, I am leaving on the twenty-first to go spend (this is just between us) two days at Lafayette's,[1] and from there I go to Geneva. You have written a charming eulogy of M. de Lalande.[2] I have only glanced through your writings,[3] and I find them charming. You are a soul and a mind of a rare calibre. May God bless you, and me also. I have been suffering for a long time. Adieu.

[No signature]

On the reverse:

M. du Pont de Nemours

NOTES

1 Mme. de Staël canceled her plans to visit Lafayette at La Grange, as we learn from a letter written in April 1807 to Mme. de Tessé, the aunt of Mme. de Lafayette. Mme. de Staël, who was then illegally and, so she thought, clandestinely in Paris, believed that Mme. de Tessé had betrayed her by sending a friend to the Minister of Police to inquire about Mme. de Staël's visit to Paris en route to exile in Geneva. Mme. de Tessé defended her action in a long letter probably written soon thereafter. See J. F. Marshall, "Madame de Staël et Madame de Tessé," *Revue d'Histoire littéraire de la France*, No. 1 (January–March 1967), pp. 114–22.

2 Joseph-Jérôme Le François de Lalande (1732–1807), the French astronomer. In August 1792, du Pont de Nemours, as a result of his efforts to defend Louis XVI and of his general moderation in the growing disorder of the Revolution, was forced to hide in order to save his life. Lalande and Harmand, the former's student and a relative of du Pont, arranged to conceal him in the attic of the Institut, where he remained several weeks.

Du Pont's eulogy of Lalande (quoted by Adrien Jean Quentin Beuchot, *Notice biographique sur M. de Lalande* [Paris?, 1807?], pp. 15–16) praises Lalande for the assistance he gave du Pont in this incident and for his honor, courage, and love of humanity.

3 These writings are probably du Pont's *Quelques mémoires sur différents sujets lus ou communiqués à l'Institut* (Paris, 1807). They consist mainly of papers on natural history (Gustave Schelle, *Du Pont de Nemours et l'école physiocratique* [Paris, 1888], pp. 427–28).

❂

111

du Pont de Nemours to Madame de Stael

28 April 1807

From excerpts in Le Marois, *Cahiers*, pp. 510–11

28 avril 1807

Nous nous entendrons et nous aimerons de loin comme de près, parce que vous êtes bonne, grande et sensible et que je ne suis ni méchant, ni petit, ni glacé.

Il est ignoble dans une telle circonstance de parler d'affaires—mais il faut en être au courant. Vous savez les miennes. Si je réussis en totalité ou en partie à l'emprunt pour lequel vous avez écrit à Pavant . . . Je payerai les billets que vous m'avez donnés.

.   .   .   .

Vous m'avez offert de prêter Cernay à Mme Du Pont, cela est bien bon. Nous ne sommes pas assez riches pour l'habiter. Louez-le. Mais quoi que vous fassiez, gardez-moi votre bienveillance et quant à celle-là rien ne peut m'enlever le moyen de la payer.

TRANSLATION

April 28, 1807

We shall understand each other and love each other from a distance as well as close at hand, because you are good, great, and sensitive, and I am neither bad, nor small, nor cold.

It is ignoble, in such a circumstance, to talk about business, but one must keep informed. You know my business. If I succeed entirely, or in part, in getting the loan about which you wrote to Pavant . . . I shall pay the notes that you have given me.

.   .   .   .

You offered to lend Cernay to Mme. du Pont. That is very kind. We are not rich enough to live in it. Rent it. But whatever you do, keep your benevolence for me, and as for the latter, nothing can take from me the means of paying for it.

112

du Pont de Nemours to Madame de Staël

19 May 1807

From a draft, WMSS 2/6

A Mme de Stael

19 may 1807

Vous prennez trop au tragique ma belle et bonne amie, ce que je vous ai demandé.

Vous m'ecrivez comme si la propriété de vos enfans était en danger. Vous me parlez de vous donner une securité positive en France ou en amerique pour le capital et pour les interets et il ne s'agit ni du capital ni des interets mais d'un delai peut etre de quelques mois peut-être d'un an pour une cinquantaine de livres.

Vous avez la securite positive que vous desirez.

Vous êtes par vos deux actions proprietaire du trentieme d'un domaine territorial sur lequel est etablie une grande usine qui valait il y a dix huit mois cinq cent quarante mille francs au moins, qui augmente de valeur tous les ans, et qui certainement en vaudra beaucoup plus de six cent mille quand la Societe finira.

Ainsi quant a votre capital, la securite est positive et parfaite.

Je l'ai rendue telle pour vous et pour tous mes autres action-naires en renoncant a tout ce qui me reviendrait de ma portion dans la societe dont j'avais fait une sixieme des fonds, en y renon-cant ce que ceux qui ont ete mis par mes associes fussent remplis; me faisant ainsi *assureur* du capital des compagnons. Je ne veux point le leur payer à mon compte unique et jusqu'à extinction de

toute ma fortune les pertes qui ne sont pas de ma faute et qui constatent même combien les operations avaient eté avantageuses,
puis que ces pertes provenant d'une puissance irresistible montent
a une somme qui excede de soixante mille francs la totalité de la
caisse primitive de la societe et qu'il reste cependant a celle ci ce
dont je viens de vous rendre compte.

A l'egard du capital vous devez donc etre hors d'inquietude.

Et quant aux interets stipulés sur un taux très elevé pour le tems
actuel vous etes en beaucoup meilleure position que tous nos
autres associés qui peuvent s'en trouver privés ou etre obliges de
les reduire pendant quelque tems si les rentrées n'y suffisent pas;
car c'est pour cela et à cette condition qu'on est en société. Tandis
que les votres sont *assurés* par des billets qui ne sont pas susceptibles de réduction et doivent etre acquittés des fonds de la societe
quand même les autres actionnaires et [*sic*] n'auraient point d'interets à repartir entre eux.

Sous un certain aspect je paraitrais avoir à me reprocher de vous
les avoir ainsi alloués, et de vous avoir pour ces interets donné
privilege sur nos autres associés, mais j'ai considere et je leur
exposerai lors de nos comptes défini[ti]fs que les fonds avaient êté
prêtés à la societe, qu'ils devaient etre rendus par elle, que ç'a êté
une condescendance de M^r votre pere d'avoir consenti à prendre
une partie du remboursement en actions. Je crois que cela vous
place pour vos interets dans un cas particulier.

Et cela m'a empeché de refuser de vous les assurer par des billets
au nom social.

Je n'ai point du tout annoncé comme vous paraissez le croire
que ces billets ne seraient pas payés.

Bien au contraire, vous avez sçu que je cherchais et sans la
caution d'un de nos amis communs tres riche,[1] des fonds dont
l'objet etait est de mettre au courant les comptes d'interets et tout
ce qui peut rester d'embarras à la Société.

Je vous ai donc seulement priée de ne pas négocier les billets en
vous prevenant qu'à moins que je ne reçusse des fonds d'Amerique
ou de France je ne pourrais vraisemblablement pas payer *a
l'echeance* celui de cette annee; ce qui suppose et dit implicitement
que je le payerai *après l'echeance* des premiers fonds que je pourrai
y employer. Je vous ai priée d'attendre les cinquante mille livres

dont il est question. Si je vous avais prié de me preter cinquante louis vous l'auriez fait et c'est precisement la même chose.

Jugez mon amie de notre position et notre delicatesse respective. Ma societé devait a M^r votre Pere environ cinquante mille francs. J'ai eu avec lui au sujet de leur remboursement une correspondance très active. Je lui ai exposé la perte enorme que me causait le gouvernement et que ma Société en etait en serait alterée très genée—non pas ruiné, mais exposée a l'etre si on la poursuivait.

Il avait beaucoup d'ordre et n'aurait ni tenu ni pu tenir cette correspondance sans avoir sous les yeux le billet de mon fils qui etait le titre de sa creance en nombres très rompus de 48 678 F. 55 centimes et mes lettres y relatives.

Il me voulait du bien et m'honorait de beaucoup d'estime. Sa haute experience savait d'ailleurs que pour tout recouvrement il y a de l'avantage a se preter aux circonstances du debiteur. Il a supprime dans ses derniers momens le billet et mes lettres faisant ce double raisonnement—si Mr du Pont ne peut pas payer à present je ne veux pas qu'il soit poursuivi; et s'il peut payer à present ou plus tard il payera tout de même.

Il nous a rendu justice a tous deux.

Je vous ai avertie comme je le devais. Je vous ai payé comptant vingt sept mille cinq cent francs sur le capital et tous les interets échus environ trente mille francs au total. Vous avez pris pour le surplus les deux actions qu'il avait acceptees.

Malgre nos malheurs qui se sont encore aggraves depuis qui pouvaient suspendre ou affaiblir ou aneantir comme dans toutes societes par action les interets et des bones-gens associés j'ai rendu la somme des votres. Mais où aller parer des billets à ordre dont j'en ai dejà acquitté un?[2]

J'ai besoin d'un delai pour le payement d'un autre de ces billets. Vous savez pourquoi j'ai ce besoin, et comment je dois sortir de son urgence. Vous avez taché d'y cooperer.

La somme est peu considerable. De vous à moi, il n'y a pas là d'affaire et je ne sais pas pourquoi vous avez cru en voir une et une grande qui coute à chacun de nous une longue lettre. Il n'y a qu'une occasion de bienveillance et de reconnaissance.

Voulez vous faire reellement une affaire qui vous donne la

double certitude en France et en Amerique qui parait vous occuper.

Vous avez à vendre Cernay. Pretez moi l'argent que vous en tirerez, je reprendrai en même tems vos deux actions au pair et de ces deux actions comme pour celle de [. . .].[3] Je vous donnerai outre l'engagement cernay que vous y ajouteriez ainsi que le paye-ment des interets sur notre propriete americaine la caution de cette valeur de Mr de Talleyrand dont je peux encore disposer; le capital remboursable lors de ma liquidation en 1811. C'est ce dont je vais causer avec Mr de Pavant.

Je ne vous parlerai point aujourd'hui de Corinne[4] quoique je l'aie lue et relue comme un bel ouvrage avec un tres grand plaisir mais il ne faut pas meler le plaisir aux affaires. Ce sera pour une autre fois.

J'ai eu connaissance d'une lettre qui m'a beaucoup affligé me laisse pour le moment, mon excellente ami peu d'esperance du succes de celle que vous avez ecrite et dont vous me parlez.[5] Je baise votre belle main.

TRANSLATION
    To Madame de Staël

                                                        May 19, 1807
    You take too tragically, my beautiful and good friend, what I have asked you.

    You write to me as if the property of your children were in danger. You speak to me of giving you a positive security in France or in America for the capital and interest, and it is not a question either of capital or of interest but of a delay of perhaps a few months, perhaps a year, for about fifty francs.

    You have the positive security that you wish.

    You are, by virtue of your two shares of stock, owner of a thir-tieth part of a plot of land on which is established a large factory which was worth at least 540,000 francs eighteen months ago, which is increasing in value every year, and which will certainly be worth much more than 600,000 when the company is dissolved.

    So, as for your capital, the guarantee is positive and complete.

    I made it such for you and all my other stockholders, by giving up everything that would come to me from my share in the com-pany, for which I had provided one sixth of the funds, by giving it up until those funds which were provided by my associates were completed, thus making myself the *insurer* of the capital of my companions. I do not want to pay them from my own account until my entire fortune is liquidated for the losses which are not my fault and which even establish how advantageous these operations have been, since these losses, resulting from an irresistible force, amount to a sum which exceeds by 60,000 francs the entire amount of the company's original funds, and since there remains for the company what I have just reported to you.

In regard to the capital, you have thus no cause for worry.

And as for the interest specified at a very high rate for the present time, you are in a much better position than all our other associates, who may find themselves deprived of it or obliged to *reduce* it for some time if the returns on the investment are not sufficient, because it is for that, and on that condition, that we are in a company. Whereas yours is *assured* by notes which cannot be reduced and must be paid from the funds of the company even if the other shareholders did not have any interest to distribute among them.

In a certain respect, I should seem to have to reproach myself for having granted it to you thus, and for having given you a privilege over our other associates for this interest; but I have considered, and I shall explain to them at the time of our final accounting, that the funds had been lent to the company, that they should be returned by it, that it was a condescension on your father's part to have agreed to take a part of his reimbursement in shares of stock. I believe that that places you in a special case for your interest.

And this has prevented me from refusing to insure it for you by notes in the name of the company.

I did not state, as you seem to believe, that these notes would not be paid.

Quite the contrary. You have known that I was seeking, without the guarantee of one of our very rich mutual friends,[1] some funds whose purpose was and is to settle the interest accounts and any other remaining troubles for the company.

I asked you only not to negotiate these notes, informing you that unless I received some funds from America or France, I probably could not pay the one for this year *at the due date,* which supposes and says implicitly that I shall pay it *after the due date* with the first funds that I can use to do so. I asked you to wait for the 50,000 francs in question. If I had asked you to lend me fifty louis, you would have done so, and this is exactly the same thing.

Consider, my friend, our positions and our respective difficulties.

My company owed your father about 50,000 francs. I had a very active correspondence with him on the question of their repayment. I explained to him the enormous loss that the government caused me, and that as a result, my company was, and would be, disturbed and very embarrassed financially—not ruined, but in danger of being so if action were taken against it.

He was very orderly and would not have carried on, or been able to carry on, this correspondence without having before him my son's note, which was the certificate of his credit in carefully itemized figures for 48,678.55 francs, as well as my letters concerning it.

He wished me well and honored me with much esteem. From his great experience, he knew, moreover, that for any collection of debts there is an advantage in adapting oneself to the circumstances of the debtor. In his last moments, he destroyed the note and my letters for these two reasons: if M. du Pont cannot pay at present, I do not want him to be sued, and if he can pay now or later, he will pay just the same.

He did justice to both of us.

I informed you as I should. I paid you 27,500 francs in cash on the capital and all the interest due, about 30,000 francs altogether. You took for the remainder the two shares that he had accepted.

In spite of our misfortunes, which have become worse since then, and which could suspend or weaken or destroy, as in every stock company, the interest and those good people, our associates, I have paid on your account, but where can one go to avoid promissory notes, one of which I have already paid? [2]

I need an extension of time for the payment of another of these notes. You know why I need this, and how I must get out of this emergency situation. You have tried to cooperate.

The sum is not very large. Between you and me, there is not any *business affair* in this; and I do not know why you thought you saw one, and a big one which costs each of us a long letter. This is only an opportunity for benevolence and gratitude.

Do you really want to make a business arrangement which will give you the double security in France and in America which seems to concern you?

You have only to sell Cernay. Lend me the money that you get from it. I shall take back, at the same time, your two shares at par and of these two shares as for that of [. . .].[3] I shall give you, besides the agreement based on the sale of Cernay that you would add to it, the payment of the interest on our American property, and the guarantee of M. de Talleyrand for this asset of which I can still dispose, the capital being payable at the time of my liquidation in 1811. That is what I shall discuss with M. de Pavant.

I shall not speak to you today about *Corinne*,[4] although I have read and reread it as a fine work with very great pleasure, but one must not mix pleasure with business. This will be for another time.

I have learned about a letter which disturbed me very much and leaves me, for the moment, my excellent friend, with little hope for the success of the one which you mention to me that you wrote.[5] I kiss your beautiful hand.

NOTES

1 The friend in question was probably Talleyrand; see the third paragraph from the end of this letter.
2 This is a very difficult paragraph to decipher, with insertions on top of insertions and many cross-outs.
3 An illegible word crossed out.
4 *Corinne* had just been published.
5 Probably an allusion to the letter written at this time by Mme. de Staël to Napoleon, in which she tried to obtain permission to remain in France and return to Paris by praising and flattering him. The letter had no effect upon him. It was supposedly confidential, but everyone in Paris seems to have known about it (Henri Guillemin, *Madame de Staël, Benjamin Constant et Napoléon* [Paris, 1959], pp. 97–98).

113

Madame de Staël to du Pont de Nemours

3 June 1807

WMSS 2/19

ce 3 juin C[oppet]

Vous ne m'avez point dit mon cher dupont, que vous demandiez quelques mois de dèlais pour l'intéret que vous me devez mais vous m'avez fait entendre (ce que je savais dèja par des lettres d'amèrique) que le fonds comme le capital sont exposés. Vous avez raison de dire que je vous prèterois 53 livres avec grand plaisir et bien que l'emprunt forcé soit moins agrèable que volontaire je consens au retard de six mois que vous demandez, mais je ne consens pas au moins autant qu'il est en ma puissance à rester dans une position qui m'expose à une perte trés considèrable et qu'il ne m'est pas possible de supporter. Je voudrois donc qu'il vous fut possible de me donner une sècuritè pour le fonds et les intérets et je prèfèrerois la caution de M^r de talleyrand à la propriètè de vos actions. Je rendrois volontiers les deux actions pour me placer comme crèancière avec sa caution. Je vous observe que vous avez eu tort envers moi en me faisant payer un enregistrement trés considèrable l'année dernière pour me donner en payement d'une somme que *vous me deviez à l'instant* des actions dont vous saviez mieux que moi la foible valeur car c'est peu de jours après la conclusion de notre acte que j'ai appris que l'un de M^{rs} vos fils avoit suspendu ses payements en amèrique.[1] Ce n'ètoit donc pas un bon procèdè que de me donner en payement des actions si douteuses et de me faire payer pour cela un enregistrement considèrable. Ce n'est pas non plus un bon procèdè que de prètendre que mon père a voulu vous faire un prèsent qui n'ètoit en aucune manière en proportion ni avec sa fortune ni avec vos relations—quand j'ai *trois fois* ècrit de sa main des dètails sur vos rapports ensemble quand *vous avez des lettres de lui* qui vous prouvent son anxiètè sur cette dette enfin quand je vous ai donnè *ma parole d'honneur que cette conjecture ètoit fausse.* Si quelque chose pouvoit me porter à en agir comme un crèancier rigoureux c'est une supposition blessante pour moi, mais laissons cela je vous prie *une fois pour tout* et revenons aux affaires. Le dèlai que vous demandez pour l'intéret n'est pas la difficulté mais la difficulté c'est que mes cousins[2] comme moi nous sommes trés inquiets de notre capital, et que nous pensons les uns et les autres que n'ètant entrès dans cette affaire que par considèration pour votre caractère personnel c'est sur ce caractère que nous devons compter pour nous tirer du danger que nous courons. Vous me proposez de vendre Cernay (ce que je ne veux point espèrant l'habiter) pour tripler mon capital. Je ne veux ni ne dois me permettre un tel hasard. Mes cousins, (qui sont aussi selon les loix de ce pays mes tuteurs) s'y opposent absolument mais si vous me donniez la caution de M[r] de talleyrand pour la totalité de ma crèance actions et billets je prendrois avec vous l'engagement de ne passer ces billets à personne. Il me semble que votre sociètè trouveroit de l'avantage à avoir en circulation 9 mille livres de lettres de change de moins, et à se libèrer de deux actions. Il me semble qu'il y a autant d'avantage à payer une dette qu'à avoir de l'argent nouveau, car pour un homme tel que vous, la dette ne pouvant jamais cesser d'ètre obligatoire reprèsente la somme que l'on vous prèteroit aujourd'hui. Rèflèchissez je vous prie mon cher du pont, à cette proposition qui me paroit la seule convenable. Je m'engage en attendant à ne pas passer votre billet à personne avant le 1er de janvier 1808. Employez ce tems à arranger l'affaire que je dèsire et qui me paroit raisonnable et juste sous tous les rapports. Adieu, mon cher du pont, je voudrois bien n'avoir aucune affaire à vous, et seulement examiner ce que ma position me permet de faire pour vous ètre utile. Je ne connois rien de si triste que des affaires d'argent avec ses amis, et sous ce rapport encor j'aimerois à me voir affranchie du triste devoir que j'accomplis malgrè moi. Mille amitiès.

[Sans signature]

TRANSLATION

June 3, Coppet

You did not tell me, my dear du Pont, that you were asking for a few months' delay on the interest that you owe me, but you gave me to understand (as I already knew from some letters from America) that the land as well as the capital are in danger. You are right to say that I would lend you 53 francs with great pleasure; and although a forced loan is less pleasing than a voluntary one, I consent to the six months' delay that you request; but I do not consent, at least as much as it is in my power, to remain in a position which exposes me to a very considerable loss and which it is impossible for me to bear. I should like, if it were possible, for you to give me a guarantee for the funds and the interest, and I should prefer the guarantee of M. de Talleyrand to the ownership of your stock. I should gladly return the two shares in order to become a creditor with his guarantee. I point out to you that you wronged me by making me pay a very considerable registration fee last year in order to give me, in payment of an amount that *you owed me at once,* some shares of stock whose little value you knew better than I, for it was only a few days after the conclusion of our transaction that I learned that one of your sons had stopped payment in America.[1] It was therefore not a good procedure to give me such dubious shares of stock in payment and to make me pay a considerable registration fee for that. It is not a good procedure either to claim that my father wanted to make you a gift which was not in any manner proportionate with his fortune or with your relations, when I have some details in his handwriting about your relations together *on three occasions,* when *you have letters from him* which prove to you his anxiety about that debt, finally, when I gave you *my word of honor that that conjecture was false.* If anything could cause me to act like a harsh creditor, it is a supposition which is insulting to me; but let us forget that please *once and for all* and return to business. The delay that you ask for the interest is not the difficulty, but the difficulty is that my cousins,[2] like me, are very uneasy about our capital, and that we all think that, having entered this affair only out of consideration for your personal character, we must count on this character to get us out of the danger that we face. You propose that I sell Cernay (which I do not wish to do, since I hope to live in it) in order to triple my capital. I do not want and must not permit myself such a risk. My cousins (who are also, according to the laws of this country, my guardians) are absolutely opposed to it; but if you gave me the guarantee of M. de Talleyrand for the total amount of my credit, shares, and notes, I should agree not to transfer these notes to anyone. It seems to me that your company would find it advantageous to have 9,000 fewer francs of promissory notes in circulation and to get rid of two shares of stock. It seems to me that there is as much advantage in paying a debt as in having some new money, since for a man like you, debt must always be binding and represents the sum that we would lend you today. Please think, my dear du Pont, about this proposition, which seems to me to be the only suitable one. I agree, meanwhile, not to transfer your note to anyone before January 1, 1808. Use this time to settle the matter as I desire, which seems to me to be reasonable and just in every respect. Adieu, my dear du Pont. I should like not to have any business with you, and only to examine what my position permits me to do to be helpful to you. I know of nothing so sad as financial matters with one's friends; and in this connection also, I should like to see myself freed from the sad duty that I carry out in spite of myself. A thousand friendly greetings.

[No signature]

NOTES
1 Victor du Pont's firm had failed in 1805.
2 Jacques Necker de Saussure and Horace-Bénédict Rilliet.

114

Necker de Saussure to du Pont de Nemours

14 July 1807

WMSS 2/19

Geneve le 14 juillet 1807

Monsieur,

J'ai reçu dans son tems votre lettre du 21 Juin qui renfermoit un mandat de f 1420 par solde des interets dus et echus le 1er 7bre 1806 sur nos deux actions. J'en ai fait part a mon beau frere. Nous avons vu votre peine. Ce que vous annoncez sur l'impossibilité ou vous etes d'acquitter les interets de cette année & l'esperance que vous nous donnez sur le capital la diminue un peu. Il serait fort triste d'avoir a regretter que mon pere se fut laissé entrainer a son obligeance naturelle & eut ainsi compromis une somme considerable. Il nous semble aussi Monsieur que si la maison de New York a fait des pertes malheureusement par sa faute la manufacture de poudre ne peut pas avoir ete dans le meme cas & qu'a cet egard les interets de ses actions doivent etre regulierement payes. Nous avons sur cela besoin de quelques explications & nous vous prions de vouloir bien nous les donner car nos deux actions sont divisées l'une sur la maison de Paris l'autre sur la manufacture. Recevez Monsieur mes salutations empressè[e]s.

J. Necker de Saussure

On the reverse:

A Monsieur
Mr Dupont de Nemours
a Paris

Postmark:

99 Genève, 19 Juillet 1807

TRANSLATION

Geneva, July 14, 1807

Sir,

I have received, in due course, your letter of June 21, which enclosed a money order for 1,420 francs in payment of the interest due on September 1, 1806, on our two shares of stock. I have informed my brother-in-law about it. We have seen your difficulty. What you announce about how you cannot pay the interest for this year and the hope that you give us about the capital diminishes it a little. It would be very sad to have to regret that my father had let himself be carried away by his natural kindness and had thus compromised a considerable sum of money. It also seems to us, Sir, that if the company in New York has had some losses, unfortunately by its own fault, the powder factory cannot have been in the same situation and that, on this account, the interest on its stock must be regularly paid. We need some explanations about that, and we beg you to be so kind as to give them to us, for our two shares are divided, one in the company in Paris and the other in the factory. Receive, Sir, my attentive greetings.

J. Necker de Saussure

On the reverse:

To Monsieur
M. du Pont de Nemours
in Paris

Postmark:

99 Geneva, July 19, 1807

115

du Pont de Nemours to Necker de Saussure and Rilliet Necker

13 June 1808

From a draft, wMSS 2/19

a MM. Necker de Saussure et Rilliet Necker

13 juin 1808

Messieurs,

Très reconnaissant de ce que vous avez bien voulu me faire marquer par Mr Pictet,[1] je viens de déposer chez Mr Grivel selon vos instructions quatorze mille francs pour les deux actions, l'une de ma Société, l'autre dans la fabrique de poudre à feu de mon fils Irenée du Pont dont vous êtes proprietaires comme heritiers de feu Mr Necker de Germany.

Il faudra que vous ayiez la bonté d'envoyer pareillement à Mr Grivel les deux actions avec procuration pour en operer *le transfer.*

Cette procuration devra être donnée conjointement par Madame Rilliet et par Mr Rilliet autorisant Madame parceque c'est elle qui est heritiere.

Je me trouve heureux de diminuer un peu pour vous Messieurs, pour les heritiers de Mr de Germany l'influence du malheur dont mon fils ainé a été la victime.

Salut et respectueux attachement.

TRANSLATION

To Messrs. Necker de Saussure and Rilliet Necker

June 13, 1808

Gentlemen,

Very grateful for what you have kindly had M. Pictet[1] inform me, I have just deposited with M. Grivel, according to your instructions, 14,000 francs for the two shares of stock which you own, as heirs of the late M. Necker de Germany, one in my company and the other in my son Irénée du Pont's powder factory.

It will be necessary that you have the kindness to send, on your part, the two shares to M. Grivel with a power of attorney in order to effect *the transfer.*

This power of attorney will have to be given jointly by Mme. Rilliet and M. Rilliet authorizing her, because she is the heiress.

I am happy to diminish a little for you, gentlemen, for the heirs of M. de Germany, the influence of the misfortune whose victim my older son has been.

Greetings and respectful attachment.

NOTE

1 Marc-Auguste Pictet-Turrettini (1752–1825), a natural scientist from Geneva. He founded the periodical *Bibliothèque britannique,* later called the *Bibliothèque universelle,* which contained translations of British scientific articles and analyses of recent British discoveries. When Geneva lost its independence in 1798, Pictet was one of fourteen citizens chosen to arrange the conditions. He became a tribune under the Consulate and one of the inspector generals of the Imperial University.

From correspondence in the Eleutherian Mills Historical Library, Pictet seems to have delivered, on several occasions, letters between du Pont de Nemours and the heirs of Necker de Germany. The letter following this one, written by du Pont to Pictet on the same day, reveals that Pictet acted as an agent for du Pont on this occasion. I reproduce the letter to Pictet not only because of its information about the repayment of the debt but also because of its interesting revelation of du Pont's character

116

du Pont de Nemours to Pictet

13 June 1808

From a draft, WMSS 2/6

13 juin 1808

A Mr M. A. Pictet

Mon cher Philosophe,

J'ai reçu de vous deux lettres, l'une pour me recommander Mr *Tissot*[1] sur le visage et dans la voix duquel j'ai lu la trace des malheurs qu'il a éprouvés. Je n'ai ôsé l'interroger sur leur nature, je l'ai fortement recommandé à Mr *Meslant* qui vous connait très bien, qui a eu souvent vos ouvrages *entre les mains,* qui est sans comparaison le premier des Relieurs de Paris.

Je suis extrêmement touché des sentimens que m'exprime votre autre lettre, du succès de votre négociation avec MM Necker de Saussure et Rilliet Necker, de la maniere noble et simple dont ces Messieurs terminent leur affaire avec ma société et celle de mon fils.

Je crois faire de mon côté tout ce qui peut être le plus avantageux pour eux et le plus conciliatoire de leur interêt et de celui de mes autres associés.

La vie est un pays de montagnes escarpées et de vallees obscures. Il faut gravir les unes, et chercher le plus droit chemin à travers les sinuosités des autres: eclairé seulement par la conscience et par cette raison, *lumiere,* comme dit St Jean, *que* DIEU *ne refuse à aucun homme venant au monde* et il faut remercier sans cesse ce DIEU BIENFAITEUR de ce qu'il nous a permis d'être, de sentir, de penser, d'etudier ses loix augustes, d'aimer, d'etre aimés surtout, de connaitre le bien et d'en faire quelque peu, d'aider nos freres et nous mêmes, de mériter quelquefois un regard de son indulgente et secourable bonté.

C'est ce qui me garantit des afflictions trop profondes, et soutient mon courage pour tacher de devenir plus sage et meilleur et de mieux faire.

Je régle tous les jours mes comptes avec la GRANDE et *Suprême*

Intelligence et je la bénis. De tems en tems ma faiblesse trouve un peu long le drame dont elle nous a faits acteurs; je sens que je bénirai aussi la fin de mon rôle. Mais je vois que tous les Rôles ont été donnés par un excellent Maitre. Ma reconnaissance l'adore avec tendresse comme ma raison avec justice.

Il ne faut pas juger notre sort par les souffrances qui toutes sont journellement payées, ou l'ont été d'avance par de très doux plaisirs. Son plus grand avantage est dans les occasions et la faculté qu'il nous donne de nous améliorer, de nous elever ainsi dans la chaine des êtres, même au sein de notre espece, peut-être un jour jusqu'à des especes supérieures. Qui sait si ce que nous appellons le malheur quand il est supporté sagement et sans murmure, n'est pas le chemin ouvert par des loix naturelles, ou même par une protection speciale vers la plus haute fortune? *Nature* dit le Sʳ Marc-Aurele *le fruit que tu m'apporteras ne sera jamais pour moi ni trop vert² ni trop mur.*

Me voila bien loin, mon cher Philosophe, de nos petits comptes en argent. Ils ont cependant aussi leur place marquée dans ce grand tout et dans ce bel enchainement de devoirs. La preuve en est qu'ils se traitent par *doit* et *avoir.* Faites moi donc le plaisir de remettre l'incluse a MM Necker et Rilliet.

Je vous embrasse avec un inviolable attachement. Mon respect a Madame Pictet, a Madame [. . .],³ a Mesdames vos filles et vos nieces dont tous les mariages me rejouissent parce que je suis convaincu qu'ils seront tous heureux beaux et bons [. . .].⁴

TRANSLATION

June 13, 1808

To M. M. A. Pictet

My dear philosopher,

I have received two letters from you, one recommending to me M. *Tissot*,¹ in whose face and voice I read the result of the misfortunes that he has experienced. I did not dare ask him about their nature. I recommended him highly to M. *Meslant*, who knows you very well, who has often had your works *in his hands,* who is without comparison the leading bookbinder in Paris.

I am extremely touched by the sentiments that your other letter expresses for me, by the success of your negotiation with Messrs.

Necker de Saussure and Rilliet de Necker, by the noble and simple manner in which these gentlemen are ending their business with my company and that of my son.

I believe I am doing, on my part, everything that can be most advantageous to them and most conciliatory for their interest and that of my other associates.

Life is a country filled with steep mountains and dark valleys. One must climb the former and seek the straightest road through the windings of the latter, enlightened only by conscience and by reason, *the light,* as Saint John says, *which* GOD *refuses to no man coming into the world;* and one must thank unceasingly that BENEFICENT GOD for what He has permitted us to be, to feel, to think, to study His august laws, to love, above all to be loved, to know good, and to do a little good, to help our brothers and ourselves, and to deserve sometimes a glance from His indulgent and helpful kindness.

That is what sustains me against afflictions which are too great and sustains my courage to try to become wiser and better and to do better.

Every day I settle my accounts with the GREAT and *Supreme Intelligence,* and I bless it. From time to time, my weakness finds the drama in which it has caused us to be actors a bit long. I feel that I shall also bless the end of my role. But I see that all roles have been distributed by an excellent Master. My gratitude adores Him with tenderness as my reason does with justice.

We must not judge our fate by the sufferings which all are paid for each day, or which have been paid for in advance by very sweet pleasures. Its greatest advantage is in the opportunities and the ability that it gives us to improve ourselves, to raise ourselves thus in the chain of being, even in the bosom of our species, perhaps some day to superior species. Who knows whether what we call misfortune, when it is borne wisely and without complaint, is not the road opened by natural laws, or even by a special protection, toward the highest fortune? *Nature,* said MARCUS AURELIUS, *the fruit that you bring me will never be either too green[2] or too ripe for me.*

Here I am, my dear philosopher, quite far away from our little financial accounts. Their place, however, is also indicated in that great unity and in that fine chain of duties. The proof of it is that they are dealt with as *debits* and *credits*. Please deliver the enclosed letter to Messrs. Necker and Rilliet.

I embrace you with an inviolable attachment. My respects to Mme. Pictet, to Mme. [. . .],[3] to your daughters and your nieces, whose marriages delight me because I am convinced that they will all be happy, beautiful, and good [. . .].[4]

NOTES

See Letter 115, note 1, on Pictet. The pious tone of this letter may be explained by the fact that Pictet was an ardent Calvinist.

1 I have been unable to identify this person.
2 An uncertain reading. *Acid* has also been suggested.
3 This name is illegible.
4 Several illegible words follow. The following reading has been suggested: *sur les bases et issus de felicite* ("on the foundations and by-products of happiness").

117

du Pont de Nemours to Madame de Staël

4 April 1809

From a draft or copy, WMSS 2/6

Paris 4 Avril 1809

M^de Stael

Mon excellente amie,

J'ai eu le plaisir de voir deux ou trois fois M. de Stael,[1] et ce plaisir m'a été très doux. Il m'a parru un homme plein de sens et de raison, de caractère dans l'âme de suite dans les idées.

Sa douce gravité, la mesure de ses expressions, son calme qui montre la pensée reussissent parfaitement aux Etats unis. Il est Américain.

Vous qui êtes primitivement française, et à beaucoup d'egards Italienne, vous y porteriez deux langues dont Franklin aurait entendu la premiere, et le Général Hamilton la seconde. Mais tous deux sont morts et n'ont point laissé d'héritiers. Vous seriez en pays perdu. Lorsqu'a la fin du diner, on vous renverrait dans votre sallon, ou bien l'on serait étonné de vous voir rester à table, vous vous trouveriez également désappointée: dans le premier cas par l'ennui; dans le second par la gêne des convives, puis par les mauvais propos de toutes les autres dames qui diraient que vous êtes venue deranger les mœurs du pays.

Restez avec nous belle, vive, et poëtique Européenne.

Quant à moi l'Amérique me plait; parceque j'aime mieux la liberté que l'influence, et que ma liberté est beaucoup augmentée par l'indifference des gens qui ne sont pas mes amis particuliers. J'espere que j'irai mourir dans le pays de ces hommes qui ne se genent point, qui ne me gênent point, qui me font l'honneur de ne pas prendre garde à moi, et de me laisser à mes enfans et à mon travail.

J'ai eu la faiblesse ou la folie de tant entreprendre d'ouvrages qui tous ont leur importance, que je n'aurai jamais trop, jamais assez de solitude pour le reste de ma vie.

J'ai expliqué à M. votre fils que ma société dans laquelle vous étes intéressée, n'a aucune relation avec les affaires de mon fils ainé, que la perte trop vraisemblable des fonds qu'elle lui avait prêtés et que j'ai lieu de croire qui sera compensé *quant au Capital* par notre intérêt des deux tiers dans la manufacture de mon second fils, dont la prospérité est audessus de nos espérances.

Je vous ai personnellement garanti les intérêts.

Et je me tiens pour assuré qu'en sacrifiant ou trois ou quatre, ou s'il est nécessaire la totalité des actions que j'ai mises dans notre société, l'intérêt de mes associés dans l'entreprise heureuse de mon bon Irenée leur fournira le remboursement des fonds qu'ils m'avaient confiés et qui eussent doublé si Victor Du Pont eut pu être payé des avances auxquelles il a été entrainé par son zele patriotique.

Je vous présente mon respect et à Mad[emoise]lle de Stael [2] qui n'est plus un enfant.

Dites pour moi quelque chose à celui de MM vos fils que je connais moins,[3] mais auquel je suis et serai aussi attaché que je dois l'être à tout ce qui vous appartient.

Je salue Mr Schalegel.[4]

Conservez moi quelque bienveillance.

Je donnerai pour vous une lettre à M. de Morgenstern,[5] Allemand Conseiller de la cour de [Russie],[6] Professeur à l'Université de Dorpatte,[7] qui desire beaucoup l'honneur de vous être présenté, et ira dans un mois a Geneve et à Coppet.

TRANSLATION

Paris, April 4, 1809

Madame de Staël

My excellent friend,

I have had the pleasure of seeing M. de Staël[1] two or three times, and this pleasure was very sweet for me. He seemed to me to be a man full of sense and reason, of character in his soul and of order in his ideas.

His gentle seriousness, the moderation of his expressions, his calm, which shows thought, will succeed perfectly in the United States. He is an American.

You, who are originally French, and Italian in many respects, you would take there two languages, of which Franklin would have understood the first, and General Hamilton the second. But both are dead and did not leave any heirs. You would be in a backwater country. Whether, at the end of dinner, you were sent to your drawing room, or you astonished people by remaining at the table, you would find yourself equally disappointed; in the first case, by boredom; in the second, by the uneasiness of the guests; then by the slander of all the other ladies, who would say that you had come to upset the customs of the country.

Stay with us, beautiful, lively, and poetic European that you are.

As for me, America pleases me, because I prefer liberty to influence and because my liberty is greatly increased by the indifference of people who are not my special friends. I hope that I shall go to die in the land of those men who do not bother each other, who do not bother me, who do me the honor of paying me no attention, and of leaving me with my children and my work.

I have had the weakness, or the folly, of undertaking so many works which all have their importance, that I shall never have too much, never enough solitude for the rest of my life.

I explained to your son that my company, in which you are involved, has no relation to the business of my older son, except for the only too likely loss of the funds that it had lent him, which I have reason to believe will be compensated, *as for the capital,* by our two-thirds interest in the factory of my second son, whose prosperity is above our hopes.

I have personally guaranteed the interest to you.

And I consider it certain that by sacrificing either three or four, or, if necessary, all the shares that I invested in our company, the interest of my associates in the fortunate enterprise of my good Irénée will provide for them the repayment of the funds that they had entrusted to me, which would have doubled if Victor du Pont had been paid for the advances to which he was incited by his patriotic zeal.

I present my respects to you and to Mlle. de Staël,[2] who is no longer a child.

Please remember me to that son whom I know less,[3] but to whom I am, and shall be, as attached as I must be to everything that belongs to you.

I send greetings to M. Schlegel.[4]

Keep some kind thoughts for me.

I shall give a letter for you to M. de Morgenstern,[5] a German, Councillor at the [Russian] [6] court, and professor at the University of Dorpat,[7] who wishes very much to have the honor of being introduced to you, and who will go to Geneva and to Coppet in a month.

NOTES

The text of this letter is taken from a draft or copy in a clerical hand at the Eleutherian Mills Historical Library.

1 Auguste de Staël.

2 Albertine de Staël.

3 Albert de Staël.

4 August Wilhelm Schlegel (1767–1845), the famed German Romantic writer, who was tutor of Mme. de Staël's children for many years.

5 Charles von Morgenstern (1770–1852), professor of classical philology at the University of Dorpat, who wrote extensively, mainly on classical subjects.

6 This word is covered by an ink blot. It can only be *Russie*.

7 Tartu, Estonia, known as Dorpat in German and Swedish.

118

Madame de Staël to du Pont de Nemours

1 May [1809?]

WMSS 2/19

> ce 1er de may
> genève

Mon fils[1] va à paris mon cher du pont et je l'autorise à terminer avec vous les affaires que nous avons encor ensemble.[2] Je ne puis rien laisser en arriere sur le continent et il me semble d'ailleurs facile pour vous de tout arranger en amérique. Ce que je souhaite c'est un interet dans la manufacture des poudres de votre fils qui puisse me dèdomager des deux actions qui n'ont plus de valeur et qui rèduiroient à rien les vingt mille livres que vous me devez.[3] Il me semble que l'ensemble de ma situation le malheur qui m'exile de tout ce qui ètoit ma vie doit vous porter à contribuer en tout ce que vous pouvez à l'ètablissement heureux de mon fils en amérique. Cher du pont que de choses nous aurions à nous dire! Il faut bien que je sois condamnèe à ne faire qu'ècrire pour vous parler seulement de nos affaires mais je vous envoye mon petit reprèsentant mulatre[4] pour vous dire de mille manières combien je pense et sens comme vous. J'ai vu le titre d'un poème intitulé le dernier homme.[5] Cette place inverse de celle d'adam me paroit vous ètre rèservèe. Adieu, adieu.

> [Sans signature]

On the reverse:

Auguste de Staël
Monsieur
Monsieur Dupont de Nemours

TRANSLATION

> May 1
> Geneva

My son[1] is going to Paris, my dear du Pont, and I am authorizing him to terminate with you the business that we still have together.[2] I cannot leave anything behind on the Continent, and it seems to me, moreover, easy for you to settle everything in America. What I want is an interest in your son's powder factory which can repay me for the two shares of stock which have no more value and which would reduce to nothing the 20,000 francs which you owe me.[3] It seems to me that my whole situation, the misfortune which exiles me from everything that was my life, ought to cause you to contribute in every way you can to the fortunate settlement of my son in America. Dear du Pont, what a lot of things we should have to say to each other! I really must be condemned to do nothing but write in order to speak to you only of our business, but I am sending my little mulatto representative[4] to you to tell you, in a thousand ways, how much I think and feel like you. I have seen a poem entitled *The Last Man.*[5] That place, the opposite of Adam's, seems to me to be reserved for you. Adieu, adieu.

[No signature]

On the reverse:

Auguste de Staël
Monsieur
M. du Pont de Nemours

NOTES

1 Auguste de Staël.

2 In a letter to Victor du Pont dated May 29, 1808 (WMSS 2/6), du Pont de Nemours had commented on his financial difficulties, his desire to return to America, his desire to finish his edition of the works of Turgot, and the problem of obtaining a passport. He had also observed:

> Mais un autre danger me pend sur la tête.
>
> .   .   .   .
>
> Je dois seize cent quatre vingt seize francs tous les ans au douze juillet à Mme de Stael pendant quatre ans. Elle a mes billets à ordre, j'ai les fonds de cette année, mais l'année prochaine elle pourra me faire mettre en prison.
>
> .   .   .   .
>
> Donc si le travail que je devais à la mémoire de M. Turgot et qui m'a retenu en France, n'est pas terminé avant la fin de l'année, et si je ne puis partir cet hiver, il y a trente à parier contre un que mes premieres lettres de 1809 seront datées de La Force ou de Ste Pelagie.
>
> C'est une chose à laquelle mes enfans doivent s'attendre et se résigner comme moi. Si elle a lieu, je ne pourrai esperer la liberté qu'à la paix générale.

(But another danger hangs over my head.

. . . .

I owe Mme. de Staël 1,696 francs every year on July 12 for four years. She has my promissory notes. I have the funds for this year, but next year she may have me put in prison.

. . . .

Therefore if the work that I owed to the memory of M. Turgot and which kept me in France is not finished before the end of the year, and if I cannot leave this winter, the chances are thirty to one that my first letters in 1809 will be dated from La Force or Sainte Pélagie.

It is a thing which my children must expect and to which they must resign themselves, as I have. If it happens, I shall not be able to hope for freedom until the general peace.)

La Force and Sainte Pélagie were two prisons in Paris.

3 Du Pont de Nemours will eventually be forced, in 1811, to give Mme. de Staël part of his interest in the American powder mills of E. I. du Pont, in exchange for her two shares in his company.

4 Auguste de Staël, who had very dark hair and a dark complexion.

5 *Le Dernier Homme,* a work in two volumes written by J. B. F. Grainville, appeared in Paris in 1805.

119

Madame de Staël to du Pont de Nemours

7 May 1810

WMSS 2/20

ce 7 may
chaumont[1] par ecure[2]
dep. de loir et cher

Vous avez parlé avec mon fils my dear sir, de nos affaires et je voudrois bien qu'il vous eut imposé pour condition de venir me voir ici. J'ai diverses objections à faire aux propositions que vous avez discutées ensemble et je vous prie d'abord de me *les expliquer* avant que j'y rèponde. Pourquoi ne venez vous pas à Nemours et de là à Blois? Nous causerions sérieusement quelques minutes et le reste du tems littérature. "Je vais donner une heure aux soins de mon empire et le reste du jour sera tout à Zaïre." Lequel de nous deux est Zaïre? Je vous aime. Je vous regrette et je ne puis traiter d'affaire avec vous sans m'interrompre pour vous le dire.

[Sans signature]

On the reverse:

Monsieur
Monsieur Dupont de Nemours
Rue du F^b Poissonniere n° 50
Paris

Postmark:

40 Ecure 10 Mai 1810

TRANSLATION

May 7
Chaumont,[1] near Ecure[2]
Department of Loir and Cher

You have spoken with my son, my dear sir, about our business and I should have liked him to have imposed as a condition that you come see me here. I have various objections to make to the proposals that you discussed together, and I beg you first to *explain them* to me before I answer them. Why do you not come to Nemours and from there to Blois? We should chat seriously for a few minutes and about literature for the rest of the time. "I am going to give an hour to the concerns of my empire, and the rest of the day will belong entirely to Zaïre." [3] Which one of the two of us is Zaïre? I love you. I miss you, and I cannot discuss business with you without interrupting myself to tell you so.

[No signature]

On the reverse:

Monsieur
M. du Pont de Nemours
50, rue du Faubourg Poissonnière
Paris

Postmark:

40 Ecure. May 10, 1810

NOTES

1 In April 1810, after announcing her intention of leaving for the United States, Mme. de Staël received permission to pass through France en route to a French port, provided that she did not travel via Paris. Before her proposed departure, however, she rented the château of Chaumont, one of the finest Renaissance

structures of the Loire valley, from her friend and American business agent, James Le Ray de Chaumont. She remained there several months while she completed *De l'Allemagne* for publication.

2 Ecure was a small post office which no longer exists.

3 The main character in Voltaire's tragedy of the same name.

The play was obviously inspired by *Othello,* with its theme of jealousy and misunderstanding. The action takes place in Jerusalem during the Crusades. Zaïre, a French girl held captive by the Saracens since childhood, is in love with and about to marry Orosmane, the sultan. Suddenly she learns, however, that she is the daughter of Lusignan, an old Crusader whose release from prison she has just obtained, and the sister of Nérestan, another French captive. Her father and brother successfully urge her to abandon the Moslem religion, in which she has been reared, to become a Christian. Orosmane, whose suspicions have been aroused by her request to postpone their marriage, intercepts a letter from Nérestan to Zaïre which seems to reveal her infidelity to her betrothed. He stabs Zaïre and then commits suicide upon learning the truth of the situation.

Mme. de Staël is quoting here the last two lines of the first act of *Zaïre,* spoken by Orosmane. *Zaïre* was one of the plays most frequently performed in the theatricals given by Mme. de Staël and her friends during these years.

120

du Pont de Nemours to Madame de Stael

18 May 1810

From a copy, WMSS 2/6

18 May 1810

A Mme de Stael

Auriez vous cru mon excellente amie aurais-je pu croire qu'une lettre de vous fut restée plus de huit jours dans mes mains sans qu'il me fut possible d'y repondre.

Vous me parlez *des soins de votre Empire*. Ce sont les *soins du mien* qui ont si étrangement absorbé presque toutes mes minutes de jour et de nuit.[1] Et le *mien* est peuplé d'environ cent mille pauvres âmes dont les corps aveugles, septuagenaires, paralytiques, manchots, epileptiques, pulmoniques, où les uns dans la premiere ou dans la derniere enfance, ont un besoin préssant de pain, de vêtemens, de bouillon. Nous n'avons pour leur en donner tres peu qu'encore moins d'argent; et nous tâchons d'y suppléer en imaginant d'abord les moyens de distinguer ceux qui exagerent de ceux qui n'exagerent pas leurs maux, puis la maniere d'adoucir les maux réels par un peu de travail proportionné aux forces, ou a la faiblesse de tels travailleurs, et qui en même tems rende libres une partie des fonds dont on ne saurait refuser le secours a ceux qui ne peuvent pas travailler du tout.

Votre adorateur le Baron de Voght[2] qui ne vous adore pas plus que je ne fais serait peut-être aussi embarrassé que moi dans une ville six fois plus grande et plus peuplé que son hambourg et relativement à sa population trois fois moins riche.

Vous comprenez bien qu'au milieu d'une telle compagnie je n'ai pas la moindre prétention de ressembler *à Zaire* autant que vous qui en jouez le Rôle a merveille.

Je ne ressemble pas même à *Orosmane* car quoique j'aye êté et soit [*sic*] peut-être encore capable d'aimer passionnement, et que j'aye souvent eû de violens mouvemens de colere contre mes rivaux je n'ai jamais pu concevoir l'idée de poignarder ma maitresse même infidelle.

"C'est un grand tort mais faut il qu'on la noye." [3] Je ne peux pas faire du mal a qui m'a fait du bien et je ne veux pas depeupler le monde.

Quand aux questions que vous me faites et m'avez deja fait faire par M fourcaut pavant et par M[r] votre fils sur vos actions dans ma société, j'ai déja eû l'honneur de répondre à l'un et à l'autre que la seule proprieté qui restat à ma societé etait, est son interêt des deux tiers ou de douze actions dans la manufacture de poudre de mon second fils irennée; et que j'ai les plus fortes raisons de croire que ces douze actions dans la societé d'irennée en vaudront *trente six* de la mienne qui n'en a que *trente neuf* dont six a moi d'ou suit qu'en perdant la moitié de mon capital je pourrai sauver a mes associés la totalité du leur.

Par rapport aux interêts,[4] j'ai a votre egard la consolation de vous les avoir payés a six et a huit pour cent en mes propres billets que j'ai acquittés et acquitterai quand mes autres associés n'en ont touché aucun.

Je me suis fait assureur de mes *Partners,* mon amie, et de vous plus que des autres. J'ai cru devoir a la confiance personnelle qu'ils avaient eû en moi cette preuve claire que je la meritais. Il n'y aura que moi et mon fils ainé de ruinés. Vous savez comme mes autres associés qu'il n'y a pas de ma faute. M[r] votre Pere a constamment approuvé ma marche dont je lui ai plusieurs fois rendu compte.

J'ai fait a ce sujet il y a environ deux ans un exposé général de toutes les opérations de ma compagnie; de sa situation et des evenemens qu'elle a supportés. Je ne les joins pas a cette lettre qu'il grossirait de maniere à en rencherir beaucoup le prix, et a exciter la curiosité de la poste qui n'a aucun interêt a s'entremettre dans vos affaires personnelles et pecuniaires.

Je le remettrai a Monsieur votre fils en y joignant les autorisations et tous les documens nécéssaires pour liquider avec mes enfans, moyennant un tiers d'action de la manufacture pour une action qu'il équivaudra de ma societé primitive.

Laissez aller en Amérique ce bon, sage, et aimable jeune homme,[5] qui aura le bonheur d'y plaire a tout le monde.

N'allez point vous même perdre dans la masse de vos richesses la bonne opinion que vous avez des américains. Ce sont des français et même des parisiens qu'il vous faut.

Il n'y a aux Etats Unis depuis le district de Maine jusqu'à la Georgie, ni chez les hommes ni chez les femmes, aucuns des Elemens propres à juger à sentir votre merite. Partant vous ne pourriez pas concevoir le leur. Vous en reviendriez mecontente excedée d'humeur et d'ennui.

Peut-être seriez vous un peu moins malheureuse a la Louisianne. Mais les francais y sont deja dans une grande minorité et la gravité Americaine y domine.

A New-Yorck il y a un homme qui vous conviendrait. C'est un suedois Mr Gahn;[6] et a Philadelphie un autre qui vous entendrait Mr *Vaughan*.[7] Il y a encore Mr *Church*[8] à qui vous ne seriez pas etrangere. Mais trois personnes sur six millions: ce n'est point assés pour vous. Restez ou l'on sait votre langue, et où tout le monde même ne la sait pas. Je l'entends au moins. C'est ce qui fait que je vous aime et vous respecte.

DPDN

TRANSLATION

May 18, 1810

To Madame de Staël

Would you have believed, my excellent friend, could I have believed, that a letter from you would have remained in my hands for more than a week without my being able to answer it?

You speak to me *of the concerns of your empire*. It is the *concerns of mine* which have so strangely absorbed almost my every minute both day and night.[1] And *mine* is populated by about 100,000 poor souls, some in their first or second childhoods, whose blind, septuagenarian, paralytic, one-armed, epileptic, tubercular bodies have an urgent need of bread, clothing, and soup. We have only very little of that to give them, and still less money; and we try to replace it by imagining, first, the ways of distinguishing those who exaggerate from those who do not exaggerate their woes, then, the means of softening the real woes by a bit of work in proportion to the strength or the weakness of such workers, which at the same time, frees a part of the funds whose help one could not refuse to those who cannot work at all.

Your adorer, the Baron de Voght,[2] who does not adore you any more than I do, would perhaps be as embarrassed as I in a city six times larger and more populous than his Hamburg, and in relation to its population, three times less rich.

You can very well understand that, in the midst of such company, I have not the slightest claim of resembling *Zaïre* as much as you, who play the role marvelously well.

I do not even resemble *Orosmane,* for although I have been, and perhaps still am, capable of loving passionately, and I have often had violent feelings of anger for my rivals, I have never been able to conceive of stabbing my mistress, even if she were unfaithful.

"It is a great wrong but is it necessary to drown her?" [3] I cannot harm anyone who has done good to me, and I do not want to depopulate the world.

As for the questions you ask me and have already had M. Fourcault Pavant and your son ask me about your stock in my company, I have already had the honor of informing both of them that the only property my company had left was, and is, its two-thirds interest, or twelve shares of stock, in the powder factory of my second son, Irénée, and that I have the strongest reasons to believe that these twelve shares in Irénée's company will be worth *thirty-six* of mine, which has only *thirty-nine,* of which six belong to me, with the result that, by losing half of my capital, I shall be able to save for my associates the total amount of theirs.

In regard to the interest,[4] I have the consolation, where you are concerned, of having paid it to you at 6 and at 8 per cent with my own notes, which I have paid off and shall pay off when my other associates have not received any at all.

I have made myself the insurer of my *partners,* my friend, and of you more than the others. I thought I owed to the personal confidence that they had in me this clear proof that I deserved it. Only I and my older son will be ruined. You know, as do my other associates, that it is not my fault. Your father constantly approved my course, which I explained to him several times.

On this subject, I made a general statement about two years ago on all the operations of my company, on its situation and the events that it had to put up with. I am not including it in this letter, because it would make it so heavy as to increase greatly the postage and arouse the curiosity of the post office, which has no business meddling in your personal and financial matters.

I shall deliver it to your son, including in it the authorizations and all the necessary documents in order to settle with my children, by means of one third of a share in the factory for the one share that it would be worth in my original company.

Let this good, wise, and likeable young man, who will have the good fortune of pleasing everyone, go to America.[5]

Do not go yourself to lose, as one of your riches, the good opinion that you have of the Americans. It is French people and even Parisians whom you need.

There is not in the United States, from the District of Maine to Georgia, either among men or women, any of the elements fitting to judge or feel your merit. Consequently, you could not conceive of theirs. You would return, unhappy and worn out with bad humor and boredom.

Perhaps you would be a bit less unhappy in Louisiana. But the French there are already in a great minority and American seriousness dominates.

In New York there is one man who would suit you. He is a Swede, Mr. Gahn;[6] and in Philadelphia another one who would understand you, Mr. *Vaughan.*[7] There is also Mr. *Church,*[8] to whom you would not be a stranger. But three people out of 6,000,000! That is not enough for you. Remain where people know your language, and where, even so, everyone does not know it.

I understand it at least. That is what causes me to love you and respect you.

DPDN

NOTES

The copy from which the text of this letter is taken was made by Mme. du Pont de Nemours.

1 France was increasingly feeling the devastating effects of the Napoleonic wars. The problem of the poor and disabled had become acute, and public institutions could no longer care for them. Du Pont de Nemours was appointed administrator of the *Secours à domicile,* which attempted to take care of the indigent in their homes. In 1810 he was helping 117,000 people and working long hours every day (B. G. du Pont, *Du Pont de Nemours, 1739–1817* [Newark, Del., 1933], II, 102).

2 Caspar, Baron von Voght (1752–1839), the German philanthropist and admirer of Madame de Staël. The director of a business house inherited from his father, Voght founded, in 1785, several institutions to aid the poor of Hamburg. In 1807, the French government requested him to make a study of French charitable institutions and suggest improvements. At this time, Voght was a guest of Mme. de Staël at Chaumont.

3 I have been unable to identify the source of this quotation.

4 In a letter written to his family in America dated October 11, 1809, du Pont de Nemours mentions that he will have to pay 1,696 francs to Mme. de Staël in June 1810. In another letter, dated April 10, 1810, he again mentions this sum and remarks that he has not a sou for this purpose. A letter written on August 24, 1810, reveals that E. I. du Pont had sent him the necessary funds. On September 20, 1810, he requests his sons to send him $1,600 each year, of which part is to be used to pay the yearly interest to Mme. de Staël. (Unpubl. letters, Eleutherian Mills Historical Library.)

5 Auguste de Staël.

6 Henrick Gahn (1774–1834), a Swedish businessman and consul of his country in New York.

He arrived in Philadelphia from Spain in 1794 with his friend Ulric Wertmüller, the Swedish painter. After traveling about the country to decide upon a place in which to settle, he founded a business in New York, and in 1797, became Swedish consul there (Adolph B. Benson and Naboth Hedin, eds., *Swedes in America 1638–1938* [New Haven, 1938], p. 573). The du Ponts seem to have become acquainted with him shortly after their arrival in the United States. Du Pont de Nemours, in a letter to E. I. du Pont dated October 6, 1801, mentions that Gahn is quite willing to let the du Pont company use his name for consignments (*E. I. du Pont,* V, 292). Among Gahn's friends were John Vaughan, Dr. Casper Winter, Joseph Priestley, and Nicholas Collin (*The Journal and Biography of Nicholas Collin, 1746–1831,* trans. Amandus Johnson [Philadelphia, 1936]). Gahn appears, in the latter work, as an urbane, intelligent, cultured gentleman.

7 John Vaughan (1765–1841), an Englishman, came to Philadelphia in 1783, where he became a wine merchant and also acted as a business agent for E. I. du Pont. He served as treasurer of the American Philosophical Society for fifty years and founded the First Unitarian Church of Philadelphia. He was active also in a

vast number of scientific, cultural, and philanthropic organizations (Elizabeth M. Geffen, *Philadelphia Unitarianism, 1796–1861* [Philadelphia, 1961]). Vaughan counted the du Ponts, Washington, Jefferson, Jay, Priestley, and Talleyrand among his friends.

8 John Barker Church (1739–1818), another Englishman, also settled in America and served with the American forces during the American Revolution as Commissary General to the French allies. One of the few American officers who understood French, he acted as interpreter between Washington and Rochambeau. He married Angelica Schuyler, the daughter of General Philip Schuyler, and thus became the brother-in-law of Alexander Hamilton. After the Revolution, Church returned to England, was elected to Parliament, and became a prominent figure in London society. He befriended Talleyrand while Talleyrand was in England during the French Revolution, and it was at his home that the plot to rescue Lafayette from Olmütz was hatched. Returning to the United States in 1797, Church became known as one of the richest men in the country.

His son, Philip Church (1778–1861), graduated from Eton and studied law at the Temple in London. He also returned to America, where he served as a captain in the Army for a time and practiced law. Later, he abandoned his legal career in order to develop 100,000 acres of land which he had acquired in Western New York. There he founded the town of Angelica on his holdings (*Prominent Families of New York* [New York, 1897], pp. 116–17).

Soon after their arrival in New York, the du Ponts became friends of the Church family, and the two families engaged in various joint business enterprises. When Victor du Pont's business in New York failed, he and his family settled at Angelica at the instance of Philip Church. Friendly relations eventually ceased between the two men, and the Victor du Ponts left Angelica to join E. I. du Pont in Wilmington. (B. G. du Pont, *Lives of Victor and Josephine du Pont* [Newark, Del., 1930], p. 155; *E. I. du Pont,* vols. VI–VIII.)

121

Madame de Stael to du Pont de Nemours

28 May 1810

WMSS 2/20

ce 28

chaumont par ècure

Dep. de loir et cher

Certainement mon cher du pont, vous vous ètes conduit aussi bien qu'il est possible votre entreprise ayant manquèe mais nèanmoins vous avez mieux traité encor le fils de mon oncle[1] que moi puisqu'ils sont à peu près payès de tout. Quoi qu'il en soit voici

ce que je voudrois si vous le pouvez un an de plus d'intéret payè
par vous à fin que nous eussions le tems nécessaire pour nous faire
payer en amèrique et la cession de votre part dans la société jusqu'à
la concurrence de la liquidation de notre dette que ce soit tiers
ou quart ou moitiè d'une action n'importe. Mon fils ira à paris
un de ces jours et discutera ces propositions avec vous. Ce qui
m'attriste c'est la crainte de ne pas vous voir avant mon grand
dèpart. Je voudrois vous dire tous mes motifs et vous savez bien
que rien ne s'ècrit. Adieu cher du pont. Je ne puis jamais cesser
de vous aimer.

Il va sans dire que si nous ètions liquidès les intérets cesseroient
à l'instant mème ou seroient rendus s'ils ètoient payès.

[Sans signature]

On the reverse:

Monsieur
Monsieur Dupont de Nemours
Rue du Fb, Poissonnière
n° 50 Paris

Postmark:

31 Mai 1810

TRANSLATION

the 28th

Chaumont near Ecure

Department of Loir and Cher

Certainly, my dear du Pont, you have conducted yourself as
well as possible in view of the failure of your company, but nevertheless you treated my uncle's son[1] better than me, since they have
been paid almost everything. Be that as it may, here is what I
should like, if you can do it: one more year of interest paid by
you so that we might have the necessary time to be paid in America and the transfer of your share in the company up to the amount
of the liquidation of our debt; whether it is a third or a fourth
or a half of a share does not matter. My son will go to Paris one
of these days and will discuss these proposals with you. What sad-
dens me is the fear of not seeing you before my grand departure.

I should like to tell you all my motives, and you know very well that nothing can be written. Adieu, dear du Pont. I can never cease loving you.

It goes without saying that if your debt were settled, the interest would cease at once or would be returned if it were paid.

[No signature]

On the reverse:

Monsieur
M. du Pont de Nemours
50, rue du Faubourg Poissonnière
Paris

Postmark:

May 31, 1810

NOTE
1 Jacques Necker de Saussure.

122

du Pont de Nemours to Madame de Stael

9 October 1810

From excerpts in Le Marois, *Cahiers,* p. 511

9 octobre 1810

Ah! Madame, quel cruel voyage.

Par quelle inconcevable fatalité, un ouvrage composé dans un sens que vous jugiez devoir vous être favorable, a-t-il été accueilli dans un sens tellement contraire?[1]

.   .   .   .

Vous ririez et vous me plaindriez peut-être de me voir établi dans une mauvaise chambre d'auberge où la fumée me fait perdre les yeux et où les rats me font perdre le sommeil, dépensant tous mes jours dans l'exercice des plus minutieux détails, buvant l'ennui goutte à goutte, dans l'espoir d'un meilleur avenir dont l'incertitude ne compensera peut-être jamais le sacrifice du présent.

Ah! ce qui ferait mon bonheur serait de vous voir, Madame, et surtout de vous voir heureuse et satisfaite; quant à moi, je crois bien qu'il faut que je sois encore quelque temps chrysalide, avant de devenir papillon. Je ne voudrais pourtant pas être de ces vers à soye que l'on fait mourir obscurément dans l'enveloppe qu'ils ont si péniblement filée.

Adieu, Madame, croyez que la Dame de Coppet est souvent la dame de mes pensées; donnez-moi, de grâce, de ses nouvelles, priez-la de m'aimer un peu, en me permettant de l'aimer beaucoup. Rappelez-moi au souvenir de tous ceux qui l'entourent, et faites en sorte qu'elle agrée l'hommage du bien vif et tendre attachement avec lequel je suis pour la vie,

Votre ob[éissant] serviteur et fidèle

D. de Nemours

TRANSLATION

October 9, 1810

Ah! Madame, what a cruel journey!

By what inconceivable adversity has a work, composed in a way that you thought would be favorable to you, been received in such a contrary way?[1]

.   .   .   .

You would laugh and perhaps pity me if you saw me settled in a wretched room in an inn where the smoke ruins my eyes and the rats make me lose sleep, spending all my days in the exercise of the most minute details, drinking boredom drop by drop, in the hope of a better future, whose uncertainty will perhaps never compensate for the sacrifice of the present.

Ah! what would make me happy would be to see you, Madame, and especially to see you happy and satisfied. As for me, I believe that I must be, for still some time, a chrysalid before becoming a butterfly. I should not want, however, to be one of those silkworms killed in darkness in the envelope that they have so painfully spun.

Adieu, Madame, believe that the Lady of Coppet is often the lady of my thoughts. Give me, please, news of her; beg her to love me a bit, while permitting me to love her a great deal. Remember me to all those who surround her, and arrange that she may accept the homage of the very strong and tender attachment with which I am for life,

Your faithful and obedient servant

D. de Nemours

NOTES

This is apparently the last letter du Pont de Nemours wrote to Mme. de Staël. On March 31, 1811, du Pont writes to his two sons that he is giving two-thirds of a share in the powder mill to Mme. de Staël (unpubl. letter, Eleutherian Mills Historical Library).

In a postscript dated July 1, 1811, to a letter written June 27, 1811 (WMSS 2/6), du Pont states:

> J'ai trouvé à emprunter *cinq cent francs* pour payer mon billet à Madame de Stael et ne pas craindre un protest, si scandaleux pour un Ancien Président de la Chambre du Commerce, et qui serait si fâcheux encore pour un Administrateur des secours à domicile, que ses amis même ne traitent fort bien que parce qu'ils le croient au dessus de ses affaires et dans une sorte de médiocre aisance, qu'il ne pourrait désavouer en leur racontant ses charges et ses embarras sans réfroidir terriblement cette apparente amitié et détruire tout son édifice de considération, cependant méritée.

> (I have found *500 francs* to borrow in order to pay my note to Mme. de Staël and not fear a protest, so scandalous for a former President of the Chamber of Commerce and so disgraceful also for an administrator of the *secours à domicile,* whom even his friends treat well only because they believe him to be above his business problems and in moderately easy circumstances, which he could not disavow by telling them about his burdens and his worries without terribly chilling this apparent friendship and destroying the whole edifice of his standing, however much deserved.)

On December 1, 1811 (WMSS 2/6), he wrote to Victor du Pont:

> Il faut qu'après ma mort mes Fils et mes petits Fils disent: *Il etait plus viril encore que nous ne le croyions.* Il faut que mes filles et mes petites Filles ajoutent *ce n'était pas pour rien qu'on le nommait* BON PAPA. Il faut que les bons citoyens des Etats Unis puissent écrire: *Ces du Pont de Nemours ont été pour nous une noble acquisition;* et que dans quelques siecles ceux de l'Europe puissent mettre sur les marges: *Il est fâcheux que nous l'ayions perdu.*
> Vous voyez, mes Enfans, que mon ambition n'est pas éteinte.

> (After my death, my sons and grandsons must say: *"He was even more virile than we thought."* My daughters and granddaughters must add: *"It was not for nothing that we called him* DEAR PAPA." The good citizens of the United States must be able to write: *"These du Ponts have been a noble acquisition for us";* and in a few centuries, those of Europe must be able to put in the margin: *"It is regrettable that we have lost him."*
> You see, my children, that my ambition is not dead.)

1 Mme. de Staël's *De l'Allemagne* had just been seized by the police, and she had been ordered into exile once more.

✦

123

Auguste de Staël to E. I. du Pont

1 March 1813

LMSS 3/5

Genève ce 1ᵉʳ Mars 1813

Monsieur,

Il y a déjà longtems que j'aurois eu l'honneur de vous écrire, si je n'avois pas espéré d'un moment à l'autre que j'aurois l'avantage de faire connoissance avec vous aux E[tats] U[nis]. La bonté que Monsieur vôtre pêre m'a toujours témoignée m'auroit rendu cette nouvelle relation bien précieuse.

Mʳ vôtre pêre vous a sans doute mandé que par un arreté de compte signé par lui le 20 May 1811 il a abandonné aux actionnaires de la société dont il a été le gerant les 12 actions que cette société possédoit dans la manufacture de poudre que vous dirigez. De cette maniére trois actions de l'ancienne société se trouvent représentées par une des vôtres et par conséquent ma mêre qui posséde 2 actions de la société Dupont de Nemours P[ère] et f[ils] & C[ompagni]e a maintenant à reclamer auprès de vous ⅔ d'une de vos actions.

Permettez-moi donc de vous demander pour ma mêre quels arrangements il vous convient de prendre à cet égard? Qu'elle est l'êpoque du remboursement des actions de vôtre manufacture; à qu'el [*sic*] prix voudriez vous racheter maintenant ces deux tiers d'action aux quels m'à mêre à droit? Veuillez, avoir la bonté de répondre à ces questions en adressant vôtre lettre à ma mêre sous le couvert de Mess. Doxat & Divett[1] de Londres. Je ne désespêre pas Monsieur, du bonheur de vous recontrer une fois dans le beau pays que vous habitez. Voudrez vous bien recevoir en attendant l'expression des sentiments distingués avec les quels j'ai l'honneur d'être

Vôtre t[rès] h[umble] et t[rès] o[béissant] s[erviteur]
Auguste de Staël H[olst]ein

Monsieur E. Irenée Dupont

On the reverse:

Monsieur
Monsieur E. I. Dupont
à Eleutherian Mill sur la R[ivière] Brandywine
E[tat] de Delaware
par Gen[era]l Marion[2]

Postmark:

New Bedford M[assachusett]s
May 17

TRANSLATION

Geneva, March 1, 1813

Sir,

I should have had the honor of writing to you a long time ago, if I had not hoped, from one moment to the next, that I should have the advantage of making your acquaintance in the United States. The kindness that your father has always shown me would have made that new relationship very precious.

Your father has doubtless written to you that by a settlement of accounts signed by him on May 20, 1811, he turned over to the stockholders of the company of which he was the manager the twelve shares of stock which that company had in the powder factory that you direct. In this way, three shares of the former company are represented by one of yours, and consequently, my mother, who owns two shares of the du Pont de Nemours, Père et Fils & Cie., now has to claim from you two-thirds of one of your shares.

Permit me, therefore, to ask you on behalf of my mother what arrangements it suits you to make in this regard? When is the repayment of the shares in your factory, and at what price would you now want to repurchase this two-thirds of a share to which my mother has a right? Please have the kindness to answer these questions by addressing your letter to my mother in care of Messrs. Doxat and Divett[1] in London. I do not despair, Sir, of having the happiness of meeting you sometime in the beautiful country in which you live. Will you please receive, meanwhile, the expression of the distinguished sentiments with which I have the honor of being

Your very humble and very obedient servant
Auguste de Staël Holstein

Monsieur E. Irenée du Pont

On the reverse:

Monsieur
M. E. I. du Pont
at Eleutherian Mill on the Brandywine River
State of Delaware
Via the *General Marion*[2]

Postmark:

New Bedford, Massachusetts
May 17

NOTES

1 A banking firm in London. Mme. de Staël was in Stockholm at this time en route to London.
2 In another handwriting. The *General Marion* was presumably the ship on which the letter was carried.

124

Auguste de Staël to E. I. du Pont

22 February 1814
Eleutherian Mills Historical Library, Acc. 146, File 95

Londres le 22 Fevrier 1814

Monsieur,

J'apprends par Messrs Le Roy & Bayard qu'en réponse à la lettre que j'ai eu l'honneur de vous adresser le 1er mars 1813 vous avez bien voulu ecrire deux fois à ma mére: mais vos lettres ayant été adressées en France ne nous sont jamais arrivées; permettez moi donc de vous prier d'en faire parvenir une copie à ma mere par le moyen de Messrs Le Roy & Bayard.

J'ai eu l'avantage de vous informer que ma mere se trouvoit, par cession de Monsieur votre pere, avoir droit à ⅔ d'Action dans votre manufacture de poudre; je prenois la liberté de vous demander quelle étoit l'époque du remboursement de ces actions et s'il entreroit dans vos arrangements de racheter maintenant la portion que possède ma mere: permettez moi de vous renouveller les mêmes questions.

Tournez vous souvent les yeux vers votre ancienne patrie; la grande crise est sur le point d'être décidée.[1] La pauvre France souffre cruellement et ce qui afflige surtout c'est que parmi les chances de l'avenir on n'en apperçoit guéres qui soient favorables à la liberté.

Recevez je vous prie, Monsieur, l'assurance de la considération distinguèe avec la quelle j'ai l'honneur d'être

Votre t[rès] h[umble] et t[rès] o[béissant] S[erviteur]

Auguste de Staël

Mr Irenée Dupont

On the reverse:

Irenée Dupont Esqre
Wilmington
London
February 22nd 1814
Auguste de Staël[2]

Postmark:

New York May 31

TRANSLATION

London, February 22, 1814

Sir,

I learn from Messieurs Le Roy and Bayard that, in reply to the letter which I had the honor of sending you on March 1, 1813, you have kindly written twice to my mother; but your letters, having been sent to France, have never reached us. Permit me then to ask you to send a copy of them to my mother in care of Messrs. Le Roy and Bayard.

I had the honor of informing you that my mother, by the transfer made by your father, found that she had a right to two-thirds of a share in your powder factory. I took the liberty of asking you the time of repayment of these shares and whether it would suit your arrangements to repurchase now the part that my mother owns. Permit me to repeat the same questions to you.

Do you turn your eyes often to your former country? The great crisis is about to be decided.[1] Poor France suffers cruelly, and what grieves one above all is that, among the possibilities for the future, there are scarcely any which would be favorable to liberty.

Receive, I beg you, Sir, the assurance of the distinguished consideration with which I have the honor of being

Your very humble and very obedient servant

Auguste de Staël

M. Irénée du Pont

On the reverse:

Irénée du Pont, Esq.
Wilmington
London
February 22, 1814
Auguste de Staël [2]

Postmark:

New York, May 31

NOTES
1 By this time, the Allies had invaded France. Paris was to fall on March 31, 1814.
2 The last three lines are in another handwriting.

125

Auguste de Staël to du Pont de Nemours

29 July 1814

WMSS 2/21

Je vous sais un peu mauvais gré, cher Monsieur, de m'avoir ecrit comme à un Baron diplomate[1] et non pas comme à Auguste de

Staël plein de dévouement et si vous me le permettez d'amitié pour vous. Toutefois vous recevrez dans la journée ma réponse officielle qui est que le Roi[2] vous permet le plus volontiers du monde de reprendre dès à présent la décoration de l'O[rdre] de Vasa.[3] Mais comme il faut que votre cordon, pendant qu'il a été loin de vous ait produit des intérêts, le Bar[on] de Wetterstedt[4] m'a promis, à son retour à Stockholm, de demander pour vous le cordon de commandeur.

Tout à vous,
Auguste de Staël

Vendredi 29 Juillet

On the reverse:

Monsieur
Monsieur Dupont de Nemours
Conseiller d'Etat de S[a] M[ajesté] T[rès] C[hrétienne] [5]
N° 23 Rue de Surenne

TRANSLATION

I am rather offended with you, dear Sir, for having written to me as to a baron and a diplomat[1] and not to Auguste de Staël, full of devotion, and if you permit it, friendship for you. Nevertheless, you are receiving today my official reply, which is that the King[2] permits you, with the greatest pleasure in the world, to resume right away the decoration of the Order of Vasa.[3] But as your ribbon must have acquired some interest while it was away from you, Baron Wetterstedt[4] promised me, on his return to Stockholm, to ask for the ribbon of a commander for you.

Cordially yours,
Auguste de Staël

Friday, July 29

On the reverse:

Monsieur
M. du Pont de Nemours
Councillor of State to His Very Christian Majesty[5]
23, rue de Surenne

NOTES
1 On May 20, 1813, Mme. de Staël had written to Benjamin Constant that Auguste de Staël had been appointed secretary to the Swedish legation in the United

States; but on February 25, 1814, she wrote Mme. Necker de Saussure from London that Auguste was no longer interested in going to America and that she was also in favor of some other appointment (*Lettres de Mme de Staël à Benjamin Constant* [Paris, 1928], p. 40; Pierre Kohler, *Madame de Staël et la Suisse* [Lausanne, 1916], p. 627). Auguste de Staël arrived in Paris from London on March 10, 1814 (*Journaux intimes,* p. 399), and Constant notes on June 1, 1814: "Mme de St[aël] postule un ordre pour son fils." (*Ibid.,* p. 404. "Mme. de Staël has applied for an order for her son.")

In a letter written on April 26, 1814, to his family in the United States (WMSS 2/7), du Pont de Nemours states: "Mr de Stael est à Paris, et vraisemblablement n'ira pas prendre possession de sa place de Consul général de Suede aux Etats Unis. Avec treize cent et quelques dollars je retirerai la propriété de ses deux actions." ("M. de Staël is in Paris and probably will not go to assume his position as Consul General of Sweden in the United States. With a little more than $1,300, I shall buy back his two shares.")

2 Charles XIII, King of Sweden.

3 King Gustavus III of Sweden had made du Pont de Nemours a member of the Order of Vasa on May 23, 1775, because of his interest in du Pont's liberal economic theories (B. G. du Pont, *Du Pont de Nemours, 1739–1817* [Newark, Del., 1933], I, 96).

In the summer of 1814, du Pont de Nemours wrote the following note to Louis XVIII (WMSS 2/7):

> Au Roi.
>
> Sire,
>
> Sa Majesté le Roi Louis XVI, sur la demande formelle du Roi de Suede Gustave III, avait bien voulu me permettre de recevoir et porter L'Ordre de Vasa, dont j'ai joui plus de quinze ans. Sa Majesté le Roi Charles XIII vient de me faire écrire qu'Elle approuvait que j'en reprisse la décoration.
>
> La Lettre officielle a été mise sous les yeux de Son Excellence Monsieur le Comte de Blacas, et y est encore.
>
> Je supplie Votre Majesté de me continuer la Permission accordée par son Auguste Frere.
>
> (To the King.
>
> Sire,
>
> His Majesty King Louis XVI, at the formal request of the King of Sweden, Gustavus III, had been so kind as to permit me to receive and wear the Order of Vasa, which I have enjoyed for more than fifteen years. His Majesty King Charles XIII has just written to me that His Majesty approved my wearing the decoration again.
>
> The official letter has been shown to His Excellency M. the Comte de Blacas and is still in his possession.
>
> I beg Your Majesty to continue the permission granted by his August Brother.)

4 Baron Gustavus Wetterstedt (1776–1837), the Swedish diplomat who represented his country in the signing of the treaty ending the Napoleonic wars.

5 In 1814, after France's collapse, du Pont de Nemours was named secretary of the Provisional Government headed by his old friend Talleyrand (Ambrose Saricks, *Pierre Samuel Du Pont de Nemours* [Lawrence, Kans., 1965], p. 339). Louis XVIII soon restored him to his former position on the Council of State (*ibid.,* p. 341).

✿

126

Auguste de Stael to du Pont de Nemours
26 April 1815
WMSS 2/21

Paris 26 Avril 1815

Si j'ai été tristement désappointé, most dear Sir, en ne vous trouvant plus à Paris, j'ai du moins admiré votre noble et courageuse résolution.[1] Si le peu de moments que j'ai à rester ici me laissoient le loisir de vous ecrire avec quelque développement je crois que vous trouveriez dans ma lettre de nouveaux motifs de Vous applaudir du parti que Vous avez pris; mais les éléments divers qui vont agiter notre Europe se sont tellement multipliés et compliqués que l'espace d'une lettre est très insuffisant pour en parler d'une maniere digne de Vous.

Madame Dupont a du avoir la bonté de Vous exprimer de ma part l'importance que met ma mere à ce que Votre 1ere traite sur M^r votre fils soit acquittée cette année à l'échéance. Le bouleversement de ses espérances de fortune en France,[2] et la chute rapide des fonds anglois et de la Livre Sterling, qui lui rend impossible de tirer maintenant sur l'Angleterre, font qu'elle manque tout à fait d'argent sur le continent et que Vos 7000 f.[3] lui deviennent entièrement nécessaires. Je ne doute pas que du beau pays de liberté que Vous avez le bonheur d'habiter vous apprecierez ces motifs, et que Vous voudrez bien prendre les mesures nécessaires pour que Votre traite soit régulièrement acquittée. Soyez assez bon pour répondre à ma mere ou à moi sous le couvert de Messrs Delessert.

Permettez Vous à un humble soldat de l'honorable parti dont vous êtes un des chefs de Vous parler de sa haute estime et de son respectueux attachement pour Vous.

Auguste de Staël

Monsieur Dupont de Nemours

On the reverse:

Dupont de Nemours Esqre
Eleutherian Mill
near *Wilmington*
State of *Delaware*

TRANSLATION

Paris, April 26, 1815

If I was sadly disappointed, most dear Sir, in no longer finding you in Paris, I admired, at least, your noble and courageous resolution.[1] If the few moments that I have to remain here left me the time to write you at some length, I believe that you would find in my letter some new motives to praise you for the decision that you have made; but the various elements that are going to disturb our Europe have been so multiplied and complicated that the space of a letter is quite insufficient to speak about them in a manner worthy of you.

Mme. du Pont must have had the kindness to tell you, on my behalf, of the importance which my mother attaches to the first draft on your son being paid this year on the due date. Because of the upset of her hopes of fortune in France[2] and the rapid decline of English funds and the pound sterling, which makes it impossible for her to draw now on England, she completely lacks money on the continent, and your 7,000 francs[3] become entirely necessary to her. I do not doubt that, from the beautiful land of liberty in which you are fortunate enough to live, you will understand these motives, and that you will kindly take the necessary measures to pay your draft on time. Be kind enough to answer my mother or me in care of Messrs. Delessert.

Do you permit a humble soldier of the honorable party of which you are one of the leaders to speak to you of his great esteem and of his respectful attachment to you?

Auguste de Staël

M. du Pont de Nemours

On the reverse:

du Pont de Nemours, Esq.
Eleutherian Mill
near *Wilmington*
State of *Delaware*

NOTES

1 On Napoleon's return from Elba, du Pont de Nemours hastily decided to leave for the United States, even though he had to leave Mme. du Pont behind because an injury to her hip prevented her from traveling. He sailed from Le Havre on March 30, 1815, and arrived in New York on May 3 (B. G. du Pont, *Du Pont de Nemours, 1739–1817* [Newark, Del., 1933], II, 120–22).

2 With the return of the Bourbons, Mme. de Staël saw the possibility of finally
collecting the two million francs Necker had lent the government. Eager to
marry her daughter, Albertine de Staël, to Victor de Broglie, she needed 600,000
francs for Albertine's dowry (Henri Guillemin, *Madame de Staël, Benjamin
Constant et Napoléon* [Paris, 1959], p. 174). Napoleon's return from Elba dashed
the hopes of collecting the debt.
3 In 1814 E. I. du Pont purchased the stock which Mme. de Staël owned in the
powder company (du Pont de Nemours to E. I. du Pont, October 30, 1814,
unpubl. letter, Eleutherian Mills Historical Library). In the same year, du Pont
de Nemours had signed two drafts of 7,000 francs each on his son, and Mme. de
Staël had purchased these. See Letter 130.

127

du Pont de Nemours to Auguste de Stael

[29?] June 1815

From a draft, WMSS 2/7

a M^r le Baron de Stael

Monsieur,

J'ai recu avec reconnaissance et le plus grand interet votre lettre
du 26 avril et son duplicata et j'avais déja recu celle de Madame du
Pont du 25 sur le même sujet.

Cette année est pour nous tous celle des contretemps et doit etre
celle des efforts de notre part pour nous et nos amis.

Il y a trois semaines que notre principal moulin a sauté. Neuf
hommes ont péri, cinq femmes sont restées veuves et un grand
nombre d'enfans orphelins. Il faut en prendre soin, et faire des
pensions aux meres.

La pluspart des autres ouvriers ont pris la terreur, et quittent
le service de sorte que jusqu'à ce [que] cet effroi soit calmé et
qu'on ait trouvé ou formé d'autres ouvriers, nous ne pourrons
guere faire executer aux troit moulins qui nous restent qu'environ
la moitié du travail qu'ils faisaient auparavant.

Nous estimons cette perte en réparations et chaumage a environ
cent mille francs.

Et sans votre lettre nous nous serions certainement renfermes
pour cette annee dans la teneur de notre acte qui nous autorise a
servir les interets a six pour cent des payemens qui n'auraient pas
pu etre effectués à leur echeance désirée.

Mais vous savez ce que sent mon cœur *non ignarus mali*.[1] Celui
de mon excellent Fils Irenee est tout semblable.

Voici la position entre les deux Pays et le parti que nous prenons.

Pour vous envoyer du Papier, il nous faudrait donner neuf mille cinq cent francs effectifs afin d'en avoir sept mille francs a deux mois de vue: tel est le cours actuel sur la France dans l'inquietude qu'on a sur l'Europe et le peu de commerce qui se fait.

Nous donnons ordre à la Nouvelle Orleans de charger à bord d'un vaisseau qui va y etre en partance une partie de coton qui vaudra plus de sept mille francs. Nous esperons qu'il arrivera avant l'echeance, mais nous ne pouvons pas dire en quel Port parce que l'instruction du capitaine est, si les circonstances politiques peuvent rendre l'arrivée en France dangereuse, de pousser a Anvers ou dans tel autre port etranger.

Il devra mettre le coton à l'ordre de M^r delessert pour la valeur etre a la disposition de Madame du Pont.

Je mande a celle ci de vous donner provisoirement et au recu de ma lettre un a-compte de mille francs.[2] Je ne peux lui demander davantage son voyage etant malheureusement retombé par sa nouvelle blessure.

M^r delessert jugera quelle pourra etre la maniere la plus prompte de réaliser six mille francs sur le coton et de vous les faire tenir.

Le surplus de ce que le coton pourra rendre sera remis a Madame du Pont.

Je suis bien aise que vous ayiez eté content de ma conduite.

J'ai toujours pensé que dans les evenemens politiques les résolutions devaient etre promptes et courageuses et que la seule chose a ne pas mettre en risque etait l'honneur car pour peu qu'il soit compromis, il faudrait de plus perdre la vie.

Presentez a Madame votre mere et à Mademoiselle votre sœur l'hommage de mon très respectueux attachement.

Je vous salue et vous embrasse.

TRANSLATION
    To the Baron de Staël
Sir,

I have received with gratitude and the greatest interest your letter of April 26 and its duplicate, and I had already received Mme. du Pont's of the 25th on the same subject.

This year is one of disappointments for all of us and must be one of efforts on our part for us and our friends.

Our main mill exploded three weeks ago. Nine men perished, five women were left widows, and a great number of children, orphans. We must take care of them and pay pensions to the mothers.

The majority of the other workers became terrified and are leaving their work, so that until this fright is calmed and we have found or trained other workmen, we shall scarcely be able to have the three remaining mills do more than half the work they were doing before.

We estimate this loss in repairs and unemployment at about 100,000 francs.

And without your letter, we should certainly have restricted ourselves this year to the terms of our deed which authorize us to pay 6 per cent interest on the payment which could not be effected at the desired due date.

But you know what my heart feels: *non ignarus mali.*[1] That of my excellent son Irénée is quite the same.

Here is the situation between the two countries and the decision that we are making.

To send you bills, we would have to give 9,500 francs in order to obtain 7,000 francs for a term of two months. Such is the present rate on France in view of the uneasiness that people have about Europe and the little commerce that is being carried on.

We are sending an order to New Orleans to place on board a ship which is going to sail from there a load of cotton which will be worth more than 7,000 francs. We hope that it will arrive before the due date; but we cannot say at what port because the captain's instructions are to sail on to Antwerp or to some other foreign port if political circumstances make arrival in France dangerous.

He will place the cotton to the order of M. Delessert for its value to be put at the disposal of Mme. du Pont.

I am writing to her to give you, in the meantime, and on receipt of my letter, an installment of 1,000 francs.[2] I cannot ask her for more, since her voyage has unfortunately been postponed by her new injury.

M. Delessert will decide what can be the quickest way to realize the 6,000 francs on the cotton and to remit them to you.

The remainder of what the cotton is able to bring will be given to Mme. du Pont.

I am very happy that you have been pleased with my conduct.

I have always thought that in political events, resolutions should be prompt and courageous and that the only thing not to jeopardize was honor, for if it be compromised ever so little, life must be lost as well.

Present to your mother and your sister the homage of my very respectful attachment.

I greet you and embrace you.

N O T E S

The powder mill explosion mentioned in this letter occurred on June 8, 1815 (*E. I. du Pont*, X, 93). Since du Pont de Nemours states that he is writing this letter three weeks later, the date of the letter must be about June 29.

1 A variation of the famous line spoken by Dido in the *Aeneid: Non ignara mali, miseris succerrere disco* ("Knowing misfortune myself, I know how to aid unfortunate persons").

2 In a letter written to his wife on June 19, 1815 (LMSS 8/A/3), du Pont de Nemours states:

> Si tu crois cependant sans te gêner trop pouvoir donner un à compte de *mille francs* à Madame de Stael fais le de suite comme un hommage de ton cœur et du mien; plus ne se pourrait.
>
> J'aurais cru que le sacrifice de Benjamin Constant au Conseil d'Etat aurait renoué l'affaire de Mme de Stael avec le tresor public, et que cette affaire en avait été un des mobiles les plus determinans. L'acquisition d'un homme tel que Benjamin valait cela.
>
> Du reste dis à elle et à son aimable et sage fils mille choses affectueuses pour moi. Je leur suis très attaché. Leurs terres en amérique seront pour eux peu de ressource. C'est de la richesse pour leur posterité, non pour leur vie. Tous les acquereurs de le Ray de Chaumont sont dans l'embarras.

> (If you believe that, without inconveniencing yourself too much, you can give a payment on account of 1,000 francs to Mme. de Staël, do so at once as an expression of homage from your heart and mine; to pay more would be impossible.
>
> I should have believed that the sacrifice made by Benjamin Constant to the Council of State would have renewed the affair of Mme. de Staël with the Treasury, and that that affair had been one of the most determining motives for it. The acquisition of a man such as Benjamin was worth that.
>
> Moreover, tell her and her likeable and good son that I send them most affectionate greetings. I am very much attached to them. Their land in America will be of little value to them. It is wealth for their descendants, but not for the present owners. All those who bought land from Le Ray de Chaumont are in difficulty.)

During the Hundred Days, Constant found it expedient to back Napoleon, who appointed him to the Council of State and gave him the task of writing a new constitution for France. Du Pont de Nemours evidently believed that Constant had compromised his principles in an effort to aid Mme. de Staël recover the urgently needed two million francs.

128

du Pont de Nemours to Auguste de Staël

3 August 1815

From a copy, WMSS 2/7

à M^r le B[ar]on de Stael

Eleuthérian Mills
Near Wilmington Delaware
3 aout 1815

M^r

Nos ordres sont arrivés trop tard à la Nouvelle Orléans. Le navire était chargé et n'avait pas même pû contenir toute la cargaison qui lui était destinée. Il n'y avait pas moyen d'y charger en outre pour six mille francs de coton.

Nous nous sommes trouvés fort embarassés. Point du tout de Papier sur France à Philadelphie, ni à Newyork: et s'il y en avait eu, il aurait coûté trente pour cent à soixante jours de vûe.

Nous avons pris le parti de vous envoyer des Stocks des Etats-Unis. Les dernières gazettes nous ont dit qu'ils ne perdaient que cinq pour cent en Europe. Et peut-être perdront-ils moins à présent que, les hostilités étant commencées, les Etats-unis sont le seul Gouvernement civilisé en paix: car leur guerre avec les Algériens n'est qu'un badinage.[1] Leurs officiers de Mer et leurs Matelots sont à present les meilleurs du Monde; et, dans la guerre qui vient de finir, ils ont toujours eu l'avantage sur les Anglais même.

Nous joignons donc à cette lettre

Stocks		Dollars	Francs au Pair
N° 653		1,000	5300
N° 644		100	530
N° 645		100	530
Intérêts de deux mois ½		15	79.50
		1,215	6439.50
	Perte supposée à 5 p[our] cent		321.97½
	Boni		117.52½

Si la perte était plus forte, M[a]d[am]e Du Pont vous en tiendrait compte. Si elle était effectivement de 5 p[our] cent au moindre, vous auriez la bonté de lui remettre le *boni*.

Le Vaisseau *La Medora* qui porte ce pacquet, part dimanche prochain 6 août. Les traversées des Etats-unis en Europe sont plus courtes que celles d'Europe aux Etats-unis. Nous avons donc lieu d'espérer que vous recevrez vos Stocks avant le 15 7bre. L'habileté de MM. de Lessert vous en fera défaire dans le plus court délai. Vous jouirez plus tôt qu'avec du Papier à deux mois.

Vous verrez que ce papier ne peut pas être perdu, parcequ'il est en nom propre et enrégistré, et n'est transférable qu'en Personne ou par *Attorney:* de sorte qu'en le vendant, il faut que ce soit par devant Notaire avec la procuration *d'Attorney*.

C'est une formalité de plus; mais qui parait compensée par la certitude d'être à l'abri du feu et des Naufrages.

Voudrez vous bien presenter mes respects à M[a]d[am]e votre mere.

D.P.d.N.

TRANSLATION

The Baron de Staël   Eleutherian Mills
                                    Near Wilmington, Delaware
                                    August 3, 1815
Sir,

Our orders arrived too late at New Orleans. The ship was loaded and had not even been able to hold all the cargo that was destined for it. There was no way to load 6,000 francs worth of cotton in addition.

We found ourselves in a very embarrassing situation. No bills at all on France in Philadelphia, or in New York; and if there had been any, it would have cost 30 per cent for a period of sixty days.

We have decided to send you some bonds of the United States. The latest newspapers have informed us that they would lose only 5 per cent in Europe. And perhaps they will lose less at present, since, hostilities having begun, the United States is the only civilized government at peace, for their war with the Algerians is only a joke.[1] Their naval officers and their sailors are the best in the world today, and in the war that has just ended, they always had the advantage, even over the English.

We enclose, therefore, in this letter:

Bond	Dollars	Francs at par
No. 653	1,000	5,300
No. 644	100	530
No. 645	100	530
Interest for 2½ months	15	79.50
	1,215	6,439.50
Supposed loss at 5 per cent		321.97½
Bonus		117.52½

If the loss is greater, Mme. du Pont would take that into account with you. If it is, in effect, 5 per cent less, would you have the kindness to give her the *bonus?*

The ship *Medora,* which is carrying this package, is leaving next Sunday, August 6. The crossings from the United States to Europe are shorter than those from Europe to the United States. We have cause to hope that you will receive your stock before September 15. With their skill, Messrs. Delessert will be able to dispose of it for you in the shortest possible time. You will receive your money sooner than with bills for two months.

You will see that these papers cannot be lost, because they are in my name and registered, and are transferable only in person or by an *attorney,* so that their sale must be effected in the presence of a notary with a power of *attorney.*

That is an additional formality, but it seems to be compensated for by the certainty of being protected against fire and shipwrecks.

Will you be so kind as to present my respects to your mother?

D. P. d. N.

NOTES

There are two copies and a draft of this letter in the Eleutherian Mills Historical Library. Although the draft is in du Pont de Nemours' handwriting, it is incomplete. The copy from which I have taken the text is not in du Pont's hand, but it appears to be a copy of the final form of the letter.

1 An allusion to the Algerine War in 1815 against the Barbary States.

129

Auguste de Stael to du Pont de Nemours

12 September 1817

wmss 2/22

Paris 12e Septembre 1817

J'ai compté sur votre intérêt et sur votre pitié, cher monsieur, dans l'horrible malheur qui nous a frappés.[1] Vous regrettez, j'en suis sur une personne qui vous étoit si tendrement attachée et qui apprécioit si vivement toutes les nobles qualités qui vous mettent hors de pair.

Le testament de ma mere m'a autorisé à rendre public son mariage avec mon ami Mr de Rocca[2] et à présenter à sa famille le fils qui en est né.[3] Je vous demanderai un jour d'étendre à mon frere Alphonse votre bonté pour moi: il est encore trop enfant pour en sentir le prix.

La publication des Considérations sur la Révolution françoise, que ma mere étoit sur le point d'achever, sera le travail au quel je vais consacrer cet hyver, en commun avec Mr Schlegel et Victor de Broglie.[4] Je m'occuperai ensuite d'une édition complette de ses œuvres et de celles de mon grand-pere. Les deux premiers volumes de son ouvrage politique[5] sont heureusement terminés: le troisième est en entier écrit de sa main; mais elle n'a pu en revoir qu'une partie.

Les divers engagements pécuniaires que ma mere me laisse à remplir, m'obligent à réaliser une portion considérable de sa fortune. C'est ce qui me fait vous prier instamment de vouloir bien me faire payer votre billet de f 7,000, échu depuis le 15 sept. 1816. J'en ai parlé à Madame Dupont qui a du vous en écrire de son coté.[6]

Pourquoi faut-il, cher monsieur, que ma lettre aille vous chercher si loin. Je conçois tout le prix que Messieurs vos fils mettent à vous garder auprès deux; mais bien des liens doivent vous rattacher à un pays qui est le vôtre et où vous êtes si généralement aimé et respecté. Je n'ai point renoncé, du reste, au desir de voir l'Amerique; et ce sera certainement ma premiere pensée lorsque j'aurai rempli les devoirs qui me retiennent en Europe.

Recevez encore avec bonté l'expression de mon tendre et respectueux attachement.

A. Staël

Monsieur Dupont de Nemours

On the reverse:

Monsieur
Monsieur Dupont de Nemours
Eleutherian Mill sur la Brandywine
Etat de Delaware

TRANSLATION

Paris, September 12, 1817

I have counted on your interest and your pity, dear Sir, in the horrible misfortune that has befallen us.[1] You mourn, I am sure, a person who was so tenderly attached to you and who appreciated so very much all the noble qualities which make you a man without a rival.

My mother's will has authorized me to make public her marriage to my friend, M. de Rocca,[2] and to introduce to her family the son who was born of it.[3] I shall request you one day to extend to my brother Alphonse your kindness toward me. He is still too young to appreciate the value of it.

The publication of the *Considerations on the French Revolution,* which my mother was about to finish, will be the work to which I shall consecrate this winter, together with M. Schlegel and Victor de Broglie.[4] I shall then busy myself with a complete edition of her works and of those of my grandfather. The first two volumes of her political work[5] are fortunately completed; the third is entirely written in her hand, but she was able to revise only a part of it.

The various financial obligations that my mother leaves me to carry out force me to convert a considerable portion of her fortune. That is what causes me to request you urgently to be so kind as to pay me your note for 7,000 francs due since September 15, 1816. I have spoken about it to Mme. du Pont, who must have written to you about it, on her part.[6]

Why must my letter, dear Sir, go so far away to seek you? I understand all the value that your sons attach to keeping you near them, but many ties must attach you to a country which is yours and where you are so generally loved and respected. I have not yet abandoned the hope of seeing America; and it will certainly be my first thought when I have fulfilled the duties that keep me in Europe.

Receive again with kindness the expression of my tender and respectful attachment.

A. Staël

M. du Pont de Nemours

On the reverse:

Monsieur
M. du Pont de Nemours
Eleutherian Mill on the Brandywine
Delaware

NOTES

1 Mme. de Staël had died on July 14, 1817. Although Auguste de Staël was unaware of the fact at the time he wrote this letter, du Pont de Nemours had died on August 7, 1817. He had insisted on doing his part to extinguish a fire in one of the powder mills shortly before, and the exertion proved too much for him, especially since he had been in poor health for the past year as a result of a fall into the Brandywine while crossing the river.

2 She had married John Rocca secretly in 1816. On September 16, 1817, Mme. du Pont de Nemours, unaware of her husband's death, wrote to du Pont de Nemours (LMSS 1/4): "Je t'ai dit que Mme de Staël avait laissé un enfant de cinq ans né d'un mariage avec M Rocca. Qu'elle singuliere fin pour cette dame. M. Rocca a fait quelque ouvrage, je ne sais quoi. On le dit bel homme mais d'une mauvaise santé." ("I have told you that Mme. de Staël had left a child five years old born from a marriage with M. Rocca. What a strange end for that lady! M. Rocca has written some work, I do not know what. People say he is a handsome man but in bad health.")

At the instigation, and probably with the assistance of Mme. de Staël, Rocca had published *Mémoires sur la guerre des Français en Espagne* (London, 1814) and *Campagne de Walcheren et d'Anvers, en 1809* (Paris, 1815). At this time, Rocca was composing *Le Mal du pays,* which has never been published. (For an account of this work, see Comtesse Jean de Pange, "Un Manuscrit inédit de Jean Rocca," *Mélanges Baldensperger* [Paris, 1930].) Rocca died of tuberculosis six months after Mme. de Staël's death.

3 Louis Alphonse Rocca was born on April 7, 1812. On the baptismal registers, he was listed as the son of a Mr. and Mrs. Giles of Boston. He was placed in the care of a Swiss clergyman and his wife shortly after his birth.

4 The two million francs had finally been repaid to Mme. de Staël, and Albertine de Staël married Victor de Broglie on February 15, 1816. See Letter 126, note 2.

5 The *Considérations sur les principaux événemens de la Révolution française.*

6 Unaware of du Pont de Nemours' death, Mme. du Pont de Nemours wrote to

him on September 8, 1817 (LMSS 1/4): "Tu auras scu la perte de Mme de Staël. Son fils est venu me voir. Il voudrait beaucoup les 7000 f et m'a prié de te l'écrire. Veux tu qu'en place de ce que je t'ai dit sur l'impression de l'Arioste je lui donne quelque a Compte?" ("You will have learned about the death of Mme. de Staël. Her son came to see me. He would like very much to have the 7,000 francs and asked me to write you to that effect. Do you want me, in place of what I told you about the printing of the Arioste, to give him some payment on account?")

Du Pont de Nemours had spent many years translating Ariosto's *Orlando furioso*. The *Essai de traduction en vers du Roland furieux de l'Arioste, 1er chant* had appeared in 1781, and the *Essai de traduction en vers du Roland furieux de l'Arioste, Chants I à III* appeared in 1812. Du Pont was planning a new edition at this time (*E. I. du Pont*, X, 225, 249, 261).

130

Auguste de Staël to E. I. du Pont

22 January 1818

LMSS 3/6

Paris 22 Janvier 1818

Monsieur,

Quoique je n'aie pas l'honneur d'être connu de Vous, j'ose espérer que vous voudrez bien me compter parmi ceux qui ont pris la part la plus vive à votre malheur.[1] La longue amitié qui a existé entre Monsieur votre pere et mes parents m'a rendu plus douleureuse qu'à un autre une perte qui a été Generalement ressentie; et le souvenir de ses bontés pour moi et des conseils qu'il a quelquefois daigné me donner, ne s'effacera jamais de mon cœur.

Je n'oserais pas, Monsieur, Vous importuner en Vous parlant d'affaires, si en qualité d'executeur des dernieres volontés de ma mere, je ne devais pas maintenant rendre compte de la gestion de sa succession.

Par suite d'un acte signé en Septembre 1814 entre ma mere et Monsieur Votre pere agissant en votre nom: Mr Votre pere a souscrit deux traites sur vous de 7,000 f. chaque, payables au domicile de Messrs Perregaux La Fitte Cie [2] les 15 Sept. 1815 et 1816. La premiere de ces traites a été acquittée; la seconde ne l'est pas encore: et j'ai tout lieu de craindre qu'une lettre que j'écrivais à Mr Votre pere pour en réclamer le payement[3] ne soit arrivée trop tard.

J'envoie cette traite à Messrs Le Roy & Bayard à New York[4] et j'ose Vous prier de vouloir bien Vous entendre avec ces Messieurs soit pour payer entre leurs mains la valeur de l'effet, soit pour l'acquiter à Paris, ainsi qu'il est stipulé. Les nombreux engagements pécuniaires que la succession de ma mere a à remplir nous obligent à rassembler tous nos capitaux.

Permettez moi de Vous parler encore, Monsieur, de tous les sentiments distingués qui sont dus à Vous même et au nom que Vous portez; et veuillez recevoir l'assurance de l'estime particulier avec la quelle j'ai l'honneur d'être

Votre très humble et très obeissant serviteur
A. Staël

Monsieur Irenée Dupont

On the reverse:

Monsieur
Monsieur Irenée Dupont
Eleutherian Mill sur la Brandywine
Wilmington
Delaware

TRANSLATION

Paris, January 22, 1818

Sir,

Although I do not have the honor of being known by you, I dare to hope that you will kindly count me among those who shared most strongly your misfortune.[1] The long friendship which existed between your father and my family made sadder for me than to another a loss which has been felt generally; and the memory of his kindness to me and the advice that he sometimes deigned to give me will never be erased from my heart.

I should not dare, Sir, to bother you by mentioning business, if, as the executor of the last wishes of my mother, I were not now obliged to render an account of the management of her estate.

As the result of a deed signed in September 1814 between my mother and your father acting in your name, your father signed two drafts on you for 7,000 francs each, payable at Messrs. Perregaux La Fitte and Company[2] on September 15, 1815 and 1816. The first of these drafts has been paid; the second is not yet paid;

and I have every reason to fear that a letter I wrote to your father to request payment[3] arrived too late.

I am sending this draft to Messrs. Le Roy and Bayard [4] in New York, and I dare ask you to be so kind as to come to an agreement with those gentlemen, either to pay them the value of the note, or to pay it in Paris, as it is stipulated. The numerous financial obligations that the estate of my mother has to fulfill require us to collect all our capital.

Permit me to speak to you again, Sir, of all the distinguished sentiments which are due to you and to the name which you bear; and please receive the assurance of the special esteem with which I have the honor to be

Your very humble and very obedient servant

A. Staël

M. Irénée du Pont

On the reverse:

Monsieur
M. Irénée du Pont
Eleutherian Mill on the Brandywine
Wilmington
Delaware

NOTES

1 The death of du Pont de Nemours.
2 A Paris banking firm.
3 Letter 129.
4 In the Eleutherian Mills Historical Library there are seven letters from Le Roy, Bayard and Company, dated March 26, 1818; April 23, 1818; May 11, 1818; July 21, 1818; October 30, 1818; February 9, 1819; and April 29, 1819, requesting payment of the money due Auguste de Staël. There is a receipt dated May 14, 1819, for $1,610.27 in settlement of this debt.

Index

Index

Abbema, Balthasar Elias: investment in du Pont de Nemours, Père et Fils & Cie., 181, 185, 197, 201; identified, 187$n11$

Aboukir, Battle of, 75$n10$

Achilles, 214–15

Acosta, château of. *See* Aubergenville

Aeneid. See Virgil

Aiguillon, Emmanuel-Armand, Duc d', 160$n8$

Alexander I, Czar, 79, 81, 82$n5$

Alexandria, Virginia, 67, 72

Algerine War: DPDN's comments on, 380, 381, 382$n1$

Almaviva, Comte: quoted by DPDN, 33, 39, 43$n6$

Alphonsine, ou la Tendresse maternelle. See Genlis, Mme. Stéphanie-Félicité, Comtesse de Brusbart de

American Philosophical Society, 361$n7$

Amiens, Peace of, 114$n1$

"L'Amitié, l'amour, les amours." *See* du Pont de Nemours, Pierre Samuel

"L'Amour et l'amitié." *See* du Pont de Nemours, Pierre Samuel

Anchises, 9, 10

Apthorp, Charles, 86, 89; identified, 90$n3$

Apthorp, Charles Ward (son of Charles): land belonging to, 86, 88–89; identified, 90$n3$; Victor du Pont's acquaintance with, 90$n4$

Apthorp, Mrs. Charles Ward (née Mary McEvers), 90$n3$

Ariosto: DPDN's translation of *Orlando furioso*, 317$n1$, 386$n6$

Atala. See Chateaubriand, François-René de

Atys, 10, 11, 12$n4$

Aubergenville, France, 313, 314, 314$n2$, 315–18 *passim*, 325$n1$

Auckland, Lord. *See* Eden, William

Auxerre, France, 304, 305, 306$n1$, 309, 310, 311$n1$

Baden, Carl Friedrich, Margrave of: letter from DPDN to, xxi

Bank of New York: Necker's inquiry about, 22, 23–24, 23$n1$; theft at, 65, 70, 74$n3$

Bank of the United States, 24$n1$, 65, 70

Banque territoriale: DPDN's role in its liquidation, 169, 171, 172, 173$n1$, 176

Barbé-Marbois, François, Marquis de, 28, 30, 79, 81–82; identified, 31$n6$

Barber of Seville. See Beaumarchais, Pierre-Augustin Caron de

Barthélemy, Jean-Jacques, Abbé: his *Voyage du jeune Anacharsis en Grèce*, 320, 322, 323$n1$

Baudin, Nicolas, 36, 42; identified, 44$n22$

Bauduy, Eugene, 205$n7$

Bauduy, Louis-Alexandre-Amélie, 197, 201; identified 205$n7$

Bauduy, Peter, 197, 201; identified, 205$n7$

Bayard, Catherine (née McEvers), 14$n2$

Bayard, Colonel William (father of William), 14$n2$

Bayard, William, 84–85, 87–88; identified, 14$n2$

de Staël-du Pont Letters

Correspondence of Madame de Staël
and Pierre Samuel du Pont de Nemours
*and of other members of the Necker and
du Pont families, edited and translated
by* JAMES F. MARSHALL

In the course of her lifelong devotion
to literature, politics, and the cultivation
of sentiment in the fervent style peculiar
to the late eighteenth and early nine-
teenth centuries, Germaine de Staël accu-
mulated a large, varied circle of friends.
The business dealings of her father,
Jacques Necker, financial minister during the reign of Louis XVI and during
the early stages of the French Revolution, provided her with one of those who
engaged her affection, Pierre Samuel du
Pont de Nemours, the French economist
and entrepreneur, who was indulging in
land speculation and other ventures in
America. Necker had invested in the du
Ponts' American enterprises, including
the gunpowder factory, E. I. du Pont de
Nemours and Company. While the father
guarded his investment by letter, the
daughter and the financier exchanged
news and ideas, maintaining a flirtatious
and affectionate correspondence. At
Necker's death, Mme. de Staël inherited
his financial interests, and the letters she
exchanged with du Pont came to have a
more businesslike tone, but their original
grace and charm persisted.

James F. Marshall has compiled this
document of Revolutionary affairs, span-
ning the years 1778–1818, from original